GENDER
AND CLASS
IN MODERN
EUROPE

GENDER AND CLASS IN MODERN EUROPE

EDITED BY

Laura L. Frader
and Sonya O. Rose

CORNELL UNIVERSITY PRESS

ITHACA AND LONDON

First published 1996 by Cornell University Press.

Printed in the United States of America

Library of Congress Cataloging-in-Publication Data
Gender and class in modern Europe/edited by Laura L. Frader and
  Sonya O. Rose.
      p. cm.
    Includes bibliographical references and index.
    ISBN 0-8014-2922-6 (cl. : alk. paper).—ISBN 0-8014-8146-5 (pb.
  : alk. paper)
      1. Women—Employment—Europe—History—Case studies. 2. Working
  class—Europe—History—Case studies. I. Frader, Laura Levine,
  1945– . II. Rose, Sonya O.
  HD6134.C58 1996
  331.4'094—dc20   95-52529

♾ The paper in this book meets the minimum requirements of the American National Standard for Information Sciences—Permanence of Paper for Printed Library Materials, ANSI Z39.48-1984.

Contents

Contents

Acknowledgments

We are indebted to the contributors to this book for their creative efforts, their hard work, and their patience while the project came to fruition. We thank Ava Baron for her encouragement as we began the volume and M. J. Maynes for her superb critical readings. Peter Agree of Cornell University Press has been supportive of our work and enthusiastic about the project in each of its phases. Northeastern University and the University of Michigan provided partial support. The Center for European Studies at Harvard University provided a congenial and stimulating place to meet and work. We thank Kristina Pfefferle, research assistant in the Department of History, Northeastern University, who helped at one stage of the project, and Patricia Preston, of the Sociology Department's Center for Research on Social Organization at the University of Michigan, who came to our rescue on more than one occasion.

L. L. F. *and* S. O. R.

Introduction: Gender and the Reconstruction of European Working-Class History

Laura L. Frader and Sonya O. Rose

Developments in feminist scholarship have moved gender as an analytical category from the periphery of scholarship into the spotlight of historical inquiry. At the same time, class, which had held pride of place in the conceptual tool kit of labor history, has been subjected to increasingly critical scrutiny as scholars have explored new theoretical approaches that have challenged earlier frameworks. This book demonstrates how the study of gender both transforms the ways we think about working-class history and reinvigorates the study of topics that have long been of interest to labor and social historians. The chapters examine the significance of gender in the processes of industrial, social, and political transformation in the United Kingdom and Ireland, France, Germany, Russia, and Italy with the emergence of industrial capitalism, the nature of work and of social and class relations underwent major shifts. As states attempted to regulate their economies, working-class and middle-class movements attempted to expand citizenship and political participation through both parliamentary processes and revolution. The contributors to this volume consider how gender meanings and relations shaped and were in turn shaped by these intertwined economic, social, cultural, and political transformations.

The focus on gender suggests that paradigms of labor history that are based on the universal category "worker" and privilege productive relations need to be replaced by new ways of thinking about the subjects and subject matters of history. Thus the chapters also attend to the importance of language and culture in social life, illuminating how political identities are constituted and social categories are created, contested, and changed. At the same time, and without being reductive, they show that gender has been a central dimension of the social practices and power relations that have had profound consequences for people's lives.

The "new labor history" has produced a rich and varied portrait of the European working class that has yielded new understandings about collective action; democratic and socialist political movements and ideological developments; working-class culture, sociability, and leisure; household structures and their formation; changes in the content of work and the labor process; and the efforts of individual labor movement leaders. We now know a considerable amount about glassblowers, hatters and tailors, metalworkers, automobile workers, agricultural laborers, textile workers, coal miners, and domestic servants in Britain, France, Germany, and Russia. We have learned how economic conditions, workplace structures, and community institutions were transformed over the course of the nineteenth and twentieth centuries, and about the social contexts in which workers organized or participated in movements to change their political and social conditions. Social historians have chronicled the rise of socialist and labor parties in France, Britain, Germany, and Russia. They have portrayed the waxing and waning of collective action and protest and the fates of organized labor movements in all of those countries. They have examined the nature of worker organization in Russia before and after the Revolution.[1]

1. Among the major works are Michael Hanagan, *The Logic of Solidarity: Artisans and Industrial Workers in Three French Towns, 1871–1914* (Urbana, 1980); Steven Laurence Kaplan and Cynthia J. Koepp, eds., *Work in France: Representations, Meaning, Organization, and Practice* (Ithaca, 1986); Joan Scott, *The Glassworkers of Carmaux* (Cambridge, Mass., 1975); Leonard Berlanstein, *The Working People of Paris, 1871–1914* (Baltimore, 1984); Eleanor Accampo, *Industrialization, Family Life, and Class Relations in Saint-Chamond, 1815–1914* (Berkeley, 1989); Molly Nolan, *Social Democracy and German Society* (New York, 1981); David Crew, *Town in the Ruhr: A Social History of Bochum* (New York, 1979); Jürgen Kocka, *Lohnarbeit und Klassenbildung: Arbeiter und Arbeiterbewegung in Deutschland, 1800–1875* (Berlin, 1983); Gerhard A. Ritter, ed., *Geschichte der Arbeiter und der Arbeiterbewegung in Deutschland seit dem Ende des 18 Jahrhunderts* (Bonn, 1984–90); E. P. Thompson, *The Making of the English Working Class* (Harmondsworth, 1968); Eric Hobsbawm, *Labouring Men: Studies in the History of Labour* (London, 1964); Hobsbawm, ed., *Workers: Worlds of Labour* (New York, 1984); James E. Cronin, *Labour and Society in Britain, 1918–1979* (London, 1984); John Foster, *Class Struggle and the Industrial Revolution* (London, 1974); Patrick Joyce, *Work, Society, and Politics: The Culture of the Factory in Later Victorian England* (Brighton, 1980); William G. Rosenberg and Lewis Siegelbaum, *Social Dimensions of Soviet Industrialization* (Bloomington, 1993); William Chase, *Workers, Society, and the Soviet State: Labor and Life in Moscow, 1918–1929* (Urbana, 1987); Diane P. Koenker and William G. Rosenberg,

Scholars have disagreed as to the relative importance of economic or cultural factors and the differential significance of institutions, organizations, traditions, and communities in historical analyses of European work and workers. The centrality of the concept of class and the ontological status of the "social," however, seemed secure during the 1970s and early 1980s. Although there were indications even then of serious ruptures in what seemed to be a consensus on the boundaries of the field, scholars optimistically searched for a grand synthesis in labor and working-class history.[2]

Increasingly, however, historians are arguing that the field has entered a period of crisis (or if not crisis, then certainly doldrums) that contrasts with the vitality and innovation of the 1970s and 1980s.[3] To be sure, part of that crisis, if crisis it is, has to do with the weakening of labor movements and left political formations in Europe and the rest of the world that provided models and aspirations for a generation of new labor historians, and the failure of the working class to function (as many hoped) as the vanguard of progressive social change.[4] At the same time, an increasing number of scholars have challenged the analytical paradigms of the field by emphasizing the importance of language and discourse in social life. Their work questions the validity of class as a subject of analysis and the value of political economy as a framework for historical understanding.[5]

Strikes and Revolution in Russia, 1917 (Princeton, 1989); Victoria Bonnell, *Roots of Rebellion: Workers' Politics and Organizations in St. Petersburg and Moscow, 1900–1914* (Berkeley, 1983); Lewis H. Siegelbaum and Ronald Grigor Suny, eds., *Making Workers Soviet: Power, Class, and Identity* (Ithaca, 1994); Laura Engelstein, *Moscow, 1905: Working-Class Organization and Political Conflict* (Stanford, 1982); Chris Ward, *Russia's Cotton Workers and the New Economic Policy* (New York, 1990).

2. On the question of synthesis, see Gérard Noiriel, *Les Ouvriers dans la société française* (Paris, 1987); Ira Katznelson and Aristide R. Zolberg, eds., *Working-Class Formation: Nineteenth-Century Patterns in Western Europe and the United States* (Princeton, 1986). For early critiques of sociological social history, see Tony Judt, "A Crown in Regal Purple," *History Workshop* 7 (Spring 1979): 66–94; Geoff Eley and Keith Nield, "Why Does Social History Ignore Politics?" *Social History* 5, no. 2 (1980): 249–72; Gareth Stedman Jones, "Rethinking Chartism," in his *Languages of Class* (Cambridge, 1983), pp. 90–178.

3. See Leonard Berlanstein, "Working with Language: The Linguistic Turn in French Labor History," *Comparative Studies in Society and History* 33 (1991): 426–40, and the essays in *Rethinking Labor History: Essays on Discourse and Class Analysis*, ed. Berlanstein (Urbana, 1993), esp. Berlanstein's Introduction, pp. 1–14; William H. Sewell Jr., "Towards a Post-Materialist Rhetoric for Labor History," pp. 15–38; and Michael Hanagan, "Commentary: For Reconstruction in Labor History," pp. 182–99.

4. Berlanstein, Introduction, provides a succinct formulation of the problem and of the relationship between recent political events and the new intellectual challenges to labor history (p. 5).

5. For a good overview of developments in labor history see ibid. Historians whose ideas about language and history have contributed to current questions about the usefulness of

It has become increasingly clear that much of the new labor history was itself a story of exclusions. These important and often path-breaking works rarely included women; the vast majority of studies focused on men, and if they dealt with women at all, they viewed their work and labor activism through conceptual prisms that highlighted their differences from men. As members of the working class and as workers, women were defined and shaped by gender, in contrast to men, whose subjectivity was defined by their work. Mainly, however, women were absent from or marginal to the historical narratives about labor and the working class in Europe.

Whereas the old labor history, the history of organized labor and the men who led it, quite clearly had a selective and particular focus, the new labor history cast a seemingly wider light that illuminated workers' workplaces and communities as well as their unions. Following a path blazed by Edward P. Thompson, European historians wrote labor history as the history of working-class formation. They produced a wealth of studies that detailed how working people came ᵗ ᵈevelop a class identity and political solidarity by struggling collectivei₁ against the ravages of economic inequality and industrial transformation.[6]

While historians took a variety of tracks, they were all guided by the same conceptual map. Central to the narratives of working-class formation has been the idea that it was accompanied by or was a consequence of proletarianization—the growth of waged labor and workers' progressive loss of control over work at the point of production. Deeply embedded in this cartography of labor and working-class history is the public/private dichotomy—the presumed separation of domestic and public arenas of social life that were the significant sites of the different activities and sensibilities of men and women. Centering historical narratives on the story of proletarianization and incorporating the nineteenth-century ideology of separate, oppositional, and gendered spheres as a foundational assumption of the discipline has had problematic consequences for labor history.

---

the concept of class include Gareth Stedman Jones, Patrick Joyce, and Joan Scott. For a thoughtful assessment see Eley and Nield, "Why Does Social History Ignore Politics?" For an essay that questions social historians' approaches to the Bolshevik Revolution see Ronald Grigor Suny, "Revision and Retreat in the Historiography of 1917: Social History and Its Critics," *Russian Review* 53 (April 1994): 165–82. Also on the continuing importance of the study of class relations, Ira Katznelson, "Working-Class Formation: Constructing Cases and Comparisons," in Katznelson and Zolberg, *Working-Class Formation*.

6. See, e.g., Katznelson and Zolberg, *Working-Class Formation*.

PROLETARIANIZATION

Scholars who have focused on proletarianization have emphasized two aspects of industrial and social transformation. Some have been concerned with the inexorable separation of working people from the means of subsistence as they became waged workers for capitalist industries.[7] Others, especially after the publication of Harry Braverman's *Labor and Monopoly Capitalism*, have focused on the workplace and have made changes in the labor process and deskilling central to their narratives.[8] Historical studies of work in Europe and the United States have called attention to the development of technologies and production processes that first obliterated trades and revolutionized household production in towns and rural areas, then proceeded to transform urban artisanal occupations and eventually skilled factory jobs.[9] Studies have focused on the transition from workshop to factory, on the decline of artisanal livelihoods, and on the impact of the growth of waged labor on household

7. See, e.g., Charles Tilly, Louise Tilly, and Richard Tilly, *The Rebellious Century* (Cambridge, 1975); Louise Tilly and Charles Tilly, eds., *Class Conflict and Collective Action* (Beverly Hills, 1981); Michael Hanagan, *Nascent Proletarians: Class Formation in Post-Revolutionary France* (Oxford, 1989). Scholars concerned with demographic history have also focused on proletarianization as a major process shaping family formation and household strategies. See, e.g., David Levine, *Family Formation in the Age of Nascent Capitalism* (New York, 1977).

8. Scott, *Glassworkers of Carmaux*; Hobsbawm, *Labouring Men*; Ronald Aminzade, *Class, Politics, and Early Industrial Capitalism: A Study of Mid-Nineteenth-Century Toulouse, France* (Albany, 1981); Crew, *Town in the Ruhr*; Jürgen Kocka, "Problems in Working-Class Formation in Germany: The Early Years, 1800–1875," in Katznelson and Zolberg, *Working-Class Formation*, pp. 279–351; K. Ditt, *Industrialisierung, Arbeiterschaft und Arbeitbewegung in Bielefeld, 1850–1914* (Dortmund, 1982); Heather Hogan, "Class Formation in the St. Petersburg Metalworking Industry: From the 'Days of Freedom' to the Lena Goldfields Massacre," and S. A. Smith, "Workers against Foremen in St. Petersburg, 1905–1917," both in Siegelbaum and Suny, *Making Workers Soviet*.

9. Embedded in the histories of class formation and proletarianization are conflicting views of the relationship between skilled and unskilled workers and politics. The view that skilled workers threatened with proletarianization dominated the organized labor and socialist movements has been reflected in numerous studies. See, e.g., Bernard Moss, *The Origins of the French Labor Movement, 1830–1914: The Socialism of Skilled Workers* (Berkeley, 1976); Hanagan, *Logic of Solidarity*; Claude Willard, *Les Guesdistes: Le Mouvement Socialiste en France, 1893–1905* (Paris, 1965); Robert Bezucha, *The Lyon Uprising of 1834: Social and Political Conflict in a Nineteenth-Century City* (Cambridge, Mass., 1974); Christopher Johnson, *Utopian Communism in France: Cabet and the Icarians, 1839–1851* (Ithaca, 1974); Rolande Trempé, *Les Mineurs de Carmaux*, 2 vols. (Paris, 1971); Donald Reid, *The Miners of Decazeville: A Genealogy of Deindustrialization* (Cambridge, Mass., 1985); Dick Geary questions the relationship between proletarianization and political radicalism in Germany, and suggests that deskilling and proletarianization were less prominent in Germany than in some other countries before 1914 in "Socialism and the German Labour Movement before 1914," in *Labour and Socialist Movements in Europe before 1914*, ed. Geary (New York, 1989), pp. 101–36.

arrangements and family life, community structures, and political group-
ings.[10] With few exceptions it was assumed that these processes occurred,
however unevenly, in a similar way in all kinds of work, and that they
affected men and women equally, and without distinction of race or
ethnicity.[11] On the basis of a dominant paradigm of European working-
class formation, then, historians argued that the processes of proletarianization altered the worlds of the working classes.[12]

Furthermore, in an effort to explore working-class agency in the dynamics of history, scholars related the story of industrialization's impact
on labor as one of male workers defending themselves against skill-
killing new technologies and management strategies. The struggle between capitalists and workers over the labor process was at the center of
historical analysis, and according to the dominant tradition in working-
class history, it was in the context of the changing structures of artisanal
production that workers became politicized.

A good deal of historical analysis has focused on precisely how the
politicization of the working class came about. The new working-class
historians and sociologists called attention to culture as a foundation of
working-class politics. Scholars who followed the lead of E. P. Thompson
emphasized how workers participated in cultural and religious institutions. They also emphasized how the developing working class called on
community- and trade-based traditions of protest to deal with the ravages

10. See Aminzade, Class, Politics, and Michael Hanagan and Charles Stephenson, eds.,
Proletarians and Protest: The Roots of Class Formation in an Industrializing World
(Westport, Conn., 1986).

11. Harry Braverman, Labor and Monopoly Capitalism (New York, 1974), for example,
focused on the development of scientific management and the technological consequences
of the division of labor; see his chaps. 4–5, 8–10. See the essays in pt. 2 of On Work:
Historical, Comparative, and Theoretical Approaches, ed. R. H. Pahl (New York, 1989).
See also Alain Cottereau, "The Distinctiveness of Working-Class Cultures in France,
1848–1900," in Katznelson and Zolberg, Working-Class Formation, pp. 111–54;
Thompson, Making of the English Working Class; Duncan Bythell, The Handloom Weav-
ers (Cambridge, 1969); Laura Lee Downs, Manufacturing Inequality: Gender Division in
the French and British Metalworking Industries (Ithaca, 1995). Also see her "Industrial
Decline, Rationalization, and Equal Pay: The Bedaux Strike at the Rover Automobile
Company," Social History 15 (January 1990); Miriam Glucksman, Women Assemble
(London, 1990). For an excellent example of work that challenges the assumed linear
progression from peasant to proletarian and simultaneously examines the complexity of
class formation through the examination of household labor and gender, see Jean Quataert,
"The Politics of Rural Industrialization: Class, Gender, and Collective Protest in the
Saxon Oberlausitz of the Late Nineteenth Century," Central European History 20 (June
1987): 91–124.

12. For an insightful critique of proletarianization as the dominant paradigm of working-class history, see Margaret R. Somers, "Narrativity, Narrative Identity, and Social
Action: Rethinking English Working-Class Formation," Social Science History 16 (Winter
1992): 591–630.

of industrial transformation.[13] Some, following Charles Tilly or exploiting insights from a range of sociological analyses of the organizational basis of collective action, focused on the corporate basis of the artisanal trades and the alliances that such workers formed.[14] Still others demonstrated the influence of both approaches by examining the intersection of cultural formations, community solidarities, and working-class political and economic structures.[15] Regardless of the path chosen, however, the bulk of the historiography featured male artisans and skilled workers as primary figures.

Some scholars have come to doubt the validity of this focus on artisans. Jacques Rancière maintains that in France male workers created an idealized portrait of artisanal workshops that did not reflect a way of life that was passing, but rather was a politically motivated romanticization of that way of life.[16] Feminist historians have raised questions about the consequences of studying artisans without problematizing their status as community spokesmen. Sally Alexander has suggested, for example, that the very language used by the male workers who have been the subjects of British labor history constructed the working class as masculine.[17] Feminist scholars have shown, in addition, that the category of "skill," so essential to the history of labor as a "deskilling" or proletarianizing story, was socially constructed and politically delineated.[18]

13. E.g., I. J. Prothero, *Artisans and Politics in Early Nineteenth-Century London: John Gast and His Times* (Folkestone, 1979); Geoffrey Crossick, *An Artisan in Victorian Society: Kentish London, 1840–1880* (Totowa, N.J., 1978); Hobsbawm, *Labouring Men*; Hanagan, *Logic of Solidarity*; Kocka, *Lohnarbeit und Klassenbildung*; John Merriman, *Red City: Limoges in the Nineteenth Century* (New York, 1986); Diane P. Koenker, "Urbanization and Deurbanization in the Russian Revolution and Civil War," *Journal of Modern History* 57 (1985): 424–50.

14. E.g., Aminzade, *Class, Politics*; Craig Calhoun, *The Question of Class Struggle: Social Foundations of Class Radicalism during the Industrial Revolution* (Chicago, 1982).

15. See, e.g., Alf Lüdke, "Organizational Order or *Eigensinn*? Workers' Privacy and Workers' Politics in Imperial Germany," in *Rites of Power: Symbolism, Ritual, and Politics since the Middle Ages*, ed. Sean Wilenz (Philadelphia, 1985), pp. 303–33; Laura Levine Frader, *Peasants and Protest: Agricultural Workers, Politics, and Unions in the Aude, 1850–1914* (Berkeley, 1992); William H. Sewell Jr., *Work and Revolution in France: The Language of Labor from the Ancien Régime to 1848* (New York, 1981).

16. Jacques Rancière, *The Nights of Labor: The Workers' Dream in Nineteenth-Century France*, trans. John Drury (Philadelphia, 1989); also see Rancière, "The Myth of the Artisan," and responses by William H. Sewell Jr. and Christopher J. Johnson, *International Labor and Working-Class History* 24 (Fall 1983): 1–47, and responses by Edgar Leon Newman and Nicholas Papayanis and Rancière's reply, *International Labor and Working-Class History* 25 (Spring 1984): 37–46.

17. Sally Alexander, "Women, Class, and Sexual Difference," *History Workshop* 17 (Spring 1984): 125–49.

18. See the special issues of *Mouvement Social* edited by Michelle Perrot, no. 105 (October–December 1978), "Travaux des femmes dans la France du XIXᵉ siècle," and no. 140 (July–September 1987), "Métiers des femmes." Also see Anne Phillips and Barbara

The narrative of proletarianization not only led to a focus on particular workers but also had embedded within it a story about modernization, advance, and progress. Much labor history focused on institutions (unions and parties), organizations, and leaders who were public men and who succeeded in dominating movements and institutions. Thus the historiography of the labor movement was for many years dominated by the story of the formation of socialist parties, labor parties, socialist party congresses, and the rise and fall of labor leaders.[19] Within this institutional focus, the narrative of labor history bore a distinctly teleological cast: labor history was written as the rise of the working class, as the progressive development of working-class organizations, as the final coming to consciousness of workers, with the working class as a major agent of progressive social change; it was written as a drama of triumph or defeat. In part the teleological thrust was the legacy of nineteenth-century labor and socialist theorists themselves, most prominently Karl Marx, with his vision of history based on the progress of capitalism and on class conflict as the driving force of historical development leading to socialism.

Whereas institutional labor history was often informed by a kind of heroic impulse, the new labor history just as often incorporated a teleological vision. Even though it focused less on particular organizations and leaders, it was informed by the presumption that the common experience of disadvantage, produced by capitalist relations of production, would or should eventually produce organized resistance and change. As the Indian working-class historian Dipesh Chakrabarty has suggested, European labor and working-class history was structured as an Enlightenment emancipatory narrative.[20]

The histories of labor and class often were, as a consequence, oriented around the idea of "exceptionalisms."[21] British and French nineteenth-

---

Taylor, "Sex and Skill: Notes Towards a Feminist Economics," *Feminist Review* 6 (1980): 79–88; Gail Braybon, *Women Workers in the First World War* (London, 1981); Penny Summerfield, *Women Workers in the Second World War: Production and Patriarchy in Conflict* (London, 1984); Glucksman, *Women Assemble.*

19. The literature is voluminous. Some examples are Willard, *Guesdistes*; Harvey Goldberg, *The Life of Jean Jaurès* (Madison, Wis., 1962); Jonathan Schneer, *Ben Tillett: Portrait of a Labour Leader* (Urbana, 1982); F. F. Ridley, *Revolutionary Syndicalism in France: The Direct Action of Its Time* (Cambridge, 1970).

20. Harvey J. Kaye and Keith McClelland, *E. P. Thompson: Critical Perspectives* (Philadelphia, 1990); Dipesh Chakrabarty, *Rethinking Working-Class History: The Case of Bengal Jute Workers* (Princeton, 1989).

21. Friedrich Lenger, "Beyond Exceptionalism: Notes on the Artisanal Phase of the Labour Movement in France, England, Germany and the United States," *International Review of Social History* 36 (April 1991): 1–23. Also see Aristide Zolberg, "Many Exceptionalisms?" in Katznelson and Zolberg, *Working-Class Formation.*

century working-class historians, for example, were concerned with why, once the working class had presumably been formed, workers became oriented toward reform. Explanations have included various theories of the labor aristocracy, including the domination of working-class parties and organizations by artisans with exclusionary, corporatist traditions, the idea that working-class culture either drained the working class of its revolutionary fervor or was itself a hidden mode of radicalism, and the idea that the working class did not become truly class conscious until the twentieth century, with the rise of the new unionism in England, the expansion of revolutionary syndicalist unions in France, and the emergence of labor as a political force.[22] German labor historians posited the notion of negative integration to explain the reformist orientation of German workers; the parliamentary success of the German Social Democratic Party allowed workers to operate through legal reform rather than revolution.[23] Regardless of how the story was told, however, labor historians seemed to agree on who the relevant social actors were in this drama, and what the drama itself ought to look like. Absent from such histories was an analysis of the exclusions that were central to the organizations, the political movements, and the men who emerged as leaders.

Even those historians who did not write from an explicitly Marxist perspective but who wrote working-class history with modernization or economic development as a central concern constructed their stories as evolutionary tales. Such narratives proceeded from the assumption that modernization involved the separation of work from the domestic arena

22. For one version of the argument of the labor aristocracy, see Foster, *Class Struggle;* Eric Hobsbawm initially made the argument for the existence of a labor aristocracy in his *Labouring Men,* pp. 272–315; see also Hobsbawm, *Workers,* chaps. 11–13. Debates over the labor aristocracy include exchanges between Alastair Reid and H. F. Moorhouse in *Social History* 3 (1978): 61–68 and 4 (1979): 481–93, and subsequent contributions by Gregor McLennan and Moorhouse, 6 (1981): 71–81, 229–33. See the critical survey of these debates by Robert Gray, *The Aristocracy of Labour in Nineteenth-Century Britain, c. 1850–1914* (London, 1981). On deference and the working class in mid-Victorian England see Joyce, *Work, Society, and Politics,* and the debate between Joyce and Richard Price in *Social History* 8 (1983): 57–75 and 9 (1984): 67–76. On working-class culture and the decline of working-class politics, see Gareth Stedman Jones, "Working-Class Culture and Working-Class Politics in London, 1870–1900: Notes on the Remaking of a Working Class," in his *Languages of Class,* pp. 179–238. On French workers' reformism see William H. Sewell Jr., "Artisans, Factory Workers, and the Formation of the French Working Class," and Cottereau, "Distinctiveness of Working-Class Cultures," both in Katznelson and Zoiberg, *Working-Class Formation;* Peter N. Stearns, *Revolutionary Syndicalism and French Labor: A Cause without Rebels* (New Brunswick, N.J., 1971).

23. See Dieter Groh, *Negative Integration und revolutionärer Attentismus: Die deutsche Sozialdemodratie am Vorabend des ersten Weltkreiges* (Frankfurt am Main, 1973); Richard J. Evans, *Proletarians and Politics: Socialism, Protest, and the Working Class in Germany before the First World War* (New York, 1990).

with the transition from proto-industrial forms of production to industrial capitalism over the course of the nineteenth century, as factories displaced small family-run workshops and increasing numbers of artisans became waged workers.[24] This paradigm was problematic from two perspectives. First, much of the work on proto-industrialization adopted a functionalist approach to the proto-industrial household and focused on the family as a harmonious and equitable productive unit, dominated by its male head. Rarely did historians question the distribution of power within the household system of production or the control of or access to resources, or ask who benefited from household labor.[25] Second, the insistence on the disappearance of the proto-industrial form and the emergence of factory industry as the essential ingredients in the development of a modern economy led historians to underestimate the persis-

24. The term "proto-industrialization" is usually credited to Franklin Mendels, "Proto-industrialization: The First Phase of the Industrialization Process," *Journal of Economic History* 32 (1972): 241–61. See also Peter Kriedte, Hans Medick, and Jürgen Schlumbohm, eds., *Industrialization before Industrialization*, trans. Beate Schempp (New York, 1981); Medick, "The Proto-industrial Family Economy: The Structural Functions of Household and Family during the Transition from Peasant Society to Industrial Capitalism," *Social History* 3 (1976): 291–315. For a more nuanced approach, see David Levine, *Reproducing Families: The Political Economy of English Population History* (New York, 1987), chap. 3, and *Family Formation*. Michael Sonenscher, *Work and Wages: Natural Law, Politics, and the Eighteenth-Century French Trades* (Cambridge, 1989), and "Journeymen's Migration and Workshop Organization in Eighteenth-Century France," in Kaplan and Koepp, *Work in France*, pp. 74–96, questions the stability and harmony of the proto-industrial workshop in eighteenth-century France. Much work has challenged the notion that household-based and small workshop handicraft production disappeared at the beginning of the nineteenth century. See Kaplan and Koepp, *Work in France*, esp. Ronald Aminzade, "Reinterpreting Capitalist Industrialization: A Study of Nineteenth Century France," pp. 393–417. See also Leslie Clarkson, *Protoindustrialization: The First Phase of Industrialization?* (London, 1985); Rudolph Braun, "Early Industrialization and Demographic Change in the Canton of Zurich," in *Historical Studies of Changing Fertility*, ed. Charles Tilly (Princeton, 1978), pp. 289–334.

25. More nuanced approaches to the study of proto-industrialization include Accampo, *Industrialization, Family Life*, and Gay Gullickson, *Spinners and Weavers of Auffay* (Cambridge, 1986). Even the picture of self-exploitation provided by some of the ethnographies in Pierre Guillaume Frédéric Le Play's studies of proto-industrial households in *Les Ouvriers européens*, 6 vols. (Tours, 1884), raised serious questions about the harmony of the domestic arrangement. See the excerpt from his vol. 6, *Les Ouvriers de l'occident: Populations désorganisées*, in *Victorian Women*, ed. Erna O. Hellerstein, Leslie Parker Hume, and Karen Offen (Stanford, 1981), pp. 318–23. See also Louise A. Tilly and Joan W. Scott, *Women, Work, and Family* (New York, 1987), pt. 1. Among works that do problematize the household from the standpoint of gender, power, and resources are Jean Quataert, "Teamwork in Saxon Homeweaving Families in the Nineteenth Century: A Preliminary Investigation into the Issue of Gender Work Roles," in *German Women in the Eighteenth and Nineteenth Centuries: A Social and Literary History*, ed. Ruth-Ellen B. Joeres and Mary Jo Maynes (Bloomington 1986), pp. 3–23; Joan W. Scott, "Work Identities for Men and Women: The Politics of Work and Family in the Parisian Garment Trades in 1848," in her *Gender and the Politics of History* (New York, 1988), pp. 93–112.

tence of proto-industrial or domestic, family-based handicraft production well into the nineteenth century.[26] They have hence tended to ignore the important role of women and children in the industrial economy outside of nineteenth- and twentieth-century factories.

PUBLIC AND PRIVATE IN LABOR HISTORY

Along with proletarianization, the public/private dichotomy, linked to the distinction between male and female, has been a foundational presupposition of both institutional labor history and the new labor history conceptualized as the study of working-class formation.[27] These analytical categories were encoded in a range of social theories, including those derived from or consonant with both liberal political theory and Marxian social theory. In addition, historians have tended to accept as fact rather than ideology the public/private dichotomy that nineteenth- and early twentieth-century observers and reformers constructed and diffused among their contemporaries of both the middle class and working class.[28] Finally, more recent historical scholarship has suggested that the very public sphere that scholars identified as the chosen subject or venue of their investigations was itself created on the basis of exclusions.[29]

26. We do not mean to conflate proto-industrial work with late nineteenth- or early twentieth-century homework; the division of labor and the organization of the family with respect to work were very different, though both forms of labor were performed in the home and by women. On the persistence of domestic production—or industrial homework, as it is sometimes called—well into the nineteenth century, see Sally Alexander, "Women's Work in Nineteenth-Century London: A Study of the Years 1820–1850," in *The Rights and Wrongs of Women*, ed. Juliet Mitchell and Ann Oakley (Harmondsworth, 1976), pp. 59–111; Marilyn Boxer, "Women in Industrial Homework: The Flowermakers of Paris in the Belle Epoque," *French Historical Studies* 12 (Spring 1982): 401–23; Barbara Franzoi, "Domestic Industry: Women's Work Options and Choices," in *German Women in the Nineteenth Century: A Social History*, ed. John C. Fout (New York, 1984), pp. 256–69; Robyn Dasey, "Women's Work and the Family: Women Garment Workers in Berlin and Hamburg before the First World War," in *The German Family*, ed. Richard J. Evans and W. R. Lee (London, 1981).

27. See Sonya O. Rose, "Gender and Labor History: The Nineteenth-Century Legacy," *International Review of Social History* 38, suppl. (1993): 145–62.

28. Examples of labor history that does look at the complex interrelationships between public and private life are Accampo, *Industrialization, Family Life*; Sonya O. Rose, *Limited Livelihoods: Gender and Class in Nineteenth-Century England* (Berkeley, 1992); Tilly and Scott, *Women, Work, and Family*; Kathleen Canning, "Gender and the Politics of Class Formation: Rethinking German Labor History," *American Historical Review* 97 (June 1992): 736–68. As Jean Quataert points out, the applicability of the public/private distinction, esp. to people who were both peasants and workers, is questionable. See Quataert, "Politics of Rural Industrialization," pp. 98–99.

29. See, e.g., Joan Landes, *Women and the Public Sphere in the Age of the French Revolution* (Ithaca, 1988); Geoff Eley, "Nations, Publics, and Political Cultures: Placing Habermas in the Nineteenth Century," in *Habermas and the Public Sphere*, ed. Craig

The public sphere was conceptualized in liberal political theory as the site of public opinion, citizenship, and democratic participation. It was imagined as a realm in which autonomous individuals behaved as rational political and economic actors. The public sphere, in other words, was gendered male. The private sphere, by contrast, was a realm of natural order based on the hierarchies of age and sex. It functioned as a "residual category" of social life, and as the domain of "natural" feminine attributes: emotion, nurturance, domesticity, and piety.

Though Marx was deeply critical of bourgeois social contract theory, he, too, presumed a public/private split, identifying forces and relations of production—located in the public or social sphere—as fundamental to historical transformation. Marx and Engels appear to have presumed that politics was located in the public sphere.[30]

The notion of gender-related oppositional spheres of human life in political and social theory was also elaborated as ideology by historical subjects. It was developed by the European middle classes in the eighteenth century and amplified in the nineteenth, and then over the course of the century it was taken on by the members of the working class as well. The ideology of separate spheres identified male activity and masculinity with the public sphere of politics and the market, and female activity and femininity with the private, domestic sphere of the household and reproduction.[31] Nineteenth-century discourse frequently invoked an idealized, orderly feminine private domain as the essential support for male activity in the public world and as a counterweight to the perceived evils of industrial capitalism, among them the increasingly visible participation of women in the labor force, especially in the insalubrious and exploitive conditions of factory labor. Nevertheless, the

Calhoun (Cambridge, Mass., 1992). See Jürgen Habermas, "The Public Sphere," *New German Critique* 3 (1974): 49–55, for an extremely abbreviated version of his definition of the public sphere.

30. For an excellent discussion of Marx's thinking about the public and private see Hal Benenson, "Victorian Sexual Ideology and Marx's Theory of the Working Class," *International Labor and Working-Class History* 25 (1983): 1–23.

31. The best discussion of the creation of the English middle-class public sphere is Leonore Davidoff and Catherine Hall, *Family Fortunes: Men and Women of the English Middle Class, 1780–1850* (London, 1987). Also see Catherine Hall, "Private Persons versus Public Someones: Class, Gender, and Politics in England, 1780–1850," in her *White, Male and Middle Class: Explorations in Feminism and History* (Cambridge, 1992), pp. 151–71. On working-class notions, see, e.g., Estelle B. Friedman and Erna O. Hellerstein, Introduction to pt. 2, pp. 118–33; Leslie P. Hume and Karen M. Offen, Introduction to pt. 3, pp. 272–91; and documents in pts. 2 and 3 of Hellerstein et al., *Victorian Women*; Michelle Perrot, "L'Eloge de la ménagère dans le discours des ouvriers français au XIXe siècle," *Romantisme*, special issue, "Mythes et représentations de la femme au XIXe siècle" (1977), pp. 105–21.

private sphere, though valorized, appeared to contemporary minds as a "secondary arena" of social relations.[32]

Numerous feminist historians and theorists have maintained for some time that the dichotomy obscured the historical relevance of the private, domestic sphere. Women's historians have produced a wealth of research on the centrality of family life to working-class communities. In addition, they have shown that the household was itself a site of conflict, contestation, and politics. Furthermore, feminist historians have long insisted that the so-called public and private arenas of life activity were not independent or autonomous. In the mid-1970s, for example, Joan Kelly maintained that rather than two spheres of social reality, there are in fact different sets of social relations.[33]

A wealth of work by feminist historians has revealed the relevance of family life to trade union activism, as well as to the structuring of labor forces and industries.[34] The expansion of industrial homework in the late nineteenth and early twentieth centuries suggests that the presumed separation of household and workplace (often used as a rationale for the significance of the public/private distinction) was not an inevitable feature of industrial capitalism. Furthermore, domestic manufacture, crucial to capitalist development in numerous countries,

32. On the creation of a domestic, feminine alternative to industrial capitalism, see Bonnie Smith, *Ladies of the Leisure Class* (Princeton, 1981).

33. See, e.g., Ellen Ross, " 'Fierce Questions and Taunts': Married Life in Working-Class London, 1870–1914," *Feminist Studies* 8 (Fall 1982); Ross, "Survival Networks: Women's Neighborhood Sharing in London before World War I," *History Workshop Journal* 15 (1983); Patricia Hilden, *Working Women and Socialist Politics in France, 1880–1914: A Regional Study* (Oxford, 1986); Tilly and Scott, *Women, Work, and Family*; Scott, "Work Identities"; Dasey, "Women's Work," and other essays in Evans and Lee, *German Family*; Anna Clark, *Women's Silence, Men's Violence: Sexual Assault in England, 1770–1840* (London, 1987); Nicky Hart, "Gender and the Rise and Fall of Class Politics," *New Left Review* 175 (1989): 19–46. For a discussion with respect to the concept of family strategies, see "Family Strategy: A Dialogue," *Historical Methods* 20 (1987): 113–25. For a discussion of conflict concerning the daughter's wage earning and the concept of family strategy, see Diane Lauren Wolf, *Factory Daughters: Gender, Household Dynamics, and Rural Industrialization in Java* (Berkeley, 1992); Joan Kelly, "The Double Vision of Feminist Theory," *Feminist Studies* 5 (Spring 1979): 216–27.

34. On the relevance of family life to trade union activism in Britain see Joanna Bornat, "Home and Work: A New Context for Trade Union History," *Oral History* 5, no. 2 (1977): 101–23. The idea that women's family ties actively promoted their trade union participation has been explored by U.S. feminist working-class historians. See, e.g., Carole Turbin, *Working Women of Collar City: Gender, Class, and Community in Troy, 1864–86* (Urbana, 1992), esp. chaps. 3 and 4. For France, see Frader, *Peasants and Protest*, chaps. 5 and 7; and Hilden, *Working Women*. On the relationship of family life, fertility practices, and the proliferation of homework industries, see Rose, *Limited Livelihoods*, chap. 4.

persisted well into the twentieth century throughout Europe.[35] In addition, feminist analysis of the demand for the family wage, a staple of trade union rhetoric in many countries, indicates the relevance of family life for male workers. In other words, not only were the public and private or domestic arenas not independent of each other, but the frequent claim that political consciousness was motivated in men by workplace problems and in women by domestic concerns is wide of the mark.

A substantial body of feminist writing stresses the historical importance of the relations of reproduction—or, more broadly, social reproduction—but years passed before historians noted that what scholars understood to be the public sphere was actually constructed on the basis of exclusions. In fact, the oppositional construction of public/private was used to justify excluding women from both politics and the market and denying them the right to vote as well as access to education and certain kinds of employment. Indeed, Geoff Eley points out, the public sphere itself, "in its classical liberal/bourgeois guise, was partial and narrowly based . . . and constituted from a field of conflict, contested meanings, and exclusions."[36] These exclusions were characteristic not only of the middle-class public sphere but of the working-class public sphere as well. Thus women (and certain men) were marginalized in trade union and working-class politics.[37]

Historians who studied the men who created and acted in the public sphere have conflated the activities of individual historical subjects with the abstract categories of the "social" and the "political" that have been the central focus of labor and working-class history—those identified as the significant factors in accounting for social change.[38] Institutional labor historians, for example, in focusing on unions and parties, paid attention to the men who succeeded in dominating social and political movements and organizations as the natural objects of historical

35. Quataert, "A New View of Industrialization: 'Protoindustry' or the Role of Small-Scale, Labor-Intensive Manufacture in the Capitalist Environment," *International Labor and Working-Class History* 33 (Spring 1988): 3–22; Barbara Engel, "Women, Work, and Family in the Factories of Rural Russia," *Russian History* 16 (1989): 224–25; Rose, *Limited Livelihoods*, pp. 72, 130–32.

36. Eley, "Nations, Publics, and Political Culture," p. 307.

37. See ibid., p. 313; Sonya O. Rose, "Respectable Men, Disorderly Others: The Language of Gender and the Lancashire Weavers' Strike of 1878 in Britain," *Gender and History* 5 (Autumn 1993): 382–97; Hilden, *Working Women*; Charles Sowerwine, *Sisters or Citizens? Women and Socialism in France since 1876* (Cambridge, 1982). The German story is somewhat different. See Jean Quataert, *Reluctant Feminists in German Social Democracy* (Princeton, 1974).

38. Geoff Eley, "Is All the World a Text?" in *The Historic Turn in the Human Sciences*, ed. Terrence McDonald (Ann Arbor, 1995), and "Nations, Publics, and Political Cultures"; Rose, "Gender and Labor History."

inquiry.[39] By not making issues of gender and the construction of political identities problems for study, labor historians have mistaken the particular for the universal.

While the new labor history examined workers' lives outside of formal organizations and their places of employment, historians in this tradition also focused on activists and leaders of working-class communities, and particularly on public and organized militancy. Forms of resistance and political activity were rarely problematized in ways that would permit recognition of the inclusions and exclusions on which those activities were based. To define their status as citizens and make the case for male suffrage, for example, working-class men in nineteenth-century Britain and France maintained that they held property in their labor, distinguishing themselves from both women and children. In this way they elaborated a notion of class that excluded women. The history of how this gendered idea of class was articulated in relation to the claim of citizenship rights and how these exclusions came into being has only begun to be written.[40] To summarize, the public-driven narrative, like the idea of proletarianization, privileged a certain group of workers as the subjects of study, for the most part male artisans and male industrial workers, as though telling the story of skilled male workers and their proletarian brothers were to tell a comprehensive story about the working class.

39. Richard Price, "The Future of British Labor History," *International Review of Social History* 36 (1991): 249–60.

40. Although Dorothy Thompson's work was critical in bringing women into the history of Chartism, she did not consider the gendered assumptions revealed in the rhetoric of both men and women Chartists. See Thompson, *The Chartists: Popular Politics in the Industrial Revolution* (New York, 1984). And see Joan Scott, "Language and Working-Class History," in her *Gender and the Politics of History*, pp. 62–63. Scott's critical assessment of Gareth Stedman Jones's work suggests that historians' attempts to attend to the importance of language in the construction of the meanings of class do not necessarily lead them to notice that those meanings are constructed on the basis of gender. An excellent study of the role of gender in Chartist discourse is Anna Clark, "The Rhetoric of Chartist Domesticity: Gender, Language and Class in the 1830s and 1840s," *Journal of British Studies* 31 (January 1992): 62–88. The literature on Chartism is voluminous. See, e.g., Asa Briggs, ed., *Chartist Studies* (New York, 1965); most of the essays in *The Chartist Experience: Studies in Working-Class Radicalism and Culture, 1830–1860*, ed. James Epstein and Dorothy Thompson (Atlantic Highlands, N. J., 1982). A happy exception to the universalistic vision of British radical politics among the Owenites is Barbara Taylor, *Eve and the New Jerusalem* (London, 1983). For France, see Steven C. Hause and Anne R. Kenney's *Women's Suffrage and Social Politics in the French Third Republic* (Princeton, 1984). Hause, *Hubertine Auclert, the French Suffragette* (New Haven, 1987), delves more deeply into Auclert's attempt to win recruits among socialists and working-class women. See esp. chap. 3. See also Amy Hackett, "The German Women's Movement and Suffrage, 1890–1914: A Study of National Feminism," in *Modern European History*, ed. Robert J. Bezucha (Lexington, Mass., 1972), pp. 354–86; Karen Hagemann, "La 'Question des femmes' et les rapports masculin-féminin dans la social-démocratie allemande sous la République de Weimar," *Mouvement Social*, no. 163 (April–June 1993): 25–44.

Forms of resistance that were not part of formal institutions such as labor unions and political parties or massive social movements were neglected.[41] Privileging public institutions and activities marginalized the private realm as both a site of resistance and an arena of social formation for the working class and for the development of class identities.

Most important, implicit models used by historians presumed that the category "worker" was universal, although in fact the subjects of labor history were particular. Most often, they were a fairly select group of men, the artisans and skilled workers who organized and engaged in public protest to articulate their grievances. The narratives often presumed that these particular subjects spoke for their more silent and less active counterparts, and that their experiences at work were the experiences of all workers. They were, in other words, quintessential workers.

WOMEN'S HISTORY

The findings of nearly twenty years of women's history and feminist inquiry challenge these foundational assumptions of working-class and labor history. This book builds on this legacy. An early and continuing strand of this vital historiography recovers the histories of the women workers who had been omitted from the historical record. European women's historians have been concerned to show women as significant participants in economic life and in collective protest and as contributors to working-class politics and working-class culture. They have countered the image of workers as quintessentially male, have contested the rationale for excluding women's occupations from histories of work, and have shown that the gendered distinction between public and private was more an ideological construct and contemporary worldview than an accurate description of actual social relations.

 Numerous investigations have revealed the significance of women workers in a host of industries and occupations. Women's labor force participation contributed to the expansion of various processes of capitalist production in factories and workshops, from textiles and garment

41. Work by women's historians on the French Resistance during World War II has called attention to the importance of the private realm in redefining and broadening the notion of resistance. See Paula Schwartz, "Redefining Resistance: Women's Activism in Wartime France," in *Behind the Lines: Gender and the Two World Wars*, ed. Margaret Randolph Higonnet, Jane Jenson, Sonya Michel, and Margaret Collins Weitz (New Haven, 1987), pp. 141–53; see also Temma Kaplan, "Female Consciousness and Collective Action: The Case of Barcelona," *Signs* 7 (1982): 545–66, on the relation of domestic concerns to women's public protest.

manufacture to small metalwares and pottery, and they made up the majority of the domestic servants and laundresses whose work was essential to middle-class domesticity in the nineteenth century.[42] They also joined the ranks of the unemployed as industries were transformed and during periods of economic decline or crisis. Women workers were central figures in rural manufacturing, and in the twentieth century they were employed in industries that were in the vanguard of industrial transformation—those that adopted scientific management and the moving assembly line—and played a crucial role in the making of a service-sector economy.[43]

Women's historians have focused on the links between women's work and family lives, and on the patterns of economic and domestic activity that marked them. They have shown the significance of women and the household division of labor in proto-industrial households, and have examined the changes in women's economic roles with the decline of domestic industry and the rise of factory production.[44] Investigations into women's work have also shown that industrial homework persisted into the late nineteenth century in certain feminized trades (lingerie, flower making, garment making, and textile manufacture, for example), sometimes increasing in periods of economic decline or developing as an

42. See, e.g., the special issues of *Mouvement Social*, nos. 105 and 140; Marie-Hélène Zylberberg-Hocquard, *Féminisme et syndicalisme en France* (Paris, 1978) and *Femmes et féminisme dans le mouvement ouvrier français* (Paris, 1981); Madeleine Guilbert, *Les Femmes et l'organisation syndicale avant 1914* (Paris, 1966); Louise A. Tilly, "Paths of Proletarianization: Organization of Production, Sexual Division of Labor, and Women's Collective Action," *Signs* 7 (1981): 400–417; Claire Auzias and Annik Houel, *La Grève des ovalistes* (Paris, 1982); Annie Fourcaut, *Femmes à l'usine en France dans l'entre-deux-guerres* (Paris, 1982); Mary Lynn Stewart, *Women, Work, and the French State: Labour Protection and Social Patriarchy, 1879–1919* (Montreal, 1989); Rachel G. Fuchs, *Poor and Pregnant in Paris: Strategies for Survival in the Nineteenth Century* (New Brunswick, 1992); Rachel G. Fuchs and Leslie Page Moch, "Pregnant, Single, and Far from Home: Migrant Women in Nineteenth-Century Paris," *American Historical Review* 95 (October 1990): 1007–31; Theresa McBride, *The Domestic Revolution: The Modernization of Household Service in England and France, 1820–1920* (London, 1976); Susan Bachrach, *Dames Employées: The Feminization of Postal Work in Nineteenth-Century France*, vol. 8 of *Women and History* (New York, 1983); Anne-Martin Fugier, *La Place des bonnes: La Domesticité féminine à Paris en 1900* (Paris, 1979); Laura Strumingher, *Women and the Making of the Working Class, Lyon, 1830–1870* (St. Albans, Vt., 1978).

43. See Ellen Jordan, "Female Unemployment in England and Wales, 1851–1911: An Examination of the Census Figures for 15–19-Year-Olds," *Social History* 13 (May 1988): 175–90; Downs, "Industrial Decline, Rationalization, and Equal Pay" and esp. her *Manufacturing Inequality*; Glucksman, *Women Assemble*.

44. Tilly and Scott, *Women, Work, and Family*, pts. 2 and 3; Bachrach, *Dames Employées*; McBride, *Domestic Revolution*; Gullickson, *Spinners and Weavers*; Sonya O. Rose, "Gender Segregation in the Transition to the Factory: The English Hosiery Industry, 1850–1910," *Feminist Studies* 13 (Spring 1987): 163–84.

outgrowth of industrial expansion.[45] The role of women in eighteenth-century bread riots and in strikes and demonstrations throughout the nineteenth and twentieth centuries has been the subject of historical analysis. Women's historians have also examined working women's roles in the labor movement, in suffrage campaigns, and in socialist politics in the late nineteenth and early twentieth centuries. Such studies contest the presumption that women's association with domesticity prevented their involvement in public or political affairs.[46]

A continuing focus in women's labor history has been on the sexual division of labor in both the workplace and the household. Numerous studies have attempted to unravel the causes and consequences of occupational sex segregation and its persistence. After Heidi Hartmann's landmark study in the mid-1970s, various historians and sociologists debated the relative impact of employers, male workers, and family needs and strategies on the sexual division of labor in employment.[47] While these studies and debates suggest that the reasons for the development and persistence of occupational segregation are complex, collectively they attest to the centrality of gender segregation in the structuring of industrial capitalism.

Taking the sexual division of labor in the household and the workplace in nineteenth- and twentieth-century European societies as a starting point, some women's historians have directed their attention to the experiences that were unique to women. Women's historians have ex-

45. Judith G. Coffin, *The Politics of Women's Work: The Paris Garment Trades, 1750–1915* (Princeton, Forthcoming). Also see Ute Daniel, "Women's Work in Industry and Family: Germany, 1914–1918," in *The Upheaval of War: Family, Work, and Welfare in Europe, 1914–1918*, ed. Richard Wall and Jay Winter (New York, 1988), pp. 267–96; Nancy Grey Osterud, "Gender Divisions and the Organization of Work in the Leicester Hosiery Industry," and Jenny Morris, "The Characteristics of Sweating: The Late Nineteenth-Century London and Leeds Tailoring Trade," both in *Unequal Opportunities: Women's Employment in England, 1800–1918*, ed. Angela V. John (New York, 1986); Shelly Pennington and Belinda Westover, *A Hidden Workforce: Homeworkers in England, 1850–1985* (London, 1989).

46. Charles Sowerwine, "Workers and Women in France before 1914: The Debate over the Couriau Affair," *Journal of Modern History* 55 (September 1983): 411–41; Zylberberg-Hocquard, *Féminisme et syndicalisme* and *Femmes et féminisme*; Guilbert, *Femmes et l'organisation syndicale*; Tilly, "Paths of Proletarianization"; Auzias and Houel, *La Grève des ovalistes*. Kaplan, "Female Consciousness," argues that women's domestic activities actually propelled them into public action. See also Laura L. Frader, "Beyond Separate Spheres: Women, the Family, and Protest in Nineteenth- and Twentieth-Century France," in *Private/Public Spheres: Women, Past and Present*, ed. D. R. Kaufman (Boston, 1989).

47. This debate focused principally on the sexual division of labor in England. See Heidi Hartmann, "Capitalism, Patriarchy, and Job Segregation by Sex," *Signs* 1 (1976): 137–69; Jane Humphries, "Class Struggle and the Persistence of the Working-Class Family," *Cambridge Journal of Economics* 1 (1977): 241–58; Jane Lewis, *Women of England, 1870–1950: Sexual Division and Social Change* (Bloomington, 1984).

plored women's domestic lives, their relations with neighbors, and their work experiences.[48] They have stressed working-class women's agency, and they demonstrate the centrality of sex as well as class to their experiences and to an inclusive understanding of working-class life.

Though these studies in European women's history have shown that a comprehensive picture of work, workers, and working-class communities, as well as working-class politics, cannot exclude women, they have not displaced or led to serious modification of the frameworks of working-class and labor history. At least some working-class and labor historians are making an effort to include women in their historical accounts, but generally they continue to write history within a framework guided by the old class formation model, erected on the presumption of gendered separate and oppositional spheres. Indeed, as feminist commentators have pointed out, many women's historians have accepted the public/private distinction uncritically.[49] As a result, scholars have treated capitalism and patriarchy as dual systems of oppression, operating independently in the public and private realms, respectively. "Dual systems theorists" looked to capitalism as the primary locus of class oppression, neglecting the ways in which gender was imbricated in the practices of capitalism as it developed.[50] Such foundational assumptions have been blinders for traditional labor historians and have helped to ghettoize or marginalize the findings of women's historians, as well as the role of gender in labor and working-class history.

48. Ross, "Survival Networks" and "'Fierce Questions'"; Elizabeth Roberts, *A Woman's Place: An Oral History of Working-Class Women, 1890–1940* (New York, 1984).

49. Leonore Davidoff, "'Adam Spoke First and Named the Orders of the World': Masculine and Feminine Domains in History and Sociology," in *Politics of Everyday Life: Continuity and Change in Work and the Family*, ed. Helen Corr and Lynn Jamieson (New York, 1990), pp. 222–23. Critiques of the public/private paradigm include Linda Kerber, "Separate Spheres, Female Worlds, Women's Place: The Rhetoric of Women's History," *Journal of American History* 75 (1988): 9–39; Dorothy O. Helly and Susan M. Reverby offer a perspective on the usefulness of the dichotomy for studying the history of women in their "Introduction: Converging on History," in *Gendered Domains: Rethinking Public and Private in Women's History*, ed. Helly and Reverby (Ithaca, 1992), pp. 1–26, as do many of the essays in that volume. See also Carole Pateman, "Feminist Critiques of the Public/Private Dichotomy," in *Feminism and Equality*, ed. Anne Phillips (New York, 1987), pp. 103–26. Valuable critiques of the gendered terms in which the public sphere and ultimately citizenship were conceived by eighteenth- and nineteenth-century political theorists and the consequences of these formulations are found in Landes, *Women and the Public Sphere*, and Carole Pateman, *The Sexual Contract* (Stanford, 1988).

50. A critique of dual systems theory is found in R. W. Connell, *Gender and Power* (Stanford, 1987). See also Mari Jo Buhle, "Gender and Labor History," in *Perspectives on American Labor History: The Problem of Synthesis*, ed. J. Carroll Moody and Alice Kessler Harris (De Kalb, Ill., 1989), pp. 64–65; Sylvia Walby, *Patriarchy at Work* (Minneapolis, 1986).

NEW DIRECTIONS IN FEMINIST SCHOLARSHIP

Historians who stress the importance of gender as a fundamental feature of social relationships have challenged the models and assumptions of "traditional" labor and working-class history.[51] With gender as a focus of research in working-class history, the foundational assumptions we have discussed become problematic. Gender analysis leads historians to question how such crucial categories as "workers," "wages," "skill," "men," "women," and "class" have been socially and culturally constructed.

By "gender" we mean the cultural meanings associated with perceptions of sexual difference, and the ways in which sexual difference forms the basis for social exclusions and inclusions and constitutes inequalities in power, authority, rights, and privileges.[52] Gender as a social characteristic is a fundamental element of all social relationships, although its significance in the creation of political identities varies. The meanings of gender are often contested because the cultural markers with which they are invested as well as the lived experiences and practices that they constitute are themselves changeable and contradictory. The historical meanings of gender change as gender is inflected by class, race, ethnicity, culture, and sexuality.[53] The term "gender," therefore, refers to both historically and socially constituted relationships and to a tool of analysis that historians can use to understand how social relationships and cultural categories are constructed. "Just as the history of blacks in the

51. The confluence of poststructuralism, literary theory, and feminism have been important here and are represented most deliberately and powerfully in the work of Joan Scott. See Scott, "Gender: A Useful Category of Historical Analysis," in her *Gender and the Politics of History*, pp. 28–50. See also Ava Baron, "Gender and Labor History: Learning from the Past, Looking to the Future," and the other essays in *Work Engendered: Toward a New History of American Labor*, ed. Baron (Ithaca, 1991); Alice Kessler-Harris, "A New Agenda for American Labor History: A Gendered Analysis and a Question of Class," in Moody and Kessler-Harris, *Perspectives on American Labor History*; Connell, *Gender and Power*; Françoise Collin, Introduction to "Le Genre de l'histoire," *Cahiers du Grif* 37–38 (Spring 1988): 5–7; Davidoff and Hall, *Family Fortunes*.

52. Obviously not all societies construe gender on the basis of sexual difference in the same way, just as not all societies operate in terms of the binary notions of gender that characterize Western European and many North American cultures. See Christine Ward Gailey, "Evolutionary Perspectives on Gender Hierarchy," in *Analyzing Gender*, ed. Beth Hess and Myra Marx Feree (Beverly Hills, 1988); Scott, "Gender: A Useful Category of Historical Analysis." Judith Butler offers provocative reconsideration of the unstable nature of gender in *Gender Trouble: Feminism and the Subversion of Identity* (New York, 1990).

53. See Iris Berger, Elsa Barkley Brown, and Nancy Hewitt, "Intersections and Collision Courses: Women, Blacks, and Workers Confront Gender, Race, and Class" (symposium), *Feminist Studies* 18 (Summer 1992): 283–326; Evelyn Brooks Higgenbothem, "African-American Women's History and the Metalanguage of Race," *Signs* 17 (Winter 1992): 251–74.

United States is both separate from and a part of the history of racism," Alice Kessler-Harris has pointed out, "so the history of women workers, which describes an aspect of cultural diversity, must be distinguished from that of gender."[54] As feminist historians have maintained, gender is present even when women are not. The study of gender inquires into the cultural construction of the categories "man" and "masculinity" as searchingly as it probes the cultural construction of "woman" and "femininity."[55]

More than a subject of historical analysis, however, gender is also an analytic framework. As Kessler-Harris notes, "gendered exploration of the past explores how the social relations of men and women create and inhibit expectations and aspirations and ultimately help to structure social institutions as well."[56] Joan Scott and others have pointed to the significance of gender as an analytical category that enables us to pay attention to the ways in which sexual difference is used to create and justify forms of power; for, in Scott's terms, "gender is a primary way of signifying relationships of power." Because sexual difference contributes to the organization of social life symbolically and in material terms, gender can provide a lens through which to analyze social organization, cultural practices, social behavior, and politics. As Scott has pointed out, a gendered analysis of authoritarian regimes (such as the old regime in eighteenth-century France and the Nazi state of the 1930s and 1940s) could help us to understand how those regimes maintained authority on the basis of inequalities founded on sexual difference.[57] Thus attention to gender can help us see how, in the 1930s, the Nazis dealt with the dual problems of depression-based unemployment and low fertility thorough a family policy that rewarded women for leaving the labor force and assuming a domestic role as housewives and mothers. Men who fathered children were likewise rewarded with monetary incentives and profes-

54. Kessler-Harris, "New Agenda," p. 225.

55. Among inquiries into the social or cultural construction of "woman," see Carolyn Steedman, Cathy Urwin, and Valerie Walkerdine, Introduction to Language, Gender, and Childhood, ed. Steedman et al. (Boston, 1985), and Denise Riley, Am I That Name? Feminism and the Category of "Women" in History (Minneapolis, 1988). For an excellent discussion of the contribution of feminist theory to a feminist social and labor history with particular reference to the United States, see Baron, "An 'Other' Side of Gender Antagonism at Work: Men, Boys, and the Remasculinization of Printers' Work, 1830–1920," in Baron, Work Engendered, pp. 47–69. On the social construction of masculinity, see Michael Roper and John Tosh, eds., Manful Assertions: Masculinities in Britain since 1800 (London, 1991); Jeffery Weeks, Sex, Politics, and Society: The Regulation of Sexuality since 1800 (New York, 1981); Mark C. Carnes and Clyde Griffen, eds., Meanings for Manhood: Constructions of Masculinity in Victorian America (Chicago, 1990).

56. Kessler-Harris, "New Agenda," p. 225. On the problems of defining gender, see Rose, Limited Livelihoods, pp. 11–13.

57. Scott, "Gender: A Useful Category," pp. 42, 45–48.

sional promotions.[58] Similarly, other studies have illuminated how welfare state policies have been formulated and implemented on the basis of perceptions of sexual difference.[59]

To understand gender as a *process* through which the perception of sexual difference structures organizations, affects social and political relationships, and becomes intrinsic to the construction of significant social categories and political identities requires us to attend seriously to the role that discourse plays in social life. Discourses constitute ideologies as well as cultural meanings that are articulated in material practices. These ideologies and cultural meanings are crucial in the formation of political identities, and they are the means by which some subjects are included and others are excluded from sites of power, influence, and political consequence. By analyzing gender as it is symbolically constructed, labor and working-class historians have begun to explore issues that reformulate the boundaries of the field, in two ways. First, gender analysis reveals that the practices that previously have been interpreted as universal and gender-neutral were both particular and dependent on constructions of sexual difference. Second, it exposes how historical subjects constructed crucial political categories such as "worker" and "citizen" by defining who was to be included in those categories and who was to be excluded from them. In this way feminist historians have begun to examine the ways in which class, skill, the wage, and activism, in addition to the family, unions, and political discourses and practices, have all been inflected by gender.[60] They have begun to challenge the dichotomization of production and consumption, and the rigid distinction between production and reproduction as well, in thinking about such concepts as the family wage. They have also begun to question how gender shaped both notions of citizenship and the policies and practices of states, such as protective labor legislation and welfare provision.

This book builds on and extends such scholarship. Four interrelated historical processes integral to the economic transformations and statebuilding that occurred in Europe between roughly 1800 and 1930

58. See Claudia Koonz, *Mothers in the Fatherland* (New York, 1987), pp. 149–51, 185–200. Similar policies were adopted by the Vichy regime in France during World War II. Married women were forced out of the labor force and employers penalized men who failed to produce children by denying them promotions or raises. See Robert Paxton, *Vichy France: Old Guard and New Order* (New York, 1972), pp. 165–68.

59. See, e.g., Elizabeth Wilson, *Women and the Welfare State* (London, 1977); Jane Lewis, *The Politics of Motherhood: Child and Maternal Welfare in England, 1900–1939* (London, 1980); Susan Pederson, *Family, Dependence, and the Origins of the Welfare State in France and Britian* (New York, 1993).

60. See Scott, *Gender and the Politics of History*; Canning, "Gender and the Politics of Class Formation"; and Rose, *Limited Livelihoods*. See also Quataert, "Politics of Rural Industrialization."

form the overarching field of inquiry that unites its chapters: proto-industrialization and proletarianization as two central elements of working-class formation and re-formation in both the emergence of industrial capitalism and the twentieth-century restructuring of capitalist economies; the complex relationship between public and private spheres as allegedly gendered domains of human activity, which was articulated and rearticulated along with economic shifts and changes in social and cultural practices; and the interrelated processes of the expansion of citizenship rights and state intervention on behalf of gendered subjects. The authors destabilize the functionalist model of the proto-industrial household based on complementarity and harmony between the sexes; they challenge the notion that proletarianization is a universal and gender-neutral process; and they dissolve the oppositional categories of public and private. Finally, they demonstrate that both the expansion of state authority and the early battles for the extension of citizenship rights in nineteenth-century Europe occurred with reference to gendered subjects and thus created new forms of exclusion. Together, they show the power of gender analysis to illuminate European working-class history and suggest new ways of thinking about work and workers that could revitalize the field.

Proto-industrialization and proletarianization were complementary processes that touched the vast majority of European workers over the course of the eighteenth and nineteenth centuries. In some areas, proto-industrialization, that stage of industrial development during which merchant capitalism both fed and benefited from rural household production during the eighteenth century, permitted the accumulation of enough capital to establish large-scale manufacturing. Proletarianization, one outcome of the decline of proto-industrial forms of production, as we have suggested, took many forms as working people were progressively separated from the productive apparatus, lost control over apprenticeship, hiring practices, and the labor process, and eventually experienced deskilling and the reorganization of work itself. In England, for example, textile manufacture was significantly modified by industrial capitalist organization from the end of the eighteenth century and the emergence of factory production in large urban agglomerations such as Leeds, Manchester, and Salford. Large numbers of women and men, many of them formerly spinners and weavers in their own cottages, left their spinning wheels and handlooms behind to sell their labor to a factory owner. These developments, in part related to early capital accumulation, population growth, and the agricultural revolution, distinguished English industrial development and the process of proletarianization of English workers from that of much of the rest of the world in timing, pace, and amplitude. In Ireland and in France capitalist development was

much more uneven. Despite the development of industrial textile production in Belfast and in French centers such as Lille, Roubaix,
Tourcoing, and Troyes in the 1830s, substantial proto-industrial sectors
of domestic textile production subsisted in both countries, in some cases
well into the nineteenth and even early twentieth centuries. In Ireland,
in rural areas of the north, population growth and land subdivision
encouraged the development and persistence of domestic textile production; in France, household textile production likewise survived well into
the nineteenth century in the traditionally Catholic Vendée, in the west.
Women's labor was central to the domestic economies of both countries.
Yet even household-based proto-industrial workers such as those examined by Jane Gray and Tessie Liu in this volume did not escape the
process of proletarianization.

The chapters in Part I contest the utility of the concept of proto-
industrialization based on a unitary and harmonious household operating
without respect to sex difference. They also call into question labor
historians' all too frequent assumption that proletarianization occurred
without respect to gender and with substantially the same consequences
for women as for men. In Chapter 1 Jane Gray shows that the history of
rural linen weavers in nineteenth-century Ireland raises questions about
proto-industrialization models that attempt to explain the course of
industrial development. Gender relations, she shows, were a fundamental component of regional patterns of industrial transformation. Gray
examines the role of gender difference from two perspectives: first, from
the standpoint of unequal exchange relationships between areas relying
primarily on women's labor at the spinning wheel and those that relied
primarily on men's labor at the loom, and their consequences for both
capital accumulation and workers' collective identities; and second, from
the perspective of the cultural practices that were part of the construction of workers' identities.

Unlike Britain, France never experienced an "industrial revolution,"
but rather industrialized slowly from about the 1830s. Moreover, the
unevenness of industrial development left behind pockets of rural protoindustry that persisted into the twentieth century, especially in certain
sectors of textile production, as in Ireland. In Chapter 2 Tessie P. Liu
examines the gendered relations of production in linen weavers' households in the Choletais region of western France at the turn of the twentieth century. Departing from flexible specialization theorists who argue
for the positive aspects of small-scale production in industrial economies, Liu points to the highly exploitive "sweated" aspects of domestic
industry. Much as in Ireland, gender inequalities in French weavers'
households facilitated male workers' resistance to industrial capitalism
and thus resulted in uneven proletarianization. Liu shows that women's

proletarianization allowed male artisans to remain independent, but it also led to regional underdevelopment. Investigations of family-based domestic textile production in both Ireland and France demonstrate that neither the development of industrial capitalism nor working people's responses to it can be fully understood unless gender is taken into account. The processes by which wage labor was produced were anything but gender neutral.

Where family-based household textile production gave way to factory production in other parts of France, later in the nineteenth century and during the twentieth century, gendered skill identities also resulted in different—gendered—work trajectories and opportunities for women and men. In Chapter 3 Helen Harden Chenut examines changes at the point of production and shifts in the conceptualization of skill in the Troyes knitting industry to show how the skill and work identities of men and women were redefined as employers introduced new technology and new forms of work organization between 1880 and 1936. This process, accompanied by the feminization of the labor force, resulted in the devaluation of women's skills and hence the devaluation of most women's occupations by the late 1930s.

Much labor history has understandably focused on the point of production, but that history does not exhaust or even necessarily encompass all that was significant in the lives of working people in the past. The history of the European working class is also the story of the articulation and rearticulation of complex relationships between gendered public and private domains in workers' lives, as the chapters in Part II demonstrate.

Throughout Western Europe, but especially in France and Britain, the notion of a separation between public and private spheres and their gender ascriptions prevailed at least from the late eighteenth century through much of the twentieth century. As industrial capitalism expanded in Europe, rendering women's wage labor more visible than ever before, the idealization of the family (and of women's role within it) as a private domain of social reproduction (as opposed to production), separate from the public and male world of production, appeared in the discourse of a wide spectrum of social observers, from such middle-class writers as John Ruskin, Mrs. Sarah Stickney Ellis, and Elizabeth-Felicité Bayle-Mouillard (Mme Celnart) to delegates to the 1879 French Socialist Workers' Congress.[61] In Britain, the idealization of the "respectable"

---

61. See, e.g., Hellerstein et al., *Victorian Women*, pts. 1 and 2; John Ruskin, "Of Queen's Gardens," in his *Sesame and Lilies* (New York, 1875); Mrs. Sarah Stickney Ellis, *The Women of England: Their Social Duties and Domestic Habits* (London, 1835); *Séances du Congrès ouvrier socialiste de France 3ᵉ à Marseille* (Marseille, 1879), and Laura L. Frader, "Engendering Work and Wages," in this volume.

working-class family contained a certain moral imperative that could be seen as a reaction to the social consequences not only of industrialization but also of colonial immigration, with its potential threat to domestic racial order.[62] Contributors to Part II of this volume examine how gendered meanings of consumption and production, debates over the right to work and the importance of family, and views of gender, race, and the family in working-class communities dissolve the frequently assumed dividing line between public and private domains.

In Chapter 4 Judith G. Coffin explores how the invention and marketing of the sewing machine in late nineteenth- and twentieth-century France broke down the boundary that allegedly separated the private domain of the household from the public domain of labor. Entrepreneurs and advertisers marketed portable sewing machines, one of the few machines ever to be gendered "female," for both housewives and potential industrial homeworkers. Coffin examines the important links between women's "public" wage earning in the garment industry and the expansion of working-class household consumption made possible by the development of installment buying in the late 1880s. For French seamstresses who could buy a machine on credit, the frontier between consumption and production disappeared. Coffin shows that this development did not lead to the restoration of family-based homework, although it did demonstrate the intimate relationship between women's waged and unwaged labor.

The family wage constitutes another arena in which the concept of oppositional public and private spheres broke down. The family wage figured prominently in labor movement claims in both nineteenth-century Britain and the United States and contributed to the construction of gender difference at work in these countries; these debates figured much less prominently in France.[63] Laura L. Frader shows in Chapter 5 that before World War I, workers' defenses of the family wage in France arose sporadically in highly skilled trades threatened by technological change or where male workers viewed women as competitors. Support of the family wage by some sectors of the labor movement was intimately linked to male workers' attempts to redefine work as a masculine activity. It also demonstrated the extent to which male workers defined their interests and identities as workers in terms of private—family—concerns. Frader shows how the politicization of the family after World War I dissolved the frontier between public and private realms. Attempts to

62. See, e.g., Vron Ware, *Beyond the Pale: White Women, Racism, and History* (London, 1992).

63. See Hal Benenson, "The Family Wage and British Working Women's Consciousness in Britain, 1880–1914," *Politics and Society* 19 (March 1991): 71–108; Rose, *Limited Livelihoods*, pp. 130–32.

enlist the working-class family (and eventually all families) in the battle against the decline of the French population led to employer and state-regulated family allowances that weakened the labor movement's appeals for a family wage. Even where population and family policy were not immediate issues, the boundaries of the family often dissolved before the sharp eyes of state and social investigators, as in Britain.

Social observers' definition of the family as an essential component of public order came into conflict with working-class families in interracial British working-class communities in seaport towns such as Liverpool and Cardiff during the first half of the twentieth century. In Chapter 6 Laura Tabili examines the significance of interracial marriage within the web of imperial, racial, and capitalist relations.[64] She shows how race inflected gender and class relations in merchant shipping communities where seamen from Britain's far-flung colonies married and set up households with white working-class British women. Indeed, Tabili shows not only that race inflected gender and class relations but that in the minds of government officials and social investigators, race and class together helped to construct gender, by redefining masculinity and femininity. The discourse that social investigators developed to marginalize and pathologize interracial marriages was simultaneously gendered as well as raced and classed.

Part of the process of state-building in virtually every Western European country included regulation of both capital and labor and the emergence of systems of social provision, with different intentions and outcomes for women and men. The chapters in Part III examine such intervention and regulation in the nineteenth and twentieth centuries. These developments follow the uneven pace of state-building across Europe, but throughout Western Europe, industrialization precipitated widespread concern about the negative effects of factory labor on women's health and reproductive capacities and about the decline of the working-class family. Much feminist scholarship has already revised our

---

64. Although there is a substantial and growing body of literature on race and working-class history in the United States, and many feminist U.S. labor historians are incorporating race as well as gender in their analyses, the study of race or ethnicity in working-class life in the European context is still in its infancy. See, e.g., David Roediger, *Wages of Whiteness: Race and the Making of the American Working Class* (London, 1991) and *Towards the Abolition of Whiteness: Essays on Race, Politics, and Working-Class History* (London, 1994); Earl Lewis, *In Their Own Interests: Race, Class, and Power in Twentieth-Century Norfolk, Virginia* (Berkeley, 1991); Robin D. G. Kelly, *Hammer and Hoe: Alabama Communists during the Great Depression* (Chapel Hill, 1990) and *Race Rebels: Culture, Politics, and the Black Working Class* (New York, 1994); Joe William Trotter Jr., *Black Milwaukee: The Making of an Industrial Proletariat, 1915–1945* (Urbana, 1985); Dolores Janiewski, *Sisterhood Denied: Race, Gender, and Class in a New Southern Community* (Philadelphia, 1985); Patricia Cooper, *Once a Cigar Maker: Men, Women, and Work Culture in American Cigar Factories* (Urbana, 1987).

understanding of state programs of social provision and the gender-specific laws that regulated private life and women's status as legal subjects.[65] Feminist scholars have likewise examined the debates about state regulation of women's employment and the consequences of protective labor legislation for women. These studies have demonstrated that the state is not a gender-neutral social institution; gender is part of the very process of state-building.[66] Indeed, Britain passed the first substantial body of gender-specific factory legislation the 1830s and 1840s. French republicans, once they gained control of the French state and definitively established a republic, also used the state to regulate women's and children's labor some eighty years later. The establishment of a unified German state in 1871 opened the door to industrial regulation with similar debates over women's work in the last quarter of the nineteenth century. Both French and German social observers and state officials focused on the detrimental effects of factory labor on women's bodies, the French arguing that motherhood was vital to the national interest. In both countries socially constructed definitions of femininity and class were embedded in national policy.

In Chapter 7 Sonya O. Rose examines the history of factory legislation in Britain. Concentrating on laws limiting the hours of labor, she argues that their gender-specific focus was crucial to the processes by which the liberal state in Britain legitimated its rule. Debates about the Factory Acts centered on the rationale for considering male workers as autonomous economic agents and female workers as dependents who needed state protection. Rose suggests not only that state regulation of women's work was crucial in the construction of male and female workers as different legal and ideological categories but that regulation was achieved through legislative initiatives that were central to the formation of the liberal state in Victorian Britain.

65. For an excellent discussion of both "gender-blind" studies and feminist analyses of the welfare state, see Linda Gordon, "The New Feminist Scholarship on the Welfare State," in *Women, the State, and Welfare,* ed. Gordon (Madison, Wis., 1990), pp. 9–25. See also Susan Pedersen, *Family, Dependence, and the Origins of the Welfare State: Britain and France, 1914–1945* (Cambridge, 1993); Jane Lewis, *The Politics of Motherhood* (London, 1980) and "The Working-Class Wife and Mother and State Intervention, 1870–1918," in *Labour and Love: Women's Experience of Home and Family, 1850–1940,* ed. Lewis (Oxford, 1986); Judith Walkowitz's discussion of the Contagious Diseases Acts in *Prostitution in Victorian Society* (New York, 1982); Mary Lyndon Shanley, *Feminism, Marriage, and the Law in Victorian England* (Princeton, 1989).

66. See Stewart, *Women, Work, and the French State;* Mariana Valverde, *The Age of Light, Soap, and Water: Moral Reform in English Canada, 1885–1925* (Toronto, 1991); Rose, *Limited Livelihoods.* For a theoretical statement, see R. W. Connell, "The State, Gender, and Sexual Politics," *Theory and Society* 19, no. 5 (1990): 507–44. See also essays in *Gender and History* 5 (Summer 1993) and *Feminist Review* 44 (Summer 1993).

German legislators and social observers began to address the issue of women's work and the female body from the 1870s, as Kathleen Canning demonstrates in Chapter 8. Canning examines the multiple discourses that focused on the place of women in German society and on the status of working women. She addresses two interrelated aspects of welfare state policy: the contesting and rearticulating of the relationship between public and private domains, and the centrality of women's bodies, sexual morality, and domesticity to debates about protective legislation. Canning maintains that the "social question" and the discourses about gender on which it focused figured prominently in the creation of the German welfare state. But, as Canning argues, these developments went "far beyond the realm of governing" to modify as well the relationship of working women to class politics.

Unlike Britain, where the form of the state was clear from at least the late seventeenth century, France saw a series of shifts from empire to constitutional monarchy to republic and back to empire within the space of some seventy years. Nonetheless, the discourse with which French reformers and legislators addressed the issue of women's factory labor bore a striking similarity to those of British and German reformers. Judith F. Stone argues in Chapter 9 that the building of the Third Republic involved the definition of a new model of the state, intimately connected with republican ideals of the family and a gendered social order. Stone examines the way in which definitions of masculinity and femininity shaped both republican ideology and republican policy, particularly with reference to protective legislation. She explores the gendered foundations of the republican concept of citizenship and the ideological contradictions that emerged when radical republicans attempted to respond to the circumstances of working women. Stone concludes that the twin issues of motherhood and political equality were crucial contested arenas that shaped the early Third Republic.

Nineteenth- and twentieth-century movements to extend citizenship rights constituted another arena in which class and gender intersected beyond the realm of capitalist production. Part IV examines the ways in which working-class claims to citizenship were simultaneously informed by notions of masculinity and femininity as well as by class. As middle-class men gradually acquired the vote, working-class men and women began to demand the same privilege. In Britain, workers of both sexes mobilized to extend full citizenship rights at the time of the First Reform Bill (1832) and carried their struggle into the late nineteenth century. Working women, initially part of Chartist suffrage movements and hopeful that they would be included in the Reform Bill of 1867, eventually disappeared from both. In France, where male citizenship implied the exclusion of women from the public sphere, the founding of the Third Republic in 1870 and the restoration of voting rights to all adult men opened new possibilities for the inclusion of women as full citizens. But these possibilities were not realized until 1944.[67] After World War I, the granting of suffrage to women and the formation of Communist parties in the aftermath of the Bolshevik Revolution broadened the bases of citizenship and forced a redefinition of working-class women's status as political actors. Communists across Europe as well as in the Soviet Union made broad appeals to women, eager to establish mass class-based parties.

Early British mobilizations for suffrage are the subjects of Chapters 10 and 11. Anna Clark explores the radical political rhetoric of Chartist activists in Britain in the 1830s and 1840s in an effort to understand why the radical possibilities for women's inclusion in Chartist claims to citizenship were not borne out. Most previous studies of early nineteenth-century Chartism have tended to accept contemporaries' masculine definitions of citizenship as normative. With the exception of Dorothy Thompson and a very few others, historians of Chartism virtually ignored women's presence in the movement.[68] Yet even historians who included women in the narrative did not question assumptions about masculinity and femininity that were central to the movement and its participants. The discourses of hierarchy and difference that emerged in Chartist rhetoric when male Chartist activists articulated their ideas about citizenship and class, or when they spoke about limited suffrage for women, have not been part of the classic histories of this movement for male citizenship rights. Clark argues that the Chartists' definitions of citizenship became increasingly more masculine as a consequence of conflict with their opponents. It was language in use, according to Clark, that transformed what could have been an inclusive understanding of "citizen" into one that emphasized masculine political dominion.

<hr />

67. French women had spoken out for the right to vote after the revolution of 1830, during the 1840s, and in 1848, but not until 1876 was a formal pro-suffrage organization established. See Patrick Kay Biddleman, *"Pariahs Stand Up!" The Founding of the Liberal Feminist Movement in France, 1858–1889* (Westport, Conn., 1982); Michelle Riot-Sarcey, *La Démocratie à l'épreuve des femmes* (Paris, 1994).

68. Dorothy Thompson, "Women and Nineteenth-Century Radical Politics: A Lost Dimension," in Mitchell and Oakley, *Rights and Wrongs of Women*, pp. 112–38, and *The Chartists*, esp. chap. 7; Malcolm I. Thomis and Jennifer Grimmett, *Women in Protest, 1800–1850* (London, 1982), chap. 6. On the discourse of "property in labor" see Alexander, "Women, Class, and Sexual Difference"; John Rule, "The Property of Skill in the Period of Manufacture," in *The Historical Meanings of Work*, ed. Patrick Joyce (Cambridge, 1987); and Joan Scott's critiques of Gareth Stedman Jones and E. P. Thompson in *Gender and the Politics of History*, pp. 53–90. For women in Chartism see Jutta Schwartzkopf, *Women in the Chartist Movement* (New York, 1991); and Clark, "Rhetoric of Chartist Domesticity." For the significance of the links between citizenship and manhood for working-class politics in England in the 1870s see Rose, "Respectable Men, Disorderly Others."

Keith McClelland takes the story of the construction of the male working-class citizen further by exploring the implications of defining as "respectable" and "independent" the men who were enfranchised by the 1867 Reform Bill. During debates about reform and as a consequence of the bill's passage, activists linked political equality to the idea that rights came in exchange for obligations to the state, such as taxpaying and military defense. The definition of equality that qualified some working-class men to vote simultaneously excluded all women, paupers, and "lunatics." Whereas Clark shows how, within a popular movement for the expansion of citizenship, Chartist men defined citizenship and class in gendered terms, McClelland concludes that initiatives emerging from both civil society and state social policies were fundamental in redefining and legitimizing the independent workingman as a citizen.

In contrast to France, Britain, and Germany, where the construction of masculine citizenship was central to the formation of the bourgeois liberal state, in Russia the Revolution of 1917 triggered a major shift in the notion of civil society. The "building of socialism" in the new Soviet Union also involved a reconsideration of gender politics as the Bolshevik Party struggled to integrate women into the new society as citizen-workers. Elizabeth A. Wood shows in Chapter 12 how the issue of organizing women became central to debates between Party functionaries and trade union leaders in the 1920s. She examines how the Bolsheviks grappled with the problem of how to integrate newly enfranchised women into the revolutionary state: should women be organized separately, as women, or should they be organized as integral members of the working class? Conflicts between women organizers and trade unions over this issue were exacerbated by relations with the Bolshevik Party. For the Party, Wood argues, played off each group against the other in order to enhance its own hegemonic position within the revolutionary state. Gender was an arena in which the Party worked out issues of control and discipline.

In other European countries as well, Communist discourses between the two World Wars relied on gendered representation of the Party activists. In Chapter 13 Eric D. Weitz examines the gendered iconography of the Communist parties of France, Germany, and Italy. In the 1920s, visual images of powerful, productive working-class men were accompanied by images of strong, athletic women workers. By the 1930s, however, although representation of the masculine worker remained the same, representations of women began to reflect the maternalist discourses prevalent in European society more generally in that period. In explaining the shifting representations of women and more stable representations of men, Weitz shows how iconographic representations of gender corresponded to political strategies and alliance-building. Like Elizabeth Wood and Kathleen Canning, Weitz demonstrates how political groups manipulated notions of gender and gendered notions of class in the process of constructing agendas and policies.

This book proposes a new agenda for working-class and labor history. It suggests that by making gender (and race/ethnicity) a focal point of analysis, historians can begin to interrogate the conceptual categories of work and workers. When these categories are made problems for study rather than deployed as preformed and unitary identities, scholars will not mistake the particular for the general. They will produce a less unified and more multifaceted view of working people's lives. By focus-ing on how the categories "work" and "worker" were constituted by historical subjects, moreover, scholars will glimpse how these subjects attempted to manipulate their social worlds, and the technologies of power that they used in doing so.

To make sense of these fundamentally political activities, scholars will have to examine how discourses worked to constitute political identities. By examining these discourses, historians will be in a position to deter-mine the inclusions and exclusions that are central to the creation of political identities, and to the making of solidarities. Working-class and labor historians cannot remain wedded to a view of labor history that focuses only on the workers who were organized as the significant agents of history. The fates of unions and radical parties in the contemporary period suggest that it is a mistake to imagine that organized workers are always the vanguard of social change. The same may also have been the case in the past, when opposition to capitalist power relations was spo-radic, and developed most often in organizations whose leaders and active members constituted a minority of workers. This does not mean that labor historians should ignore trade unionism and social movements for political and social rights. Rather, we need to pay greater attention to the way allegiances were forged—to those who did not join as well as those who did; to those who were excluded as well as those who were included. It is important to recognize that the people who were marginal to those organizations and movements actually may have been central to the dynamics of labor's history.

Though we propose that attention to gender and language is important to a reimagined labor and working-class history, this book suggests why we cannot afford to dispense with the study of political economy. Indeed, Gray, Liu, Chenut, and Tabili demonstrate that our unders-tanding of economic and social development is enhanced when we recognize the centrality of gender and race to these processes. Historians who have devoted attention to social and economic conditions and how they change without examining the role played by gender and race/ethnicity have missed crucial aspects of those processes and changes.

Such studies are critical even for those historians who focus primarily on culture and politics, because they can help scholars understand the contexts in which political identities are forged and the conditions under which categories are contested and changed.[69] This does not mean that these conditions or contexts by themselves produce the politics. Rather, social conditions create the impetus for politics without determining the specific form they take. In other words, to be able to assess the inclusions and exclusions that are the stuff of collective identities, scholars need to know, at the very least, who was there to be included or excluded. In the effort to map and understand discursive shifts, the way forward is to know something about the changing social contexts from which revised cultural understandings emerge.[70] Instead of abandoning the study of political economy and the enterprise of social history, we need to examine the symbolic processes that are involved in the structuring of the material world. At the same time, as we argued earlier, critical attention to the political process is fundamental to a reimagined working-class history. Incorporating gender in such studies is a crucial beginning.

69. Kathleen Canning makes this point in "Feminist History after the Linguistic Turn: Historicizing Discourse and Experience," *Signs* 19 (Winter 1994): 368–404.

70. Marshall Sahlins elucidates how cultural categories change in the context of their use, when, as he puts it, "word meets world": *Islands of History* (Chicago, 1985).

I

RETHINKING
PROLETARIANIZATION

I

Gender and Uneven Working-Class Formation in the Irish Linen Industry

Jane Gray

In a poem first published in 1804, the Irish weaver-poet James Orr nostalgically portrayed life in a linen manufacturing household "in years of yore."

> He weav'd himsel', an' keepet twathree gaun,
>   Wha prais'd him ay for hale weel-handled yarn;
> His thrifty wife an' wise wee lasses span,
>   While warps and queels employ'd anither bairn;
> Some stript ilk morn an' thresh'd, the time to earn
>   To scamper wi' the houn's frae hill to hill;
> Some learn'd the question-beuk in nybr'ing barn—
>   Christy wrought unco close, whyles took a gill,
> But when his wab was out had ay a hearty fill.[1]

1. James Orr, *The Posthumous Works of James Orr of Ballycarry, with a Sketch of His Life* (Belfast, 1935), p. 173. For an extended analysis of this poem, see Jane Gray, "Folk Poetry and Working Class Identity in Ulster: An Analysis of James Orr's 'The Penitent," *Journal of Historical Sociology* 6 (1993): 249–76.

> He weaved himself, and kept two or three going,
>   Who praised him for strong, well-handled yarn,
> His thrifty wife and wise wee lasses span,
>   While warps and quills employed another child;
> Some stripped each morn and threshed, the time to earn
>   To scamper with the hounds from hill to hill;

This rich stanza depicts a prosperous farmer-weaver household in which relations between husband and wife, father and children, farmer and cottiers are simultaneously complementary and hierarchical. Each member provides an essential input to the small enterprise in which the rhythm of production is task-oriented. The boys work especially hard in the mornings in order to "earn" time to go hunting, while Christy, their father, a skilled weaver, finishes the piece before indulging his appetite for alcohol.

The account is both nostalgic and romanticized. Orr sets his tale in a legendary time that only Brice, "the auld herd on the moor," can remember.[2] Yet social scientists have often adopted a similar image of the preindustrial household as a self-contained, harmoniously functioning unit. This "ideal type" has tended to obscure the inequalites that existed within and between households and, in turn, the significance of gender in the process of working-class formation. Nostalgic images of an ideal domestic sphere, like that found in Orr's poem, should be understood not as descriptions of household production in past time but as interventions in gender and class politics at the time of writing.

Two influential perspectives on the formation of the European working class are the theory of "proto-industrialization" as it has been developed by Peter Kriedte, Hans Medick, and Jürgen Schlumbohm, and E. P. Thompson's "cultural" approach to the development of class consciousness.[3] Gender must be made central to both perspectives if they are to explain regional and social differentiation in industrialization and class formation.

My analysis of the cultural changes associated with class formation centers on the gendered meanings attached to the consumption of beer and tea in the poems of "rhyming weavers" from the northeast of Ireland.[4] These works, published by subscription during the first half of the

---

Some learned the question-book in neighbouring barn—
Christy wrought very fine, at times drank a gill,
But when his web was out had a hearty fill.

2. This is probably a reference to Edward Brice, who became the first Presbyterian minister to preach in Ireland when he settled in Orr's parish of Templecorran in the early seventeenth century. See the memoir by James Boyle reproduced in *Ordnance Survey Memoirs of Ireland*, ed. Angélique Day, Patrick McWilliams, and Nóirín Dobson, vol. 26 (Belfast, 1994), p. 107. The poem is an account of how a weaver and his family are saved from dissipation by their conversion to Methodism, but Orr was himself a Presbyterian.

3. Peter Kriedte, Hans Medick, and Jürgen Schlumbohm, *Industrialization before Industrialization*, trans. Beate Schempp (Cambridge, 1981); E. P. Thompson, *The Making of the English Working Class* (New York, 1966).

4. For a general discussion and anthology of works by Ulster's folk poets, see John Hewitt, *Rhyming Weavers, and Other Country Poets of Antrim and Down* (Belfast, 1974). For a discussion of the uses of folk poetry for historical research, with special reference to James Orr, see Donald H. Akenson and William H. Crawford, *Local Poets and Social History: James Orr, Bard of Ballycarry* (Belfast, 1977).

nineteenth century, give unique clues to how ordinary people understood and represented the changes surrounding the transition to centralized production. They also impose limitations on the analysis of changes in the relations between men and women. First, discussion of the construction of gendered working-class identities is confined to that part of rural industrial Ireland which made the transition to factory industry, and further to the descendants of Scots and English settlers who were privileged in comparison with native inhabitants of Ireland, and who had higher levels of literacy. Second, while a strong case can be made that individual weaver-poets were representative of their communities,[5] both weavers and poets were male. Sarah Leech appears to have been the only spinner who published poems in the tradition of the rhyming weavers.[6] The value of folk poetry, however, lies less in its articulation of individual attitudes than in its expression of the cultural values and ideals of ordinary people. The poems should be read as texts embedded in a broader popular discourse. By obliging us to think about class formation in the language of everyday life, they help ensure that our analyses are "held tightly in check by the voices of the past."[7]

GENDER IN THE DEVELOPMENT OF THE IRISH LINEN INDUSTRY

By 1800, the Irish linen industry might be said to have reached both its zenith and a turning point. Originating in the Scots and English settler communities of the northeast and nurtured by favorable British trade regulations, commercial flax spinning and linen weaving provided two of Ireland's most important export commodities throughout the eighteenth century. Generally furnishing their own raw materials, Irish rural households sold the woven cloth to drapers, who had it finished before reselling it to merchants in Belfast and London. Yarn not consumed within the household was bought up by jobbers, who transported it for resale to weavers or to merchants for direct export to Britain, where it was used as warp in the manufacture of cotton cloth. At the turn of the nineteenth century Irish linen cloth exports continued to rise, but yarn exports had declined significantly, partly as a result of competition from British

---

5. See Akenson and Crawford, *Local Poets*.

6. Hewitt, *Rhyming Weavers*, pp. 40–41. Women were much less likely to be literate than men. In the west of Ireland late in the nineteenth century, folklorists collected songs that women sang as they gathered at their spinning wheels. For a discussion of Irish spinning songs, which were subject to continual improvisation, see Jane Schneider, "Rumpelstiltskin's Bargain: Folklore and the Merchant Capitalist Intensification of Linen Manufacture in Early Modern Europe," in *Cloth and Human Experience*, ed. Annette B. Weiner and Jane Schneider (Washington, D.C., 1989), pp. 177–213.

7. Natalie Zemon Davis, *The Return of Martin Guerre* (Cambridge, Mass., 1983), p. 5.

machine-spun yarn and partly because it had become possible to spin cotton yarn strong enough to use as warp. The industry was regulated by the trustees of the Linen Board, a body established by the Irish parliament in 1711.

Almost all households in the northern half of Ireland had some connection with the linen industry by this time, and the social organization of linen production took the form of a series of uneven relationships across space and between social groups. First, the sexual division of labor between spinning—women's work—and weaving—men's work—confined women to the most labor-intensive and poorly remunerated end of the production process. Second, this sexual division of labor coincided with a regional division of labor between the northeast, where most of the cloth was produced, and the northwest, which depended largely on supplying yarn to the weaving districts (despite a dramatic increase in weaving in County Mayo at the end of the eighteenth century). Within the weaving districts some households were dependent on entrepreneurial farmers and drapers who put out bought yarn to be woven by the piece. In the vicinity of Belfast, moreover, a fledgling cotton industry was thriving, and many weavers had been induced by high wages to weave cotton put out by mill spinners. Religious difference cross-cut these relationships, with Catholics likely to be overrepresented at the lowest ends of the production line, among cottier-weavers and spinners.[8]

What were the social processes through which this complex division of labor had emerged? The most powerful theoretical account of rural industrialization to date is that of "proto-industrialization." Hans Medick and his colleagues expanded the idea, first put forward by Franklin Mendels, into a comprehensive theory of rural industry as a transitional mode of production in its own right.[9] They argued that rural industry

8. General accounts of the Irish linen industry may be found in Conrad Gill, *The Rise of the Irish Linen Industry* (Oxford, 1925); William H. Crawford, *The Handloom Weavers and the Ulster Linen Industry* (Belfast, 1994); and Louis M. Cullen, *An Economic History of Ireland since 1660* (London, 1972). In an important article Brenda Collins demonstrated the relationship between sexual and regional divisions of labor. See Brenda Collins, "Proto-Industrialization and Pre-Famine Emigration," *Social History* 7 (1982): 127–46. The extent and form of class differentiation among weaving households has been the subject of controversy. For the most authoritative discussion see William H. Crawford, "The Evolution of the Linen Trade in Ulster before Industrialization," *Irish Economic and Social History* 15 (1988): 32–53. For a more explicitly theoretical discussion see Marilyn Cohen, "Peasant Differentiation and Proto-Industrialization in the Ulster Countryside: Tullylish, 1690–1825," *Journal of Peasant Studies* 17 (1990): 413–32.

9. Schlumbohm disagreed with Medick and Kriedte on this point, preferring not to think of proto-industrialization as a single system. See Introduction to their *Industrialization before Industrialization*, pp. 1–11. See also Franklin F. Mendels, "Proto-Industrialization: The First Phase of the Industrialization Process," *Journal of Economic History*, 32 (1972): 241–61.

developed on the basis of a contradiction between the subsistence-oriented strategies of rural households and the profit motive of merchant capitalists. The availability of income from commodity production encouraged earlier marriage and land subdivision, leading to population growth and increasing dependence on industrial earnings, thus ensuring a permanent oversupply of labor. Merchants extracted surplus profits from cottage producers, according to the theory, because the cottagers' small farms and gardens enabled them to sell their products at less than the cost of household reproduction. Under these circumstances there was little incentive to raise productivity through capital investment, and producers often found themselves in a downward spiral of impoverishment, indebtedness, and self-exploitation—a process described by David Levine as "industrial involution."[10] The limitations as well as the advantages of rural industry lay in the subsistence orientation of household production units. Merchants could respond to increased demand only by expanding into new areas of the countryside. Proto-industrialization thus reached its limits when the costs of spatial expansion became too great and merchants turned increasingly toward direct control over the labor process in factory production.

Two major problems have since been identified with the proto-industrialization thesis, both of which are evident in the Irish case. First, the thesis does not account for regional differences and interdependencies in rural industrialization and deindustrialization. While the linen industry does seem to have been associated with the "classic" proto-industrial trends of population growth and land subdivision, there was considerable local variation. Moreover, the thesis cannot by itself explain why some regions made the transition to centralized factory production while others experienced deindustrialization and decline. Second, the proto-industrialization thesis excludes almost by definition the possibility of capital accumulation and class differentiation among household producers themselves—both processes that occurred to some extent in the Irish northeastern weaving districts.[11]

10. David Levine, *Family Formation in an Age of Nascent Capitalism* (New York, 1977), p. 14. For an application of the concept of involution to Ireland see Eric L. Almquist, "Mayo and Beyond: Land, Domestic Industry, and Rural Transformation in the Irish West" (Ph.D. diss., Boston University, 1977).

11. The literature on proto-industrialization is extensive. For critical overviews see Myron Gutmann and René Leboutte, "Rethinking Proto-Industrialization and the Family," *Journal of Interdisciplinary History* 14 (1984): 587–607; Leslie Clarkson, *Proto-Industrialization: The First Phase of Industrialization?* (London, 1985); Stanley L. Engerman, "Expanding Proto-Industrialization," *Journal of Family History* 17 (1992): 241–51; Maxine Berg, *The Age of Manufactures, 1700–1820: Industry, Innovation and Work in Britain* (London, 1994), pp. 66–72; Tessie Liu, *The Weaver's Knot: The Contradictions of Class Struggle and Family Solidarity in Western France, 1750–1914* (Ithaca, 1994), pp. 22–44. Kriedte and his colleagues have recently "revisited" proto-industrialization in a

These shortcomings originate in two flawed assumptions in the model of household production at the core of the theory.[12] First, households are assumed to be characterized by the functional interdependence of their members. By stressing family cooperation, Medick and his colleagues did not fully recognize the significance of unequal relations of production within households. The second problematic assumption is that households are bounded entities. By developing their analysis on the basis of an abstract "normal" type, the theorists of proto-industrialization failed to take into account relations between household production units, both locally and regionally.[13]

In the Irish case, relations within and between households were structured by gender. Brenda Collins has shown that the regional division of labor between spinning and weaving districts emerged as a consequence of the sexual division of labor, which generally confined women to spinning and men to weaving.[14] Because spinning was a more labor-intensive task than weaving, the demand for women's labor exceeded that for men's. At least four spinners were required to supply a full-time weaver with yarn. Weaving households faced with a shortage of women's labor might add female relatives or servants to the core nuclear family, or

comprehensive survey of the literature. See Peter Kriedte, Hans Medick, and Jürgen Schlumbohm, "Proto-Industrialization Revisited: Demography, Social Structure, and Modern Domestic Industry," *Continuity and Change* 8 (1993): 217–52. For critical applications of the thesis to the Irish case see Collins, "Proto-Industrialization"; Eric L. Almquist, "Pre-Famine Ireland and the Theory of European Proto-Industrialisation: Evidence from the 1841 Census," *Journal of Economic History* 39 (1979): 699–718; Leslie Clarkson, "The Environment and Dynamic of Pre-Factory Industry in Northern Ireland," in *Regions and Industries: A Perspective on the Industrial Revolution in Britain*, ed. Pat Hudson (Cambridge, 1989), pp. 252–70; Cohen, "Peasant Differentiation."

12. These two problems with "naturalistic" conceptions of the household were identified by Olivia Harris. See her "Households as Natural Units," in *Of Marriage and the Market: Women's Subordination in International Perspective*, ed. Kate Young, Carol Wolkowitz, and Roslyn McCullagh (London, 1981), pp. 49–68. For an excellent discussion of how representations of the peasant household as "natural economy" have obscured the unevenness of working-class formation, see William Roseberry, "The Construction of Natural Economy," in his *Anthropologies and Histories: Essays in Culture, History, and Political Economy* (New Brunswick, N.J., 1989), pp. 197–232.

13. For an extended version of this argument see Jane Gray, "Rural Industry and Uneven Development: The Significance of Gender in the Irish Linen Industry," *Journal of Peasant Studies* 20 (1993): 590–611. Kriedte et al. have observed that "the connection between the work-process and the family as the reproductive unit turns out to be more complex than was assumed by the original model." In particular they note that "the co-operative division of labour did not invariably occur within the household, but could also occur between households: and households could adapt to the requirements of work and survival not only through the demographic acts of marrying and begetting children, but also through the social acts of single children leaving home or the admission of people who did not belong to the nuclear family": "Proto-Industrialization Revisited," pp. 223–24.

14. Collins, "Proto-Industrialization," pp. 133–37.

even hire itinerant spinners on a temporary basis. As the weaving industry intensified in the northeast, however, the demand for yarn could not be met by local women. Population growth and land subdivision made weaving households increasingly dependent on the produce of their looms, and correspondingly greater quantities of yarn were imported from outlying districts. Thus even remote, mountainous places, where subsistence agriculture prevailed, were incorporated in the commercial linen industry by the sale of a few hanks of yarn to jobbers who supplied the weaving districts. Spinning was actively promoted by landlords, who sought to increase both the amount of rent paid in money and the quantity of rent overall.[15]

The growth of the Irish linen industry in the eighteenth century thus depended on a much greater spatial expansion of spinning than of weaving precisely because of the division of tasks by sex within rural industrial households. Furthermore, the relationship between women and men, and therefore between spinning and weaving districts, was an exploitive one. The sexual division of labor not only led to imbalances in weaving households, it also ensured that while women did much of the work of cultivating flax and preparing it for the loom, the most capital-intensive and highly remunerated stage of the household production process was monopolized by men. A loom, which cost at least five times as much as a spinning wheel, represented a far greater investment. Spinning was more labor-intensive: it took up to six days' worth of spinning to produce yarn for a day's worth of weaving. Finally, spinning was poorly remunerated in comparison with weaving. According to Arthur Young's estimates, a weaver could earn from 10 pence a day to a shilling and 4 pence for fine work in the late eighteenth century, whereas a spinner could earn just 3 or 4 pence a day.[16] Nevertheless, witnesses to the 1825 British Parliamentary Select Committee on the Linen Trade of Ireland calculated that spinning contributed at least half the value of linen.[17] When it is considered that women were also responsible for many of the

15. Land was subdivided in the weaving districts (especially in the proximity of major markets) because the availability of income from weaving encouraged farmers to apportion their holdings among all their children, and to sublet greater portions of their land to cottiers. It also enabled these same cottiers to outbid the farmers for their plots when leases came up for renewal. See William H. Crawford, "The Influence of the Landlord in Eighteenth-Century Ulster," in *Comparative Aspects of Scottish and Irish Economic and Social History*, ed. Louis M. Cullen and Thomas C. Smout (Edinburgh, 1976), pp. 193–203. In spinning districts the prevalence of the communal landholding system known as "rundale," together with the income from spinning, fostered subdivision. See Almquist, "Mayo and Beyond."

16. Arthur Young, *Tour in Ireland, 1776–1779*, ed. Arthur W. Hutton (London, 1892).

17. George Grier reckoned that spinning accounted for half the value of linen, and James Twigg estimated that women doubled the value of flax by their work: "Report from the Select Committee on the Linen Trade of Ireland," pp. 20, 31, H.C. 1825 (463), V.

tasks involved in cultivating and preparing the flax for spinning, it is clear that the Irish linen industry was built on the under- and often unremunerated labor of women.[18]

This exploitation of women transcended individual households to drive the uneven regional development of the industry as a whole. The supply of underpriced yarn from the northwest fostered the growth of linen weaving and facilitated class differentiation in the northeast. Population growth and land subdivision made weaving households increasingly reliant on yarn imported from outlying districts. This demand in turn created openings for entrepreneurial farmers and drapers who put out yarn to be woven into cloth. Most of these "manufacturers" operated on a very small scale, employing from five to twenty weavers on average.[19] These processes were escalated by changes in the technology of bleaching which allowed for weaving to be a year-round rather than a seasonal activity.[20]

Petty accumulation in the weaving districts was built on industrial involution in the yarn districts. Irish witnesses to the Select Committee on the Linen Trade insisted to the incredulous commissioners that "independent" spinners produced yarn more cheaply than outputters could. "They set little value on their own labor," said Peter Besnard.[21] In fact, women's labor input responded to household requirements rather than to market value. Observers noted that a temporary need for cash often led women to sell their yarn for little more than the price of raw flax.[22] Households integrated to the market through women's work thus remained subsistence-oriented while at the same time the availability of income from spinning fostered population growth, land subdivision, and ultimately immiseration.

The low cost of women's labor also provided the Irish linen industry with its competitive edge, discouraging investment in technology comparable to that already occurring in Britain. One of Ireland's earliest mill spinners told Edward Wakefield that "the leading cause against the extension of machinery, is the low price of labor. Yarn spun by women is sold here much cheaper than the same article manufactured by machinery in England."[23] Therefore, though finishing the cloth had been partially mechanized in Ireland from the middle of the eighteenth century,

18. See William H. Crawford, "Women in the Domestic Linen Industry," in *Women in Early Modern Ireland*, ed. Margaret MacCurtain and Mary O'Dowd (Dublin, 1991), pp. 255–64.

19. Crawford, "Evolution of the Linen Trade," p. 45.

20. Edward R. R. Green, *The Lagan Valley, 1800–1850* (London, 1949), p. 69.

21. Commons, "Report on the Linen Trade," p. 116.

22. Edward Wakefield, *An Account of Ireland, Statistical and Political*, vol. 1 (London, 1812), p. 684.

23. Ibid., p. 684.

spinning mills did not appear in any number in the northeast until the 1820s. These early water-driven mills were limited in scope and did not immediately threaten domestic production. By contrast, when steam-driven mills were established around Belfast in the 1830s, the hand-spinning of yarn rapidly became obsolete, depriving many outlying households of their sole source of income. Because of their distance from the mills, weavers outside the northeast could not compete with the households of the "core" weaving district, who survived by weaving mill-spun yarn under increasingly impoverished conditions, until the introduction of power looms in the 1860s. In the yarn districts, the loss of income from spinning left many households particularly vulnerable to the failure of the potato crop in the mid-1840s. In testimonies to the Poor Inquiry of 1836, witnesses reported that spinners could no longer earn a living "on account of the mills around Belfast."[24]

Just as gender relations were at the heart of uneven rural industrial growth, and eventually of deindustrialization in the yarn districts, so the transition to factory production and working-class formation in the weaving districts were fundamentally gendered processes. As weavers and manufacturers relied increasingly on imported yarn, the significance of women's labor in weaving households declined. Women no longer provided the decisive labor input, so that their income had acquired the status of "pin money." In County Armagh Charles Coote found that women's earnings were spent on "finery" because "the men's labor procures them provisions."[25] Women were thus in a sense "freed" from the demands of the household economy to become mill workers. In 1838 almost 70 percent of all employees in Irish flax spinning mills were female.[26] Mechanization ultimately altered the division of labor in weaving households, as women began working at the loom in significant numbers. The sexual division of labor that had served to maintain exploitive relations between women and men and between spinning and weaving households had become irrelevant once the production process was controlled by mill owners.

Medick recognized that women and children provided the crucial marginal work effort that made possible the "super-exploitation" of proto-industrial households—that is, the purchase of commodities produced in such households at less than the cost of household reproduction.[27] Be-

24. "Poor Inquiry, Ireland, Appendix D, Employment of Women and Children," p. 84, H.C. 1836 [36], XXXI.
25. Sir Charles Coote, *Statistical Survey of the County of Armagh* (Dublin, 1804), p. 253.
26. "Return of All the Mills and Factories . . . ," p. 339, H.C. 1839 (41), XLII.
27. Hans Medick, "The Proto-Industrial Family Economy," in Kriedte et al., *Industrialization before Industrialization*, p. 62.

cause they continued to see the household in functionalist terms, however, the theorists of proto-industrialization failed to appreciate the full significance of gender relations for the overall growth and transformation of rural industrial production. In Ireland, exploitation on the basis of gender crossed the boundaries of individual households, as manufacturers and weavers benefited from the work of spinners in the yarn districts, as well as the work of women and children in their own households. Medick and his colleagues focused on the contradictions between merchant capitalism and the family economy of rural households to explain the dynamic of rural industrial growth and decline. My analysis shows that, at least in the Irish case, unequal gender relations within and between households must be placed at the heart of the thesis if it is also to account for differentiation in both rural industrial development and the transition to capitalist industry.

Household producers in the northeast of Ireland both resisted and adapted to these changes. In creating new working-class identities they were responding to and effecting changes in gender relations. Nostalgic images of an ideal domestic sphere (and of ideal relations between women and men) played an important part in this process.

GENDER IN THE TRANSFORMATION OF
EVERYDAY LIFE

Early in the nineteenth century, upper-class observers of the weaving community in northeast Ireland noted a cultural transition from disorderly, task-oriented patterns of work and leisure to a new regularity and sobriety in everyday life. When Arthur Young toured the weaving districts in the late 1770s, he found precisely the contradiction, emphasized by Medick, between producers' preference for leisure and the profit motive of traders. "When provisions are very cheap the poor spend much of their time in whiskey houses," he reported from Lurgan, County Armagh. "All the drapers wish that oatmeal was never under 1d. a pound." From Maghan, in the same county, he reported that weavers were "licentious and disorderly." Their public and crowded leisure activities included such amusements as cockfighting and bullbaiting. Fairs and markets were occasions for courtship, drinking, and brawling. Hunting hares on foot was the favorite pursuit of young men. Young was the astonished witness of such a hunt in Maghan, where he learned to his disapproval that "a pack of hounds is never heard, but all the weavers leave their looms and away they go after them by hundreds."[28]

28. Young, *Tour in Ireland*, pp. 128, 127.

Observers in the early 1800s, by contrast, emphasized that weaving households had abandoned such work and leisure habits in favor of time-disciplined labor and "respectability." Sir Charles Coote compared the inhabitants of County Armagh with those of "the poorer counties" in respect to their greater time discipline: "In this county, a steady industry affords a sufficiency for the moderate comforts of life, and will admit of a redundancy for other purposes, without exhausting nature at such a sedentary business as the loom."[29] Joseph Ferguson similarly applauded the industriousness of the weaving population in Ballymoyer, attributing their well-being to their own sober lifestyle: "Those little luxuries may be justly considered as the rewards of industry and sobriety, as there is not a single public house in the parish, where spirits are sold."[30] By the 1830s, the Ordnance Survey memorialists were usually able to report that such pastimes as cockfighting, bullbaiting, and cardplaying were no longer popular.[31]

What can account for this remarkable transformation in the everyday life patterns of industrial producers in the northeast? In his account of the lifestyles and political behavior of proto-industrial producers, Medick relied heavily on E. P. Thompson's notion of "plebeian culture."[32] Thompson applied the term to the social layer of workers and small employers in eighteenth-century England. He argued that rural artisans and early manufacturing workers were less in a position of dependence, more free from discipline at work, and more free to choose between work and leisure than they had been before or were to be in the early decades of factory production. They established their own relatively autonomous way of life, in which "physical and emotional needs, work and pleasure were not yet separated from each other."[33]

The transition to factory production involved a struggle on the part of employers to impose "discipline"—and particularly regularity of timekeeping—on this refractory working population. The task-oriented work rhythms of cottage producers waited on the necessities of family life, on seasonal change, and on the specific task to be completed. Centralized production, by contrast, introduced a quantifiable notion of time and led to a conceptual distinction between "work" and "life" which would have been meaningless under the proto-industrial

29. Coote, *Survey of Armagh*, p. 264.

30. Joseph Ferguson, "Parish of Ballymoyer," in *Statistical Account or Parochial Survey of Ireland*, vol. 2, ed. William Shaw Mason (Dublin, 1816), p. 81.

31. See Sean J. Connolly, "Religion, Work-Discipline and Economic Attitudes: The Case of Ireland," in *Ireland and Scotland, 1600–1850*, ed. Thomas M. Devine and David Dickson (Edinburgh, 1983), pp. 235–45.

32. Medick, "Proto-Industrial Family Economy," pp. 64–73; Edward P. Thompson, "Patrician Society, Plebeian Culture," *Journal of Social History* 7 (1974): 382–405.

33. Medick, "Proto-Industrial Family Economy," p. 66.

system.[34] The advent of the factory was therefore accompanied by the suppression of plebeian culture. With it came the adoption of more methodical habits in everyday life, a decline in the significance of festivals and holidays, and a movement toward a sobriety and respectability that was to lay the foundation for more organized class resistance. According to Thompson, Methodist evangelism played a crucial role in this process through its celebration of a "methodical discipline in every aspect of life," and of labor as a "pure act of virtue." Working people, he argued, turned to Methodism in response to the political disillusionment surrounding the failure of the French Revolution.[35]

For Thompson and Medick, then, the cultural transformation that occurred in northeast Ireland should be understood as a fundamental component of the process of working-class formation. Sean Connolly has argued that Protestant evangelical clergy in Ulster succeeded in reforming the habits of their parishioners only because successful industrialization had already begun, whereas the parishioners of their Catholic counterparts throughout Ireland were, economically speaking, "not so ready to play their parts."[36]

I suggest, however, that this argument, as it stands, is overly linear and deterministic. The adoption of "respectable" habits of work and leisure by a segment of the Irish rural industrial population cannot be understood as a response to the imposition of a capitalist labor process, because that process was not in place for most workers until much later in the nineteenth century. Moreover, though Protestant evangelicalism clearly did play an important role in introducing new everyday life patterns in Ulster, it also had a part in the revolutionary ideas abroad in the rebellion year of 1798.[37] These cultural changes cannot, therefore, be seen simply as the "chiliasm of despair." Instead, they represented a strategic effort by segments of the rural industrial community to carve out a separate cultural space in the face of threatening political, social, and economic changes. Folk poems indicate that gender constituted one important dimension of these changes.

34. See Edward P. Thompson, "Time, Work-Discipline and Industrial Capitalism," *Past & Present* 38 (1967): 56–97.

35. Thompson, *Making of the English Working Class*, pp. 362, 388.

36. Connolly, "Religion, Work-Discipline and Economic Attitudes," pp. 243–44.

37. See David Hempton and Myrtle Hill, *Evangelical Protestantism in Ulster Society, 1740–1890* (London, 1992), pp. 20–44. Eric Hobsbawm noted a "peculiar parallelism" between religious revivalism and the advance of political radicalism in England: *Worlds of Labour* (London, 1984), p. 32. But see Thompson, *Making of the English Working Class*, pp. 389–91, for a response to this observation. Joan Scott has pointed out that Thompson's analogy between his work and a biography is revealing of the extent to which he saw working-class formation as a linear and teleological process. See Scott, "Women in the Making of the English Working Class," in her *Gender and the Politics of History* (New York, 1988), p. 72.

Medick observed that the conspicuous consumption of urban luxuries was one way in which rural industrial producers set about establishing their own way of life.[38] Indeed, consumption items, from the mundane (potatoes and whiskey) to the luxurious and exotic (fine clothing and tea), were a common theme in the poetry of Ulster's rhyming weavers. The poets used consumption items as symbolic vehicles through which they represented and organized their perceptions of the social environment and their sense of identity. This is most obvious in some of David Herbison's poems, where he uses the device of lamenting a worn-out object to conjure up the sense of loss generated by the machine's destruction of a way of life.[39] Similarly, in some of James Orr's poems, tea, potatoes, and beer provide the foci for humorous and extraordinarily detailed accounts of everyday life.[40] In many of the poems, attention to the meanings surrounding valued objects provides insights to the *social* meanings by which the poet's community constructed its sense of identity. Here I am particularly interested in how those meanings were organized by gender, and in turn organized gender relations.

Alcohol consumption was pivotal to public amusements, in which, as Medick has written, the rural industrial community culturally reproduced itself.[41] Gay Gullickson found that in the Caux region of northern France, women were generally excluded from public leisure activities, but descriptions of Irish fairs, markets, and other gatherings in the early nineteenth century indicate that women were active participants and, indeed, were active drinkers.[42] This is reflected in James Orr's celebration of plebeian culture, "Ballycarry Fair," where "bargains, courtships, toasts, huzzas, / Combine in blythe disorder, O!"[43]

Like his father, Orr (1770–1816) was a weaver and small farmer who lived near Ballycarry in the Presbyterian parish of Templecorran, on the east coast of County Antrim. Known to local people as the Bard of Ballycarry, Orr supported the uprising of United Irishmen in 1798, and spent a few months in exile in America to avoid arrest for treason. Disillusioned by his experience with rebellion, Orr increasingly emphasized the importance of moral reform for curing his countrymen's ills. Interestingly, he wrote in a letter to a friend that "I wish B'carry Fair in particular never had been written."[44] Orr's revised attitude toward alcohol is found in "The Foundered Farmer" (first published posthumously in

38. Medick, "Proto-Industrial Family Economy," pp. 68–69.
39. See, e.g., "Michael Queen to his Auld Shoes," in David Herbison, *Midnight Musings, or Thoughts from the Loom* (Belfast, 1848), pp. 51–57.
40. Orr, *Posthumous Works.*
41. Medick, "Proto-Industrial Family Economy," p. 67.
42. Gay Gullickson, *Spinners and Weavers of Auffay* (Cambridge, 1986), p. 85.
43. Orr, *Posthumous Works*, p. 156.
44. Quoted in Akenson and Crawford, *Local Poets*, p. 70.

1817), where he describes how, as a result of a drunkard's death, his mother sickens and dies, and the girl he planned to marry loses her mind.[45] The poet did not follow his own moral strictures: he died a bachelor and "well-beloved drunk."[46]

Orr was not unique among the rhyming weavers in condemning drunkenness. Hugh Porter grimly describes "the drunkard's fate"—death in a "dirty, roofless byre":

> The value o' a virtuous life
> Owre late he learns,
> So, leaves a broken-hearted wife
> An' beggar'd bairns.[47]

Porter's dedication of the poem to a patron raises the question whether negative accounts of drinking in the folk poems were designed to please upper-class readers. Whiskey consumption does not seem to have declined in northeast Ireland; in fact, it continued to increase overall through the 1820s.[48] On the other hand, the comments of upper-class observers suggest an increase in sobriety, at least among some segments of the rural industrial community. John Dubourdieu insisted that drunkenness was a vice "daily losing ground" in County Antrim, and that in County Down "the inhabitants are growing daily more sober."[49]

It seems reasonable to infer that at least some segments of the rural industrial population were now paying lip service to the idea of temperance. Moreover, the poetry of the rhyming weavers does not suggest a shift toward the celebration of abstinence, but rather a change in the social meaning of drinking. There is an interesting contrast between the excoriation of the public house in Thomas Beggs's "Village Ale-House" and its celebration in his "On Saturday Night."[50] Beggs (1789–1847) was the son of a farm laborer (and second cousin of James Orr) in Glenwhirry, County Antrim. He lived a colorful life, spending some time at sea, but

45. Orr, *Posthumous Works*, pp. 251–53.
46. Akenson and Crawford, *Local Poets*, p. 10.
47. Hugh Porter, "The Drunkard's Fate," in *Poetical Attempts by Hugh Porter, a County of Down Weaver* (Belfast, 1813), pp. 75–79.

> The value of a virtuous life
> Too late he learns,
> So, leaves a broken-hearted wife
> And beggared children.

48. See Elizabeth Malcolm, *Ireland Sober, Ireland Free: Drink and Temperance in Nineteenth-Century Ireland* (Syracuse, N.Y., 1986), pp. 21–25.
49. John Dubourdieu, *Statistical Survey of County Antrim* (Dublin, 1812), p. 499, and *Statistical Survey of County Down* (Dublin, 1802), p. 260.
50. Thomas Beggs, *The Second Part of the Minstrel's Offering: Original Poems and Songs* (Belfast, 1836), pp. 17–18, 55–56.

later finding employment at a number of bleachworks near Belfast.[51] "The Village Ale-House" is Beggs's rewrite of part of Oliver Goldsmith's "Deserted Village," a critique of rural social change in England.[52] Goldsmith laments the current state of affairs by contrasting it to an idealized village of the past (thought to have been modeled on his birthplace in Ireland). Of the alehouse he writes, "Thither no more the peasant shall repair / To sweet oblivion of his daily care." Beggs, however, subtitles his version "Goldsmith's 'Country Ale-House' contrasted" and describes the pub as a place where "starvling weavers oft in groups repair / to banish reason and to bring despair."

In contrast to this image of a place where "village wretches pass away the night, / In vile obscenity and brawling fight," in Beggs's "On Saturday Night" the alehouse provides the company of true friends, which is "a gem on life's fast-ebbing tide, / And the best in the casquet of Time." The differences between the kinds of sociability described in the two poems center on the twin themes of time and reason. The very title of "On Saturday Night" suggests that its pleasures take place only within the context of time-disciplined labor, "when the week is away, / And its trouble and toils are gone by." Whereas in "The Village Ale-House" sense "expires," reason is "banished," and madness "raves," in "On Saturday Night" "he who has sorrow and care to allay, / He may taste the wine-cup and be sage." Goldsmith wrote in "The Deserted Village," "Yes! let the rich deride, the proud disdain, / These Simple blessings of the lowly train." Beggs echoes this sentiment in "On Saturday Night" when he celebrates the value of true friendship in the alehouse, "Though the dull ones may blame, and the proud ones despise."

James Orr's poem "Address to Beer," where he contrasts the virtues of that beverage to the evils of whiskey, is another effort to change the social meaning of drinking toward moderation and decency.[53] Though beer was never widely consumed in Ireland, especially not in the northern counties, it was considered to be a healthy drink, and it is in this context that we must read Orr's assertion that "Renown'd Reformer! thou has freed / Frae suffrin's tragic, / Unnumber'd fools, wha turn'd their head / Wi' Whiskey's magic."[54] The virtues he extolls in beer are its lack of potency and its cheapness.[55] There is a sense in which beer is the

51. Hewitt, *Rhyming Weavers*, pp. 69–72.

52. Oliver Goldsmith, *The Collected Works of Oliver Goldsmith*, vol. 4, ed. Arthur Friedman (Oxford, 1966), pp. 287–304.

53. This poem was originally published in the *Belfast Commercial Chronicle* in 1809. It is reproduced in Akenson and Crawford, *Local Poets*, pp. 63–65.

54. See Malcolm, *Ireland Sober, Ireland Free*, p. 22, and Akenson and Crawford, *Local Poets*, p. 63.

55. The reference to cheapness may be ironic, however. According to Malcolm, beer was more expensive than illegal whiskey, which was being manufactured in increasing

honest workingman's drink, in contrast to whiskey, which impoverishes its crazed victims, and punch, which is favored "mang nice tea-parties." Thus Orr's beer, like Beggs's alehouse, posits a social identity that is below polite society but above those who desperately seek to forget their poverty and misery in drink. Alcohol consumption remains an important component of cultural reproduction, but that culture, once characterized by spasmodic indulgence, has come to be (ideally) characterized by regulated moderation.

Central to the critique of intemperance in these poems is alcohol's impact on the domestic scene. Whereas Goldsmith had presented the alehouse as a place where coy maidens flirt with their beaux, in Beggs's version it becomes the site of marital infidelity and only "pert haridans" seek to be "pressed." Orr celebrates beer because its adherents do not linger in the alehouse: "An' spen 'thrifts wont to stay a week in / The house of pleasure, / On tenpence worth set hameward streekin,' / An' hain their treasure." The respectable beverage is thus associated with private virtue and the restriction of women to the domestic sphere, in contrast to that unrespectable drink, whiskey, which is associated with plebeian disorder in the public sphere.

In "The Penitent," Orr's great poem on the theme of moral improvement, the central character's wife is described as a helpless victim of his addiction to "plebeian" amusements, including drunkenness. Worst of all, perhaps, he drives her to indulge in vices of her own:

> Mary ne'er min't the house—mair like a byre,
>   But clash'd wi' nyber wives. Unkent to him
> For tea, an' snuff, the troubled dames desire,
>   She'd smuggled meal an' seeds; tho' hunger grim
> Devour'd the duddy weans, now in a wretched trim.[56]

Just as the meaning of alcohol changed in the cultural transformation associated with class formation, so the poems suggest a shift in the meanings surrounding tea, which was culturally associated with women. Specifically, tea drinking came to be identified with women's addic-

---

quantities. She quotes Arthur Guinness to the effect that beer consumption was confined to the urban working classes (in towns mostly outside Ulster) in 1823. The poor could not afford it. See her *Ireland Sober, Ireland Free*, pp. 25–26.

56. Orr, *Posthumous Works*, p. 175.

> Mary never minded the house—more like a byre,
>   But clashed with neighbor wives. Unknown to him
> For tea, and snuff, the troubled dame's desire,
>   She'd smuggled meal and seeds; though hunger grim
> Devoured the ragged children, now in a wretched trim.

tion to luxuries and consequent abdication of their domestic responsibilities.[57]

Once again, James Orr's work exemplifies this transition. In his poem titled simply "Tea" he emphasizes the role of tea in the cultural reproduction of the community and the household.[58] Tea eases the tensions between women and men, deflecting the malignancy of older women's gossip, making wives tolerant of their husbands' drinking, and curing men of the hangovers that otherwise would keep them from work. Though Orr makes it clear that men also drank tea, it is most strongly associated with women and with the successful functioning of the domestic sphere. Tea even features in courtship, as young women seek the identity of their "future match" from the spae-wife, who reads their fortunes in the tea leaves. In this poem (in contrast to "The Penitent") Orr specifically rejects the addictive qualities of tea: "Tea mak's man a nerveles wrig, / The doctor says—p-x on the prig!"

Sarah Leech's "Address to Bachelors," on the other hand, warns young men against the "dames of fashion," who fool those who "gape for riches" by their finery.

> Too late you may have cause to wail,
> For should the tea or whiskey fail,
> She, vixen-like, will you assail,
>   Or chide and snap,
> And swear, should you be dragged to jail,
>   She'll have her drap.[59]

For Leech, women's consumption of luxuries runs counter to their role in the household. She ends rather coyly with the announcement that she must get back to her spinning. Leech's poem has a certain poignance, for we are told in the introduction to her collection that she has become lame, and her spinning wheel is "the only means she now has to depend on for her subsistence." Born the daughter of an "industrious linen weaver" in 1804, she lived near Raphoe, County Donegal, on the outskirts of the linen-weaving district, and had formerly been a schoolteacher.[60] When "Address to Bachelors" was published, the market for hand-spun yarn was already faltering, however. Young women's in-

57. This analysis of the meanings surrounding tea is elaborated more fully in Jane Gray, "Gender and Plebeian Culture in Ulster," *Journal of Interdisciplinary History* 24 (1993): 251–70. For an account of the spread of tea drinking in Ireland see Patricia Lysaght, " 'When I Makes Tea, I Makes Tea . . .': Innovation in Food—the Case of Tea in Ireland," *Ulster Folklife* 33 (1987): 44–71.

58. Orr, *Posthumous Works*, pp. 60–63.

59. Sarah Leech, *Poems on Various Subjects* (Dublin, 1828).

60. Ibid., pp. 10–16.

creased consumption of luxury commodities went hand in hand with a decline in the significance of their labor input to weaving households as more yarn was imported from other regions and then as machine-spun yarn was introduced.

When David Herbison published "The Auld Wife's Lament for Her Teapot," "that machine that spins the yarn" had made hand-spinning obsolete.[61] Known as the Bard of Dunclug, near Ballymena, County Antrim, Herbison (1800–1880) lived through the entire period of indus-trial transformation. "At the age of fourteen I was harnessed to the loom," he wrote, "and doomed for life to be an operative weaver—an occupation at which those engaged must either toil with incessant drudg-ery or starve."[62] In "The Auld Wife's Lament," the history of the teapot symbolizes the passing of the rural industrial way of life. The teapot played its first part in the reproduction of an autonomous culture under-written by women's central role in production: the old woman had bought it herself. It was the centerpiece of village festivals, at which courtship took place in her youth. "At every party it was down, / Throughout Dunclug." By the time of her daughters' courtship, however, "sweets" had become the principal device for catching men, and the teapot was used to confine them to the home:

> Whene'er their wooers cam' to see them,
> A wee drap tea they be to gie them,
> For fear, as I thought, they would lea' them,
>   Alone to rove,
> They never fail'd wi' sweets to free them
>   Frae ithers love.[63]

This strategy worked, but at the expense of weakening the way of life represented by the teapot, which was burned thin, and which finally broke "the day the wheels began to fail." Now the old woman can no longer support herself by spinning and she contemplates the broken teapot alone.

My reading of the folk poems suggests that the gender-specific mean-ings surrounding the commodities of alcohol and tea—both once impor-

---

61. Herbison, *Midnight Musings*, pp. 42–45.
62. Ibid., p. viii.
63. Ibid., p. 43.

> Whenever their wooers came to see them,
> A wee drop tea they had to give them,
> For fear, as I thought, they would leave them,
>   Alone to rove,
> They never failed with sweets to free them
>   From others love.

tant aspects of the cultural reproduction of the rural industrial way of life in northeast Ireland—underwent a transformation in the first half of the nineteenth century. Both were increasingly perceived to have undermined the peace and stability of the household, and to have inhibited men and women from performing their appropriate roles. These shifting cultural meanings can be understood partly as a response to social changes over which the linen-weaving community had little or no control. As we have seen, changing gender relations were indeed at the heart of those processes that undermined the independence of linen-weaving households and ultimately household production itself.

Thomas Beggs's "Auld Wife's Address to Her Spinning Wheel" makes it clear that rural industrial producers understood proletarianization and the transition to mechanized industry precisely in terms of changing gender relations.[64] In this poem the "auld wife" contrasts the "pert maidens, wha ply in the mill" with "the mountain lass, at her wee bit wheel." Whereas the mill workers must "toil for men that are hard to please," the "mountain lass," who is described as "leal" (loyal), "modest," and "meek," is raised in "her ain father's cot on the green." The old woman concludes that the spinning machine "has added mair pelf [wealth] to the hoards of the great / and left those that were low in a far lower state." Thus for Beggs the misery, impoverishment, and moral decline associated with the mill is linked to the transfer of control over the labor of young women from fathers to capitalist employers.

These cultural changes must also be understood as a *strategy*, however. The lost domestic idyll that the rhyming weavers nostalgically "remembered" was at least partly an ideal created to resist the processes that threatened their way of life. The image of women as innocent, modest creatures under the protection of their fathers and husbands is belied by other images, such as that provided by Orr of the faction fight at Ballycarry Fair: "Ilk maid and matron hands her dear, / The baulder that he's hauden, O."[65] The poems suggest that at least some segments of the rural industrial community sought, by adopting a more sober, disciplined lifestyle, to establish a domestic and social space that would protect them from threatening changes. The cultural transformation that Thompson and Medick associated with working-class formation thus represented an effort on the part of the working population in the north of Ireland to resist and differentiate themselves from those changes that made women the vanguard of the industrial working class.

---

64. This poem is reproduced in Crawford, *Handloom Weavers*, pp. 82–84.

65. Orr, "Ballycarry Fair," in his *Posthumous Works*, p. 157. "Each maid and matron hands her dear, / The boulder that he's holding, O."

CONCLUSION

If we are to explain why the transition to capitalist industry and working-class formation were uneven and differentiated processes, gender must be placed at the heart of our analyses. By representing the household as a bounded, harmoniously functioning unit, the proto-industrial thesis obfuscates the dynamic part played by unequal gender relations in the uneven growth and transformation of rural industrial production. Furthermore, unilinear models of working-class formation have tended to ignore the centrality of gender in the experience of ordinary people, and in the cultural construction of working-class identities.

The growth and uneven regional development of the Irish linen industry was rooted in an exploitive sexual division of labor which came to coincide with a regional division of labor between spinning and weaving districts. The former experienced industrial involution and eventually deindustrialization, whereas the latter experienced some degree of class differentiation and ultimately became the site of mechanized, centralized production. Just as gender had structured the growth of rural industrial production, so working-class formation in the northeast was a gendered process. Within weaving households, the significance of women's labor input declined as greater quantities of yarn were imported from outlying districts, so that women were in a sense "freed" to become workers in the first spinning mills. With the introduction of mechanized spinning, women became weavers in significant numbers for the first time, as the sexual division of labor that had underwritten the regional configuration of rural industrial growth became obsolete.

Folk poems produced in the part of Ireland that experienced the transition to factory industry suggest that gendered meanings were in turn at the heart of the cultural changes associated with working-class formation. Some rural industrial producers represented these social changes in part as a disruption of appropriate gender roles, constructing a nostalgic image of the domestic sphere which was also an ideal. By means of changes in everyday life, they hoped to establish just such a safe space, which would distance them from threatening external forces they were powerless to control.

2

What Price a Weaver's Dignity? Gender Inequality and the Survival of Home-Based Production in Industrial France

Tessie P. Liu

In the countryside south of the Loire in the Department of Maine-et-Loire, handloom weaving survived more than a hundred years after textile production elsewhere was mechanized. "Several old hand weavers," a local socialist wrote in the early twentieth century, "seized by the love of liberty and pride in their independence and ancestral virtues, have eluded the discipline of the power loom imposed by the bosses. They have installed one or two looms in their own shops and work at their own pace. *They were their own masters.*"[1]

The place is the Pays des Mauges, best known to historians as the heart of the Vendée counterrevolutionary insurrection in 1793. Today, as an important center of light industry in western France, the region is more often called the Choletais, taking its name from the most important city of the area, Cholet. Small family workshops and home-based manufacturing have a long history in this region. The tradition began with linen weaving for overseas markets in the seventeenth and eighteenth centuries and continues today with clothing, shoes, electronic assembly, and furniture making.

Although economists and historians generally agree that the persis-

---

1. François Simon, *Petit histoire des tisserands de la région de Cholet* (Angers, 1946), p. 82; emphasis added. Simon was a schoolteacher, a socialist activist, and a historian of his native region, the Pays des Mauges.

tence of small-scale manufacturing is a characteristic feature of French industrialization, scholars disagree as to how to explain the phenomenon.[2] Mechanization was slow in the Choletais because small producers successfully fought the incursion of large-scale manufacturing.[3] Indeed, the history of manufacturing in the region is the story of weavers' resistance to capitalist relations of production. In the 1840s, for example, handloom weavers defeated attempts by local industrial mill owners to mechanize weaving. In 1850, after a decade of continued unrest, during which the army was regularly called in to protect property and keep the peace, industrialists withdrew from cloth production. This action brought the first wave of mechanization to an abrupt halt, reinforcing the handicraft character of local weaving. Even though power looms triumphed in the end, introduced slowly in the 1860s at a moment when weavers were weakened politically, industrial manufacturing did not completely displace hand production.[4] Handloom weavers found ways to adapt to markets dominated by industrial producers, often by accepting lower rates and specializing in cheaper goods.

Thus unlike theorists of technological dualism who maintain that the survival of small-scale production in industrial economies marks a positive alternative to factory-based mass production, I emphasize the "sweated" end of the process.[5] Although we can understand why small-

2. See Christian Le Bas, *Histoire sociale des faits économiques: La France au XIXᵉ siècle* (Lyon, 1984); and Patrick Fridenson and André Straus, *Le Capitalisme français, XIXᵉ–XXᵉ siècle: Blocages et dynamismes d'une croissance* (Paris, 1987). Older studies remain helpful; see, e.g., Claude Fohlen, "The Industrial Revolution in France, 1700–1914," in *The Emergence of Industrial Societies*, vol. 4 of *Fontana Economic History of Europe*, ed. Carlo M. Cippolla (London, 1973), pp. 7–75; and Rondo E. Cameron, ed., *Essays in French Economic History* (Homewood, Ill., 1970).

3. See Tessie Liu, *The Weaver's Knot: The Contradictions of Class Struggle and Family Solidarity in Western France, 1750–1914* (Ithaca, 1994).

4. See Claude Fohlen, *Les Industries textiles au temps du Second Empire* (Paris, 1956). In France the power loom was not introduced in the linen trades until the 1860s, approximately forty years after it came into wide use for weaving cotton cloth, and did not take hold until the 1880s. The delay is attributed to the difficulties of perfecting machines capable of weaving linen because of the brittleness of the fiber. In addition, consumers in the first part of the nineteenth century preferred cottons. Linen markets did not revive until the 1860s and 1870s. By the early twentieth century, however, mechanized production dominated the entire industry. See also Albert Aftalion, *La Crise de l'industrie linière et la concurrence victorieuse de l'industrie cotonnière* (Paris, 1904).

5. For an optimistic view of small-scale production, see Charles F. Sabel and Jonathan Zeitlin, "Historical Alternatives to Mass Production," *Past and Present* 108 (August 1985): 133–76. On the economics of the sweated trades, see Albert Aftalion, *Le Développement de la fabrique et le travail à domicile dans les industries de l'habillement* (Paris, 1906), and Duncan Bythell, *The Sweated Trades: Outwork in the Nineteenth Century* (London, 1978). For a description of dispersed production in France, see Valentine Paulin, "Homework in France: Its Origins, Evolution, and Future," *International Labor Review* 37 (February 1938): 192–225.

scale production endures by looking at entrepreneurial strategies in stratified product markets, the existence of niches for small firms in an industrial economy does not unproblematically call forth producers and workers willing and able to fill them. Theorists of technological dualism must also take into account the role of unequal power relations between firms and between groups of workers, particularly at the low-waged, "sweated" end of the spectrum.

Since handloom weaving was not economically attractive in the Choletais, why did handloom weavers fight so hard to remain in their trade? Particularly relevant are the meanings attached to skill and proprietary rights over the production process; that is, what it meant for weavers to be small producers. Weavers manifested this craft identity not only in protest and politics but also in their family and work relations.

Gender relations in weaving families enabled weavers to survive as their own masters. Despite rapidly declining piece rates, older male weavers refused to take other forms of paid labor. Their determination to remain at their looms forced their daughters and wives to seek wage work to supplement the declining household incomes. By the early twentieth century, a new form of labor-intensive outwork specializing in ready-made shoes and garments for urban markets developed to take advantage of this captive newly proletarianized female labor force. These new specialties formed the basis of the region's current manufacturing economy. Looking at power relations within weaving families allows us to see how gender can mark a class divide. Not only did family dynamics segment the local labor market, but the conditions under which women entered the labor market shaped the possibilities for further economic development in the region. These entrepreneurial strategies that relied on cheap female labor reinforced the region's poverty even as they created new jobs.[6]

THE SURVIVAL OF HANDLOOM WEAVING IN THE
AGE OF POWER LOOMS

In 1904, during a government inquiry on conditions in the French textile industry, weavers explained that when power looms were first introduced in the region, industrialists used them to enforce a new division of the product market.[7] Within a decade, machines produced the

6. For a similar discussion of the connections between domestic struggles, proletarianization, and economic development, see Belinda Bozzoli, "Marxism, Feminism, and South African Studies," *Journal of South African Studies* 9 (April 1983): 139–71.

7. Archives Nationales (AN), C7318: Chambre des Députés, Euquête sur l'industrie textile en France, 1903–4, régions non-visités, Maine-et-Loire (Enquête textile 1904), the

medium-weight linen used for the sheets, trousers, and shirts once made on handlooms. Handloom weavers were forced into the cheapest end of the market, making the coarse linens used for sacks, dishcloths, napkins, and tablecloths. At the other end of the product market, the finest linens, known as *linon* and *batiste*, remained the domain of handloom weaving, but consumers were increasingly substituting machine-made fine-grade cottons for luxury linens, thus reducing the demand for these specialties. Yet, the numbers of handloom weavers in the region did not decline as quickly as one might have expected. About 10,000 handlooms were in operation in the 1870s (supporting 13,000 to 15,000 men, women, and children), and by 1904 there were still 7,000 to 8,000.[8] Handwork thus found refuge in the coarsest grades that were not profitable enough to mechanize and in the finest grades for which machines were not skillful enough to produce. In addition, industrialists used the handloom sector to protect themselves from the vicissitudes of market demand by subcontracting work to handloom weavers to meet seasonal variations, rush orders, and small runs. Finally, some handloom weavers specialized in working with low-quality yarns that were too brittle and uneven for machine work. Under the watchful eye and skilled hands of a weaver, defective materials could be transformed into cloth of passable quality. But in product markets dominated by machine-made cloth, most of the remaining specializations were not lucrative to handloom weavers. In the first decades after mechnanization, the incomes of handloom weavers fell by a quarter to a third of their former level. By the early twentieth century, weaving incomes were halved, falling to around 1 franc a day.

A deposition from handloom weavers in Saint-Léger-sous-Cholet exposed the inadequacy of their incomes. The average 1 to 1.25 francs a day they earned, even the occasional 2 francs, weavers complained, could not sustain a family. "For a father of a family to survive with two or three children and his wife, and pay his suppliers regularly, he must be able to earn 3 francs a day. And we must tell you that even working 12 hours a day, [we cannot earn this amount]. We earn so little in return [for

---

depositions of the Bourse du Travail, the Chambre Syndicale de Cholet, the Union des Syndicates Professionnels, and the *juge de paix* of Cholet. On the division of product markets between machine labor and handwork, see Aftalion, *Crise de l'industrie linière.* Michael J. Piore develops a similar argument in *Dualism and Discontinuitities in Industrializing Societies,* ed. Suzanne Berger and Michael J. Piore (Cambridge, 1980).

8. Between 1878 and 1904 the number of power looms in the region grew from 260 to 2,000. AN, F12 4516B: Situation industrielle de Maine-et-Loire, reports 1879–88; AN, C7318: Enquête textile 1904, deposition of the Union des Syndicats Professionnels.

our labor]."[9] The family budgets of other workers in the region indicate that the handloom weavers' situation was difficult indeed. A survey of the local shoe industry conducted between 1909 and 1911 revealed that a male shoeworker who earned 983 francs a year could barely support his wife and three young children.[10] Even with aid from the city of Cholet (a modest 38 *francs* a year), the family still could not meet its expenses, which amounted to just a little above 1,150 francs a year. For weavers in Saint-Léger-sous-Cholet, who earned between 375 to 600 francs a year, 900 francs a year (or three francs a day) represented the good life, one that was no longer attainable. Indeed, many weavers earned even less. Some averaged as little as 75 centimes a day. An annual income of 225 francs (or 75 centimes a day) was barely enough to purchase bread to feed a shoeworker and his family. Comparing these incomes to the cost of living, a member of the Bourse du Travail asked passionately:

> How can a father of a family with two children live honorably after deducting from an average annual income 115 francs for rent, 70 francs for fuel, 200 francs for bread?
>
> Even for the highest paid handloom weaver, what is left to maintain the household of four people? There's no use to mention stew [*fricot*], because it's only made of potatoes and dry beans and greens filched from neighboring fields.
>
> For the poorest paid in the countryside, three-fourths of the basic necessities of life are pilfered from farmers by moonlight. Seeing such great misery, the farmers dare not complain. Who has the right? It's sad to report, but it's exactly the truth. How can it be otherwise with such vile rates?[11]

Certainly stealing cabbages and turnips was a desperate solution to the crisis, but one that effectively dramatized the weavers' plight. If we take weavers at their word, and there is sufficient evidence to corroborate their reports on wages and cost of living, we are led to wonder how, indeed, did weaving families survive? If staying at their looms meant that children must go hungry, how did weavers justify their choice? To answer these questions, we need to look more precisely at the nature of the crisis in weaving and what happened to weaving families.

9. AN, C7318: Enquête textile 1904, deposition of the Chambre Syndicale of Saint-Léger-sous-Cholet.
10. Office du Travail, *Enquête sur le travail à domicile dans l'industrie de la chaussure (1909–1911)* (Paris, 1919), p. 188.
11. AN, C7218: Enquête textile 1904, deposition of the Bourse du Travail and the Chambre Syndicale of Cholet.

TABLE I
Weaving households in Villedieu-la-Blouère, 1846–1911, by age of
household head (percent)

Year	Number	Age of household head					
		<25	25–34	35–44	45–54	55–64	65+
1846	38	7.7	25.6	35.9	12.8	12.8	5.1
1881	130	0.0	12.9	30.5	19.1	26.7	10.7
1911	114	0.0	8.8	11.4	20.2	33.3	26.3

Source: Archives communales de Villedieu-la-Blouère, censuses of 1846,
1881, 1911.

THE CHANGING PROFILE OF HANDLOOM
WEAVING HOUSEHOLDS

In the last decades of the nineteenth century, the expectations of
weavers and the lives of weaving families changed significantly.[12] We can
trace these transformations through the household-by-household surveys
of the population census of the commune of Villedieu-la-Blouère, a typical rural community in the interior of the Choletais. Between 1881 and
1911, a period of rapid change in the textile trade, most handloom
weavers in the commune remained in their trade. The population census
of 1881 recorded 130 weaving households. Thirty years later, in 1911, the
census taker listed 114 handloom weavers as heads of households.
Though this slight decline mirrors the relative constancy in the number
of handloom weavers we observed at the regional level, the general
characteristics of weavers as a group had changed. On the whole, the
population of handloom weavers had aged. The average age of heads of
weaving households increased from 49 in 1881 to 55 in 1911. The aging
of handloom weavers is even more pronounced when we consider that
the average age of the male head of household in Villedieu-la-Blouère, in
1846 was 40. This aging was accompanied by a decline in average household size, from 3.4 to 3.1.

Table I shows the distribution of weaving households over several
historical phases of textile production. Over the nearly six decades represented in Table I, the proportion of weaving households in the early
phases of the family life cycle (those with household heads aged 25–34
and 35–44) declined sharply. Equally striking is the increase in older
households (55–64 years and over 65 years). Particularly in the decades
between 1881 and 1911, when piece rates declined most rapidly, the

12. The following household information comes from the manuscript censuses of
Villedieu-la-Blouère, 1881 and 1911. The households described are actual households,
though I have changed the names of their members.

relative proportion of weaving households remained most stable in those phases of the life cycle in which the household had access to the labor of grown children—that is, during the 45–54 and 55–64 stages. The decline in the proportion of younger households was substantial in this period, as was the rising proportion of households in the oldest category. The growing difficulties young male weavers faced in sustaining dependent children through weaving is reflected in the decline in the number of young weaving households.

Even more significant than the general aging of the population of weavers was the change in the internal organization of weaving itself. In 1881, 93 percent of weaving households were family production units. That is, every working member of the household held some occupation connected to cloth production, either as a weaver or in an auxiliary task. Three percent of weaving households consisted of older weavers living alone. In the remaining 4 percent of households headed by weavers, other members of the household were employed in different trades. Thirty years later, only 44 percent of the 114 weavers were heads of family production units. In 46 percent of the households headed by weavers, children and (less frequently) wives were employed in another occupation, up from 5 percent in 1881. The number of elderly weavers living alone increased to 10 percent of all weaving households.

These patterns can be traced through individual lives. According to the population census of Villedieu-la-Blouère conducted in 1881, Jean Pineau, a 30-year-old handloom weaver, lived with his wife, Marie, and two young sons, Louis and Jean. Marie aided Jean in his work. Most probably, the couple expected that when Louis and little Jean reached early adolescence, they, too, would weave. Three decades later, in 1911, we find that Jean *fils* and Louis have both married and live in their own households as handloom weavers. Louis's wife helps him in weaving, and Jean's wife takes in embroidery work in addition to helping her husband. The census taker listed her as an embroiderer. Jean Pineau *père*, now widowed, lives with three sons born after the 1881 census. The father continues to weave, but not all the sons living under his roof practice his trade. Henri, 29, and Joseph, 23, are weavers, but the youngest, Georges, has become a shoeworker. Though Jean *fils* and Louis both followed in their father's profession, they themselves are not heads of household production units—households in which all adults perform some part of the weaving production process. This experience was typical of their generation.

François Sécher was 18 in 1881. He lived with his widowed mother and five siblings. François, his mother, and his older brothers were listed in the 1881 census as weavers. His sisters also worked within the family production unit. In 1911, François Sécher has married and continues the trade he practiced as an adolescent. We do not know how many children he and his wife, Julie, had in total. In 1911 only one 15-year-old daughter lives with them. The daughter is a shoeworker. François's brother Henri also continues to weave. Henri Sécher is the head of a weaving household production unit consisting of himself and his 26-year-old nephew.

As the lives of Jean Pineau and François Sécher suggest, handloom weavers who apprenticed under their fathers and older brothers in the last decades of the nineteenth century still practiced their trade in the early twentieth century, but they could no longer replicate the family work patterns of their youth. To the extent that handloom weaving was a viable occupation in the early twentieth century, it had become the occupation of the head of the household, who was able to stay at his loom only because other members of the household made up for the diminishing returns from weaving. The casualty of economic hardship was weaving as a family enterprise. Those weavers who complained most bitterly in the depositions taken in 1904 were probably no longer young. The image of a young weaver and his family held symbolic importance for older weavers.

Clearly male weavers did not respond to declining piece rates by switching occupations or even looking for supplemental incomes. In fact, these weavers refused work in the shoe industry even when jobs were offered. As one disgruntled and perplexed shoe entrepreneur, René Chené, explained, he had initially conceived of slipper making as a good venture, anticipating the number of weavers who would flock to this new opportunity, with its better wages. But he discovered to his dismay that weavers left their looms with great reluctance. Many tried three or four times to take on work in the shoe trade but returned each time to weaving. Attributing this behavior to the force of habit and to the weavers' inherent suspiciousness of new ways, shoe entrepreneurs solved their problem by hiring women instead.[13]

Yet we should not be surprised that established weavers would resist work in the shoe industry. They resisted proletarianization on all fronts. To assume that weavers could have easily switched from making cloth to making shoes would in effect be to deny the reality of their grievances and belittle their determination to struggle on as weavers. Even at the peak of their mobilization to defend piece rates, when militant factory workers joined their struggles, many weavers were so attached to their sense of themselves as independent producers that they hesitated to admit the possibility of common interests with factory workers. During a general strike that paralyzed local textile production in the fall of 1887,

13. René Chené, *Les Débuts du commerce et de l'industrie de la chaussure dans la région de Cholet* (Maulévrier, Maine-et-Loire, 1980).

industrialists were able to break the coalition so carefully nurtured by socialist handloom weavers, for whom the coalition united those who worked with their hands against those who lived off the labor of others. By offering concessions on piece rates for handloom products and refusing to negotiate on rules and work hours that affected factory discipline, industrialists exploited the differences that divided small producers from proletarians. Many handloom weavers willingly accepted the separate treatment, insisting on the status difference between themselves and proletarians. Unlike factory operatives, handloom weavers coordinated the production process, they owned the means of production (even though the capital investment for handlooms was negligible), and they were skilled at producing cloth rather than tending machines. Weavers were proud of these distinctions—proud enough to forgo the political gains and economic utility of maintaining a coalition with factory workers. Their behavior suggests that weaving was more than a job. Property relations and notions of skill were bound up with social identities.[14]

WEAVING AS A MASCULINE IDENTITY

In their indictments of declining piece rates, male weavers presented themselves simultaneously as weavers and as fathers. Indeed, they made little distinction between the two roles. When the weavers of Saint-Léger-sous-Cholet said, "for a father of a family to survive with two or three children and his wife . . . ," they subsumed the survival of children and wife within the survival of the weaver in his trade. The word order in this sentence is significant. It poses the problem as the survival of fathers, and then considers the welfare of children and wives as dependent on attainment of the first goal. We can find a more explicit expression of this reasoning in the stirring words with which members of the Chambre Syndicale concluded their testimony:

> What does the honest and hardworking worker want? It is to live by the work of his profession, to raise his family honestly, to give to our beloved France soldiers robust in body and spirit, and mothers who possess the moral energy to raise their children. It is greed that grows in society and perhaps [in all] humanity; all society should be based on the three grand words of human thought, Duty in all things, Justice, and Reason.
> For us, the cost of labor must be raised to where the worker has a

14. For a longer discussion of the strike and conflicts among handloom weavers over their status in an industrial economy, see my *Weaver's Knot*, chap. 7.

proportional part of the boss's profits because they contribute to the wealth of the latter.[15]

It is important to note here that the handloom weavers of Saint-Léger-sous-Cholet placed their profession first. They did not indicate that their first duty was to their families, and consequently that they would take any work to support them. For many handloom weavers, the struggle to maintain and raise piece rates was a battle for justice. In their view, a just society would give the weaver his fair share, a share that would allow him to carry on his profession *and* adequately fulfill his duty to his family. The perception of the crisis in weaving thus revealed an order of priorities that subsumed family interest in the individual professional identity of the father, who could not conceive of family interest independent of that identity. In this sense, the ability of adult male weavers to continue weaving came to stand for the survival of the production unit. The strategies employed by household members to meet their collective subsistence were regarded as means to attain that goal.

By defining the family interest in accordance with the prerogatives of the father, weavers revealed that for them, masculinity, skill, and the status of household head were indivisibly entwined.[16] Traditionally, members of weaving households distinguished between male and female tasks. Male heads of households were "weavers" or "master weavers," younger males were "apprentice weavers" or simply "weavers." Female members of the household were identified by ancillary tasks in cloth-making; those who mounted the warp were *ourdisseuses*; those who wound the skeins were *dévideuses*. Embedded in this division was a notion of male "skills" linked to craftsmanship—that is, knowledge and adeptness at making cloth—and of female "activities" that were helpful to the producers but not directly responsible for the quality and production of the actual product.

It mattered little that in day-to-day production, who performed which tasks was a flexible matter.[17] Occupational titles did not necessarily govern or limit the kinds of tasks people performed. Rather it is more useful to conceive of occupational titles, in this case, as signifying relationships. That is, although *ourdisseuse* and *dévideuse* denote specific

15. AN, C7318: Enquête textile 1904: Réponse de la Chambre syndicale des ouvriers tisserands de Saint-Léger-sous-Cholet.

16. Joan W. Scott, "Work Identities for Men and Women: The Politics of Work and Family in the Parisian Garment Trades in 1848," in her *Gender and the Politics of History* (New York, 1988), pp. 93–112. For a similar analysis see Keith McClelland, "Masculinity and the 'Representative Artisan' in Britain, 1850–80," in *Manful Assertions: Masculinities in Britain since 1800*, ed. Michael Roper and John Tosh (London, 1991), pp. 74–91.

17. For a description of work routines in weaving families, see François Simon, *Département de Maine-et-Loire, Commune de la Romagne* (Anger, 1927), p. 58.

activities, the names actually specified the relationship of those who bore those titles with those who were named *tisserands* (weavers). It was *tissage* that gave the household its social identity, not *ourdissage* or *dévidage*. The notion of male craftsmanship or skill in clothmaking integrated members of the household into the production process through a clear authority structure. This underlying logic subdivided tasks by sex and generation, affirming the power of men over women, of older men over younger men.

The equation between masculinity and skill was not unique to the male handloom weavers of the Choletais. Sally Alexander and Barbara Taylor have observed that Chartist tailors and bootmakers in nineteenth-century England made the same claims about their activities, especially when they wished to exclude women from their trades.[18] The frequency of this pattern has led John Rule to conclude that most artisans believed that they held "property" in their skills, but that this property was thought to inhere in men exclusively.[19] To extend the analogy further, skill is not just any possession: I liken it to patrimony. Like patrimonial property, it does not signal simple individual ownership. Patrimony centers kin relations on the patriarch and orders the relationships of individual family members with one another.[20]

This arrangement rested on a conception of moral order. Like all such constructs, it described the "ought" in the system rather than the "is." The belief did not ensure the actual authority of fathers as heads of households, nor did it describe how compliance and cooperation were actually achieved. Nor was it a matter of personal gain that fathers

18. Sally Alexander, "Women, Class, and Sexual Differences in the 1830s and 1840s: Some Reflections on the Writing of Feminist History," *History Workshop Journal* 17 (Spring 1984): 125–49; Barbara Taylor, " 'The Men Are as Bad as Their Masters': Socialism, Feminism, and Sexual Antagonism in the London Tailoring Trade in the 1830s," in *Sex and Class in Women's History,* ed. Judith I. Newton, Mary P. Ryan, and Judith Walkowitz (London, 1983), pp. 187–220. An extensive literature documents the association of skill with masculinity. See, e.g., Anne Phillips and Barbara Taylor, "Sex and Skill: Notes towards a Feminist Economics," *Feminist Review* 6 (1980): 79–88; Cynthia Cockburn, *Brothers: Male Dominance and Technological Change* (London, 1983); Sonya Rose, "Gender Antagonism and Class Conflict: Exclusionary Strategies of Male Trade Unionists in Nineteenth-Century Britain," *Social History* 13 (1988): 191–208; and Ava Baron, "Contested Terrain Revisited: Technology and Gender Definitions of Work in the Printing Industry, 1850–1920," in *Women, Work, and Technology,* ed. Barbara Drygulski Wright et al. (Ann Arbor, 1987), pp. 58–83.

19. John Rule, "The Property in Skill in the Period of Manufacture," in *The Historical Meaning of Work,* ed. Patrick Joyce (Cambridge, 1987), pp. 99–118. See also Wally Seccombe, "Patriarchy Stabilized: The Construction of the Male Breadwinner Wage Norm in Nineteenth-Century Britain," *Social History* 11 (1986): 53–76; and Harriet Friedmann, "Patriarchal Commodity Production," *Social Analysis* 20 (December 1986): 47–55.

20. Pierre Bourdieu, "Marriage Strategies as Strategies of Social Reproduction," in *Family and Society,* ed. Robert Forster and Orest Ranum (Baltimore, 1976), pp. 117–44.

Table 2
Occupations of weavers' sons and daughters, Villedieu-la-Blouère, 1911

	Sons		Daughters	
Occupation	Mean age	Number	Mean age	Number
Weaver	24.3	23	30.8	6
Shoeworker	22.1	9	21.5	23
Needleworker	0.0	0	24.3	10
Other wage work	0.0	0	17.0	1
None	8.3	22	8.2	29
All occupations	17.4	54	17.1	69

Source: Archives communales de Villedieu-la-Blouère, census of 1911.

Table 3
Mean ratio of men to women (over age 12) in weaving households, Villedieu-la-Blouère, 1911, by age of household head

	Age of household head				
	25–34	35–44	45–54	55–64	65+
Not in family production unit	0.50	0.43	0.37	0.53	0.51
In family production unit	0.50	0.57	0.68	0.57	0.50

Note: One-person households are excluded.
Source: Archives communales de Villedieu-la-Blouère, census of 1911.

should assume responsibility for the family enterprise. Certainly not all fathers lived up to or even welcomed this responsibility. As evidenced in their language, however, the patriarchal sense of self was very real in the moral self-perception of handloom weavers.

THE DIFFERENT FATES OF WEAVERS' SONS
AND DAUGHTERS

The tenacious hold of craft identity over handloom weavers required their children to make up the shortfall in income. The children must have felt obligated to find remunerated work earlier and felt pressed to stay longer in the parental household. Turning again to census data from Villedieu-la-Blouère, we see in Table 2 that sons were far more likely than daughters to devote themselves to weaving (twenty-three sons in weaving households but only six daughters were themselves weavers). Daughters concentrated mostly on wage work in the shoe and needle trades, while a small number of weavers' sons worked as shoeworkers. The differences in the occupations of daughters and sons explains why the sex ratios in weaving households that remained family production units tended to favor males. As evidenced by the higher ratio of men to women in weaving family enterprises in Table 3, sons who stayed with their parents stayed as weavers, not as wage earners in another profession.

These patterns suggest that weaver fathers conceived of the contributions of sons and daughters in terms of different strategies and goals. A preference for sons to continue in weaving is consistent with notions of male identity in weaving households. Craft continuity from father to son is but an extension of the inextricable entwining of masculine identity with headship of household and craftsmanship. It would have been a sign of defeat for the head of the household to enter another profession, and his sons, in a sense, carried the burden of the father's struggle. The identification of the skills and social identity of the household with patrimony assumes a new significance here: integral to the value of patrimonial property is the fact that it is passed on, as a concrete symbol of the success of the father. That daughters became proletarianized workers laboring at home and in factories is also consistent with the way gender identities were constituted in weaving households. Women in those households were conceived of as helpers and secondary producers in the process of clothmaking. Although certainly many wives and daughters were adept weavers, their occupational classification as *dévideuse* or *ourdisseuse*, as we have seen, signified a marginal position in relation to the core identity of the household.[21]

A look at the overall demographic profile of households headed by weavers more fully explicates the implication of this reasoning. As Table 4 indicates, weaving households that successfully retain sons as part of the family production unit were quite rare. Fewer sons than daughters stayed, and in the critical 45–54 phase, when children were old enough to bring in resources, daughters greatly outnumbered sons. The higher con-

---

21. These were not gender identities of a predictable sort. Women in weaving households were not defined by their reproductive activities, although they clearly performed them. Instead, they were defined as producers, but secondary producers, whose specific activities were not crucial to the family's identity. The discussion of the participation of women during the formation of the Chambre Syndicale is indicative of male weavers' attitude toward women's labor. At one of the initial meetings, local handloom weavers gathered to hear the speech of an organizer from Angers. His speech urging a ban on female wage work and blaming women for low male wages was not well received by the local weavers, who insisted that their organization should include their wives and daughters. Yet, while this measure recognized women as producers, female members of the Chambre Syndicale were not given the right to vote at meetings. This was also the case in the *syndicats de prévoyance*. Women were present but silenced. So while women's contributions were recognized as productive labor, the women themselves were still viewed as dependents, subordinated to their husbands and fathers, who articulated the opinions of the household.

TABLE 4
Average number of sons and daughters in weaving households,
Villedieu-la-Blouère, 1911, by age of household head

	Age of household head				
	25–34	35–44	45–54	55–64	65+
Sons	0.4	0.8	0.5	0.6	0.3
Daughters	0.5	1.1	1.1	0.5	0.5

Note: One person households are excluded.
Source: Archives communales de Villedieu-la-Blouère, census of 1911.

TABLE 5
Size and composition of weaving households, Villedieu-la-Blouère,
1911, by age of household head

	Age of household head				
	25–34	35–44	45–54	55–64	65+
Not a family production unit					
Number of households	3	9	10	18	12
Average size	3.0	4.0	4.1	3.6	3.4
Average no. daughters	0.3	1.0	1.4	0.9	0.9
Average no. sons	0.6	0.5	0.4	0.9	0.5
Family production unit					
Number of households	5	9	6	18	12
Average size	2.8	4.3	3.3	2.7	2.2
Average no. daughters	0.6	1.1	0.5	0.1	0.0
Average no. sons	0.2	1.0	0.6	0.3	0.2

Note: One-person households are excluded.
Source: Archives communales de Villedieu-la-Blouère, census of 1911.

centration of males in Table 3 is deceptive, because it masks the generally smaller size of these households. As Table 5 indicates, there were in
fact very few sons in these households. As the parents grew older, the
number of sons in these households steadily declined.

If the average size of family production units were the same as the size
of households with mixed occupations, one might suspect that the distinction between these two types of households was purely the result of
the distribution of sons and daughters. As Table 5 indicates, however, in
older phases of the family life cycle (phases 45–54, 55–64, 65+), households with mixed occupations were consistently larger (by approximately
one person). The presence of daughters in these households was relatively constant (on the average, between 0.9 and 1.4 daughters, depending
on the phase of the family life cycle) and did not diminish appreciably as

TABLE 6
Male heads of households in shoemaking, Villedieu-la-Blouère, 1911, by age group

	<25	25–34	35–44	45–54	55–64	65+
Number	0	12	12	7	3	0
Percent	0%	35.3%	35.3%	20.6%	8.8%	0%

Source: Archives communales de Villedieu-la-Blouère, census of 1911.

parents aged. We expect those households in which all members wove to have had more sons than daughters, but in fact the number of sons was negligible and declined with the age of the parents. Thus older weaving households were actually divided between elderly couples aided by working daughters and elderly couples living alone. This fact may explain why the sex ratio of males to females in the two kinds of households (Table 3) becomes more equal as households grow older.

If we look carefully at the demographic profile of older weaving families, the absence of sons suggests that sons were leaving to establish their own households. This pattern is corroborated by Table 6, which examines the age of male heads of households in the shoemaking trades. The strong preponderance of younger households reflects the economic choices of weavers' sons who were able to set up their own households. About 90 percent of young male shoeworkers can be traced back to weaving households. That sons of weavers had a more difficult time taking up weaving as heads of their own households is demonstrated by the small number of young weaving households in the 1911 census. Many of their fathers, however, continued as weavers in the *bourg*. The small numbers of older households headed by shoeworkers also reflects the newness of the shoe industry, as well as the fact that relatively few older men entered it. The few older male shoeworkers did not come from weaving households, but were formerly independent shoeworkers in the local bespoke trade.

While sons went off to establish their own households, daughters stayed longer and were more consistently present in older households. In households in which both sons and daughters were present (the 45–54 phase), the mean age of the oldest daughter was 18, whereas the mean age of the oldest son was 14.3, suggesting that parents were holding onto their daughters longer than their sons. Unable to promise a future in handloom weaving, weaving households lost their claims on sons' presence and labor. Certainly, it served the material interest of fathers to hold onto sons, but the very notion of manhood that weavers defended stipulated that under these material circumstances sons must break away. Ironically, because daughters were peripheral to the social identity of weaving households, elderly weaving parents relied more heavily on them for support.

Undergirded by these contradictions, small-scale production enjoyed a remarkable degree of staying power. In retrospect, the resistance of handloom weavers may seem to have been doomed to fail, but the fact that many weavers who were in the prime of life in the 1880s finished their days as handloom weavers thirty to forty years later should indicate the tenacity of their grip on this identity and their notion of craft and skill. As the same time, their ability to stay rather than migrate, to remain handloom weavers and not to search out new jobs, was predicated emotionally and materially on the acceptance of the same set of associated meanings by the women in the households. The final link in the chain rested on the ties that bound these women as family members. The struggle against proletarianization was a victory only for the *père de famille*. Wives and children, especially daughters, were called upon to maintain the fiction.

The emotional and economic complexities of women's situation came from the unspoken demands on them to fill in the gaps—the shortfalls in money and ideology. Women in weaving families lived under the dual pressures of capitalist and patriarchal demands, although they would certainly not use this vocabulary. The two systems, however, did not act as one. The precapitalist handicraft economy was organized by particular sets of patriarchal principles. Capitalists did not simply take over these principles, as some feminist theorists have argued.[22] In fact, they could not do so, because patriarchal authority was inseparable from the market-based autonomy of small-scale producers, their knowledge of manufacturing processes (what we would call skill), and the sexual division of labor that allowed the household to function as a production unit. To proletarianize artisans was to attack precisely those aspects of artisanal production in which patriarchal authority was embedded. Thus the artisans' struggle against capitalist relations of production was at the same time a struggle for their notion of the father's prerogatives.

22. For an overview of this debate, see the essays in *Women and Revolution: A Discussion of the Unhappy Marriage of Marxism and Feminism*, ed. Lydia Sargent (Boston, 1981). My own position is closest to that of Ann Ferguson and Nancy Folbre, who emphasize the tensions and contradictions between patriarchy and capitalism. See also Michael Roper and John Tosh, "Historians and the Politics of Masculinity," in their *Manful Assertions*, pp. 1–24; and Alison MacEwen Scott, "Patterns of Patriarchy in the Peruvian Working Class," in *Women, Employment and the Family in the International Division of Labor*, ed. Sharon Stichter and Jane Parpart (London, 1990), pp. 198–220.

THE "SWEATED TRADES"

Weaving families provided a disporportionate number of recruits for the new shoe and garment trades in the region. They supplied the crucial labor force to sustain the new manufacturing. Of the fifty-three men working in the shoe industry listed in the population census of Villedieu-la-Blouère in 1911, 60 percent were heads of their own households. Forty percent were dependent members of households. Of these twenty-one dependent workers, nine were sons of weavers living at home, four were sons of shoeworkers, and none were the sons of cultivators. Of the shoeworkers working in 1911 whom I successfully traced back to the 1881 census (some 70 percent), nearly all (90 percent) came originally from weaving households. Of the women employed in the shoe trade (seventy-six in all), 40 percent came from weaving households, 24 percent from the households of shoeworkers, and 8 percent from farming households. The remaining 28 percent were from the households of day workers, service artisans, and small shopkeepers. We find comparable patterns in the needle trades, where of the women employed as *lingères*, *couturières*, and *brodeuses* in 1911 (78 in all), 27 percent came from weaving households, 15 percent from shoemaking households, and only 4 percent from cultivator households.

Whereas cultivators represented about 32 percent of the population of Villedieu-la-Blouère, only 6 percent of the female workers in the new "sweated trades" came from these households. No male sweated workers came from agricultural households. If we count weaving households and shoeworkers' households (themselves largely headed by children of weavers) together, we find that these households provided 52 percent of the female labor force and 100 percent of the smaller male labor force in the new sweated shoe and lingerie trades. This finding cannot be attributed to a greater number of weaving households, for they constituted about the same proportion of the population as agricultural households.

If the struggles of handloom weavers created the necessary conditions in the local labor market for the new outwork industries, the same set of struggles explains outwork from the entrepreneurial end. By the late nineteenth century, cloth manufacturers in the Choletais were under increasing pressure from urban retailers to supply finished goods. Hemmed and embroidered kerchiefs, tablecloths, napkins, bedding, and a wide array of undergarments were in great demand. This change in demand resulted from a revolution in consumption patterns pioneered by Parisian department stores in the second half of the nineteenth century.[23]

23. On department stores, see Michael B. Miller, *Le Bon Marché: Bourgeois Culture and the Department Store, 1869–1920* (Princeton, 1981). For a broader treatment of bourgeois consumer culture in France in the same period, see Rosalind Williams, *Dream Worlds:*

The instability of demand and constant changes in styles in the highly seasonal, volatile, and competitive fashion industry discouraged investment in machinery and plant space. Urban retailers and manufacturers subcontracted the work to petty entrepreneurs who organized the actual transformation. They subdivided the tasks and put them out to people who worked at home by hand or with the aid of small sewing machines. Many entrepreneurs engaged in this kind of subcontracting had been middlemen in the textile trade. When mechanization had threatened their livelihood in textiles, these middlemen found a new niche for themselves in the rapidly growing market in consumer goods. Making use of their former connections to markets and their intimate knowledge of the local population, they made "cheap productive labor" available to urban manufacturers and ultimately to Parisian department stores and other retailers in industrial cities in the North. The region's other specialization in hand-sewn slippers and other soft-soled shoes also drew its labor and entrepreneurial talent from the region's textile past.[24]

Entrepreneurs in the shoe and garment trades sustained their businesses on the processes that created this pool of female and young male workers searching for jobs to supplement weaving incomes. The low piece rates in handloom weaving kept wages low in the new manufacture. Since there was little demand for day laborers in agriculture, the rural manufacturing population had few alternatives. Piece rates were so low that homeworkers sometimes extended their workdays to fourteen hours just to earn 20 francs a month. Their highest wages reached 30 francs a month.[25] Contemporary social reformers referred to these new industries as the "sweated trades" because of their tendency to sweat greater productivity out of workers by cutting piece rates rather than investing in machinery.

It is important to note that entrepreneurs in the new trades could not have created the necessary preconditions for their industry through their own actions and schemes. They made use of the unintended conse-

---

Mass Consumption in Late Nineteenth-Century France (Berkeley, 1982). For studies of urban fashion industries, see Judith G. Coffin, "Woman's Place and Women's Work in the Paris Clothing Trade, 1830–1914" (Ph.D. diss., Yale University, 1985); Henriette Vanier, *La Mode et ses métiers: Frivolités et luttes des classes, 1830–1870* (Paris, 1960); and James Schmiechen, *Sweated Industries and Sweated Labor: The London Clothing Trades* (Urbana, 1984).

24. Chené, *Débuts du commerce*; Paul Bouyx, "Naissance de la chaussure dans le Choletais," *Bulletin de la Société des sciences, lettres et beaux-arts de Cholet*, 1948–49, pp. 145–56; P. Head, "Boots and Shoes," in *The Development of British Industry and Foreign Competition, 1875–1914*, ed. Derek H. Aldcroft (London, 1968), pp. 158–85.

25. Office du Travail, *Enquête sur le travail à domicile dans l'industrie de la lingerie*, vol. 2 (Paris, 1908). Also issued by the Office du Travail, *Enquête sur le travail à domicile dans l'industrie de la chaussure* (Paris, 1914).

quences of the handloom weavers' struggle to preserve a semblance of their independence as small-scale producers.[26] It is ironic that many social critics of industrial society, such as Frédéric Le Play and Albert de Mun, pointed to family-based production as more humane and harmonious than factory production, when in fact family-based production, under the imperatives of familial bonds, may have been able to enforce work conditions more deplorable than any wage worker in a factory would tolerate.

Local entrepreneurs, however, paid a price for resorting to outwork and sweating. In the short run, local entrepreneurs favored homework and hand labor because they had little capital. This production strategy gave them a point of entry, but in the long run it was not necessarily beneficial for the region's economy and did not necessarily promote the economic survival of the rural entrepreneur. Local producers in the Choletais were locked into the insecure end of the product market. The structure of competition from other entrepreneurs, from retailers, and from machine-made goods tended to drive down both prices and profits. Because these entrepreneurs entered at the cheap end of the product market, where returns on investments were low, it was difficult for them to accumulate enough to break out. Thus outwork and sweating tend to replicate their own marginality. Despite their successful adaptation to the changes in urban consumer markets, the region and its people remained poor and on the periphery of the wealth and well-being generated by industrial capitalist development.

By the early twentieth century, labor-intensive production in weaving and in the new outwork trades functioned in the same relation to mechanized, centralized industries. Although both handloom weavers and outworkers in the garment and shoe trades worked long hours, were poorly remunerated, and worked at home using hand technologies, we must be careful to differentiate the historical roots of each group and not see them as a single phenomenon. As impoverished producers, handloom weavers were at the end of a long, often valiant struggle against proletarian status. In the end, they earned less than industrial workers and their control over the production process meant very little compared to their dependence on merchants for supplies and access to markets. Although reality was but a pale reflection of the faded vision of proud and independent producers, the self-image of weavers remained strong.

Outworkers in the garment and shoe industries were newly proletarianized. Unlike weavers, they were not remnants of a preindustrial past;

26. For a similar discussion of gender inequalities and the segmentation of labor markets, see Jane Humphries and Jill Rubery, "The Reconstitution of the Supply Side of the Labour Market: The Relative Autonomy of Social Reproduction," *Cambridge Journal of Economics* 8 (December 1984): 331–46.

dispersed manufacturing was fostered by the new consumer revolution in ready-to-wear items, which was stimulated by the growth of industrial urban society. That the two groups existed side by side in the same family offers an important lesson for those who champion small-scale family firms for their flexibility in adapting quickly to market changes. These advocates have not examined the gender relations and social organization that allow for this flexibility. A more realistic assessment of small-scale production requires us to move beyond market-level analysis and recognize the dependence of marketplace struggles on more private struggles within families. The ability of handloom weavers to continue in their trade in the face of political failures and the continued encroachment of mechanized production rested on the unequal power relations within their families and the ability of fathers to exact sacrifices from daughters. In the end, however, reliance on these unequal power relations set off its own negative spiral. The weavers continued the region's economic underdevelopment by reinforcing its reliance on cheap labor strategies. Handloom weavers in the Choletais may have avoided giving up their looms, but given the chain of outcomes, one is tempted to ask: What price a weaver's dignity?

3

The Gendering of Skill
as Historical Process:
The Case of French Knitters
in Industrial Troyes, 1880–1939

Helen Harden Chenut

Skill is an attribute identified historically with men's work, so its attribution to women seems a contradiction in terms. Yet gendered categories of skill prevailed in most trades. Most of the historical and sociological literature on the question of skill has relegated women to the category of unskilled worker without questioning how women came to be defined as unskilled or considering whether women in fact shared

I acknowledge with gratitude the financial contribution of the French government's Centre National de la Recherche Scientifique (CNRS) to the research for this chapter, which originally appeared as a research report titled "La Construction sociale des métiers masculins et féminins dans la bonneterie Troyenne, 1900 à 1939," GEDISST-CNRS, Rapport final, December 1987. This work was also made possible by the generous support and collaboration of the members of the GEDISST-CNRS in Paris, an interdisciplinary research group with whom I debated many of the issues discussed here. Institutional support for a year's leave came from the American Council of Learned Societies and was spent at the Bunting Institute of Radcliffe College in 1993–94.

1. This is a short list from a vast literature on the subject: Charles More, *Skill and the English Working Class, 1870–1914* (New York, 1980); Harry Braverman, *Labor and Monopoly Capital* (New York, 1974); John Rule, "The Property of Skill in the Period of Manufacture," in *The Historical Meanings of Work*, ed. Patrick Joyce (Cambridge, 1987). Rule is attentive to the exclusion of women from the category of skilled labor. See also Paul Thompson, *The Nature of Work: An Introduction to Debates on the Labour Process* (London, 1989); Charles Sabel, *Work and Politics* (Cambridge, 1982); Joan Scott, *The Glassworkers of Carmaux* (Cambridge, Mass., 1974).

some skills with men.[1] Many scholars have come to question the assumptions on which skill distinctions are based.[2]

An exploration of the gendered meanings of skill contributes to the historical understanding of the transformations of work and workers' resistance to industrial capitalism. The process of skill differentiation is embedded in the nineteenth-century workplace, in the conflicting relations between capital and labor, but it is also constructed from multiple social values mediated by the family, the community, and society at large. Skill, then, is historically significant as a marker of social class, as a motor of worker mobilization, but also as a component of gender and work identity.[3] It is a key category by which workers defined themselves in relation to others in the community. Women workers, however, found themselves in the problematic position of having to affirm their skills in relation to the normative male model upheld by employers. During the nineteenth century women worked alongside men in many trades; and as auxiliaries or contingent workers, they were denied power or authority despite their significant numbers in the workforce. They were segregated in separate work spaces, assigned specific tasks, and given tools of symbolic value.[4]

In France gendered skill definitions were grounded in the notion of métier, a skilled profession within a corporative tradition. The craft tradition—or "corporate idiom," as William Sewell has termed it—goes back to the French Revolution and was carried over in modified form into the nineteenth century as a cultural matrix for the development of the French labor movement.[5] Craft, community, and skill became trans-

2. Anne Phillips and Barbara Taylor, "Sex and Skill: Notes towards a Feminist Economics," *Feminist Review* 6 (1980); Cynthia Cockburn, *Brothers: Male Dominance and Technological Change* (London, 1983), and *Machinery of Dominance: Women, Men and Technical Know-How* (London, 1985); Mary Freifeld, "Technological Change and the 'Self-Acting' Mule: A Study of Skill and the Sexual Division of Labour," *Social History* 11 (1986): 319–43; Ava Baron, "An 'Other' Side of Gender Antagonism at Work: Men, Boys, and the Remasculinization of Printers' Work, 1830–1920," in *Work Engendered*, ed. Baron (Ithaca, 1991).

3. Joan Scott, "Work Identities for Men and Women: The Politics of Work and Family in the Parisian Garment Trades in 1848," in her *Gender and the Politics of History* (New York, 1988), pp. 93–112. Scott makes the important point that "skill . . . was a relative rather than absolute description of certain kinds of work" (p. 95).

4. An Italian ethnologist, Paola Tabet, has argued that male domination over women has been constituted and maintained by the prescriptive use of tools and techniques for the production of goods, which has created a "technology gap" that allows men a monopoly of advanced knowledge and techniques. See "Les Mains, les outils, les armes," *L'Homme* 19 (July–December 1979): 5–61.

5. See William Sewell Jr., *Work and Revolution in France* (Cambridge, 1980), pp. 162–93. Sewell argues that the "corporate idiom" was an expression of the corporation as a moral community. Though trade corporations had been outlawed in 1791, workers continued to use corporate traditions, practices, and language in opposition to nineteenth-century employers' attempts to disorganize them.

formed by industrialization and revolution in France under historical conditions very different from those in England. The French path to industrialization, the specific pattern of French working-class formation, and the role of skilled artisan workers as leaders of French socialism make the French case of craft and community distinctive. It follows that gender and class relations, divisions between skilled and unskilled workers, were shaped by historical forces peculiar to the French industrial experience. Artisanal forms of work far outnumbered factory jobs until after the Paris Commune of 1871. Under these conditions the male model of the skilled artisan persisted long after the actual erosion of working conditions and the dilution of skills.[6] By the turn of the century French unions in many trades clearly expressed the notion of a skilled male worker whose identity was increasingly threatened by technological advances and by women's employment.[7] They reasoned that because skill was defined as masculine, the employment of women and children destroyed the notion of skill. Behind this reasoning lay the conflation of mechanization, deskilling, and feminization, as male workers perceived the risk of becoming redundant or of being replaced by women. As we shall see, occupational segregation of women was one measure to protect men's jobs; the gendering of tools and technology was another.

Troyes, France's primary center for the manufacture of hosiery and knitted goods, experienced intense economic growth, feminization of the workforce, and technological development from 1880 to 1939. Craft and community in Troyes created a system of internal ranking in the mills in terms of occupation and skill. This hierarchy played into a gendered work identity for men and women, valorized by class and community in the town. Skill or métier was one important component of work identity. In the French hosiery industry, the male model of métier predominated as a definition of technical aptitude, mastery, and craft. Women used the similarity of certain technical skills to claim that they too had a métier. But technical mastery that depended on machine-operative skills was not the only measure of skill. Women workers were also recognized as having different skills from men. This gender difference was sometimes

6. Studies on the nineteenth-century skilled artisan have focused on the connection between skill and political consciousness or between changing working conditions and proletarianization. See the debate between Jacques Rancière, "The Myth of the Artisan: Critical Reflections on a Category of Social History," in *Work in France*, ed. Steven Kaplan and Cynthia Koepp (Ithaca, 1986), pp. 317–35, and Christopher Johnson, "Response to Jacques Rancière," *International Labor and Working-Class History* 24 (Fall 1983): 21–25.

7. For just the textile industry see the reply from the Fédération Nationale Ouvrière de l'Industrie Textile de France to the Parliamentary Inquiry of 1902, Archives Nationales (AN), C 7321: "Workers' technical mastery in the textile industry is today eliminated by the progressive substitution of automatic machines . . . for hand labor and dexterity, in sum, for everything that constitutes men's technical mastery, which has been displaced by the employment of women and children."

valorized as "natural feminine aptitudes," sometimes diluted to a mere symbolic distinction, but it was always perceived as constituting a different but complementary work identity for women.[8] It is significant and paradoxical that the mill owners of Troyes prized the only women's occupation requiring hand skills and artistry, closely identified with a feminine ideal, as the most highly skilled of women's hosiery jobs.

As increasing numbers of women workers in Troyes were employed to keep pace with growth in productivity, related changes in the work process led to the deskilling of workers of both sexes. Women had claimed that their specialized tasks demanded skills that overlapped with men's; now they could no longer do so. In 1936 a strong Popular Front movement in Troyes gave male union leaders sufficient leverage to negotiate from a position of strength the first collective bargaining agreement in the industry's history. In the process they codified the trade, effectively preserving men's skilled status to the detriment of women's and reconstructing a hierarchy of difference.

GENDER AND SKILL

Labor historians still debate the degree to which skilled workers in France became "proletarianized" during the second half of the nineteenth century, and in the process lost control over their craft status and skills. There seems to be general agreement that the process began with the spread of the factory system and intensified with mechanization and the concentration of capital and labor. Yves Lequin suggests that workers' concern for the dilution and loss of their skills appeared with the first signs of Taylorism, which he dates in the 1880s in France.[9] Studies of skilled artisans stress the relation between the increased division of labor, changing working conditions, and the growth of classconsciousness.[10] Some historians have examined the patterns of worker unrest to determine the degree of workers' resistance to industrial capitalism in various industries.[11] Still others assume workers' resistance

8. Scott, "Work Identities," p. 107.

9. Yves Lequin, "Le Métier," in Les Lieux de mémoire, ed. Pierre Nora, vol. 3, Les France, pt. 2 (Paris, 1992), pp. 376–419.

10. Two positions on this question are represented by Christopher Johnson in "Patterns of Proletarianization: Parisian Tailors and Lodève Woolens Workers," in Consciousness and Class Experience in Nineteenth-Century Europe, ed. John Merriman (New York, 1979), and Alain Cottereau, in his Introduction to Denis Poulot, Le Sublime (Paris, 1980). See also John Rule, "The Property of Skill in the Period of Manufacture," in Joyce, Historical Meanings of Work, pp. 99–118.

11. Michelle Perrot, Les Ouvriers en grève: France, 1871–1890, 2 vols. (La Haye, 1974); William Reddy, The Rise of Market Culture: The Textile Trade and French Society, 1750–1900 (Cambridge, 1984).

to industrial discipline as the norm and seek to understand the meanings of a range of grievances and conflicts, from informal, silent resistance to the more formal collective action of strikes.[12] These historians presume skill to be gender neutral. Several French feminist historians, however, have analyzed the strike behavior of women workers in particular nineteenth-century labor conflicts.[13]

Feminist historians have long sought to explain the sexual segregation of women's waged work and its consequences (unskilled labeling, low wages, lack of mobility, devaluation, etc.) in other than purely economic terms. A whole generation of studies of women and work, both in sociology and in history, were based on the assumption that the key to understanding women's subordination in society lay in this fundamental inequality in the division of labor. They have attempted to demonstrate that Marxist categories of economic analysis have been, as Heidi Hartmann has affirmed, gender blind.[14] It is now evident that sexual discrimination predates the capitalist system and is perpetuated in the labor market even today. In seeking to explain the nonobjective and noneconomic nature of such workplace discrimination, Anne Phillips and Barbara Taylor argue that the construction of skill is a key category in the meaning of work. "Skill definitions," they affirm, "are saturated with sexual bias. The work of women is often deemed inferior simply because it is women who do it. Women workers carry into the workplace their status as subordinate individuals, and their status comes to define the value of the work they do. Far from being an objective economic fact, skill is often an ideological category imposed on certain types of work by virtue of the sex and power of the workers who perform it." [15] Phillips and Taylor point to the arbitrary way women's subordinate position in society has been used to explain women's unskilled label and low wages. Sonya Rose develops this analysis further by demonstrating how gender distinctions were constitutive of job composition and workplace organization.[16] For Rose gender distinctions created antagonisms within the working class and operated as a capitalist strategy to divide and control

12. This is particularly the approach of Alain Cottereau. See his Introduction to Poulot, *Le Sublime*, and "The Distinctiveness of Working-Class Cultures in France, 1848–1900," in *Working-Class Formation: Nineteenth-Century Patterns in Western Europe and the United States*, ed. Ira Katznelson and Aristide Zolberg (Princeton, 1986).

13. See Perrot, *Ouvriers en grève*, 1: chap. 3; Claire Auzias and Annik Houel, *La Grève des ovalistes* (Paris, 1982); and esp. Madeleine Guilbert, *Les Femmes et l'organisation syndicale avant 1914* (Paris, 1966).

14. Heidi Hartmann, "Capitalism, Patriarchy, and Job Segregation by Sex," *Signs* 1 (1976).

15. Phillips and Taylor, "Sex and Skill."

16. Sonya O. Rose, *Limited Livelihoods* (Berkeley, 1992), esp. Introduction and chap. 2; and Rose, "Gender Segregation in the Transition to the Factory: The English Hosiery Industry, 1850–1910," *Feminist Studies* 13 (Spring 1987).

rs' loyalties. She uses the example of the hosiery industry in En-
to illustrate how men and women often competed for jobs. Joy Parr,
comparative study of the knitting industry in Canada and England,
examines the gender construction of skill in relation to many variables.
She notes that the sex labeling of specific tasks is contingent, and she
points to knitting as a prime example: "In the midlands and in Ontario
knitting was made men's or women's work through a complex interaction which combined tradition from the workshop and the early factory
with social prescription about who was entitled to work for wages at all
and characteristics of the local labor market and labor organization and of
both the product market and the prevailing technology."[17] While "skill,"
then, is a key category of analysis, it is only part of a more complex
configuration in the analysis of class, gender, and work.

SKILL, CRAFT, AND INDUSTRIALIZATION

What do we mean by métier? I use this term to define skill, knowing
that the notion has its own long history and development in French
working-class culture. The term métier, rooted in the revolutions of 1789
and 1848,[18] refers to those basic social units of useful labor recognized by
the republican forces. It could be said to be "at once economic, sexual and
political," as Joan Scott has argued in the case of worker identity.[19] At the
same time, the meanings attached to métier were contested and have
evolved over time. Workers persisted in using the customs, conventions,
and practices of their trade as a way of imposing order on the competitive
individualism developed by the capitalist system. "Nineteenth-century
workers attempted to gain control over many aspects of their trades,"
Sewell notes: "job placement, the pace and processes of work, the arbitration of disputes, the quality of goods produced, recruitment into the
trade, the level of wages and piece rates paid to workers, and so on."[20] The
notion of métier, then, not only includes technical skills or shared savoir-
faire but also represents a self-defined workers' community in opposition
to industrial capitalism. The meanings attributed to the term were
shaped by changing historical conditions in the trade. Historically two
very different logics—those of capital and labor—have operated in the
defining of skills, and the antagonism between the two became expressed

17. Joy Parr, *The Gender of Breadwinners* (Toronto, 1990), p. 60; and Parr, "Dis-
aggregating the Sexual Division of Labor: A Transatlantic Case Study," *Comparative
Studies in Society and History* 30 (1988).
18. Lequin, "Le Métier," p. 377. Lequin describes the processions of trade corporations
in the early months of the Revolution of 1848.
19. Scott, *Gender and the Politics of History*, p. 96.
20. Sewell, *Work and Revolution*, pp. 179–80.

most explicitly in strikers' grievances.[21] The introduction of new technology gave employers an opportunity to erode the craft knowledge and ability that workers struggled to maintain in their jobs, the same skills that union leaders defended as training and experience. Wage demands often masked contested meanings of skill.

How can we problematize skill from the perspective of gender within this historical framework? Is métier-as-skill exclusively a male property?[22] In other words, does the notion of métier apply to women? If so, when does this notion appear in gendered terms in the Troyes hosiery industry? How do women workers represent themselves in terms of métier?

According to *Le Grand Robert* dictionary, métier refers to what constitutes or confers a profession, and the referent is a male model. But the term is also used to refer more generally to technical skills, both manual and intellectual, that are acquired through training and based on experience (avoir un métier, to have a trade). It is also used to mean work that is both recognized by society and a livelihood. This latter meaning is gendered—métier d'homme ou de femme—not in any indistinct way, but in reference to a social occupation.[23] If métier is defined narrowly as "a trade,' nineteenth-century women workers would seem not to have had one, as they were considered contingent workers whose primary ascription was to home and family.[24] Michelle Perrot has argued that the notion

21. Danièle Kergoat underscores the opposing logics in the following terms: "[Job qualification] refers to the complex set of qualities required by employers for a specific job task, and it is this definition that serves as the basis for job classification grids (therefore the wage scale) and to legitimize the division of labor; management decisions on the job classification system depend on personnel management policy and on technological imperatives; worker qualification, on the other hand, refers to the training and experience that workers deploy in carrying out their job, and it is this definition that unions refer to when they negotiate job classification": *Les Ouvrières* (Paris, 1982), p. 53.

22. Rule argues that in mid-nineteenth-century England skill was "clearly a male 'property', and in that it was the distinguishing mark separating the artisan from the common labourer, it also represented a symbolic capital": "Property of Skill," p. 108. Thus it implicitly excludes women as unskilled labor. For Sonya Rose, "honorable manhood was equated with possessing a skill and family headship." Among British skilled artisans, notions of masculinity, skilled status, breadwinning, and respectability were interrelated. See Rose, *Limited Livelihoods*, pp. 138–53.

23. Among the quotations listed to exemplify usage, *Le Grand Robert* gives three concerning women's métiers: the first relates to the fact that "women have progressively gained access to professions traditionally exercised by men"; the second refers to "the oldest profession in the world"; and the third is excerpted from Zola's *La Bête humaine* and can serve only to demonstrate the devalorization of women's work: "Doubtless, he concluded, not all women would be willing to clean public restrooms. But there is no such thing as a stupid métier": *Le Grand Robert de la langue française*, 2d ed (Paris, 1985), 6: 416–18.

24. Lequin, "Le Métier," p. 407. Lequin quotes Michelle Perrot's argument that women rarely have a métier in the male sense of the term; even if they work, the job is not a

of métiers de femmes or women's occupations took shape under the moral eye of liberal social reformers who framed the "woman question" as they simultaneously denounced the dangers and evils of the factory system for women and children.[25] These male observers noted that certain tasks were appropriate and fitting to women's "nature" but did not necessarily describe them as skilled.[26]

The process of creating gender distinctions discursively to circumscribe women's work went hand in hand with the occupational segregation of women in production. The increasing numbers of women working in certain sectors of the French economy by the turn of the century provide evidence that employers understood how their skills could be effectively exploited. According to the 1906 census, women represented 37.15 percent of the active population in France as a whole. By 1921 this figure had reached 39.6 percent, only to decline to 36.1 percent in 1936.[27] If we break down these aggregate figures for 1906, we find that 37.9 percent of women worked in agriculture, 37.7 percent in industry, and 24.4 percent in the service sector.[28] In the industrial sector the numbers of women workers remained fairly constant from 1906 to 1936, while the composition and distribution of their jobs changed. This is the case in the textile industry, which witnessed the decline of such women's tasks as embroidery and passementerie and the creation of more jobs for men and women as modern machine operators.[29]

In the hosiery industry there was a steady increase in the proportion of women in the labor force in Troyes and the department of the Aube over the first half of the twentieth century: 51 percent in 1901, 61 percent in 1921, and 57.5 percent in 1936. Women swelled the ranks notably in the category of blue- and white-collar workers (ouvriers et employés) during the 1920s and 1930s. Behind these aggregate figures we can observe new work patterns emerging for women. Employers in Troyes encouraged married women to continue working while they raised their children. Low wages made a second income a virtual necessity for most couples. The feminization of the workforce in Troyes was also linked to the increased specialization and professionalization of women hosiery workers. They were no longer auxiliaries or contingent workers. Women's

lifetime commitment that confers status and identity. See Michelle Perrot, "Qu'est-ce qu'un métier de femme?" in Mouvement Social, no. 140 (July–September 1987).

25. Perrot, "Qu'est-ce qu'un métier de femme?" p. 5.

26. Paul Leroy-Beaulieu, Le Travail des femmes au XIXe siècle (Paris, 1873).

27. Jean Daric, L'Activité professionnelle des femmes en France (Paris, 1947). I have calculated from Daric's figures for the active population in all occupations, table 1, p. 15.

28. Guilbert, Les Femmes et l'organisation syndicale, pp. 13–14.

29. Sylvie Zerner makes this point in "De la couture aux presses: L'Emploi féminin entre les deux guerres," in Mouvement Social, no. 140 (1987), pp. 8–25.

skills became redefined in a specific industrial and historical context: knitting frames geared to mass production created more task-specific jobs for women as loopers, seamers, quality control workers, finishers. Certain female occupations became categorized according to machine-specific skills, as we shall see. The fact of operating a specialized machine did not necessarily confer a skill label, but mechanization of special female tasks did allow women to master new skills and to perform as machine operatives as men did. Jobs that were identified with their machine conferred status.

Women workers could and did, claim to have a métier and a gendered work identity that overlapped to some extent with men's: bonnetier and bonnetière were generic and gendered terms for workers in the knitted-goods industry, recognized by all the Troyes industrial community. Such customary terms of collective identity connoted complementarity in the gender division of labor, similar to that employed in many old French trades, but in reality these terms blurred job composition. The generic bonnetière masked women's place in the production process, but it conveyed the idea of an independent wage earner in the Troyes mills. By 1939 bonnetier still referred to a skilled male knitter, but bonnetière had become an increasingly disparaging term for the local factory girl, tarnished by vulgarity and by her association with men in the workplace.[30] In the historical process of engendering skill, the construction of difference gradually stigmatized women hosiery workers.

Craft unions developed to defend workers' status, interests, and well-being. Even if skill was not explicitly mentioned in wage demands, the notion was implicated in this contested terrain. The question of acquiring and preserving skilled status and recognition remained a fundamental area of unresolved class and gender conflict at the end of the nineteenth century. As industrial syndicalism developed in France by the fusion between the craft workshop tradition and the new industrial proletariat, workers struggled against the leveling of working conditions in modern industry.

The textile unions in Troyes fought for employers' recognition and the right to represent labor and negotiate their demands. In the early years of the struggle to organize, the local Guesdist leaders appealed to women workers to join forces with male co-workers in strikes and to join the union. By 1895 the mixed hosiery union, the Association Syndicale des Ouvriers et Ouvrières de Toutes les Professions Se Rattachant à la Bonneterie, was making special appeals to raise female membership. A tract dating from this time was addressed specifically to women workers,

30. An interesting linguistic study of present-day terminology in the hosiery industry only partially raises this question. See Françoise Perdriset, "Recherches sur le vocabulaire de la bonneterie" (thesis, Université de Paris, 1980).

enumerating them by their gendered métiers and calling upon them as mothers, wives, and daughters of the working class.[31] The union formulated its concern over female membership in explicitly gendered terms. In Troyes, however, the male leadership in both the political parties and the unions ensured that class and labor interests predominated over gender concerns. Women workers were marginal to both sorts of political institution. Union membership was modest in 1900: 2.9 percent for France as a whole, 1.06 percent for the department of the Aube; and while women represented 32.8 percent of the Aube's active population, they constituted only 13 percent of members in the two mixed unions.[32] It was their central place in the production process that provided women a real workplace identity.

THE SEXUAL DIVISION OF LABOR

The technical complexity of knitting machines and the variety of articles they produce make knitting an intricate operation. Production in the Troyes mills was labor intensive, and that labor had to be skilled. Historically the work process had been divided into several operations assigned to men, women, and children according to their sex, age, and ability. Men appropriated the knitting frame and the technical knowledge required to repair or adjust the machine. The mechanics of knitting technology were decidedly a masculine preserve, and the technical skills so prized for their prestige and productivity were those that developed out of the craft tradition. According to the first statutes regulating the trade, established by the Corporation des Bonnetiers d'Arcis-sur-Aube in 1750, operating the hand-powered knitting frame was exclusively a male privilege.[33] The putting-out system, organized around the family unit under the direction of its male head, did not often recognize women and children as producers. In practice, however, the husband, wife, and older children operated the knitting frame as necessary to finish the week's

31. This tract can be read as a representation of women workers' place in the social order, as Joan Scott has suggested, first as members of the working class, second as members of a corporative tradition, and third as members of a family or social and economic unit in French society. See Joan Scott, "L'Ouvrière! Mot impie, sordide...": Women Workers in the Discourse of French Political Economy, 1840–1860," in her *Gender and the Politics of History*, pp. 139–63.

32. The basic figures come from Guilbert, *Les Femmes et l'organisation syndicale*, p. 30.

33. Julien Ricommard, *La Bonneterie à Troyes et dans le département de l'Aube* (Paris, 1934), p. 32. Ricommard's classic history of the Troyes hosiery industry cites these statutes as the origin of male knitters' appropriation of the frame, a privilege that went unchallenged until mill owners employed women knitters to replace men during World War I. See chapter 5 for a discussion of the custom governing the sexual division of labor.

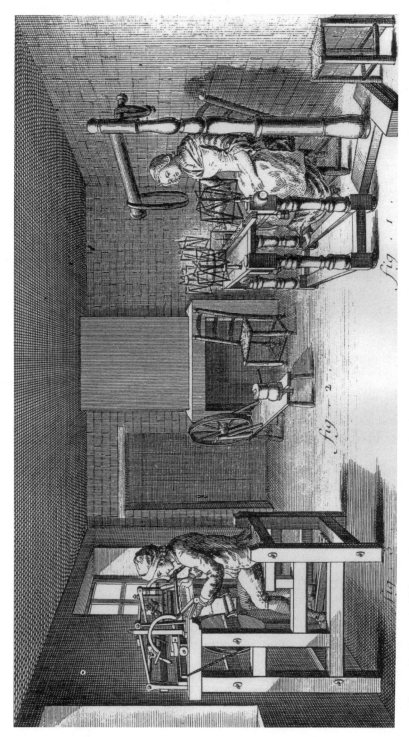

3.1. The gender division of labor in domestic knitting as represented in the *Encyclopédie* of Diderot and d'Alembert. (Archives départementales de l'Aube)

production. The household production model tends to idealize gender relations by presenting a fixed and symmetrical image of the couple, such as we find reproduced in Diderot's *Encyclopédie* (Figure 3.1). Such self-sufficient images of complementarity are misleading, because women's work was subordinate to men's in many ways.

Mill owners reproduced the sexual division of labor developed by artisans and adapted it to their needs in the mills. In the transition from an artisan mode of production to an industrial one, the male knitter maintained his privileged position at the knitting frame, the most valorized and productive machine, while women were employed to prepare the raw materials (spinning) and to seam and finish by hand the articles produced. The fact that women's tasks were only partially mechanized led to a need for increasing numbers of "nimble fingers" to sew and finish knitted goods. Seaming was labor-intensive. Employers recruited a growing number of women to execute increasingly fragmented tasks.

The first step in the work process was winding the yarn. The bobbin winder worked in tandem with the knitter and provided him with the raw material for his frame. As a women's job, bobbin winding was poorly paid and physically demanding, and it carried the social stigma attached to hard physical labor in proximity to men. Knitting was the next stage of production. Male knitters or stockingers operated both flat-bed frames for the production of fully fashioned goods and small circular machines that produced tubular stockings or continuous fabric. Most women's jobs were grouped around finishing: seaming, looping, mending, and quality control, all labor-intensive subdivided tasks that were mechanized in stages. The skills required were good eyesight, taste, the dexterity needed to work with the elasticity of knitted fabric, and knowledge of the knitting process. As we shall see, mill owners prized one group of female workers above all others: skilled menders (*raccoutreuses*), trained in the fine needlework skills of repairing flawed or damaged goods. When one considers that such goods included the expensive luxury silk stockings of the 1920s, it is easy to understand how manufacturers ranked this work as both highly profitable and the ultimate women's métier. The final operations, from matching pairs to packaging, were mainly executed by women.

The growing feminization of the Troyes workforce can also be explained by the highly organized practice of outwork in the knitting industry. Some tasks assigned to women could be done at home. Small portable seamers had been introduced around 1890 to seam heels and toes. Specialized mending of flawed products by hand was routinely done at home. Employers delivered such unfinished socks and stockings to mothers with small children to care for at home. The fact that the outwork system persisted well into the 1930s is confirmed by the collective bargaining agreement of 1936 concerning homeworkers.

The sexual division of labor in this production process evolved out of custom, craft, and convention. In comparison with women who worked in the hosiery industries of England and Canada, where operation of the circular knitting frame became a "mixed gender occupation,"[34] French women in the Troyes mills never challenged this male monopoly. During World War I, when women in industries all over France substituted for men at the front, women in Troyes replaced men on small flat-bed knitters, reputed to be simpler and lighter to operate than the large knitting frame. The substitution in this case was recognized as a response to exceptional wartime circumstances, and when the men returned to their prewar occupations, women returned to theirs. The knitting frame remained gendered as a male machine. Women continued to follow in the customary female occupations for which they had been trained by their mothers and fathers. In this hierarchy of difference, formal and informal skill training played a crucial role in the gendering of the Troyes work culture.

APPRENTICESHIP AND TRAINING IN THE
SKILLING PROCESS

By the turn of the century two forms of traditional apprenticeship and training coexisted in the Troyes knitting industry, one for technicians and workshop foremen, one for the various production jobs. The first consisted of formal training in a professional school founded by the bourgeois entrepreneurs of Troyes in 1888; the second was grounded in the emulation and example of family members or friends who worked in the trade. Obviously the second route, informal and family apprenticeship, has left little written record for historians to evaluate; we have only the experienced hand, or what the French call la mémoire de la main.[35]

Measures for institutionalized apprenticeship and training were directed almost exclusively toward men. Troyes's entrepreneurs combined foresight and personal interest in establishing the Ecole Française de Bonneterie in 1888. Many of them had attended engineering schools or

34. Parr, *Gender of Breadwinners*, p. 60.
35. This evocative phrase comes from a watchmaker cited by François Caron during a public thesis defense in June 1986 at the Sorbonne. The following paragraphs on informal training and apprenticeship are based on oral history testimony collected from a sample of men and women operatives who had worked in the Troyes mills in the 1920s and 1930s. For further discussion see Helen Chenut, "La Formation d'une culture ouvrière féminine: Les Bonnetières troyennes" (doctorat de 3ème cycle, Université de Paris VII, 1988).

the regional école des arts et métiers, and this experience led them to seek state and municipal aid for their project. Their purpose was to train young men to become captains of their industry, the model being, of course, the army.[36] The entrepreneurs were committed to a two-to-three-year general and technical education program to train a small male elite for their immediate needs in the mills. Two-thirds of the twenty students enrolled had scholarships, but the mill owners maintained absolute control over admissions. What was at stake was the kind of professional savoir-faire and autonomy that artisan knitters had sought to protect against the inroads of industrial capitalism. Workers perceived the school as an attempt by manufacturers to train their own sons, along with overseers, in the specialized and technical knowledge of the trade, thereby dividing the workforce even further into supervisors, technicians, and manual operatives. One worker delegate from Troyes to the Paris World's Fair of 1889 argued for training that would transmit an integral vision of the trade, together with a general education, free and guaranteed by the state.[37]

The norms established by mill owners for the administration of their private professional school in Troyes were contested by the Socialists when they came to power there at the turn of the century, but the town's subsidy was never called into question. Rather, local elected officials sought to strengthen the technical education programs of the public schools, and called upon individual public-spirited entrepreneurs to make inspection missions and recommendations. Ultimately the state stepped in to establish the norms that would give a legal status to apprenticeship. The state school system was to coordinate the various forms of training and administer examinations. These directives were embodied in the law of 1928 on apprenticeship. There was a price to pay, of course: workers' testimony confirmed that their families had to advance the money for their apprenticeship, and that they earned no wages during the training period.[38]

Informal and family apprenticeship provided most production workers entry into the mills. Like many nineteenth-century trades, the Troyes knitting industry was grounded in professional intermarriage or endogamy, which ensured the continuity of work skills and culture from

36. Emmanuel Buxtorf, engineer-mechanic, inventor of several accessory machines, and the school's first director, expressed their aim in these terms: "Les contre-maîtres sont à l'industrie ce que les officiers sont à l'armée": "Inauguration de l'Ecole Française de Bonneterie," *Journal de la Bonneterie Française*, November 15, 1890, Archives Municipales de Troyes (AMT), R257.

37. Report by M. Foin, "Rapport des délégués ouvriers à l'Exposition universelle de 1889," AMT, F140.

38. Testimony from Madame Aubron (August 28, 1982) and Madame Binet (August 4, 1983). See also n. 35.

one generation to the next. Children were initiated into the hand skills and work processes of the trade in the family workshop. The father as head of household trained the members of his own family.[39] But some mothers who did handwork or seaming at home trained their children to help finish certain manual tasks. Once they entered the mills, most young workers were trained on the job to acquire the factory experience that qualified workers of both sexes in the eyes of the foreman. The family network served to gain access to this type of employment at the early age of 13 (the legal school-leaving age).

For young men the first step on the established career ladder was to serve as a rebrousseur in tandem with a bonnetier, or hosier; then, around the age of 16, he became the *bonnetier*'s official apprentice. Rebroussage was a stopgap job. It was a manual task between two stages in the production of socks and stockings on the flat-bed knitter, and required nimble fingers and good eyesight. The bonnetier subcontracted the work to his rebrousseur. This practice of making a skilled worker the actual employer of his unskilled helper created tension and competition, which often resulted in conflicts over wages. Young rebrousseurs could walk off the job and effectively halt production.

Women's professions did not benefit from either institutional training or long apprenticeship in the mills. When women's work was first mechanized, on-the-job training directed by an experienced worker or forewoman provided the only formal training outside the family work-shop. By the 1920s women workers spent three to six months acquiring the skills and speed necessary to earn their living at piecework. This relatively short training period implied lower skill content and con-trasted noticeably with the longer training required for men's work. The increasing subdivision of women's work into fragmented tasks dimin-ished their opportunity to learn and improve their skills. Technical improvements introduced during the 1920s and 1930s mechanized such small operations that women learned little more than specialized me-chanical high-speed tasks, such as operating buttonholing and button-sewing machines.

There was one notable exception to this pattern of female apprentice-ship: the fine needlework skills of the mender or raccoutreuse required months of patient on-the-job training and practical experience with knit-ted fabrics. Apprentices had to learn to identify flaws in the finished knitted product, then reconstruct the stitches in such a way as to render

39. A description of the family workshop in 1900 has survived through the monograph of a rural primary schoolteacher who served twenty-two years in his community: M. Jamerey, monographie de la Commune de Maizières-La-Grande-Paroisse, Petite Industrie, Bonneterie, l'Exposition universelle de 1900, groupe XVI, classe 103, La Chambre de Commerce de Troyes.

the repair invisible. Such Penelope-like skills were highly valorized both socially and professionally. In contrast to the worker whose machine skills were gendered as masculine, the mender embodied consummate hand skills and artistry with the needle. Such skills, even if developed over a long apprenticeship, were intimately associated in mill owners' minds with women's natural attributes. Embroiderers worked alongside menders to decorate the elaborate silk stockings of the Belle Epoque. Rozsika Parker has remarked that "the art of embroidery has been the means of educating women into the feminine ideal, and of proving that they have attained it."[40] The skilled menders of the Troyes mills certainly embodied such a feminine ideal. We shall soon see how mill owners exploited this ideal in a skill competition they organized in 1930.

The short training that women received, on the job and informally, contrasts sharply with the professional training developed for valorizing and legitimizing men's skills. Women's career patterns differed from men's. More important, their informal family training did not automatically confer social status and a sense of métier. It was a status they had to legitimize through on-the-job training in the workplace. At the outset the requisite skills for their professions—hand skills and the use of tools of symbolic importance—were identified with customary feminine domestic occupations. The mechanization of knitting, together with the improvement of knitting technology, did little to reverse the historical pattern of occupational segregation. It did, however, give new meaning to specific women's occupations in the industry and empower them to claim skills that overlapped men's. Women became operatives of machines designed for their specific tasks.

GENDERED TOOLS AND TECHNOLOGY

The gendering of technology and tools provides just one strategy for creating and maintaining gender distinctions in skill. The evolution of knitting technology structured the organization of work in the Troyes mills.[41] During the period we are examining knitting frames were equipped with automatic functions and became capable of producing goods rapidly and in series. The most important invention of this period was the Cotton frame knitter from England, displayed at the Paris

40. Rozsika Parker, *The Subversive Stitch* (London, 1984), p. 1.
41. For the evolution of knitting technology see Georges Ude, *Etude générale de bonneterie* (Paris, n.d.); M. Hamant, "Les Diverses Opérations de fabrication et le matériel de finissage et d'apprêt," conférence faite à la Chambre de Commerce de Troyes, April 10, 1944; and William Felkin, *The History of the Machine Wrought Hosiery and Lace-Manufacture* (London, 1867).

World's Fair of 1867 and constructed in Troyes from 1878. The Cotton frame became the mass-production knitter of the modern mill. Once improved, it produced a wide variety of goods in series. Manufacturers were thus able to diversify production and adapt more quickly to the changing needs of fashion, while also maintaining high productivity. The Cotton frame knitter became the consummate masculine machine.

Mechanization affected both men's and women's work by increasing specialization.[42] Fewer men were needed to tend the mass-production knitters and fewer mechanical skills were needed to maintain production runs, resulting in slowdowns in production and periods of layoff. For women the number of specialized tasks increased as their work was subdivided, creating more gender-specific jobs. At the time of the Parliamentary Enquiry of 1904, the Chambre Syndicale Patronale (Employers' Hosiery Association) of Troyes listed three categories of male knitters and some twelve women's occupations with craft-specific titles.[43] The technical innovations of this period did little to upgrade the skill content of women's work. Rather, the female tasks that had been partially mechanized became valorized socially through their machine-related skills. By the interwar period employers were bridging technological gaps in the production process with semiskilled women's jobs. Production shifted from hosiery to a greater diversity of fashion clothing made from cut-up knitted fabric sewn together along an assembly line.

If we analyze two occupations, one masculine and one feminine, we can understand how women's skills, contrary to men's, were diluted when technological innovations were introduced. The "bonnetier Cotton" or knitter on the Cotton Patent frame operated the most prestigious mechanical knitting machine of the modern hosiery industry. His work required physical strength in the 1880s and 1890s because heavy gears had to be shifted between operations. The physical-strength argument underpinned the male monopoly of the machine. With the introduction of automatic commands before 1914, the Cotton Patent operator became more of a machine minder and a supervisor of the knitting process. His mechanical skills came into play at best when he had to repair or replace broken needles, for example, or to set up and restart a machine. The knitter could sit down to wait until the machine stopped for the next operation. Finally, mill owners required knitters to oversee two frames, or even the ultra-long Cotton, with twenty-four or thirty-six heads knitting simultaneously (Figure 3.2). These mass-production knitting frames

42. "Specialization" implies the fragmenting of an operation into a series of repetitive tasks that require little skill. The term reveals some of the ambiguity of skill definitions. In fact, the modern French term for unskilled worker is *ouvrier spécialisé*, or *O.S.*

43. "L'Enquête parlementaire sur l'état de l'industrie textile et la condition des ouvriers tisseurs" (1906), AN, C7318.

3.2. A Cotton Patent knitter at work in the 1950s. From an advertising brochure for Vitos, manufacturer of knitted goods, Troyes, published in 1963. (Archives départmentales de l'Aube)

accelerated the work pace but still allowed the operator to intervene in the process and preserve some technical competence. The lengthy training and workshop apprenticeship, combined with the rites of passage both into the profession and up the career ladder, all gave the Cotton Patent knitter the social and professional status of a skilled worker. As the work evolved, his skills were diluted but transferable. He was able to maintain a skill label through job recomposition over the sixty-year period dominated by the Cotton Patent frame. Ultimately, he could look back and identify with the skilled worker of the corporate tradition. In short, he belonged to a craft fraternity.[44]

If we examine the work of a typical woman machine operator, the looper or remmailleuse, and trace its evolution over the same period, the divergencies in the skilling process become clear: shorter factory apprenticeship, no formal recognition of previous sewing machine experience, a specialized piecework task, no reference to the craft tradition. It is also evident why this work was assigned to women at the outset: it involves joining two edges, stitch by stitch, onto poinçons or hooks and sewing them together. In the nineteenth century this work was done by hand with a crochet hook. It became mechanized around 1880, when the sewing machine was adapted to the seaming of knitted goods (Figure 3.3). The introduction of a specialized machine allowed women to master new technical skills. In social and cultural terms, it created a new primary identity for loopers in the workplace as machine operatives, similar to the male model. Apprenticeship on this specialized machine took place in the factory, but a significant number of women loopers were trained in the family workshop or at home by their mothers. One obvious advantage of this small seamer was its compact size and shape, which permitted it to fit easily into a domestic environment. As we have seen, many loopers were outworkers, combining child care with industrial work.

The machine-operative skills involved in this work were recognized, but there were hidden difficulties to the job that were less obvious. The manual dexterity and good eyesight needed to produce a flat, invisible stocking seam that could stretch around the heel, for example, made the looper's job a delicate one. The looper worked with her eyes riveted on tiny metal poinçons that reflected the light; working with black thread on fine knitted goods diminished her productivity; and problems with the tension of her precision machine could prevent her from making her quota for the day. Loopers were paid by the piece, and they had to pace themselves to make a living. Mill owners gradually forced the pace by the 1930s, and after 1945 a worker's productivity was controlled by a stopwatch. She had no career ladder to climb, no technical improvements to her machine to master, only an accelerating productivity norm to meet.[45]

The gendering of technology strengthened existing occupational segregation and preserved the skilled status of male knitters on the Cotton

44. Testimony from Monsieur Laborie (May 18, 1987).
45. Testimony from Madame Fournet (August 28, 1982).

3.3. A looper at work on a machine developed by Valton et Fils. (From Louis and Marie-Madeleine Boucraut's *Pierre Valton et ses fils* [Troyes, 1986], p. 114, by kind permission of Mme Boucraut)

frame machine. For women workers, mechanization brought upgraded mechanical skills that employers harnessed to production norms and to increasingly specialized and subdivided tasks. While both knitters and loopers progressively lost control over the pace and progress of work, they struggled to maintain some degree of control over the product's quality. Skill and craft sense were embedded in quality control. Labor conflicts in the Troyes mills inevitably became the means of expressing grievances over both wages and skill.

SKILL CONTESTED

By the turn of the century Troyes mill owners had established a multiplicity of wage rates for the production of knitted goods. This situation reflected the changing structure of production in the mills and the diversity of goods produced. Workers and their unions demanded uniform piece rates throughout the mills, but competition among employers and a large labor pool kept wages down. Mill owners played on the competition between male and female workers, between workers of different professions, and between factory workers and those employed in rural workshops or at home. A two-month strike erupted in February 1900 as workers demanded wage increases and uniform piece rates that would apply to all the mill workshops. In demanding unified piece rates they appealed to workers' sense of unity and craft solidarity. But they also voiced secondary grievances that revealed underlying dissatisfaction over divisions of labor, quality control, and recognition of skill. The youngest male workers, the rebrousseurs, sparked the strike in a sudden revolt against the subcontracting that bound them as unskilled helpers paid piecework rates directly by the knitters.

Twelve thousand workers left their jobs in an important demonstration of solidarity. Strikers organized according to métier and to factory workshop for the purpose of electing delegates to a general strike committee, which would present their grievances. This male pattern of corporative representation, reminiscent of the organizing strategy of workers' associations during the Revolution of 1848, was imitated by the women. Thus gender and class solidarity were framed in terms of the corporative community, embodied in a general strike committee composed of roughly equal numbers of men and women and large numbers of young rebrousseurs. The organization of the strike is significant in its reliance on craft practice for collective action to dispute age-old methods of payment, subcontracting, and workers' control over the quality of the goods they produced.[46] Union involvement was minimal. Once the strike had been declared, the unions sought to use the mobilization to recruit new members.

Critical to our understanding of the strike are the employers' practices that skilled men and women were contesting. These grievances touched on their sense of quality workmanship above and beyond the question of wages. At issue was the employers' practice of punishing what they saw as poorly executed work by peremptory wage deductions known as pour comptes. This practice was bitterly resented by women pieceworkers, who claimed the right to quality control over their own production. Seamers in the Raguet mills, for example, refused to machine-stitch camisoles without first basting them by hand.[47] They were defending their craft skills in the production of luxury knitted goods. Grievances of

46. "Grève de 1900," Archives Départementales de l'Aube (ADA), série continue 417. See also Reddy, *Rise of Market Culture*, chap. 10.
47. ADA, SC417.

this kind demonstrate workers' growing anger over the levying of fines for work over which they had less and less control.

Male knitters and other machine operatives protested fees for lighting and for the replacement of machine needles broken during production. Mill owners, they charged, were deducting more from their pay than the needles cost. Knitters were also subject to pour comptes for any defects in the knitted fabric. They, too, voiced pride in their ability to judge the quality of the products they produced. A worker delegate sent to the Paris World's Fair several months after the end of the strike complained: "All the knitted goods were locked up in display cases so it was impossible to touch them, and in the hosiery industry, touching is one of the main ways of knowing if the fabric has all the properties that appear to the eye."[48] Workers were not so alienated from the products of their labor as labor historians have thought.[49]

Mill owners, calling workers' demands "incoherent," refused to consider unifying piece rates by job category throughout the Troyes mills on the grounds that the existing system accurately reflected the diversity of hosiery production in the town. The strike took them by surprise, at a historical moment of intense capitalistic competition and restructuring locally, and of increasing government intervention through protective legislation. They refused all contact with the strike committee, denying its claim to represent "their" workers, and imposed a general lockout. After two months the workers gave in and returned to work.

From the Troyes workers' viewpoint, the strike failed in its attempt to defend the level of wages and skill and, more important, to overcome divisions within the working class. Workers had counted on a favorable political context, both locally with the Guesdist socialists seeking electoral victory in Troyes and nationally with the Waldeck-Rousseau government in power.[50] Their demands were in fact presented in piecemeal fashion by the various occupational groups and workshops. The strikers had tried to unite a craft community that in the long run was made up of separate corporative interests divided by the work process. The embryonic union, backed by the Guesdist Socialist Parti Ouvrier Français,

48. Report by Emile Caillot, "Rapports des délégués ouvriers de la ville de Troyes à l'Exposition universelle de 1900," AMT, F141.

49. Leora Auslander makes this point in her essay on furniture makers and extends it to include workers' sense of the aesthetics of the products they produced. See her "Perceptions of Beauty and the Problem of Consciousness: Parisian Furniture Makers," in *Rethinking Labor History: Essays on Discourse and Class Analysis*, ed. Lenard Berlanstein (Urbana, 1993), pp. 149–81.

50. The strike committee sent a delegation to Paris to meet with Waldeck-Rousseau and the Socialists in the Chambre des Députés. Waldeck-Rousseau refused to intervene on their behalf. The worker delegation was composed of four male knitters and one woman seamer.

never controlled the strike, because the workers refused to consider a more vertical political structure to represent their interests. Skilled and semiskilled workers were not yet organized together in sufficient numbers in an industrial union. But among the strikers there was overall solidarity between men and women in defense of wages and skill.

The strikes of 1936 were altogether different in content and style, reflecting the historical development of industrial capitalism in Troyes, with increased feminization of the workforce and development of mass-production technology. Yet wage rates and skill definitions were still major issues of dispute. A weakened labor movement, divided between Socialist-backed and Communist-led unions, had struggled in the 1930s to improve wages in Troyes, while layoffs and wage reductions at the mills kept workers of both sexes in constant flux. A reunified labor movement in 1936 and the victory of the Popular Front both in Paris and in Troyes ensured an alignment of political forces favorable to the workers' demands. Mill owners capitulated early in June, turning to the bargaining table after a relatively short period of conflict and factory occupation by strikers. They agreed to apply government reforms, granting recognition of the unions, a 40-hour workweek, paid vacations, and a 10 percent increase in wages. More important, they agreed to negotiate a collective bargaining agreement covering many practices contested by workers in the Troyes knitting industry.

The historic collective bargaining agreement of September 1936 can be said to have codified skills in the profession.[51] At least, union representatives set out to do just that in an unprecedented social and political context. The agreement produced a definition of job composition and wage rates for the entire hosiery industry: an hourly rate was to be combined with a piece rate, based on the article produced and on the type and gauge of knitting machine used. Clearly the wage part of the agreement represented a victory for the workers, who had struggled for many years to escape from employers' arbitary practices in this regard. The hourly rate provided in principle a guaranteed minimum wage, and the piece rate rewarded productivity. Moreover, an indemnity was to be granted in the case of any work stoppages "independent of male and female workers' volition." Workers might have lost control over the work process, but they would no longer be penalized for technical incidents or accidents that halted the production process.

The agreement legitimized the existing gender division of labor and skill. It can be read as both a technical and a gender description of

51. "Convention collective passée à Troyes le 18 Septembre 1936 entre les organisations patronales et ouvrières de la Bonneterie et Industries annexes du département de l'Aube, modifiée et complétée par l'additif du 3 Novembre 1936," Troyes, 1936, ADA, SC 4334A.

production jobs. Women's work was, as usual, sharply distinguished from men's. Tasks were divided, even subdivided, and then labeled by gender. Thus women would be "knitter-minders" but not "knitter-operators," the distinction being that women could not intervene to fix the circular frames on which a small number of women now worked.[52]

Customary women's occupations were classified on a scale from 1 to 8, ranging from the unskilled finishing tasks of petites mains to fine-gauge seaming on more difficult and delicate knitted fabric. Under the circumstances, skill distinctions stood out ever more sharply in the effort to define more uniform job categories. One job category was identified simply as travaux féminins, or "women's work," characterized as unskilled, task-oriented, and manual.

Though it is obvious from this account that male union leaders protected male jobs and skills, they did struggle to raise what they called the "abnormally low" wages of "women, laborers, and less skilled workers in the spinning mills and dyeworks." The unions and the mill owners' association even broke off negotiations for a short period over this question. Union leaders explained that they were pressing for a revision of women's wages and greater uniformity of compensation for the same jobs throughout the Troyes mills.[53] The unions obtained satisfaction on both demands, only to find that mill owners eroded these and other worker gains as the balance of power shifted in the following years.

GENDER AND SKILL CELEBRATED

Beyond the language of the workplace lies an elaborate cultural system of gender representations informing skill. The Troyes hosiery industry celebrated its skilled workers in two events. In 1909 the annual corporative festival called the Fête de la Bonneterie was transformed by the election of a queen by her co-workers (Figure 3.4). The festival became a popular ritual, richly symbolic in character and spectacle. Eight queens were elected over the next two decades (Figure 3.5). Then in 1930 the mill owners organized a public competition among skilled workers of certain métiers to celebrate their industry. Both of these events provided means for representing, through ritual, practice, and symbol, the social and cultural meanings of skilled work. In both celebrations we see that definitions of skilled and unskilled work were embedded as deeply in social values and gender distinctions as in the technical aptitudes of the workplace.

52. Job composition on the circular knitter was the same in the Canadian hosiery industry. See Parr's account in *Gender of Breadwinners*, pp. 72–76.
53. *Aube Ouvrière*, September 1936.

3.4. A commemorative postcard of the first Fête de la Bonneterie in 1909. This elaborate float depicts the craft tradition, with the stockinger or knitter at his frame surrounded by the women at work at their various subordinate tasks. (Archives départementales de l'Aube)

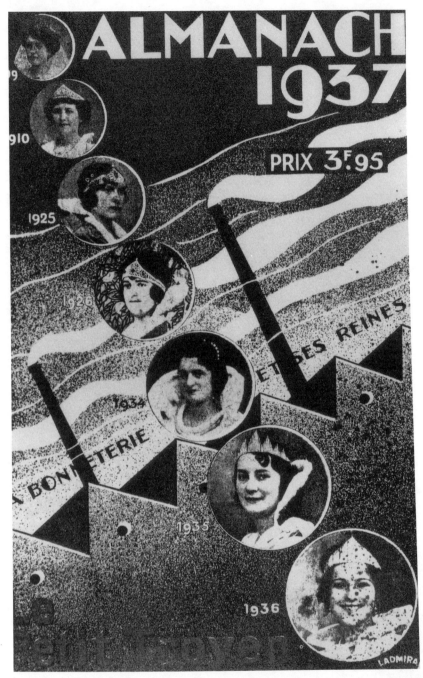

3.5. Seven queens are celebrated in *Le Petit Troyen*'s almanac for 1937. (Archives départementales de l'Aube)

The Fête de la Bonneterie was an annual tradition, held in September since the days of the guild and promoted by the decidedly male craft union, or Confrérerie des Bonnetiers. Troyes mill owners decided to mark the occasion with symbols of the industrial era. By crowning a woman worker as queen for the day to preside over this festival, they hoped to bridge class differences between employers, artisans, and workers in the aftermath of the bitter strike of 1900. The renewal of the festival tradition with the election of a new queen, each time in a different historical and political context, gave new gendered meanings to women's work. Like the strike, the traditional craft festival was a means for the working class to affirm its identity in a political context.[54] At the same time, the election provided women workers with the means to fashion a positive self-identity through the recognition of a skilled woman worker as queen.

The new version of the festival took place at a time when Troyes mill owners were attempting to consolidate their gains, mitigate social strife, and gain recognition of their town as the capital of the hosiery industry. The organizers were also eager to reconstitute the history of the Troyes industry, judging by the number of floats that evoked the origins of the trade corporation in pageantry and costume. One float featured the various métiers in a series of tableaux vivants. For the working class of Troyes the festival affirmed their identity as workers.

The first queen, chosen by ballots distributed among women workers in the factory workshops, was a skilled mender. We know from newspaper accounts that her co-workers invested a great deal of themselves in her symbolic triumph, choosing a colleague who was worthy as well as young and beautiful.[55] This form of social recognition in a small textile town stamped the young queen as representative of a skilled métier and as an independent wage earner. As the festival evolved in later decades, these symbolic meanings changed. In 1925 and 1926 the festivals were revived by the local tourist office, and commerce and consumption became their main purpose. We do not know how the new queen was selected, but in the official discourse of the festival the queen was la Reine des Travailleurs, "Queen of the Workers," symbol of an almost androgynous worker. By the 1930s the festival was once again organized by local tourism and commerce. The election of the queen took place appropriately at the Bourse du Travail, but she was chosen by an all-male jury according to obvious beauty-contest criteria. A new generation of young women had joined the workforce to fill semiskilled jobs. The

54. Didier Bigorgne, "Mouvement ouvrier et fêtes dans les Ardennes (1885–1936)," in *Fêtes et pôlitique en Champagne à travers les siècles*, ed. Sylvette Guilbert (Nancy, 1992).
55. *Le Petit Troyen* August 4 and September 13, 1909. See also "Fêtes de la bonneterie (1909)," AMT, série I, 1157–58.

queen no longer represented a skilled female métier. The social status of women on which this skill distinction was based had all but disappeared. The term bonnetière now connoted "factory girl." In the political context of the Popular Front, however, the festival queen did become an abstract symbol of the social and political order: la fille du peuple, or the body politic as legitimized by working-class unity under the Popular Front government. Politics had created a new pageant and strengthened a local symbol for reasons of legitimizing power.[56]

Thus the representations of the queen, crowned as both feminine cipher and idealized woman worker, changed over time from skilled worker to beauty queen, from class and gender symbol to consumer image. The mediated image of women and their professional skills is decidedly vulnerable in comparison with men's. Troyes women workers were celebrated as skilled when their gendered work identity was constructed as overlapping with men's within the craft tradition. In later years, as the festival became a commercial spectacle, women's skills were recast as "special natural abilities" and relegated to the symbolic.

An analysis of the skill competition of 1930 raises similar questions as to the contingency of the distinctions in women's skills. It was an exceptional event organized at the initiative of the local deputy and mill owner Léon Boisseau to reward the most skilled workers of the Troyes hosiery industry. The competition was designed to test technical, manual, and artistic skills in both male and female occupations: for men, the test combined pattern making, laymaking, and cutting garment pieces from knitted fabric; for women, mending with consummate taste specific flaws in the pattern of finely knitted silk fabric and creating an openwork design. Both tests were to be executed in the best time. An all-male jury consisted of mill owners, overseers, and workers. Newspaper accounts centered almost exclusively on the extraordinary artistry of the menders, whose openwork designs were comparable to those of the best lacemakers.[57] The organizing committee noted that some women menders in the competition had been handicapped by "timidity, fatigue, or nervousness," and urged them to demonstrate their skills by displaying their best work at a local professional exhibit (Figure 3.6). The commentary tells us more about gender distinctions than about the women who performed the work: "Our women workers are really little fairies . . . daughters of Penelope with prodigiously nimble fingers," the local

56. "Fêtes de la bonneterie (1925–1926)," AMT, série I, 1159; "Fêtes (1936)," ibid., 11511.

57. The comparison was drawn by the commentator of the *Tribune de l'Aube*, which cosponsored the competition. In fact, the mending operation is the opposite of lacemaking, for the mender must create holes to form a pattern in the existing knitted fabric. See *L'Annuaire de la Tribune de l'Aube*, 1930, p. 85.

3.6. Examples of a mender's work displayed after the 1930 competition. (Courtesy of the Musée de la bonneterie de Troyes)

newspaper boasted.[58] When the vocabulary of skill is applied to women's work, it evokes mythical images of patience, perseverance, and silent craft. Penelope becomes a timeless signifier of femininity. After mill owners lavished praise and recognition on the two prize winners, both women returned to the mill, requested promotion, and were refused.[59]

The evolution of knitting technology after 1945 was to dilute the skills required of women menders. The invention of a new tool partially mechanized their task, making it possible to speed up the work and thus to raise productivity norms. The introduction of synthetic fibers in the

58. *Tribune de l'Aube*, June 28, 1930.

59. In oral history interviews with both women I learned how difficult it was to obtain promotions in this highly skilled profession. After many years of waiting, one mender was moved in 1947 into a training position where she was to instruct apprentices in her trade. Testimony from Madame Aubron and Madame Binet; see n. 38.

production of stockings made their work less important. Nylon stockings were so cheap and resistant that they were discarded rather than mended. Skilled menders were still in demand to ensure the quality of other knitted articles, but the greater Taylorization of their training and their tasks in those postwar years represented a loss in the transmission of knitted textile culture.

THE CONTINGENCY OF SKILL DEFINITIONS

The history of the skilling process in the Troyes hosiery industry demonstrates the complex interaction between men's and women's skills, on the one hand, and variables specific to the craft culture of Troyes, to the distinctiveness of French working-class formation, and to the pattern of industrial capitalism in France on the other. To a degree it was possible for women to claim skilled status alongside men because their mastery of the new machines introduced into their métier created technical competence similar to men's. Skill was not exclusively a male property, then, since women could represent themselves as having it too. Women's skills, however, were not legitimized by formal training as men's were. Moreover, women were acknowledged as having exclusive mastery over needlework, as men could claim skilled status as operators of the Cotton Patent knitter. Occupational segregation, combined with class solidarity, reduced the possibility of gender conflict. Certainly working conditions before World War I strengthened the grounds for a shared work culture. Troyes women workers felt that their community valued their social roles, work skills, and gendered work identity together with men's.

By the 1920s, however technological changes had diluted men's and women's skills alike, while fragmentation of tasks created greater specialization and blurred skill distinctions. The number of women in the workforce employed at semiskilled tasks far outnumbered men, and this process of feminization affected the way men perceived their own skilled status. Male union leaders sought to preserve masculine skills in the first collective bargaining agreement governing the industry in 1936. The same agreement established a code of skill distinctions that segregated most of women's work in a category of unskilled tasks. It became impossible for women to claim skills that overlapped men's or to cross over into male jobs.

The engendering of skill in the Troyes knitting industry shows how problematic the meanings attached to women's work are. Gender distinctions between men's and women's skills, rooted in social and cultural values extending beyond the workplace, devalue women when conflict threatens. Men struggle to distinguish themselves from women, particularly when the feminization of their trade threatens their jobs and skilled status. Where women are concerned, skill distinctions are highly contingent on social factors related to their power and status in society. Women's skills become divorced from workplace recognition and embedded in "natural" aptitudes associated with their place in society.

The tension between the contingency of social values and gender distinctions on the one hand, and the determinism of technology coupled with deskilling on the other, need not be resolved in favor of the latter. When such problems are seen in historical perspective, it is evident that they depend on human agents of change. A nationwide nurses' strike in France in 1988 raised the question of recognition and revalorization of an ancient feminized profession. Formulating their demands outside the unions, the nurses sought to construct a new professional identity, one divorced from prescribed gender roles for women and grounded in new medical technology. They stressed the contradictions in their status and demanded retraining. In the process they appealed directly to their few male nurse colleagues for support, recognizing that the status of their profession would obtain recognition as skilled only if it were more effectively mixed.[60] The notion of separate skill tracks for men and women accounts for differences in training and technical aptitudes. But it does not deal with the contingency of social and cultural values that continues to impede real change in the engendering of skill.

60. Danièle Kergoat et al., "Les infirmières et leur coordination," research report, GEDISST-CNRS, Paris, 1990.

II

PUBLIC AND PRIVATE
IN WORKING-CLASS
HISTORY

4

Consumption, Production, and Gender: The Sewing Machine in Nineteenth-Century France

Judith G. Coffin

When Marx wrote *Capital*, the sewing machine seemed to him a "decisively revolutionary machine," destined to overthrow existing social modes of production. That it promised to transform the role of women in industry helped to rivet many nineteenth-century observers' attentions on this new technology.[1] The sewing machine, however, was not only a means of production; it was one of the first mass-produced and mass-marketed consumer durables. Inextricably linked to a revolution in clothing production, it was also bound up with a revolu-

This chapter was presented at the conference "L'Habillement, ses entreprises et ses produits: Approches locales et perspectives historiques," at Argenton-sur-Creuse, June 11–12, 1993. I thank the colleagues who organized the conference and made helpful comments, especially Michelle Perrot, Louis Bergeron, Monique Peyrière, Nicole Pellegrin, and Nancy Green. Thanks as well to Ruth Harris, Amy Dru Stanley, Sally Stein, Margaret Talbot, Bill van Benschoten, and Willy Forbath. Some material has appeared in "Credit, Consumption, and Images of Women's Desires: Selling the Sewing Machine in Nineteenth-Century France," *French Historical Studies* 18 (Spring 1994): 749–83, and in my book *The Politics of Women's Work: The Paris Clothing Trades, 1750–1915* (Princeton, 1996).

    1. Karl Marx, *Capital* (New York, 1977), 1: 603, 604, 608. For other nineteenth-century views, see Jules Simon, *L'Ouvrière* (Paris, 1861), and Paul Leroy-Beaulieu, *Le Travail des femmes au XIXe siècle* (Paris, 1873).

tion in consumption, a revolution that entailed the large-scale organization of retail, credit, and advertising, new patterns of spending, and the transformation of "the world of goods."[2] Icon of modern femininity, object of desire, and emblem of modernity, the nineteenth-century sewing machine appeared startling, almost hypnotic in its promises and appeal.[3]

Gender historians, long concerned principally with the effects of industrialization on women's work and roles, have begun to explore the ways in which new forms of consumption—changing consumer markets, new products, habits, and desires, and a new language of goods—worked as a powerful solvent on traditional structures of gender.[4] The history of the sewing machine, with its dual character as instrument of production and consumer durable, shows the importance of joining the older investigations and the new; it demonstrates the interest of widening our focus on the workplace and the forces that shaped it. Embedded in household as well as industrial labor, it obliges us to confront the distinctive character of female labor, which, as several historians have pointed out, is a hybrid of paid and unpaid work.[5] This history is of central importance, then, because the machine came to define woman's place in the nineteenth-

2. Mary Douglas and Baron Isherwood, *The World of Goods* (New York, 1979). On the revolution in consumption, its timings, and its meanings, see the different points of view in Michael Miller, *The Bon Marché: Bourgeois Culture and the Department Store* (Princeton, 1981); Rosalind Williams, *Dream Worlds: Mass Consumption in Late Nineteenth-Century France* (Berkeley, 1982); Debora Silverman, *Art Nouveau in Fin-de-Siècle France: Politics, Psychology, and Style* (Berkeley, 1989); Leora Auslander, *Taste and Power: Furnishing Modern France* (Berkeley, forthcoming); Ellen Furlough, *Consumer Cooperation in France: The Politics of Consumption, 1834–1930* (Ithaca, 1991); Whitney Walton, *France at the Crystal Palace: Bourgeois Taste and Artisan Manufacture in the Nineteenth Century* (Berkeley, 1992); Philip Nord, *Paris Shopkeepers and the Politics of Resentment* (Princeton, 1985); and the forum "Consumerism, Commercialization, and Postmodernism" with Robert Frost, Ellen Furlough, Miriam Levin, and Mark Poster in *French Historical Studies* 16 (Spring 1993).

3. Although I am concerned here with its French dimensions, this is an international history. One of the most striking descriptions of the hypnotic modernity of the sewing machine, with its nickel parts, glittering needle, and shiny varnished wood, can be found in Laura Ingalls Wilder, *Little Town on the Prairie* (New York, 1941), p. 40. The story is set in the 1880s.

4. Victoria de Grazia, *How Fascism Ruled Women* (Berkeley, 1992); "The Arts of Purchase: How American Publicity Subverted the European Poster, 1920–1940," in *Remaking History*, ed. Barbara Kruger and Phil Mariani (Seattle, 1989); and "Beyond Time and Money," *International Labor and Working-Class History* 43 (Spring 1993): 24–30.

5. E.g., Karin Hausen, "Technical Progress and Women's Labour in the Nineteenth Century: The Social History of the Sewing Machine," in *The Social History of Politics: Critical Perspectives in West German Historical Writing since 1945*, ed. George Iggers (Dover, N.H., 1985); and Jean Boydston, "To Earn Her Daily Bread: Housework and Antebellum Working-Class Subsistence," *Radical History Review* 35 (April 1986): 7–25.

century world of industry, because it distilled contemporaries' vaulting hopes and deepest fears about female wage labor, and because it compels us to explore in new ways the relationships between the history of production and that of consumption, between the history of wage work and that of domestic labor, and between the development of national industry and the changing structure of the family economy.

Nineteenth-century sewing machine manufacturers trumpeted their machines' benefits to women across the globe. The dissemination of the sewing machine, however, confronted considerable economic and cultural obstacles, particularly insofar as women were concerned. Garment workers, especially women, were poor. Women's labor (waged or unwaged, industrial or domestic) was undervalued. Women lacked systematic training and mechanical experience. The sewing machine's use in the home contravened deeply rooted ideas about machinery and craft. Its effects on the division of labor in industry, the organization of households, and women's waged and unwaged work were subjects of anxious speculation. The heady challenge of creating and tapping a female market for the machine (and one that potentially crossed class boundaries) required manufacturers to elicit, interpret, and represent "women's" needs and desires in largely unprecedented ways. This was not a simple process. The contentiousness of gender roles in the second half of the century, real uncertainties about where the markets for different sewing machines lay, and the highly experimental character of early advertising all combined to make "gendering" the sewing machine a complex enterprise. The experiments in advertising constitute a particularly interesting chapter in the history of work, femininity, and their iconography. It is a chapter with important bearing on historical interpretations of nineteenth-century conceptions of gender and their malleability.[6]

I am concerned here with the period before 1914, the early stages of consumer culture, and the way the home sewing machine was sold and used in France.[7] All of the issues broached here are broad; my purpose is simply to set out some of the key developments and to establish links between hitherto disparate subjects, suggesting how looking at these links might enrich the historiography of women's work and gender relations.

6. See Joan Scott, *Gender and the Politics of History* (New York, 1988).

7. For other approaches, see Michelle Perrot, "Machine à coudre et travail à domicile," *Mouvement Social*, no. 105 (October–December 1978); Hausen, "Technical Progress and Women's Labour"; Nicole Pellegrin, "Femmes et machine à coudre: Remarques sur un objet technique et ses usages," *Pénélope: Pour une Histoire des Femmes*, no. 9 (Autumn 1983), pp. 65–71; Monique Peyrière, "Recherches sur la machine à coudre en France, 1830–1889" (Mémoire de DEA, Histoire des Techniques, Ecole des Hautes Etudes en Sciences Sociales, Paris, October 1990).

MEN AND WOMEN IN THE NEEDLE TRADES

The sexual division of labor in the garment trades has long been uniquely fluid and contentious. Historians conceive of clothing as women's "traditional" work: women developed the skills required in the household, and prescriptive conceptions of femininity legitimated the use of those skills in the wider arena of the formal economy. Such is hardly the case. The image of sewing as an appropriately feminine activity and symbol of womanly industry (in the early modern sense of the term) seems to have appeared only in the early seventeenth century.[8] Moreover, the relation of those ideas to either the division of household tasks or economic activities for the market was tenuous at best. Throughout the early modern period, men's and women's guilds vied for the rights to make various items of clothing. No normative conception of femininity or references to a household division of labor sorted out these battles.

The abolition of the guilds in 1791 and the economic turmoil of the revolutionary decade crowded the officially "free" labor market and exacerbated antagonisms between men and women needleworkers. The early nineteenth century then brought efforts to manufacture and sell ready-made clothing (confection). To do so the manufacturer had to bypass powerful tailors, produce in the off season when underemployment drove wages down, and subcontract work to cheap labor—often but not exclusively female. These changes, coming as they did in hard times, aroused vociferous protest. The long-tumultous history of gender relations in the trades ensured that any transformation would be controversial. Experiments with sewing technology, associated from the beginning with ready-made manufacturing, thus sparked anxiety, anger, and feverish speculation. Would such developments bring more women into the trade? Or would the mechanization of sewing produce massive female unemployment? How would technological change and its attendant industrial reorganization reshape gender and craft hierarchies in the clothing industry?[9]

The first French experiments with sewing machines (enterprises that involved the French artisan Barthélemy Thimonnier, officially credited with inventing the machine) raised just such questions. In 1830, Parisian

8. Daniel Roche, La Culture des apparences: Une Histoire du vêtement (Paris, 1989), pp. 252–53; Rozsika Parker, The Subversive Stitch: Embroidery and the Making of the Feminine (New York, 1989), p. 18; Nicole Pellegrin, L'Aiguille et le sabaron: Techniques et productions du vêtement en Poitou, 1880–1950 (Poitiers, 1983).

9. On these economic developments, see Christopher Johnson, "Economic Change and Artisan's Discontent: The Tailors' History," in Revolution and Reaction, ed. Roger Price (London, 1975); Scott, Gender and the Politics of History, chap. 5.

tailors marched on Thimonnier's shop demanding work and threatening to smash what they called the *casse bras*, or "arm breakers." Over the next stormy decade, concerns shifted from male to female artisanship and unemployment. In 1845, when Thimonnier renewed his patent and began to manufacture machines in Saint-Etienne, he again courted controversy. The local *Journal de Villefranche* hailed his efforts and the machine, which was "as astonishing in its simplicity as in the grandeur of its results."[10] Yet the newspaper was soon obliged to publish a letter from an angry reader. Of all social problems, the reader wrote,

> none is greater than the inability of a single woman to support herself at work. . . . If the enormous group of women whose lives are devoted to sewing and who are incapable of doing anything else is the source of moral concern at present; if, every day, some of these poor creatures, disheartened by poverty, succumb to the deceptive promises of debauchery and seduction and debase themselves; and if those who have the courage to resist the suggestions of poverty can only earn what everyone knows is not a living wage . . . can you imagine what will happen once five in six of these women has been thrown out of work by the mechanical stitcher?[11]

If the first obstacle to sewing machines was the hostility of laboring men, a second lay in these deep concerns about the distinctive vulnerability of women workers and the fears of moral disarray that vulnerability created. Such concerns reflected the particular poverty of needleworkers, but they were magnified by nineteenth-century convictions that femininity and technology were incompatible and that women were, by their nature, poorly equipped to compete in a rapidly changing industrial world. When Thimonnier was invited to reply to the anonymous letter writer, he railed at his contemporaries' hidebound conceptions of women's roles and possibilities.

> Why should we assume that these machines are hostile to the female sex? Why not say, instead, that they have come to expand the industrial domain of women, make their forces equal to those of men, and place them at the same level of intelligence? . . . Rather than proscribe invention, let us demand reform in women's education. Let us create trade schools [*écoles d'arts et métiers*] for working women as well as working men. That way, perhaps we will abolish, or at least reduce, commensurate with their respective needs, the shocking inequalities between brother and sister and the disproportion in their wages. . . .

10. *Journal de Villefranche*, August 21, 1845.
11. Ibid., September 14, 1845.

The industrial world is changing as if by magic, and people want the
fate of the most interesting half of humanity to depend forever on the
needle.[12]

Despite this memorable exchange, Thimonnier's invention went nowhere. The most decisive obstacle was doubtless the indifference of
garment manufacturers, who were dependent on cheap labor and on
systems of putting out, which drove wages down, kept risky investments
to a minimum, and allowed them to adjust for the brutal seasonality of
the industry. Such conditions created few incentives for technological
innovation and virtually no interest in the clumsy factory device to
which Thimonnier had attached his name.[13]

In the 1850s, the Singer company fixed its eye on the French market.
The Parisian garment industry beckoned enticingly; Paris was also a
logical beachhead on the European continent. The company's initial
efforts, however, bore no fruit. In 1858, Singer's Parisian representative
took out a new patent for a small model, bringing the company's new
strategy to France. He cited the crucial need for a *machine de famille* that
could do industrial work while conforming to domestic interiors decorated with "tasteful" pieces of furniture.[14] The decision reflected several
cultural as well as economic calculations about the European market. To
concentrate on the home model was a gesture toward the organization of
the garment industry, in which outwork predominated. It was also a
decision to cut the costs of at least one model; a "family" machine meant
an inexpensive one. Finally, it marked the definition of the Singer as a
"woman's" machine and a recognition of the dual nature of women's
work—waged and unwaged. In so doing it inaugurated a rush to corner a
new female market.

From the late 1850s on, Singer and all the American manufacturers
channeled their energies into the home model sewing machine, and into
marketing rather than technological innovation. "The best foreign
houses have started to advertise in gigantic proportions," wrote one
despondent French manufacturer, "far beyond anything we are accus-

12. Ibid., September 28, 1845. Thimonnier's reply and self-defense mixed the principles
of political economy with strong doses of utopian socialism in a way characteristic of the
early nineteenth century. The exchange provides an excellent example of how technology
and political economy began to reorient the question of women's work in the nineteenth
century, machinery and mechanization raising new questions about the human body's
productivity and capacity.
13. Robert Davies, *Peacefully Working to Conquer the World: Singer Sewing Machines
in Foreign Markets, 1854–1920* (New York, 1976), pp. 24–25, and Emile Bariquand,
"Matériel et procédés de la couture," in *Exposition universelle de 1878, groupe 6, classe
58* (Paris, 1880), p. 2.
14. *Exposition Universelle de 1900. Musée Rétrospective de la classe 79: Matériaux et
procédés de la couture* (St-Cloud, 1901), pp. 18, 19.

tomed to in France. They have practically imposed certain names on the public."[15] Very gradually, Singer and other successful foreign firms were able to open up a dual market, selling not only to industry but to families. During the 1870s and 1880s, prices dropped by half. Sales rose rapidly, from 20,000 annually in 1873 to 150,000 in 1889.[16]

This history was long written as a technological success story, involving interchangeable parts, assembly-line production, and American manufacturing. Since the 1980s, however, historians of technology have thoroughly revised this account.[17] Technological advances were less decisive than new strategies regarding design, conception, and market, and these strategies were shaped—and complicated—by gender imperatives.

CLIENTS OF HUMBLE FORTUNE AND THE DEVELOPMENT OF CREDIT

Of all the obstacles facing sewing machine manufacturers, the most important was the notorious poverty of their customers. The predominance of outwork in the clothing trades created few incentives for manufacturers to invest in technological change. Virtually no working woman or man was in a position to purchase such an expensive device outright, and certainly not small, jobbing tailors and seamstresses. In the late 1870s an ordinary family model cost around 225 francs, which amounted to anywhere from one-fifth to half of a seamstress's yearly earnings.[18] The Singer company claimed to have pioneered installment payment plans

15. Bariquand, "Matériel et procédés," pp. 2–5. Bariquand singled out Singer's aggressive advertising, which by the 1870s had established the company's name abroad. Marx, too, underscored the frenetic marketing of the sewing machine and its repercussions.

16. On nationwide sales, see ibid., pp. 37–39, and Alfred Picard, *Exposition universelle de 1889 à Paris: Rapports du jury international* (Paris, 1890), 7: 113–15. Between 1860 and 1872, 54,000 sewing machines were sold in Paris: 19,020 to industrialists, 23,585 to workers, and 10,845 to "families." Another 550 machines went to convents. See *Enquête sur les conditions du travail en France pendant l'année 1872* (Paris, 1875), pp. 42–43. French sales were small in comparison with the worldwide production and sales, which quickly marched into the millions.

17. The classic technological history is David Landes, *The Unbound Prometheus* (Cambridge, 1969), pp. 307–17, persuasively criticized in David Hounshell, *From the American System to Mass Production: The Development of Manufacturing Technology in the United States* (Baltimore, 1984). See also Charles Sabel and Jonathan Zeitlin, "Historical Alternatives to Mass Production: Politics, Markets, and Technology in Nineteenth-Century Industrialization," *Past and Present* 108 (1985): 133–76; Raphael Samuel, "Workshop of the World: Hand Power and Steam Technology in Mid-Victorian Britain," *History Workshop* 11 (1977): 6–72; Dolores Greenberg, "Energy, Power, and Perceptions of Social Change in the Early Nineteenth Century," and John M. Staudenmaier, "Recent Trends in the History of Technology," both in *American Historical Review* 95 (June 1990): 693–725.

18. A small, foot-powered machine had retailed for F400 in 1867. Ten years later the price had dropped to F200, provided the customer paid cash. See Bariquand, "Matériel et

and to have done so in the name of democracy, wooing clients "of humble fortune." Every sewing machine advertisement, however, promised "easy payment," and all manufacturers were driven to dropping prices, reducing down payments, and providing credit—any effective means to keep money trickling steadily out of seamstresses', tailors', and working families' garrets and shops. The provision of credit was critical to the development of a working-class market for the machine and to technological change in the garment industry. In other words, credit provided one of the essential links between the history of production and that of consumption.

Credit was not a new practice.[19] Installment payment plans pioneered by the sewing machine industry from the 1860s on hardly entailed a new attitude toward money; it would have been a far greater novelty to persuade working people to pay for even small items with cash. Yet they formed part of a significant shift over the course of the century in the way working people borrowed and bought. Workers received their pay more frequently, reducing their need for short-term small loans, or tabs, from local merchants and café owners. At the same time, the new consumer items of the late nineteenth century, such as furniture, sewing machines, and bicycles, required much larger sums of money. Credit transactions thus became more formal.[20] Working-class needs combined with large retailers' ambitions produced a newly organized and large-scale credit industry, one that expanded beyond the boundaries and control of neighborhood grocers or wine bars.

One of the key players in the emergence of the credit industry, and a revealingly important presence in sewing machine sales, was the *grands magasins Dufayel*. By the 1880s Dufayel's was the first department store to offer all its wares on credit, and the plebeian counterpart of *grands magasins* such as the Bon Marché and the Magasins du Louvre, which

---

procédés," pp. 2–5. Prices fell another 50% in the next decade. See Grace Rogers Cooper, *The Sewing Machine: Its Invention and Development* (Washington, D.C., 1976), and Peyrière, "Recherches sur la machine à coudre."

19. See Charles Couture, *Des différentes combinaisons de vente à crédit* (Paris, 1904); Vicomte G. d'Avenel, *Le Mécanisme de la vie moderne* (Paris, 1902), 4: 364, 365, 373; Daniel Roche, *Le Peuple de Paris: Essai sur la culture populaire au XVIIIᵉ siècle* (Paris, 1981), p. 85; Michael Sonenscher, *Work and Wages: Natural Law, Politics, and the Eighteenth-Century French Trades* (Cambridge, 1989); Guy Thuillier, *Pour une histoire de la vie quotidienne au XIXᵉ siècle en Nivernais* (Paris, 1977), pp. 382, 386; Michelle Perrot, *Les Ouvriers en grève: France, 1871–1890*, 2 vols. (Paris, 1974); Eugen Weber, *Peasants into Frenchmen: The Modernization of Rural France* (Stanford, 1976), pp. 38–40; *Enquête sur les conditions du travail . . . 1872*, Questionnaire A XII, pp. 13–14; Henri Leyret, *En plein faubourg* (Paris, 1895), pp. 49–50; and Williams, *Dream Worlds*, pp. 92–94.

20. Couture, *Des différentes combinaisons*, pp. 4, 8.

accepted only cash.[21] Dufayel's domes towered over the neighborhood from the Rue de Clignancourt to the Boulevard Barbès, its credit networks extended into nearly all the popular quarters of Paris, and by 1904 the store claimed to have outlets in the principal cities of France. The system bridged old and new forms of commerce. Obviously aimed at a national market and marshaling enormous capital, Dufayel's credit network nonetheless relied on local contacts, word of mouth, and face-to-face encounters. The company sent salesmen into popular neighborhoods, inviting working families to take out "subscriptions," paying for coupons to be used at Dufayel's store with monthly payments. The company also used the information its salesmen gathered in this process to establish profiles of the working-class buying public, and to strike out in new commercial directions. Dufayel became, for example, one of the first French advertising agencies, conducting and publishing market research and compiling mailing lists.[22] The Dufayel enterprise, then, did more than simply peddle credit to the working class. It was actively involved in creating, shaping, and scrutinizing a new buying public.

The Dufayel enterprise clearly relished its revolutionary role in the ongoing transformation of consumption. The company's brochure was illustrated with an engraving of the "Galeries Principales des Caisses," or accounting department, which, the text breathlessly explained, "seems to extend as far as the eye can see. The bustle of the enormous crowd offers a glimpse of only a small part of the prodigious business of this enterprise." Tellers' booths and cash registers arrayed along perfect perspectival lines to the horizon suggested the vastness of Dufayel's operations. The entire scene, including the busy crowd and the tracklike perspective lines, evokes a railroad station—an eloquent reference to the expanded horizons, the new vistas, and the (social) mobility made possible by payment on credit.[23] The catalogue presented a wide range of available wares, from the simple to the luxurious: bicycles, pianos, watches and clocks, jewelry, and, prominently, nearly every model of sewing machine, from specialized buttonholers and pleaters to all-purpose home models. The sewing machine, indeed, helped define Dufayel's promise: credit for expensive necessities and access to a distinctively lower-middle-class and working-class "modernity."

21. See ibid., p. 79, and Dufayel brochures in the Service Recueil at the Bibliothèque Nationale.
22. By 1904 Dufayel had 3,500 regular subscribers: Couture, *Des différentes combinaisons*, p. 75. In 1893 Dufayel's trade journal, *L'Affichage Nationale*, offered, for example, lists of 600,000 Parisians classified by profession, *milieu*, or *situation*.
23. "Une Visite aux grands magasins Dufayel" (1902), Bibliothèque Nationale, collection Le Senne, 40 2117.

Dufayel sold sewing machines on credit, and he provided a model for others to follow.[24] Sewing machine manufacturers also supplied credit to their customers themselves, through more industrial networks. They reached the public directly by sending their own salesmen into the streets or the countryside. These salesmen offered potential customers a machine, a few lessons, credit, and work from one of the local clothing manufacturers. Clothing manufacturers, too, joined in helping to sell sewing machines. In areas where clothing manufacturers had large networks of handworkers, they "tried with all their power" to make women use machines and raise productivity.[25] Manufacturers discovered to their irritation, however, that doing so increased their workers' independence and bargaining power. Temporarily equipped with their own machines, seamstresses could secure work from other manufacturers who offered better or steadier pay. For the same reason, workers preferred to purchase their machines whenever possible, saying that doing so allowed them to work for whom they pleased.[26] Charitable and religious societies, persuaded that the problem with women's wages lay in the technological backwardness of the female trades, joined in the project of extending credit for sewing machines and training women to use them.[27]

Thus the dissemination of the sewing machine in France was inseparable from the expansion of *travail à domicile*, or homework, in the clothing trades in the late nineteenth century. Fueled by the search for inexpensive female labor and resistance to restrictions on female factory work, clothing manufacturing spread like wildfire into the French countryside. In the east of France, shirtmaking took root in areas that had long been centers of embroidery production; in the west, the traditional weaving region of Cholet began also to produce sewn goods for clothing manufacture; the Cher and Indre became centers of shirtmaking. The dissemination of the sewing machine helped the Walincourt region retool after the decline of other home industries. The aggressive efforts of enterprises selling sewing machines, a government study reported, had more or less furnished the local labor force with the tools of the trade

24. The advertisements in the Musée de la Publicité, Paris, document the rapid expansion of stores selling some goods on credit to working- and middle-class customers. Such cheap clothing stores as Au Classes Laborieuses, Le Bon Génie, and Les Phares de la Bastille promised "everything on credit," small down payments, and 15 to 30 months to pay.

25. Ministère du Travail et de la Prévoyance Sociale, Office du Travail, *Enquête sur le travail à domicile dans l'industrie de la lingerie* (Paris, 1911), 5: 66. On the transformation of rural outwork, see Tessie Liu's excellent *The Weaver's Knot* (Ithaca, 1994).

26. See worker monographs 44, 68, 77, and 90 in *Enquête . . . lingerie*, 5: 101.

27. *Association pour faciliter aux ouvrières l'achat d'une machine à coudre*, brochure in Bibliothèque Marguerite Durand, Paris, dossier "Machine à coudre."

and "contributed to the continuous development of the [shirtmaking] industry."[28]

The expansion of credit created countless opportunities for swindle and usury. Workers in the garment industry reckoned that sewing machines were sold at over twice their value, and surprisingly, manufacturers agreed with that estimate.[29] Wage-earning seamstresses faced a dilemma. On the one hand, not to have a sewing machine doomed one to the cheapest kind of handwork.[30] On the other hand, low wages and very high seasonal unemployment made embarking on a credit payment plan a risky venture. In some regions and trades, workers calculated that a machine simply did not justify the risk, and they refused to abandon handwork, no matter how poorly paid.[31] When workers bought machines, debt added to the burden of overwork, long days, and low wages, exacerbating the sense of *démesure* among garment trade workers. The working-class press of the late nineteenth century frequently denounced the *maisons d'abonnement*, arguing that the onus of credit perpetuated the enslavement of labor.[32]

This story underscores some of the particular characteristics of women's wage labor, its organization, and its technological advance. The cheapness of labor in the garment industry had long created powerful disincentives to mechanization, accounting for garment manufacturers' relative indifference to new sewing technologies. Women's labor in the household—sewing for the family—was similarly cheap, or undervalued. For this reason, mechanization happened only when widespread credit enabled workers, whether as wage earners or as housekeepers, to finance technological advances themselves. Consumer credit began to make it possible for them to do so in the last decades of the nineteenth century. The recruitment of women workers into industry thus was inextricable from the emergence of a working-class buying public. By the same token, particularly in France, women's wage earning was crucial to the expansion of popular consumption.

28. *Enquête... lingerie*, 5: 54, 68; 3: 421–23. See also Albert Aftalion, *Le Développement de la fabrique et le travail à domicile dans les industries de la confection* (Paris, 1906), p. 68.

29. *Enquête... lingerie*, 5: 68. Moreover, Dufayel and other retailers sold sewing machines *à tempérament*: they waived the down payment, offered free delivery, and required no payment for the first month. But this practice was considered a rental, so that customers who could not make payments lost their machines, and none of their money was reimbursed.

30. Leroy-Beaulieu, *Travail des femmes*, p. 405.

31. *Enquête... lingerie*, 5: 66–67. See also 3: 421–23.

32. Perrot, *Ouvriers en grève*, 1: 211. See also "Honteuse Exploitation," *L'Eveil Démocratique*, December 8, 1907, and Léon Bonneff and Maurice Bonneff, *La Vie tragique des travailleurs: Enquêtes sur la condition économique et morale des ouvriers et des ouvrières* (Paris, 1914), pp. 288–90.

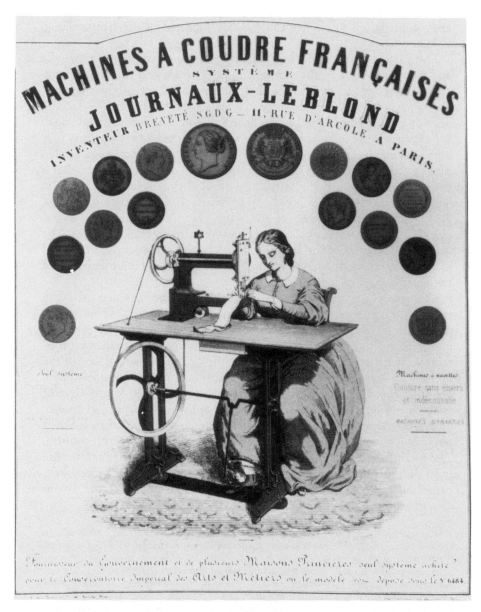

4.1. An advertisement for Journaux–Le Blond sewing machines, the "only French device accepted for the London exposition of 1862." (Cliché Bibliothèque nationale de France, Paris)

GENDERING THE SEWING MACHINE: ADVERTISING AND DESIGN

Sewing machine manufacturers were among the most aggressive advertisers of the nineteenth century (Figure 4.1). Yet how to advertise their machine, and how to represent their market, posed real dilemmas. Some of the dilemmas arose from the nexus of ideas surrounding women, technology, and the home. Medieval and early modern guild regulations had specifically banned the use of machines in the home and prohibited women from operating them. The aim of those regulations had been to combat "clandestine" (nonguild) home production and to guard trade secrets and craft hierarchies.[33] Nineteenth-century taboos were different, more concerned with preserving the tranquility of the *foyer* and with separating the home, seen as a sphere of privacy and family life, from a more intrusive industrial economy.[34] But older and newer ideas overlapped and reinforced each other. Wildly contradictory views of women's work so strongly voiced during the nineteenth century—indignation about industrial toil, for instance, and the sentimentalization of household labor—created obstacles for manufacturers and retailers to negotiate. Vague calls to "emancipate" working women all over the world were enormously popular, but actually selling female wage labor was a controversial enterprise.

Would-be sellers of a "women's" sewing machine confronted cultural as well as material obstacles. Depictions of women in the workplace, which intended to capture distinctively "female" ways of working, reveal the cultural imagery inherited by nineteenth-century advertisers. Several conventions seem to have governed those images. Engravings of women workers in the clothing trades were often a pretext for pornographic or erotic fantasies. Seamstresses' fantasies (romantic, materialistic, or both) were also favorite themes. Unlike representations of male labor, which focused on the worker and the work process, those of female labor centered instead on commerce and sales, and on women as vendors or beautiful objects. The "artistry" of working "girls" was the closest any

33. As feminist historians have pointed out, apprenticeship, technical training, and access to skilled machine work remained, in large measure, male monopolies. See, e.g., Pellegrin, "Femmes et machine à coudre"; Helen Harden Chenut, "La Formation d'une culture ouvrière féminine: Les Bonnetières troyennes, 1880–1939" (thesis, Université de Paris VII, 1988); Anne Phillips and Barbara Taylor, "Sex and Skill: Notes towards a Feminist Economics," *Feminist Review* 6 (1980); Cynthia Cockburn, *Brothers: Male Dominance and Technological Change* (London, 1983); Sonya O. Rose, *Limited Livelihoods: Gender and Class in Nineteenth-Century England* (Berkeley, 1992), pp. 24–30.

34. On nineteenth-century domestic ideology, see the important discussion in Bonnie Smith, *Ladies of the Leisure Class: The Bourgeoises of Northern France in the Nineteenth Century* (Princeton, 1981). See also Adrien Forty, *Objects of Desire* (London, 1986), chap. 5, esp. pp. 118–19.

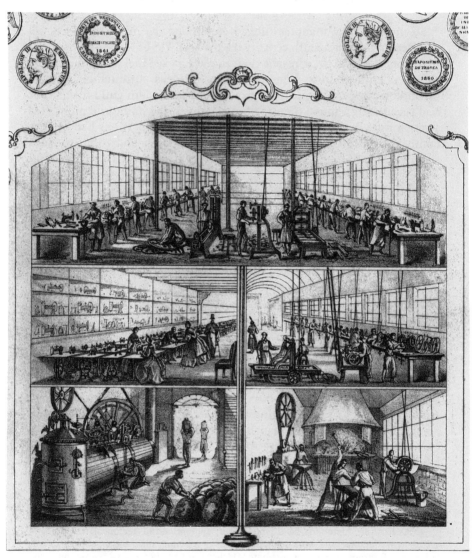

4.2. "Sewing machine factory," 1862. This engraving was the basis for advertisements published in the *Jounal des Tailleurs* and elsewhere. At the bottom we see the boiler room; the top floor houses the machine shop, where men work at lathes and drills. In the second-floor showroom women demonstrate how to use the machines. (Cliché Bibliothèque nationale de France, Paris)

came to acknowledging skill.[35] Representations of femininity endowed women with such qualities as dexterity, taste, intuition, and artistry, but sharply distinguished those attributes from craft, skills, and technological mastery, which were acquired and maintained in the masculine world of the shop. Artisan elites worked with machines, operating and repairing them; it was difficult to imagine "Jenny l'ouvrière," gazing dreamily out her garret window, doing anything of the sort. The iconographic storehouse from which advertisers and designers drew did not associate women with machinery.

In principle, the sewing machine had many possible destinations, or markets, for the garment industry had a male as well as female labor force and a mix of home and shop trades. In its infancy, the sewing machine was, to use Freud's phrase, polymorphous. In advertising, however, polymorphous tendencies were quickly repressed in favor of a more gendered identity. Sewing machine manufacturers almost immediately began to differentiate machines and markets, multiplying the number of models available, and advertising various specialized machines as male and all-purpose or "family" ones as female. These categories did not mesh with the actual division of labor in the garment trades, but they did comport with the culture's gendered notions of skill: men were trained to be specialized, they acquired expertise, and they could handle complicated technologies, while women did "all-purpose" work. An early Le Blond advertisement set this differentiation out visually: a woman sat at a family model at the center of the page, while specially adapted industrial machines circled the edge.[36] The "Singer girl," who appeared in the company's advertisements from the beginning, became the trademark of Singer's aggressive effort to associate itself with the home model and win the female market. An early advertisement for Singer's Parisian outlet also illustrates the gendering of the sewing machine (Figure 4.2). Occupying two full pages in the *Journal des Tailleurs*, it showed three floors of a Singer workshop and about thirty men at work—drilling holes, stamping out parts, molding bases, and manipulating the lathes. Amid this hum of masculine activity only a few female figures appear, in the showroom, demonstrating the use of the newly made sewing machines or considering buying one.[37] Manufacturing these machines was men's work, the advertisement insisted, but operating them was women's.

35. See the visual material on *lingères* and *couturières* in the Bibliothèque Nationale, Cabinet des Estampes, collection "Métiers" Md 43 and "Moeurs" Oa22, and at the Bibliothèque des Arts Décoratifs, collection Maciet, ser. 330, "Métiers," and 35, "Boutiques et magasins."

36. In industry women operated the specialized machines as well. In advertising, though, the woman became the mark of the home machine.

37. Tailors' journals were virtually the only ones to run advertisements in this early period; tailors and entrepreneurs were clearly expected to buy them for their wives and

The first sewing machines had been operated by soldiers. By the 1860s, though, pictorial references to men sewing were few and far between. The exceptions are interesting. A poster issued around 1900 for the Compagnie Française de la Machine à Coudre (Figure 4.3) shows a tailor sewing a Prussian flag. "Women of France, take notice!!" the caption reads. "No more foreign competition! Victory!" The "competition" was the German sewing machine industry, which by the 1890s was making serious inroads into the French market. The advertisement also tapped reservoirs of hostility to men (especially Jewish men) competing in the "women's trades," mixing anti-Semitic and nationalist commonplaces in an effort to rouse potential customers.[38] Other advertisements depicting men portrayed recognizably "picturesque" or "exotic" scenes: the "old tailors of Finistère," "Egyptians and Arabs [sic] sewing," and so on.[39]

This process of gendering also shaped industrial design, which was a crucial part of marketing. Designers graced even the tables of shop machines with curved iron legs, rounded the machine's body, polished the finish, and added artistic touches. Ornate wrought-iron stands, removable decorative "bonnets," or, for the most expensive models, rosewood or mahogany cabinets turned sewing machines into pieces of furniture. The cabinets could cost 300 to 400 francs, or double the price of the machinery, underscoring the product's value as more than simply utilitarian.[40]

The effort to create a "feminine" machine produced some revealingly strange results in the early decades. Machines appeared in Second Empire fashion plates, perched delicately on tabletops, resting under the gloved hands of elaborately dressed ladies. Advertisements combined an unusual range of products, for instance, "Dresses and scarves, perfumes, and sewing machines." The machines' femininity was exaggerated, as if they were trying on a gender for the first time.

---

women employees. Domestic magazines carried no mention of sewing machines before the mid-1860s. As design historians point out, the most crucial aspect of design is to peg the product to a specific market. See Forty, *Objects of Desire*; Penny Sharpe, *An Introduction to Design and Culture in the Twentieth Century* (New York, 1986); and Susan Strasser, *Satisfaction Guaranteed: The Making of the American Mass Market* (New York, 1989).

38. On immigrant labor in the clothing trades, see Nancy Green, *The Pletzl of Paris* (New York, 1986).

39. See the collection of postcards in the section "Couture" and Singer's advertisement "Tunis 5, Ave de France," 1892, both in Bibliothèque Forney, Paris. Advertisements continued to show soldiers wearing machine-sewn uniforms and sewing at machines.

40. Visual materials and advertising archives offer the best evidence for the evolution of design. See the Thimonnier machine in J. Meyssin, *Histoire d'une invention: La Machine à coudre* (Lyons, 1866), p. 9, and in the Musée des Arts Décoratifs, ser. 330 23, "Couturières," Musée de la Publicité, and Bibliothèque Forney.

4.3. An advertising poster for the French Sewing Machine Company, circa 1900, shows a Prussian sewing a flag, presumably to be waved in victory over the French sewing machine industry unless the French buy more French-made machines. (Collections du Musée de la chemiserie et de l'élégance masculine, Argenton-sur-Creuse, Indre, France)

Most advertisements from this early period (1850s–1870s), though, seem less contrived. To the contrary, they contributed to creating and disseminating the now familiar tropes of nineteenth-century domesticity: the contrast of public and private, industry and home, male and female. Like the Singer advertisement in the *Journal des Tailleurs*, they commonly juxtaposed descriptions or engravings of sewing machine factories, with their blast furnaces, smokestacks, and brawny men carrying rods of pig iron, with the world of women, tending their needlework and family chores in the home. They proclaimed the excitement of progress, industry, and technology, "celebrating the mass in mass production"; at the same time, they strove to wed that excitement to the reassuring imagery of separate spheres.[41] The "sewing machine girl" who regularly figured in advertisements from Singer, Le Blond, Gigaroff, and other French manufacturers was simply dressed, with a small lace collar, long dark skirt, and hair fastened neatly. She could easily have been a working woman, but not surprisingly, the advertisements cast her as a paragon of domestic industry and womanly virtue who transcended social class. The industrious portrait was especially popular in the early 1870s, when, in the aftermath of the Franco-Prussian war, French women's magazines called on their readers to work hard and eschew frivolity. Prefiguring the government of moral order, they warned that France's *redressement* (recovery) required "a stronger and less effeminate generation."[42]

The 1880s and 1890s, however, marked an important turning point in the history of advertising, bringing changes in both techniques and images.[43] Forms of advertising multiplied to include expensively produced mail-order catalogues and posters. Advertising groped its way toward a more "scientific" grounding, determined to connect advertising techniques and imagery to studies of potential consumers. New trade journals such as *La Publicité Moderne* articulated the "basic laws of advertising." These "laws" became increasingly psychological, although in the late nineteenth century few could agree on what psychology entailed. Articles discussed the importance of repetition and clarity, debated whether "harmony" or "intensity" would more effectively imprint a message, reviewed the use of symbols, and counseled advertisers

41. See, e.g., the description in John Scott, *La Génie recompensée, ou L'Histoire de la machine à coudre* (New York, 1880), or the advertisements for the Compagnie Française de la Machine à Coudre in the Centre d'Histoire des Techniques.

42. *Journal des Demoiselles*, 1872, p. 27.

43. On advertising, see Auslander, *Taste and Power*; Marjorie Anne Beale, "Advertising and the Politics of Public Persuasion in France, 1900–1939" (Ph.D. diss., University of California, Berkeley, 1991); Nord, *Paris Shopkeepers*, pp. 69, 75–78; Miller, *Bon Marché*; Williams, *Dream Worlds*; and Marc Martin, *Trois siècles de publicité en France* (Paris, 1992). See also Alain Weill, ed., *Trois siècles de l'affiche française* (Paris, 1978), Introduction.

about how to use associations and images to link their product to their target audience among a new group of consumers.[44] Articles in such journals were particularly interested in women. Women were considered particularly susceptible to suggestion. Feminine psychology seemed especially legible, providing, in Marjorie Beale's words, access to the unconscious.[45] Above all, the importance of mobilizing a female buying public seemed self-evident. Advertising journals thus directed retailers' efforts toward the home, which, many writers argued, stood at the center of female consumption. As one article in *La Publicité Moderne* put it, the "home" (they used the English word) was "the umbilical cord of our economic and social world."[46] The metaphor is revealing about gender and the economy in the era's social thought. Money spent on or channeled through the home (newly adorned as a well-appointed interior) was the emergent economy's lifeblood, and it flowed through an unmistakably gendered vessel.

Advertising in the 1890s, then, was both creating and being created by new images. Modernity, consumption, and the "new woman" who embodied them, supplied an extraordinary variety of new themes to manufacturers, industrial designers, department stores, and poster artists.[47] Even the most practical consumer good could signify something about its owner's class or status, and neither designers nor advertisers spared any effort to enhance this aspect of the machine's appeal. As late nineteenth-century brochures show, displays of sewing machines in department stores were remarkably lavish. So were the cabinets in which the machines were housed. Set in decorated wood cases, machines could metamorphose into *meubles* akin to the furniture, mirrors, and clocks that stores such as Dufayel were advertising as hallmarks of an "interior." Catalogues advertised sewing machines' "beautiful cabinetry" and their "mahogany wood." They elevated their class standing, describing them as "rich" "furnishings," "extremely elegant," that could grace "bourgeois interiors" and be suitable "in any milieu." Almost all advertisements underscored the machine's dual purpose as a *gagne pain*

44. *Publicité Moderne*, March 1908. See also "Six Principes de la psychologie," ibid., November 1907; "Les Bases scientifiques de la publicité," ibid., October–November 1908.

45. "Conquerez les femmes," *Publicité Moderne*, May 1908; "Les Femmes et l'annonce," ibid., December 1920–January 1921, pp. 301–2; Marjorie Anne Beale, "Imagining an Audience: Gender, Film, and the Physiology of Perception in France, 1900–1930," paper delivered at the meeting of the American Historical Association, San Francisco, 1994.

46. "Conquerez les femmes." From the late 1880s on, "home" became a popular term in women's magazines, a mark of fashionable English interiors and the new importance of the home in the restructuring of consumption.

47. The new woman was "modern" in being unconstrained by traditional prescriptions for domesticity and virtue; her ties to the home were those of a consumer who embellished it.

(breadwinner) and *beau décors* (handsome furnishing). One particularly emphatic line of catalogue copy read: "The sewing machine will be valued as a mode of existence [*moyen d'existence*] as well as an appliance with so many uses in the home." Thus packaged, the machine was intended to suggest, literally, a mode of existence rather than a mode of production.[48]

The catalogues were explicit about this *moyen d'existence*. Sewing machine advertisements showed cozy, well-furnished parlors in which these instruments of toil were prominently and lavishly displayed, the machines' uses purposefully blurred. By the 1890s, such advertisements beckoned to a working-class as well as a middle-class audience; they were images that represented the ways in which the working-class dwelling had become a "home." Increasingly the sewing machine was marketed as a vehicle of an emerging working-class consumerism, presented to women as a symbol of modern femininity, and framed in a picture of a new and modern working-class domesticity.

Older images of virtuous toil (such as the Singer girl of the 1860s) did not suddenly vanish from the iconographic storehouse in which commercial artists worked. Advertisements of the fin de siècle continued to use traditional imagery; they showed mothers sitting at sewing machines while their daughters gazed up admiringly, learning important skills in a familial setting.[49] By the 1890s, however, these sentimental scenes had begun to seem hackneyed, and were obliged to share the stage with more "modern" images of femininity. More and more, advertising produced new icons, such as the woman now emblematic of Belle Epoque art: "half fairy princess," a late nineteenth-century writer described her, "half *gigolette*, lips parted, eyes promising . . . enticing passers-by with sewing machines, chicory drink, petrol lamps, and sulfur waters."[50] This siren/prostitute with her drinks and soaps, bodily luxuries, material comforts, and labor-saving devices projected a euphoric vision of abundance, eroticism, and freedom that the Belle Epoque defined as "modernity."

Advertisements strove hard to summon up images of modernity, freedom, and technological advance. One Singer ad showed a winged sewing machine flying over the Eiffel Tower and a rainbow. Marianne figures (then deployed as symbols of the modernizing Third Republic) flew or danced with machines in their arms. Sewing machines were designed so

48. See the catalogues of Erda and Griga, Howe, Hurtu, Panneton Frères, A. Petit, Pfaff, Singer, Stoewer, and Wallut, all in Bibliothèque Forney.

49. See, e.g., Millet, "Les Couturières"; "La Leçon de Tricot"; H. Salmson, "Chez Grand' mère"; and many other examples in Bibliothèque des Arts Décoratifs, ser. 330.23. Such paintings and engravings sentimentalize women's roles as guardians of family traditions and familial apprenticeships.

50. Avenel, *Mécanisme de la vie moderne*, 4: 176.

4.4. "Neva: The best for families and workshops." The sewing machine offers to replace the distaff and spinning wheel. Advertising poster by Tamagno, 1880s. (Courtesy of Bibliothèque Forney, Paris)

that the treadle at the side suggested the wheel of a bicycle or car.[51] Drawings placed women at whirring sewing machines as if they were driving a locomotive or riding a bicycle; sometimes their children were shown helping to pull the fabric through. New Home's boast that its machine was *légère et rapide* had a similar purpose: by the century's end the exhilaration of speed and freedom from industrial or domestic drudgery had become more compelling sales pitches than the virtues of needlework and the duties of domesticity.

The exhilaration of speed and the image of the "new woman" that accompanied it also produced currents of anxiety, which run through many of these images. Magician figures promised to conjure away domestic chores, but they could also summon up stories of the sorcerer's apprentice and of magic and machinery out of control (Figure 4.4). The image of diabolical technology comes through in a widely reproduced New Home advertisement (Figure 4.5) playing on *Le Bon Petit Diable* by the Comtesse de Ségur. The wicked Madame MacMiche sews up the pants of her devilish orphan nephew Charles with him in them, dangling head first off the table, and mischievously pumping the machine's pedal with his arms.[52] Popular fiction hurtles into the modern world, but the image thus created seems unintentionally menacing as well as humorous.

Other advertisements used caricature, which likewise turned on elements of the grotesque. The machinery was so simple, advertisements proclaimed, that a monkey or an elephant could use it (Figure 4.6). Advertisements showed elephants clambering onto sewing machine chairs as they would onto circus pedestals, operating the sewing machines with their trunks; or monkeys, balanced atop the machines, hurtling down "loop de loops," or roller-coasters. Again, machine labor became a spectacle of dexterity, something akin to a circus performance. Yet just as the circus featured performances that were at once marvelous and freakish, so these advertisements could quickly become hostile, belittling women's skills and domestic routines. This possibility did not escape notice at the time. In 1903 *La Publicité Moderne* chided commercial artists for their tendency to ridicule their subjects, and for what the journal perceived as a rash of "bad" mothers and ugly, frightening, or "devouring" women in advertisements. The New Home sewing machine ad was singled out for criticism, and so were the circus images.[53]

51. Vigneron advertisements, Bibliothèque Forney.

52. Musée de la Publicité, no. 16269, New Home, with *medaille d'or*, 1889. This image was used in New Home advertisements in fashion and home magazines through the 1880s and 1890s.

53. *Publicité Moderne*, September 15, 1903. See Anne Martin-Fugier's interesting discussion of *les arts de la femme* and the simultaneous glorification of and disdain for women's handicrafts in *La Bourgeoise: Femmes au temps de Paul Bourget* (Paris, 1983), pp. 162–68.

4.5. The most widely used advertising poster for New Home, 1889. (Collections du Musée de la chemiserie et de l'élégance masculine, Argenton-sur-Creuse, Indre, France)

Gendering the sewing machine, then, could not be a simple process. Few could agree on the character of femininity, and perceptions of women's roles and needs were changing too rapidly. The commercial art of the fin de siècle registered a sharp rebellion against older models of domestic virtue and against older certainties about what constituted "the

4.6. Advertising poster for Elias Howe sewing machines, 1906. The monkeys in the background, representing mischief and mimicry, figured in advertising for sewing machines and representations of machinery in general. (Courtesy of Bibliothèque Forney, Paris)

feminíne." This rebellion arose from intersecting social and cultural forces. By the end of the century, a broad coalition of social reformers and public health officials were denouncing deteriorating conditions and "sweating" in the needle trades. In 1901 a surprisingly large number of Parisian seamstresses and tailors shut down shops in the fashionable women's clothing district near ·he Opéra in a strike that newspapers hailed as an "awakening" of working womanhood and a sign that women were joining the "forward movement of history."[54] Deteriorating conditions in industry, or the rising publicity given those conditions, also made it harder to sentimentalize sewing in the domestic realm. A growing number of feminists were vocally impatient with rhapsodic tributes to the glories of the needle, and they deplored teaching little girls skills that headed them toward an overstocked and poorly paid trade.[55] All of these developments sent manufacturers, designers, and advertisers scrambling to articulate and respond to "women's" new needs and discontents. Sewing machine manufacturers cast the machine as the great emancipator or the bearer of women's fantasies. Commercial graphic artists tried to visualize and package those fantasies. If some of their images were whimsical and exhilarating, others could seem frightening or ugly—a reflection of the real gender antagonisms of the period. If the new woman of the fin de siècle was feared as a sign of gender disorder, she was also hailed as a symbol of modernity and cultivated as a consumer. Finally, despite the rising controversy about sweating, advertising aimed at a working-class public could hardly ignore the centrality of female wage labor in working-class life.

CONSUMPTION, CLOTHING, AND THE FAMILY ECONOMY

By the late nineteenth century, reformers were writing from a variety of political perspectives that the sewing machine might revive a self-

54. *La Fronde*, February 18, 1901; *Le Petit Sou*, February 18, 1901; *L'Intransigeant*, February 19, 1901. The strike is well covered in the archives of the Prefecture of Police, Paris, BA 1394. Important strikes followed in 1910, 1911, and 1917. Archives Nationales, F7, 13881.

55. E.g., Madeleine Pelletier: "We should be careful not to teach knitting, crochet, lacemaking, and embroidery. Over the course of their lives, women spend thousands of hours dulling their minds on these activities. If people have money, they can easily buy these products ready-made. If they cannot buy them, they can perfectly well do without": *L'Education féministe des filles* (1914), quoted in Martin-Fugier, *La Bourgeoise*, p. 171. Or Marie Guillot: Needlework is "a useless, exhausting, and dull chore": *L'Ecole Emancipée*, May 24, 1915; and Guillot again: "Education should simplify rather than romanticizing housework": *Tribune Féministe*, June 7, 1913, p. 444. See the similarly unsentimental portrait in Jeanne Bouvier, *Mes Mémoires: Une Syndicaliste féministe, 1876–1935* (1936) (Paris, 1983).

sufficient household economy, shielding the family from the perils of modernity and the cash nexus. In 1888 the immensely popular and unusually practical household manual *Maison rustique des dames* recommended a sewing machine to any woman with a family, to be used in sewing household linens, including grain sacks for the farm, and mending clothes. The author acknowledged, however, that the expense might be prohibitive.[56] The deeply ideological *Journal des Demoiselles* also recommended general-purpose sewing machines to all its readers. The *Journal*'s editors expected that these machines would be used in "womanly arts," or unwaged domestic work. Even if ready-made clothes could be purchased, women's magazines tirelessly reiterated, many sewing tasks remained: trousseaux made at home could save a family considerable expense; little girls could embroider household linens, smocks, and blouses; socks and shirts needed to be repaired, seams restitched, holes darned, and buttons replaced.[57] They clearly hoped that sewing machines would help extract women and the home from the cash nexus: sewing for the family would encourage self-sufficiency and domestic industriousness, and brace women against the seductive power of cheap fashions and buying on credit. Similar hopes echoed through writings by social Catholic reformers, one of whom cheerfully hailed the advent of a "machine to stitch the family together."[58]

Any number of sources, however, suggest that most women who sewed did so for wages and that "womanly arts" never fortified the household against what contemporaries considered the twin perils of mass consumption and wage earning. Most of the women who wrote to the *Journal des Demoiselles* about their sewing machines were seamstresses who worked for wages or for private clients. This is not surprising. The clothing of families in France had long been inextricable from the cash nexus.[59] Middle-class women paid seamstresses to make their clothes if they could afford to do so, or hired a day worker *(femme de chambre)* to copy a seamstress's designs. In the late nineteenth century they supplemented custom-made clothing with items purchased from

56. The author's recommendation, "a sewing machine easily replaces the labor of four persons," inadvertently highlights the problem: such a replacement might make sense to a labor contractor but not to an ordinary *mère de famille*. See Cora Millet-Robinet, *Maison rustique des dames*, 13th ed. (Paris, 1888), p. 37.

57. See, e.g., *Journal des Demoiselles*, 1870, p. 222; 1872, p. 27; 1873, p. 296; 1879, p. 20; Millet-Robin, *Maison rustique des dames*, and Mme Aline Valette, "Travaux manuels pour les filles (programme du 27 juillet 1882)," in *La Journée de la petite ménagère* (Paris, 1884).

58. *Journal des Demoiselles*, 1870, p. 222; 1873, p. 296; 1879, p. 20. On social Catholics, see my "Social Science Meets Sweated Labor," *Journal of Modern History*, June 1991.

59. See references in n. 8. Sewing hardly figures in the series of engravings of *travaux ménagers* at the Bibliothèque Nationale.

mail-order catalogues. It would be a mistake to read patterns published in the fashion magazines of the Third Republic—*La Mode Illustrée, La Mode Pratique, Le Journal des Demoiselles*—as testimony to subscribers' domestic zeal or sewing skills; these patterns were usually taken to seamstresses. Women of the laboring classes had neither the time nor the skills for "womanly arts." Working-class families clothed themselves via the thriving trade in used clothes or, by the late nineteenth century, at inexpensive clothing stores such as La Belle Jardinière. Apart from seamstresses, women who worked for wages rarely did more than mend their families' clothes or sew extremely simple dresses for themselves.[60] On the eve of World War I, a working-class newspaper asked Marie Guillot (a feminist and union activist who frequently wrote on women's issues) to comment on recent changes in working women's domestic routines. Guillot wrote that the sewing machine had been a great boon, for it had reduced the purchase price of ready-made clothes. She made it clear that unless a woman were a seamstress, she was unlikely to sew clothing for her family.[61] The family economy's embeddedness in consumer markets encouraged wage work more than home sewing. So did the way families valued female labor. Wage earning weighed more heavily than labor saving in working-class family investments in expensive household devices.[62] When working-class families purchased sewing machines, they did so with an eye to bringing in wages, through piecework.

It remains impossible, however, neatly to separate women's waged and unwaged work. This difficulty is conceptual as well as empirical, and confronts all historians of female labor.[63] Third Republic debates about teaching sewing in the schools illustrate the problem. Under Jules Ferry, the Third Republic took up a characteristically modernizing project of teaching girls important domestic skills, chief among them sewing. The project proved quite controversial, for its critics claimed that these skills

---

60. On clothing practices and budgets, the best discussion is Pellegrin, *L'Aiguille et le sabaron*, p. 151. See also Martin-Fugier, *La Bourgeoise* pp. 175–77; Pierre Pierrard, *La Vie ouvrière à Lille* (Paris, 1965), pp. 169, 213; and Millet-Robinet, *Maison rustique des dames*. Similar testimony for England is found in Standish Meacham, *A Life Apart* (Cambridge, Mass., 1977), and Richard Hoggart, *The Uses of Literacy* (London, 1957). For Germany, see Robyn Dasey, "Women's Work and the Family," in *The German Family: Essays on the Social History of the Family in Nineteenth and Twentieth Century Germany*, ed. Richard J. Evans and W. R. Lee (London, 1981).

61. Marie Guillot, column in *La Vie Ouvrière*, July 5, 1913, p. 4.

62. At the same time, the economic value of housework and child care made outwork, at what all agreed were egregiously low wages, a seemingly rational way for families to use female labor.

63. See Hausen, "Technical Progress," p. 260; Boydston, "To Earn Her Daily Bread"; and Jean Quataert, "The Shaping of Women's Work in Manufacturing: Guilds, Households, and the State in Central Europe, 1648–1870," *American Historical Review* 90 (December 1985): 1122–48.

would inevitably be turned to wage earning.[64] In response, the project's defenders tried to distinguish teaching a métier, which they conceded would be indeed inappropriate for girls, from imparting "useful general knowledge," which they contended would serve in their domestic life and was rightly part of republican womanhood. School programs were not providing vocational training, they argued, only teaching modern domesticity.[65] Reformers' efforts to distinguish the acceptable from the opprobrious, however, were futile. Women's work in the family economy ran on a continuum from paid to unpaid labor. "Industrial" and "domestic" did not stand at opposite ends of a spectrum. Skills acquired in the schools would be turned to industrial use and then brought back to the home, where seamstresses could make for themselves or their daughters the dresses temptingly illustrated in ready-made catalogues and fashion magazines.

There is an important historiographical issue here. Historians, like nineteenth-century social observers, commonly describe sewing as a skill women routinely learned in the family and turned to industry in the nineteenth century. That view forms part of a larger historical picture in which the origins of the gender division of labor in industry lie in the household. The picture is distorted in important respects. As the late nineteenth-century shirtmaker and union leader Jeanne Bouvier observed in her unsentimental autobiography, sewing entailed skills that were not routinely acquired in homes.[66] More often than not, sewing skills were acquired and honed in industry, and only then brought to the home. Nineteenth-century depictions of daughterly apprenticeships, sentimentalizing a self-enclosed family unit, obscure the extent to which wage work developed women's skills—although, as in the family, within strict parameters. If women were able to fashion clothing for their families, that was usually because they had trained and worked as seamstresses.

Sewing machines, then, did not mechanize or simplify preexisting unwaged labor. Nor did they revive a family economy based on subsis-

64. Mme P. W. Cocheris, *Pédagogie des travaux à l'aiguille à l'usage des écoles de filles* (Paris, 1882); Marie Koenig, *La Couture en classe* (Paris, 1901); Bibliothéque de la tante Marguerite, *La Coupe et la couture à la maison et à l'école* (Paris, 1900); Augusta Moll-Weiss, *Le Foyer domestique* (Paris, 1902); *Le Manuel du foyer domestique* (Paris, 1923). As Moll-Weiss noted, one of the issues at stake here was whether girls should be educated by their families or by the state. Critics included Charles Drouard (inspector of primary education), *Les Ecoles de filles* (Paris, 1904). Though it was important to keep women from being idle, he said, they should not engage in wage work.

65. A. Piffault, *La Femme au foyer: Education ménagère des jeunes filles* (Paris, 1908). On similar debates in Germany see Quataert, "Shaping of Women's Work," pp. 1136–38.

66. Bouvier, *Mes Mémoires*. A reading of one of the household manuals—Valette, *Journée de la petite ménagère*, or Millet-Robin, *Maison rustique des dames*—is a healthy reminder of the skills involved in even the most basic sewing. Women were more likely to learn embroidery or knitting.

tence. Through the late nineteenth and early twentieth centuries, they seem principally to have created new possibilities for female wage work through the expansion of outwork in various branches of the garment industry.[67]

After World War I, these patterns shifted. The daily work routines of the household began to be mechanized. Salons showed new products, more companies offered new lines of credit for *electro-ménager* equipment, magazines encouraged women to think of housework as a profession, and finally, electricity made updating the household feasible, though still expensive.[68] The contraction of employment in the garment industry after the war, in combination with the acute hardships of the period, shifted the balance of waged and unwaged labor, increasing the importance of sewing for familial consumption. In the interwar context of professionalized domesticity, a more technological household, and a world where women's industrial labor (particularly in the garment trades) was contracting, *l'ami Singer* could rework its image, presenting itself as the "guardian of domestic skills" and promising to *preserve* skills and traditions and defend women's domesticity against the "reign of ready-made." It became a symbol of female traditionalism and nostalgia rather than modernity.[69]

Sales of home sewing machines seem to have peaked in the 1950s and then fallen off sharply in the 1960s. The Singer company attributed its

67. Yvonne Verdier found a direct link between the availability of sewing machines and the rising numbers of seamstresses in Minot. See her *Façons de dire, façons de faire: La Laveuse, la couturière, la cuisinière* (Paris, 1979), p. 220. In cities, where male tailoring traditions were more deeply rooted and women's work patterns different, tailors survived longer.

There are important differences between the American and French markets for sewing machines and patterns of women's work. In the United States, the standard of living was higher, credit was easier to come by, machines were less expensive, and the rates of female participation in the labor force were lower. In France, not only were sewing machines more difficult to finance, but more married women worked for wages. The number of small seamstresses and tailors was also considerably higher in France. In that situation, opportunities for wage work were greater and it was easier for families to buy relatively inexpensive clothes than to make them. In short, *la femme au foyer* was more common in the United States than in France. The character of national consumer markets and their relation to women's wage-earning and gender roles is a subject that needs more investigation. Victoria de Grazia has posed some of the crucial questions. See n. 4 above.

68. Robert L. Frost, "Machine Liberation: Inventing Housewives and Home Appliances in Interwar France," *French Historical Studies* 18 (Spring 1993): 109–30; Martine Martin, "Ménagère: Une Profession? Les Dilemmes de l'entre-deux-guerres," *Mouvement Social*, no. 140 (July–September 1987); Monique Peyrière, "Un Moteur électrique pour la machine à coudre: Une Innovation dans l'impasse," *Bulletin d'Histoire de l'Electricité*, June–December 1992; and Françoise Werner, "Du ménage à l'art ménager: L'Evolution du travail ménager et son écho dans la presse feminine française de 1919 à 1939," *Mouvement Social*, no. 129 (October–December 1984).

69. Singer brochure, 1927, in Service Receuil, Bibliothèque Nationale; Martin, "Ménagère: Une Profession?" p. 94.

plummeting fortunes in those times to the fact that women no longer had the skills required to use the machines.[70] Singer was too wedded to domestic ideology and to the image of its machine as *l'ami de la ménagère* to acknowledge the importance of women in industry. Yet it is clear that as fewer women did industrial garment work, fewer carried those skills home and transmitted them to their daughters. By the 1960s, the culture of sewing skill and technical know-how that the machine had represented atrophied.

In sewing work, the distinctively hybrid character of women's work is particularly obvious. Women's unpaid household labor cannot be understood without reference to their industrial involvement. Skills were not cultivated in a hermetically sealed household or separate women's sphere, and women could rarely afford to acquire skills solely for domestic purposes. For that reason, the sewing machine remained a "mule," its domestic and industrial purposes and markets inescapably intertwined.

CONCLUSION

The mass production of consumer goods did not begin as easily as is often argued. Nor was marketing a simple process. Advertising campaigns contributed to the gendering of sewing machines, marking at least some of them as "female" and setting off a scramble for a new women's market. Gendering, however, created as many problems as it resolved, for the ongoing problems of reaching a working-class market were considerable.[71] Such problems gave rise to new practices, chief among them credit payment, that would restructure the market for consumer goods and help create a female buying public.

Manufacturers and advertisers appealed to this new market in ways that also underscore the experimental character of this early advertising and the contentiousness of gender roles at the time. The late nineteenth century witnessed a rebellion against traditional domesticity and prescriptions about household duties and virtuous labor; and rapidly shifting conceptions of masculine and feminine complicated the process of gendering the machine. So did the emergence of modernist aesthetics, the search for a science of advertising, and the new attention given the

---

70. "Behind the Snafu at Singer," *Fortune*, November 5, 1979. By Singer's estimates, 79% of American women between 24 and 29 owned sewing machines in 1970. By 1985, Singer calculated, that figure would drop to 31%. "The high skill level required" was the principal problem. I have been unable to find comparable figures from France.

71. Early twentieth-century brochures describing interchangeable parts instructed customers to order by the part's number and *not* to write "like last time." See brochure for the Excelsior model from A. Petit, 1902, in catalogue collection, Bibliothèque Forney.

unconscious. In this unsettling cultural and social context, selling the sewing machine became an intriguingly unpredictable process. Advertisements veered from sentiment to caricature, from promises to emancipate women from domestic and industrial drudgery to reminders of the hard-nosed calculations that working families had to make, and from an individualism that celebrated the possibilities of the "modern" woman to an essentialism in which machines and femininity were radically incommensurate.[72] As Susan Strasser has shown in the American context, new products came packaged with new needs and habits.[73] Selling the sewing machine thus came perilously close to marketing women's industrial work, a controversial venture even in France, where women's work—at least in the family economy—was frankly acknowledged. Advertisers negotiated these shoals by emphasizing the machine as an emblem of consumption and modern femininity, or by playfully replacing images of labor with spectacles of performance. The turmoil these strategies involved comes through in the refreshing unfamiliarity of many late nineteenth-century advertisements. These were not simply scenes of sentimentalized domesticity or *la femme au foyer*.

Many of these advertisements appealed to a distinctively working-class vision of domesticity, offering a combination of "modern" womanhood and access to what many working-class women hoped would be better wage work. The two appeals were inseparable, for despite union men's and social reformers' increasingly adamant calls for a "family wage," women's wage earning was crucial to the family economy. Without women's work, then, the doors to the new world of goods remained firmly closed. That sewing machines both represented the new world and helped open those doors reminds us how tightly production and consumption were enmeshed.

72. From the 1870s to the 1890s, medical journals discussed at length the sexual dangers of the sewing machine. See my "Credit, Consumption, and Images of Women's Desires: Selling the Sewing Machine in Nineteenth-Century France," *French Historical Studies* 18 (Spring 1994): 749–83.

73. Strasser, *Satisfaction Guaranteed*, p. 95.

5

Engendering Work and Wages: The French Labor Movement and the Family Wage

Laura L. Frader

Labor historians have begun to document the influence exerted by notions of sexual difference on foundational concepts such as work and skill, central to the lives and work of working men and women in the nineteenth and twentieth centuries, and to uncover the ways in which sexual difference has influenced patterns of inclusion or exclusion in the workplace and in unions.[1] Fundamental to the presumptions about women's and men's capacities for work and the worth of the labor they performed were notions about women's "natural" attachment to the

I thank Helen Chenut, Nancy Green, and Michelle Perrot for critical comments on earlier drafts of this chapter.

1. For examples, see Joan Scott, "Gender: A Useful Category of Historical Analysis" and "Work Identities for Men and Women: The Politics of Work and Family in the Parisian Garment Trades in 1848," both in her *Gender and the Politics of History* (New York, 1988), pp. 28–50, 93–112; Ava Baron, "Gender and Labor History: Learning from the Past, Looking to the Future," and "An 'Other' Side of Gender Antagonism at Work: Men, Boys, and the Remasculinization of Printers' Work, 1830–1920," both in *Work Engendered: Toward a New History of American Labor* (Ithaca, 1991), ed. Baron, pp. 1–69; Sonya O. Rose, *Limited Livelihoods: Gender and Class in Nineteenth-Century England* (Berkeley, 1992); Cynthia Cockburn, *Brothers: Male Dominance and Technological Change* (London, 1983); Laura Lee Downs, *Manufacturing Inequality: Gender Division in the French and British Metalworking Industries* (Ithaca, 1995); Kathleen Canning, "Gender and the Politics of Class Formation: Rethinking German Labor History," *American Historical Review* 97 (June 1992): 736–68.

private world of reproduction and the home and men's "natural" ties to the public domain of wage work and politics.[2] However inaccurately the dichotomy described the real lives of working people, it nonetheless guided the thinking of social reformers, politicians, and, indeed, much of the European labor movement about men's and women's respective places in the world of work and the home.[3] Debates over the family wage demonstrate how those mappings of sexual difference led to the conceptualization of different rights, structured gender inequalities, and shaped male workers' claims and labor movement strategies in nineteenth- and twentieth-century France before World War II.[4]

In many European countries, as well as in North America, skilled male workers freqently raised the demand for a "family wage," the demand that male workers be paid a wage sufficient to support their unwaged wives and children. Proponents of the family wage ideal removed the wage from the domain of the individual and tied it to the interests of the collectivity, the family. They assumed that the right to provide subsistence to a family was a male right, hence workingmen should be paid wages not only on the basis of their labor, as individual workers, but also on the basis of their status as fathers and family providers. The family wage also included a strategic imperative: to ensure high wages for skilled workers and ultimately to exclude women from the public world of wage labor. Women, whose presence in the labor force many people viewed as an aberration, could then devote themselves entirely to the private work of reproduction and domestic activity. Behind the notion of the family wage was not merely opposition to women's work, although that was an important component of the family wage demand. Embedded in the concept was also an idealized notion of the family, sustained by women's private, unwaged labor in the home and by men's breadwinning in the public world of work. Indeed, this is the historical significance of

2. For nineteenth-century expressions of these assumptions, see Bonnie Smith, *Ladies of the Leisure Class* (Princeton, 1981); Michelle Perrot and Georges Ribeill, eds., *Le Journal intime de Caroline B.* (Paris, 1985); Erna Olafson Hellerstein, Leslie Parker Hume, and Karen M. Offen, eds., *Victorian Women* (Stanford, 1981); Mrs. Sarah Stinkney Ellis, *The Women of England, Their Social Duties and Domestic Habits* (London, 1835); John Ruskin, "Of Queen's Gardens," in his *Sesame and Lilies* (New York, 1875).

3. Critiques of the usefulness of the public/private dichotomy as an analytical concept include, e.g., Chapter 1 of this volume; Sonya O. Rose, "Gender and Labor History: The Nineteenth-Century Legacy," *International Review of Social History* 38, suppl. (1993): 145–62; Dorothy O. Helly and Susan M. Reverby, Introduction to *Gendered Domains: Rethinking Public and Private in Women's History*, ed. Helly and Reverby (Ithaca, 1992), pp. 1–24; Carole Pateman, "Feminist Critiques of the Public/Private Dichotomy," in *Feminism and Equality*, ed. Ann Phillips (New York, 1987), pp. 103–26.

4. See also Alice Kessler-Harris, "A New Agenda for American Labor History: A Gendered Analysis and the Question of Class," in *Perspectives on American Labor History: The Problem of Synthesis*, ed. J. Carroll Moody and Alice Kessler-Harris (De Kalb, Ill., 1989), for a slightly different formulation of this issue.

the family wage: it points to yet another way in which sexual difference leads to differential concepts of rights and structures gender inequalities in the workplace and in the family.

Historians of the British working class have noted for some time the significance of family wage demands across diverse sectors of the working class, beginning in the 1830s. With considerable regularity skilled British workers self-consciously linked their status as respectable workingmen to their ability to provide for their families.[5] This ideal received strong support among men in many sectors of the British labor movement.

British and American historians have also intensely debated the broader significance of the family wage for working-class history. Jane Humphries has argued that support for the family wage was an effort to protect the working-class family from the incursions of capitalism, and that the ideal of the family wage was based on class solidarity, not on individual workers' interest in higher wages.[6] Heidi Hartmann, in contrast, has emphasized the importance of gender to family wage demands: the family wage was a means to reinforce both male workers' privileged position in the labor market and their dominance of women.[7] Martha May has argued that both American men and women workers jointly pursued the family wage in the nineteenth century on the basis of class solidarity; not until the early twentieth century did strategic concerns lead workingmen to base their claims on gender and especially on the exclusion of women from the labor force.[8] The issue of the family wage in France, however, has been virtually ignored by historians of the French

---

5. For examples of nineteenth- and twentieth-century demands for the family wage among English workers, see Barbara Taylor, *Eve and the New Jerusalem* (London, 1983); Rose, *Limited Livelihoods*, pp. 130–32; Hal Benenson, "The Family Wage and British Working Women's Consciousness in Britain, 1880–1914," *Politics and Society* 19 (March 1991): 71–108; Jane Lewis, *Women of England, 1870–1950: Sexual Divisions and Social Change* (Bloomington, 1984), pp. 45–74; Jane Humphries, "Class Struggle and the Persistence of the Working-Class Family," *Cambridge Journal of Economics* 1 (1977): 241–58; Humphries, "The Working-Class Family, Women's Liberation and Class Struggle: The Case of Nineteenth-Century British History," *Review of Radical Political Economics* 9 (Fall 1977): 25–41; Angela John, Introduction to *Unequal Opportunities*, ed. John (Oxford, 1986), pp. 24–25. For American workers' demands for a family wage, see Martha May, "Bread before Roses: American Workingmen, Labor Unions, and the Family Wage," in *Women, Work, and Protest: A Century of U.S. Women's Labor History*, ed. Ruth Milkman (London, 1985), pp. 1–21; Ron Rothbart, "Homes Are What Any Strike Is About: Immigrant Labor and the Family Wage," *Journal of Social History* (1991): 267–84.

6. Humphries, "Class Struggle." Humphries's argument is strongly criticized by Benenson, "Family Wage."

7. Heidi Hartmann, "Capitalism, Patriarchy, and Job Segregation by Sex," *Signs* 1 (1976): 137–69; Hartmann, "The Unhappy Marriage of Marxism and Feminism: Towards a More Progressive Union," *Capital and Class* 8 (Summer 1979): 1–32.

8. May, "Bread before Roses."

working class; simultaneously, historians have left unexamined the ways notions of the idealized household, embedded in family wage discourse, helped to shape male as well as female class identities in France in the nineteenth and twentieth centuries.[9]

Demands for the family wage appeared less consistently in nineteenth- and early twentieth-century France than they did in England, and varied considerably among trades; there was no broad consensus on the issue. World War I, however, raised new concerns about the gender division of labor and the wage for French workers, concerns that surfaced in debates about the relationship of gender, family, work, and the wage in the 1920s and 1930s. Debates over the family wage in France show that work- ingmen's interests and work identities were as much informed by con- cerns of family and social reproduction as women's, despite the gendered dichotomization of public and private so heavily promoted by middle- class reformers and political economists and idealized by workers them- selves. The family played an important role in the mobilization of working-class men's labor demands.[10] In France, both class and gender interests informed male workers' discussion of the family wage and women's work; gender was a fundamental component of the articulation of class interests and class identities. Yet the family wage virtually disappeared as a demand of French male workers between the World Wars.

THE FAMILY WAGE BEFORE WORLD WAR I: A CHORUS OF DIFFERENT VOICES

The discourse of the family wage in France before World War I was not one discourse but many. Workers spoke with diverse voices on the subject and debated what was arguably a hotly contested issue. It would be impossible to say, as some investigations have said for the same period

9. One exception is Michelle Perrot, "L'Eloge de la ménagère dans le discours ouvrier au XIXᵉ siècle," in *Mythes et représentations de la femme* (special issue), *Romantisme* 13–14 (1976): 105–21. The ideal is mentioned briefly in Louise A. Tilly and Joan Scott, *Women, Work, and Family* (New York, 1987), p. 132, and in Scott, "'L'Ouvrière! Mot Impie, Sordide . . .': Women Workers in the Discourse of French Political Economy, 1840–1860," in Scott, *Gender and the Politics of History*, pp. 143–44. Somewhat more attention has been given to the British case. See Geoff Eley, "Nations, Publics, and Political Cultures: Placing Habermas in the Nineteenth Century," in *Habermas and the Public Sphere*, ed. Craig Calhoun (Cambridge, Mass., 1992), pp. 314–15, on the place of the household in the constitution of masculine privilege in politics and the workplace. As Eley points out, the family wage demand was a means by which skilled male workers not only aimed to preserve their status within the family but also asserted their difference from unskilled, unorganized workers (p. 316).

10. See Perrot, "L'Eloge de la ménagère," p. 110.

in Britain, that the family wage doctrine "underpinned . . . male trade unionists' political initiatives."[11] Demands for the family wage were specific to workers in trades that were especially threatened by women's competition or were undergoing technological change. French workers did not uniformly use the rhetoric of manhood and manliness or the respectability of the male breadwinner, as British workers did. Like British workers, however, French workers appealed to idealized notions of the family and maternity to argue for the withdrawal of women from paid work. They invoked the duty of "honest workingmen" to support their families.[12] French workers were also influenced by the widespread concern about population decline, which grew into a national debate after France's defeat in the Franco-Prussian War of 1870–71 and resurfaced with a fury after World War I. At the same time, for French workers, as for their British counterparts, the family wage and the question of women's competition contained a critical subtext: a debate over who had the right to be named as a family provider and who had a right to work. Male workers' appeals for the family wage and arguments against the employment of women demonstrated powerfully how "private" concerns about reproduction—about family and *foyer*—as well as production influenced men's work identities. Finally, in France before World War I the family wage was a male demand; it was very rarely supported by working-class women either within the labor movement or outside of it.

In the politically tense environment of the waning July Monarchy, in the 1840s, when skilled workingmen were fighting to preserve their status in trades undergoing reorganization, male workers did not universally invoke the ideal of the unwaged housewife to valorize their position as wage earners. Parisian tailors and their wives, for instance, many of them influenced by utopian socialist followers of Saint-Simon and Etienne Cabet, recognized that wives could perform tailoring work at home while simultaneously performing their domestic tasks and caring for children. The workers roughly categorized as printers, on the other hand, stood among the most vocal advocates of the family wage throughout the nineteenth century.[13]

---

11. Benenson, "Family Wage," p. 71; Benenson's n. 1 lists some of the works that demonstrate this position.

12. On British workers, see Rose, *Limited Livelihoods*, pp. 127–52.

13. See Joan Scott, "Work Identities for Men and Women: The Politics of Work and Family in the Parisian Garment Trades in 1848," in Scott, *Gender and the Politics of History*. The main innovations in tailoring in this period were not technological but rather had to do with the reorganization of work in workshops (as opposed to the home), shifts in the role of family labor, and subcontracting (in tailoring and garment work—especially subcontracting out to seamstresses in convents and prisons). The differences between printers and tailors on the family wage in this period may also have been structural. That

Historically highly skilled, typesetters, proofreaders, pri\
bookbinders fiercely defended their independence, skills,\
system of apprenticeship, and duty to support their families\
wages alone. Indeed, men's economic activity was as much con
by their position in the private sphere as it was by their acti\   ...
the public domain. "[P]aternity imposes duties; a father has the moral
obligation to feed, raise, and educate his children. To give them a
position in life."[14] For these workers, the rights of men in public were at
least in part ensured by their domination in private. Men in the book
industry believed, as one of them declared in 1842, "that women's condition can really improve only when men earn enough to support their
families, as is only right . . . so the male worker must achieve his position; he must make his real rights in society understood."[15] This attention to workingmen's status as fathers and family providers was entirely
consonant with Pierre-Joseph Proudhon's idealization of the preindustrial independent artisanal family.[16]

The identification of the male worker as a "family man" and the
assumption that support of the family was both his right and his duty
lay at the foundation of the demand for the family wage. Moreover,
implicit here was a definition of work, and hence of the wage, that
differed for men and women—a difference that early nineteenth-
century political economists such as Jean-Baptiste Say well under-

---

is, the fact that tailoring had been organized around family labor may have militated
against the myth of the male breadwinner as the sole financial support of the family.
Printing, however, had never been family based in the same way. I am grateful to Nancy
Green for sharing her thoughts with me on this structural difference. On women's defense
of their right to work, see Claire Moses, *French Feminism in the Nineteenth Century*
(Albany, 1984); Michelle Riot-Sarcey, *La Démocratie à l'épreuve des femmes: Trois Figures critiques du pouvoir, 1830–1848* (Paris, 1994), esp. p. 89. For an earlier defense of
women's right to work that distinguished between "appropriate" (home-based) and "inappropriate" (workshop or factory-based) work for women, see Charles Dupin, *Le Petit
Producteur français*, vol. 6 of *L'Ouvrière française* (Paris, 1828), esp. pp. 10–22. I thank
Michelle Perrot for this reference.

14. *Revue Républicaine* 2 (1834–35): 48, quoted in Riot-Sarcey, *Démocratie à l'épreuve
des femmes*, p. 148.

15. "Enquête: De la condition de la femme," *L'Atelier*, December 30, 1842, pp. 31–32;
Riot-Sarcey, *Démocratie à l'épreuve des femmes*, p. 152.

16. Pierre-Joseph Proudhon, *Système des contradictions économiques, ou Philosophie
de la misère* (1846), in his *Oeuvres complètes* (Paris, 1923), 1: 197–99. See also Louis
Devance, "Femme, famille, travail et morale sexuelle dans l'idéologie de 1848," in *Mythes
et représentations de la femme*, p. 96; Joseph Bernard, Grenoble workers' delegate to the
1879 Socialist Workers' Congress, in *Séances du Congrès ouvrier socialiste de France, 3ᵉ
session tenue à Marseille du 20 au 30 octobre 1879 à Salle des Folies Bergères* (Marseille,
1879) [hereafter *Congrès ouvrier de 1879*], p. 184. See Tessie Liu's description of how
family interest was subsumed within the professional identity of the male weaver in
Chapter 2 of this volume.

stood.[17] Say, whose ideas were invoked by labor activists later in the century, assumed that women's work did not create exchange value because it was performed within the home, and therefore was not "productive"; only labor that produced exchange value could be considered "wage work." Reproduction did not enter the calculus of political economy because it had no clearly defined value in the market. Women, therefore, could not be considered legitimate workers. Ideally, women's domestic labor would be reimbursed by the wages of men, which would include the cost of providing for their wives and children as well as for themselves.[18] The ideal of the woman at home, however, was completely at odds with the reality of French women's growing participation in the labor force over the course of the nineteenth century. Between 1866 and 1901, women's labor force participation in France grew by over 10 percent (from 24.7 to 34.8 percent of the labor force); by 1901, 40 percent of all married women were employed. In Britain, by comparison, women's labor force participation over the same period declined (from 27.2 percent in 1871 to 24.9 percent in 1901); only 9.6 percent of all married women were employed.[19] Men often reacted to the growing female presence in the workforce with charges that women competed with men for jobs and drove down their wages.

Male workers deployed the discourse of competition to marginalize women and protect their (own) dominant position at work. Workingmen also responded to real threats to job security. Particularly in printing, some employers barely concealed their intention of saving money by hiring women. Paul Dupont provoked a major strike in the industry when he hired women compositors in his new Clichy printshop in 1862. In 1878 and again in 1901, women compositors worked as strikebreakers in Paris and in Nancy, respectively.[20] Opposition to competition from women grew and printers raised the ideal of the family wage in arguing for the exclusion of women from the trade.[21]

17. Jean-Baptiste Say, *Traité de l'économie politique*, 6th ed. (Paris, 1841), p. 324; Scott, "'L'Ouvrière!'" p. 143. See also Perrot, "L'Eloge de la ménagère," p. 119.

18. See Scott, "'L'Ouvrière!'" pp. 145, 157.

19. See T. Deldyke, H. Gelders, and J.-M. Limbor, *La Population active et sa structure*, vol. 1 of *Statistiques internationales rétrospectives*, ed. Paul Bairoch (Brussels, 1968), pp. 167 and 169 for the French case, 183 and 185 for the British case. The high rate of married women's participation in the French labor force owed much to their employment in agriculture and in small family-based shops.

20. A strike at the Berger-Levrault printshops in Nancy drew particular attention because the strikebreakers came from a women compositors' union founded by Marguerite Durand, editor of the feminist newspaper *La Fronde*. See Marie-Hélène Zylberberg-Hocquard, *Féminisme et syndicalisme en France* (Paris, 1978), pp. 256–59.

21. See Madeleine Guilbert, *Les Femmes et l'organisation syndicale avant 1914* (Paris, 1966), pp. 50, 188–91. Madeleine Rebérioux points out that the statutes of the Fédération Française des Travailleurs du Livre in 1881 affirmed "almost unanimously—with the

The introduction of the Linotype machine about 1895, along with the opportunities it created for employing female compositors, provoked debate about women's work in printing and sparked a call for the family wage. The new machines, indeed, completely redefined skilled work by making it possible for relatively untrained women and boys to set type; some employers hired women to replace men on the new machines.[22] Printers, even those who were relatively sympathetic to women's work at union rates equal to men's wages, linked their concerns about the Linotype to women's presence in printshops and to the exploitation of improperly trained boy apprentices. Indeed, employers hired women to work on Linotype machines at much lower rates than men.[23] From 1900 on printers debated at length the question of women's work and the implications of the new machines for the gender relations of the workplace. They complained bitterly that women worked for starvation wages, without a proper apprenticeship. Condemning women's work on the Linotype machines, one speaker at the national printers' congress in 1910 demonstrated that his ideas about who had the right to work were based on his notions of sexual difference. "If this congress were able to successfully combat the wage work of married women, of women who assume male powers [*de la femme en puissance de mâle*] . . . the plague from which all workingmen suffer would immediately be eliminated." The real solution, he argued, was for the employer to raise the wages of all male workers with heavy family responsibilities.[24]

But competition was only part of the explanation for printers' hostility toward women. Equally salient was the idealization of the working-class housewife. Printers couched their opposition to women's work and their claims to a family wage in terms of women's "natural" functions as mothers and housewives, and deplored the effects of women's work on the family and maternity. At the 1888 Third National Trades Union Congress, despite the expression of strongly divergent opinions about

---

exception of Rouen—that one of its goals was to remove women from composing rooms by all legal means, including equalization of wages": "De beaux métiers," in *Les Ouvriers du livre et leur fédération: Un Centenaire, 1881–1981*, ed. Rebérioux et al. (Paris, 1981), p. 30.

22. On reactions to the Linotype, see *Compte rendu du septième congrès national de la Fédération française des travailleurs du livre* (Paris, [1895]), pp. 52, 67. On strikes against the Linotype machines and the hiring of women to work on them, see *Compte rendu du dixième congrès national de la Fédération française des travailleurs du livre* (Paris, [1910]), pp. 301, 469.

23. *Compte rendu du huitième congrès national de la Fédération française des travailleurs du livre* (Paris, 1900), pp. 25, 45.

24. *Compte rendu du dixième congrès*, pp. 464, 466. Despite expressions of hostility toward women's presence in the trade, the congress in fact took a major step forward in passing a resolution in favor of the admission of women to the trade at union rates. However, not all printers accepted women's presence as readily as their leaders did.

women's right to work, delegates passed a resolution deploring women's
and children's wage work as "a monstrosity . . . completely contrary to
the natural role of women in a well-organized society, destructive to the
physical and intellectual development of the child and the principal
cause of the moral degradation of both."[25] In 1910, August Keufer,
conservative head of the Printers' Federation, echoed this position:
"Men's wages must be sufficient for women to remain in the private
realm and fulfill . . . their natural function of mother and family educator."[26] Thus the rhetorical strategy of proponents of the family wage
was twofold: the repeated portrayal of women as invaders, based on the
conviction that work is a male privilege; and the invocation of a family
ideal based on distinct gender positions, according to which men worked
in public to provide for their families and women performed their "natural" functions of social reproduction in private to reconstitute and maintain the labor force.[27] Both ideals betrayed men's determination to
preserve their status simultaneously in the family and in the workplace
and the inflection, indeed shaping, of workingmen's interests by gender
interests.

Women's wage labor and the family wage provoked considerable dis-
agreement among workers. Although typesetters vigorously opposed
women's presence in printshops, even at wages equal to those of men,
and idealized the wife and mother, other workers in book production just
as seriously defended women's right to work, especially the right of
single women and widows who needed to support themselves, and favored women's admission to the printers' unions.[28] Bookbinders, for
instance, less threatened by women's competition, argued for women's
right to work, and defended equal pay for equal work and women's
admission to the Printers' Federation, on "socialist principles." Ultimately, bringing women into the unions would "preserve the corporation
and limit the number of women working."[29] Divisions among men in the
industry, however—among binders, relatively untouched by competition
from women, who performed tasks quite different from men; typesetters,
who were the most threatened by women's competition on Linotype
machines; and proofreaders—each group with its corporate interests to

25. *Fédération nationale des syndicats et groupes corporatifs ouvriers de France,*
troisième congrès national, Bordeaux, Octobre 1888 (Bordeaux, 1888), pp. 6–7. See also
the intervention of Auguste Keufer, *Compte rendu du huitième congrès,* p. 39.

26. *Compte rendu du dixième congrès,* p. 477.

27. On this point, see also Rebérioux, "De beaux métiers," p. 32.

28. See, e.g., reports on the congresses of 1883, 1887, 1889, and 1895 excerpted in
Guilbert, *Femmes et l'organisation syndicale,* pp. 49–51, 53–58. No women were present
as delegates at any of these congresses.

29. Congresses of 1883 and 1900, quoted ibid., pp. 37, 41, 50. See also the disagreements
at the 1905 congress, quoted ibid., pp. 59, 63.

defend, made it impossible for them to agree on the exclusion of women from the trade more generally, on the basis of either class or gender.

The debates about women's work and the family wage were most acute among printers, but leatherworkers and metalworkers also supported the family wage. In these heavily male trades, skilled workers invoked notions of masculinity as well as of femininity in arguing for male workers' right to support their families. In 1905 and again in 1907 leatherworkers condemned women's industrial homework; cutters who experienced competition from women on new machines proposed that women simply be banned from workshops.[30] But not all workingmen wanted to remove women from the leather shops, and their discussions were riddled with ambiguity. Like the bookbinders, those who were less threatened by women's competition on machines defended women's right to work and proposed instead an end to family-based domestic work and piecework with the requirement that all work should be done in a workshop.[31] Unlike garment workers in the 1840s, the leatherworkers believed that workshop labor was preferable to domestic labor because it could be more easily regulated. For leatherworkers as for printers, gendered positions in fatherhood and the family were crucial components of a workingman's identity.

Metalworkers also invoked fatherhood, the family, and an idealized balance of gender relations in criticizing competition from young boy apprentices who worked below union rates. Parisian clockmakers, members of the Metalworkers' Federation in the 1890s, appealed to the role of adult workingmen as fathers, who, undercut by boys, could not support their unwaged wives and children.[32] Women's entry into metalworking trades also disrupted workingmen's idealized vision of the relationship of masculinity, fatherhood, work, and the wage. Raising the specter of role inversion and unemployment in reaction to women's presence in metal shops, a shipyard worker from Marseille complained, "If this situation continues, the father of the family will find himself doing the cooking while his wife and children go out to work."[33] Metalworkers idealized the

---

30. *Quatrième Congrès national de la Fédération des cuirs et peaux* (Puteaux, [1905]), quoted ibid., p. 127.

31. A Parisian shoemaker, for example, argued against the elimination of women from his trade, but later expressed the hope that leatherworkers' wages would be high enough to enable their wives to remain at home: *Cinquième Congrès de la Fédération nationale des cuirs et peaux* (Paris, 1907), pp. 64, 69.

32. "Compte rendu du deuxième congrès national de la métallurgie, tenu à Paris du 23 au 27 novembre 1892," *Bulletin officiel de la Fédération nationale des ouvriers métallurgistes de France*, no. 19 (December 1892), pp. 13, 20; *Compte rendu du troisième congrès de la Fédération nationale des ouvriers métallurgistes de France* (Saint-Etienne, 1894), p. 21.

33. "Compte rendu du deuxième congrès national de la métallurgie," p. 22.

family and women's role as mother in arguing for wage increases that would permit the workingman to support a family. Jewelers' fears that unemployed men would be supported by their wives emerged, tinged with racism: "[T]he [unemployed] workingman will live like an Arab, from the meager pittance his wife earns."[34] But the debate over women's work and demands for the family wage were hardly as intense among metalworkers as among printers, largely because few women worked in metal shops and no technological innovations or changes in the labor process emerged to disrupt men's control of metalworking before World War I. The discourse of the family wage temporarily disappeared in metalworking by 1900. Moreover, in trades in which women were well represented, such as textiles, cigarette and match manufacture, food processing, teaching, and garment manufacture, or in which the gender division of labor was sufficiently marked so that men's jobs were not threatened by competition from women, workingmen did not appeal to the family wage ideal. French workers' differences and disagreements over the family wage within individual trades also appeared in national labor confederations before World War I.

Labor activists brought the issue of women's work onto the floor of virtually every major national labor congress from the 1870s until World War I. At the historic 1879 Third Socialist Workers' Congress in Marseille, delegates evoked the by-now familiar idealized image of the working-class family, and several defended the principle of the family wage in arguing against women's wage labor. Even the suffragist Hubertine Auclert, whose impassioned plea for women's rights was one of the focal points of the congress, argued for women's economic independence on the grounds of their "natural" motherhood.[35] In terms loaded with gendered images, Isidore Finance, delegate of the Paris building painters, urged "tough-fisted and hardheaded workingmen ... to demand a wage that is not simply the equivalent to the product of their labor, but sufficient to keep women and the aged at home."[36]

34. *Compte rendu du premier congrès national de la Fédération nationale des travailleurs de l'industrie de la bijouterie-orfèvrerie-horlogerie* (Paris, [1909]), quoted in Guilbert, *Femmes et l'organisation syndicale*, pp. 145–46.

35. *Congrès ouvrier de 1879*, pp. 155–56. Perrot, "L'Eloge de la ménagère," esp. pp. 110–12, emphasized the valorization of the working-class housewife at the 1879 Congress. Auclert's intervention was nonetheless a radical attack on women's economic (and legal) dependence and on the assumption that men could support their families on their wages alone. Auclert challenged the ideal of working-class fatherhood by arguing that the husband often "forgets his fatherly duties; he can even abandon his wife and children. The lover virtually always escapes the costs of paternity [se dérobe presque toujours aux charges de la paternité]." This was the same argument used some twenty-six years later in favor of a married women's property law.

36. *Congrès ouvrier de 1879*, pp. 620–21. See also Irénée Dauthier of the Paris saddlemakers, p. 179; Ferdinand Vedel of the Paris wallpaper hangers, p. 222. Dauthier was the only woman to support the family wage ideal at this congress.

Although many workers in 1879 deplored the real exploitation of young women workers—worse in some ways than the exploitation of men, given women's vulnerability to sexual harassment—not all concluded that these were grounds on which to ban women from waged work altogether. The startlingly progressive resolution in favor of women's right to work, equal wages, and freedom to choose their role in society, drafted by a mixed committee with the support of Hubertine Auclert and approved at the congress, echoed the growing defense of women's wage work by both men and women activists and congress delegates.[37]

At the 1892 congress of the National Federation of Labor Unions, women tobacco workers responded to men's hostility to their presence in the labor force and to demands for the family wage by arguing that women's right to work was essential to their independence. Although federation leaders adopted an extensive report insisting that unions bar women, the report also demanded equal wages for equal work in any area of work considered "neither unhealthy nor contrary to women's aptitudes;" a maternity leave of six weeks before and six weeks after the birth, with wages for time lost to be paid by the municipality; and the eligibility of women for election to employer-worker industrial arbitration councils.[38] These delegates did not demand a family wage, but embedded in the discussion and the accompanying resolutions was the assumption that a male wage sufficient to support a family would permit women to remain at home.

Family wage demands did, however, appear sporadically in the national congresses of the Fédération Nationale des Bourses du Travail from 1892 to 1902 and in the main labor confederation, the General Confederation of Labor (Confédération Générale du Travail, or CGT), from 1898 on.[39] In

37. Ibid., p. 804. The resolution was drafted by a committee of four women and five men. Not all women supported it. Irénée Dauthier, in particular, argued at some length for women's place in the home, as she had done at the 1876 congress. See ibid., pp. 163–80; Perrot, "L'Eloge de la ménagère," pp. 112–13. See also *Congrès socialiste ouvrier de Marseille, 1879: Compte rendu lu en assemblée corporative le 15 février 1880 par I. Dauthier, déléguée des selliers de Paris et de la Société des travaillers amis de la paix* (Paris, 1880), which contains Dauthier's critical remarks on Hubertine Auclert's intervention; *Congrès ouvrier de 1879,* pp. 184–85 (Bernard), 187–91 (Graves), 191–93 (Tranier), 196 (Godefoy), 198–99 (Monard), 199–202 (Hébrard), 202–4 (Ytier).

38. *Cinquième Congrès national des syndicats et groupes corporatifs ouvriers de France tenu à Marseille du 19 au 22 octobre 1892: Compte-rendu receuilli dans les archives de la Bourse du Travail de Marseille* (Paris, 1909), pp. 50, 164–65. See also the reports presented to the *Sixième congrès national des syndicats de France: Compte rendu des travaux du congrès tenu à Nantes du 17 au 22 septembre 1894* (Nantes, 1894), quoted in Guilbert, *Femmes et l'organisation syndicale,* pp. 167–68.

39. See Guilbert, *Femmes et l'organisation syndicale,* pp. 151–54, 169–84. The Bourses du Travail, the official labor exchanges, were established in the 1890s to serve as an employment service; in fact they became the locus of worker education initiatives and labor organization. The Bourses merged with the CGT, the Confédération Générale du

1898 the confederation resolved "that, in all areas, we should spread the idea that the husband must provide for the wife."[40] This action drew stinging criticism from Jules Guesde, the powerful head of the socialist French Workers Party (Parti Ouvrier Français, or POF), who issued a firy reproach to the rigid essentialism of his labor movement comrades.[41]

In 1900, however, despite another lively debate at the CGT national congress over the admission of women to unions, the application of protective legislation, and women's competition, a resolution on the family wage failed to pass. Marie-Joseph Eugène Guérard, national secretary of the almost entirely male railway workers' union, expressed the majority view when he argued that women would be free only when they had full control of their wages, and that to escape from their dependence on men and enjoy their freedom they must be able to work. Although debate about women's work did not cease, especially among rank-and-file workers, this would be the last time workers raised the issue of the family wage at a national labor congress before World War I.[42]

How do we explain the virtual disappearance of family wage demands? First, from the beginning of the century, women's labor force participation continued to grow. By 1911, women made up 38.9 percent of the labor force, and 48.8 percent of all married women were employed.[43] Women's presence in public, in the workplace, and in labor struggles alongside men undermined arguments about the gendered characteristics of public and private spheres. Second, male labor leaders and activists began to accept women's right to work, despite the resistance of such groups as the typesetters. Two developments illustrate this gradual acceptance. First, the CGT, partly in reaction to feminist initiatives to organize working women, took steps to appeal to women. In 1907 it created a Feminist Labor Action Commmittee, headed by Maximilienne

---

Travail, in 1902. The CGT was founded in 1895, from the Fédération des Syndicats. See ibid., pp. 171–74.

40. *Dixième Congrès national corporatif (IVᵉ de la CGT) tenu à Rennes les 26–30 septembre et 1ᵉʳ octobre 1898: Compte rendu des travaux du congrès* (Rennes, 1898), pp. 174–85; Bourse du Travail Du Havre, *Le Congrès de Rennes (la Fédération des bourses du travail et Confédération générale du travail Du Havre): Rapport par André Philippe, délégué de la Bourse du travail Du Havre* (Le Havre, 1899), pp. 69–71; "Le Mouvement syndical en France: Le Xᵉ congrès national corporatif (IVᵉ de la Confédération générale du travail) à Rennes," *Musée Social*, no. 2 (February 1899), pp. 83–84.

41. See "Mouvement syndical," p. 84, and the more complete extract of Guesde's reaction (originally published in *Le Socialiste*, October 9, 1898), in Guilbert, *Femmes et l'organisation syndicale*, p. 174n. Surprisingly, Jean Jaurès, leader of the independent socialist configuration, supported a family wage in 1904. See Tilly and Scott, *Women, Work, and Family*, p. 132.

42. On the persistence of hostility to women's work, see, e.g., Zylberberg-Hocquard, *Féminisme et syndicalisme*, pp. 260, 274.

43. Deldyke et al., *Population active et sa structure*.

Biais, to deal with women's issues.[44] In addition, the confederation began to admit women's unions when local labor federations refused them membership. This was the case with two women's printing unions that had been denied admission to local federations in 1910 and 1912.[45] Second, reactions to the Couriau affair in 1913 demonstrated that French workers had already begun to abandon the family wage ideal. Emma Couriau, who worked in a Lyon printshop at union wages, was denied admission to the local printers' union and her husband was expelled from it for allowing his wife to work in a union shop. The affair sparked a flurry of debate in the labor and feminist movements over married women's right to work, and elicited a vocal defense of women's work by major labor activists and movement leaders. The Couriau affair also elicited a systematic discussion of the need to organize women.[46] The growing number of women in the labor force, the large numbers of married women in paid employment, women's increasing presence in the labor movement before World War I, and labor leaders' acceptance of women as partners at work and in labor struggles all help to explain the soft-pedaling, if not disappearance, of demands for the family wage before World War I. Although the history of the family wage did not end with the war, the specific social and political environment of France in the interwar years and employers' wage policies shifted the focus of the debate about the links between gender, family, work, and wages.

THE FAMILY WAGE BETWEEN THE WARS

In trades that men had historically dominated, metalworking and printing, debates over the family wage resurfaced during and after the war. The introduction of women workers into arsenals and munitions factories, where they counted for about 30 percent of munitions workers by 1918, marked a radical and substantial invasion of "male territory" by women.[47] Women's activism in the strikes of May–June 1917 revived metalworkers' arguments for the rights of male breadwinners to a family

44. Zylberberg-Hocquard, *Féminisme et syndicalisme*, pp. 260–61.

45. CGT Congresses of 1910 and 1912, cited in Guilbert, *Femmes et l'organisation syndicale*, pp. 182–83.

46. Levels of women's unionization in France before World War I were extremely low: 4% in 1903 and just under 10% in 1912. See Guilbert, *Femmes et l'organisation syndicale*, pp. 420–27. See Guilbert's analysis of the press on the Couriau affair, pp. 409–12. On that affair see Charles Sowerwine, "Workers and Women in France before 1914: The Debate over the Couriau Affair," *Journal of Modern History* 55 (September 1983): 411–41; Zylberberg-Hocquard, *Féminisme et syndicalisme*, pp. 263–68.

47. Mathilde Dubesset, Françoise Thébaud, and Catherine Vincent, "Les Munitionettes de la Seine," in *L'Autre Front*, Cahiers du *Mouvement social* no. 2 (Paris, 1977), p. 191.

wage based on some of the same essentialist arguments men invoked earlier. "That women are . . . organically inferior to their [male] companions . . . is incontestable, but women's inferiority is not only physical, it is also moral and intellectual."[48] Such assertions of male superiority in the face of both women's activism and the physical and psychological devastation of war accompanied (however ambiguously) renewed idealization of the working-class family and appeals to the utopian condition of the *femme au foyer*, "the faithful guardian of . . . family traditions."[49]

Although metalworkers continued to argue for the family wage into the 1920s, printers dropped their "official" discursive opposition to women in 1919 and agreed to admit women to their unions.[50] But the war also shifted the political and discursive fields governing the relationship of gendered positions, family, work, and the wage in three ways. First, whereas workers and employers had been the major parties to debates over work and wages before the war, afterward the state, partly on the basis of its powerfully interventionist role in wartime, became an interlocutor as well. Second, the discursive boundaries between public and private became more difficult to sustain as the wartime devastation of population and France's historically low birth rate became national concerns and women (especially married women) continued to hold jobs at a relatively high rate.[51] Women's labor force participation varied between

48. Dr. Letourneau, "Contre la femme au syndicat," *Bulletin du Syndicat des Métallurgistes de Bourges*, no. 6 (August 1917), pp. 3–4 (communicated to the author by Judith Wishnia). On the 1916–17 strikes and perceptions of women, see Laura Lee Downs, "Women's Strikes and the Politics of Popular Egalitarianism in France, 1916–1918," in *Rethinking Labor History: Essays on Discourse and Class Analysis*, ed. Leonard Berlanstein (Urbana, 1993), pp. 114–48.

49. See "Discussion sur la question féminine," *Bulletin du Syndicat des Métallurgistes de Bourges*, no. 6 (August 1917), pp. 3–5; also "La Main d'oeuvre féminine et l'organisation de la femme," *L'Union des Métaux*, no. 68 (July 1918), pp. 13–14; report on the 1918 congress of the Fédération des Métaux, "Quatrième Journée," *L'Union des Métaux*, no. 69 (July 1918), p. 7. At this congress the Federal Committee resolved that the increasingly generalized "absorption of women by industry is in flagrant contradiction to . . . procreation," but nonetheless recommended the unionization of women "because it would not be a good tactic to group them outside of men's organizations."

50. See Fédération Française des Travailleurs du Livre, *Onzième congrès national tenu à Nancy du 8 au 13 septembre 1919* (Paris, 1919). Postal workers also discussed proposals for a family wage, but they do not seem to have been adopted. See, for example, Syndicat national des agents des postes, télégraphes et téléphones (confédéré), *Septième congrès tenu à Toulouse les 10, 11, 12 et 13 juin 1925* (Epernay, 1925), pp. 151–53.

51. On population concerns in interwar France, see Karen Offen, "Body Politics: Women, Work, and the Politics of Motherhood in France, 1920–1950," in *Maternity and Gender Policies: Women and the Rise of the European Welfare States, 1880s–1950s*, ed. Gisela Bock and Pat Thane (New York, 1991), pp. 138–59; and Susan Pedersen, *Family, Dependence, and the Origins of the Welfare State: Britain and France, 1914–1945* (Cambridge, 1993). See also Mary Louise Roberts, *Civilization without Sexes* (Chicago, 1994), chaps. 4 and 5.

42.3 percent of the total population in 1921 and 34.2 percent in 1936.[52] Married women's labor force participation varied between 49.6 percent in 1921 and 42 percent in 1936, and between 34.9 percent (1921) and 41 percent (1936) of all women employed in nonagricultural work.[53] However, married women's high labor force participation in the interwar years only partly explains why gender-based appeals for the family wage gradually disappeared. Third, whereas the prewar wage was based on the production of exchange value in public, the postwar wage became linked to value produced in private: reproduction, now redefined as a public issue.

The 1920s saw a major initiative on the part of a growing number of employers to meet the dual objective of stimulating the reproduction of the labor force after the unparalleled losses in the war and containing wages in a period of skyrocketing inflation. In addition to cost-of-living allowances to permit wages to keep pace with inflation and to forestall labor actions, many employers provided a family bonus (*sursalaire familial*) to workers who had worked for one month in their factory, on the basis of the number of children they had. Workers with two children could add 25 percent to their wages; those with six children received double wages.[54] This bonus, the closest French workers would ever come to a "family wage," provoked extensive debates within the labor movement and drew considerable hostility from labor leaders in both Communist and noncommunist unions from about 1923 on.

Unlike the family wage of yore, based on the labor of the workingman and on the obligation of "honest fathers of families" to provide for their

52. The proportion of women in metalworking, for example, doubled from 4.2% in 1906 to 8.4% in 1921. In the Paris region women made up as many as 14% of metalworkers in the 1920s and nearly 20% in the 1930s: Ministère du Travail, Statistique générale de France, *Résultats statistiques du recensement générale de la population, 1921* and *1926* (Paris, 1925, 1929). For figures on women's labor force participation more generally in this period, see Françoise Geuland-Léridon, *Le Travail des femmes en France* (Paris, 1964), p. 26; Jean Daric, *L'Activité professionnelle des femmes en France* (Paris, 1947), esp. pp. 12, 15–16, 26. See also Jean-Louis Robert, "Women and Work in France during the First World War," in *The Upheaval of War: Family, Work, and Welfare in Europe, 1914–1918*, ed. Richard Wall and Jay Winter (Cambridge, 1988), pp. 251–66.

53. Daric, *L'Activité professionelle*, p. 26; Deldyke et al., *Population active et sa structure*, pp. 167, 169.

54. Pedersen, *Family, Dependence*, p. 245. See also her discussion of the administration of these funds through the *caisses de compensation*, pp. 224–88. As Pedersen shows, the *caisses* grew steadily, from 15 in 1920 to 255 in 1932 (p. 231). The *sursalaire* was the most important of a series of allowances begun by employers in the 1920s; they included birth bonuses, available to workers employed by a firm for three months, and nursing bonuses, payable to nursing mothers who were employed by the firm or whose husbands were employed by the firm. See also Françoise Thébaud, "Le Mouvement nataliste dans la France de l'entre-deux-guerres: L'Alliance nationale pour l'accroissement de la population française," *Revue d'Histoire Moderne et Contemporaine* 32 (April–June 1985): 276–301.

dependents, the family bonus was not actually a wage, but rather a supplement to the wage, payable to both men and women workers. It was not based on the labor of an individual worker, but was tied to the number of dependents he or she had to support, and therefore was not the same for all workers. As such it contrasted sharply with labor unions' attempts to establish unified wage scales over which they could exercise some control in bargaining with employers. Moreover, the bonus was no measure of benevolence designed to help out needy families; it permitted employers to control and supervise the labor force. The supplement required continuity of employment, so that workers who missed a day of work or participated in a strike forfeited the bonus. The system was accompanied by an extensive program of home visits and home economics education for mothers, designed to educate them about child care and housekeeping.[55]

Labor leaders' opposition focused on three things: the symbolic meaning of the system of payment of the *sursalaire*, the strategic problem it presented to the labor movement, and employers' use of the bonus as a form of social control, with gender-based consequences. Reactions of rank-and-file workers, labor leaders, and the labor left also revealed their continued ambivalence about the relationship of gender, work, and the wage, in addition to subtle but important differences between Communist organizations belonging to the United General Labor Confederation (Confédération Générale du Travail Unitaire, or CGTU) and the noncommunist activists of the CGT. Overall, far more than the CGT, the CGTU aggressively supported women's right to work and attempted to organize women throughout the 1920s.[56]

CGT activists, for example, reacted with righteous indignation to the system of payment (among other things) that permitted wives to receive the supplement. They invoked prewar assumptions about the rights of fathers as family providers, the privilege of men to be deemed "producers," and about the kind of labor that merited remuneration. Henri Labe, secretary of the CGT Metalworkers' Federation, asked indignantly, "[H]ow can we perpetuate this method that . . . rewards an effort that *has no relation to work!* How can we accept that [employers] inflict such a gratuitous insult on producers, the fathers of families, by giving the family allowance to the wife and not giving it directly to the producer?"[57]

55. Pedersen, *Family, Dependence*, pp. 273–74.

56. The CGTU established a Women's Commission in 1922 and immediately brought the question of organizing women to the floor of confederal congresses. The CGT appointed a Women's Commission in 1929; until then Jeanne Chevenard served as the women's propaganda delegate.

57. Fédération des Ouvriers en Métaux et Similaires de France [CGT], *VIIe Congrès fédéral tenu à Paris les 23, 24, 25 août 1925: Compte rendu des travaux du congrès* (Versailles, 1925), p. 287 (emphasis mine).

Embedded in this protest was an assumed distinction between the gendered characteristics of "production," performed by men in the workplace and deemed worthy of a wage, and social reproduction, carried out by women, which did not qualify as "production" and therefore was not worthy of a wage.[58]

Labor activists also pointed to the strategic problems that the unions' positions on the issue raised for the organization of workers from 1925 on. In spite of the Communists' commitment to the organization of women, metalworkers in the Communist unions also viewed the wage through the lenses of gender, portraying the worker as a family man. A family bonus for the father of six or seven children (about 450 francs a month) was not an insignificant sum, and some workers were concerned that opposition to the *sursalaire* might actually turn people away from the unions. A metalworker argued that a real family wage would avoid the problem altogether by ensuring that "all workingmen who have family responsibilities are paid enough to support their families."[59] Metalworkers remained intransigent, but also relatively unique in their vision of a mythical working-class household, and could be found demanding the family wage for workingmen as late as 1927.[60] Others focused on the divisive influence of the bonuses and called attention to the fact that employers used them to compress wages.[61] Some workers in fact struck over reduced family bonus payments, and employers attempted to settle some metalworkers', shoemakers', and textile workers' strikes by offering increases in the *sursalaire familial* rather than across-the-board wage increases (or in exchange for smaller wage increases than workers demanded).[62]

58. This logic was not far removed from that of the nineteenth-century political economist Jean-Baptiste Say.

59. Fédération Unitaire des Ouvriers et Ouvrières sur Métaux, *Troisième congrès national: Rapports et compte rendu du 3ᵉ comité fédéral, 1–3 septembre 1925* (Paris, 1926), pp. 154–55.

60. See Fédération Unitaire des Ouvriers et Ouvrières sur Métaux, *Quatrième congrès national à Paris, 12–14 décembre 1927: Rapports et compte rendu sténographique* (Paris, 1928), p. 265.

61. Report of Georges Buisson (Fédération des Employés), CGT, *XXIIIᵉ Congrès confédéral de 1923: Compte rendu des travaux* (Villeneuve St-Georges, 1923), p. 122. See also Joseph Couergou, "Les Mensonges de la philanthropie capitaliste: Les Allocations familiales," *Le Métallurgiste*, November 1926, press clipping in Archives Nationales (AN), F7 13780; see also the debate on the *sursalaire familial* in CGTU, *Congrès national ordinaire: 3ᵉᵐᵉ Congrès de la CGTU, Paris, 26 au 31 août 1925* (Paris, 1925), pp. 524–25, 530, 541–42; Marthe Bigot, "Charges familiales," *L'Ouvrière* 1 (August 5, 1922).

62. See reports on strikes in AN, BB18 2706 (criminal justice archives), "Rapport du Juge de Paix du canton de Romans à M.le Procureur de la République à Valence," May 12, 1924; ibid., 2752, "Rapport du Procureur général, Grenoble, à M.le Garde des Sceaux, Paris," October 13, 1926, and "Rapport du Procureur général, Nancy, à M.le Garde des Sceaux, Paris," March 24, 1926; ibid., 2831, "Rapport du Procureur général, Douai, à M.le Garde

Finally, workers opposed the social-control dimension of home visiting initiatives. Not only did they resent employers' intrusion into the private domain of the family, but this aspect of the *sursalaire* also posed strategic problems for the labor movement. Here, too, their critiques rested on gender-based arguments: they blamed women's susceptibility to the supplements for men's failure of nerve in strike actions. Georges Buisson, head of the Fédération des Employés, speaking at the 1923 CGT congress, called attention to the way the system of home visiting and child-care education enabled *dames visiteuses* (women welfare workers) to enter working-class homes during the last textile workers' strike in the Nord, "while workingmen were in union meetings, to frighten the women and encourage them to get their husbands to return to work."[63] Marguerite Routier, prominent activist in the Union des Syndicats de la Seine, speaking at the Third National United Metalworkers' Federation Congress (CGTU), pointed out that as recipients of the wage supplement women could indeed encourage their husbands to abstain from labor actions that risked depriving them of this extra income. "When a man starts talking about a strike, the wife, who is sort of a minister of finance, says, 'Fine, but what if I loose the *sursalaire*?' and he replies, 'So much the worse; I won't strike!'"[64] The practice of depriving workers of the supplement for any unexcused absence from work not surprisingly affected the gender politics of working-class families, for the wife often kept the purse.

Although labor leaders recognized that rank-and-file workers with dependents welcomed family bonuses, they demanded state control of all forms of social protection—aid to large families, birth bonuses, and nursing bonuses—under the same conditions as unemployment, health, and old-age insurance.[65] CGTU activists emphasized the participation of workers in the administration of family allowances and the establishment of uniform regional rates payable to all heads of household without distinction of nationality.[66]

---

des Sceaux, Paris," July 26, 1930, on a series of strikes in the textile factories of Armentières, Houplines, and Roubaix-Tourcoing; "La Vie économique et social," *L'Humanité*, February 2, 1926; R.A., "Quelques remarques sur l'état de l'organisation du Parti dans la région du Nord," *Cahiers du Bolchévisme* (January 1, 1932): 60, on textile strikes in 1931.

63. CGT, *XXIIIe Congrès confédéral à Paris (XVIIe de la CGT): Compte rendu des travaux* (Villeneuve St-Georges, 1923), p. 123. The entire text of Buisson's report, pp. 119–25, reprises the main features of the CGT position on the *sursalaire*. It obviously did not occur to Buisson that women might have attended these meetings.

64. Fédération Unitaire des Ouvriers et Ouvrières sur Métaux, *Troisième congrès national*, p. 207.

65. CGT, *XXIIIe Congrès*, pp. 124–25.

66. See the anonymous article "Les Allocations familiales, arme patronale," *Cahiers du Bolchévisme* 3 (June 1928): 499–504.

In 1932, at the depths of the Depression, the state took over regulation of the family allowance system, making family allowances mandatory for all workers, separating them from the wage and from continuity of employment in any single firm. Although employers would continue to administer the allowance system, they agreed that no longer would any worker be denied the allowance on the grounds of a strike or an unexcused absence.[67] The establishment of a state-mandated family allowance system effectively undermined the family wage demands of even the most recalcitrant defenders of male privilege. By taking family allowances away from the exclusive control of employers and hence separating them from the wage, the state effectively rewarded social reproduction as a contribution to society, independent of the productive activities of the workplace.[68]

This move did not, however, resolve the national debate about married women's work. At the same time that a national family allowance system was being established, Catholic social action groups such as the Women's Civic and Social Union (Union Féminine Civique et Sociale) and the Catholic unions grouped in the French Christian Labor Confederation (Confédération Française du Travail Chrétien, or CFTC) campaigned for the return of married working women to the home and for an unwaged mother's allowance that would reimburse married working-class women who chose to leave paid employment.[69] Some working women reacted strongly against these attempts to restrict married women's right to work, with visible differences between Communist and noncommunist women's visions of women's rights as wage earners.[70]

Consistent with their position throughout the 1920s and 1930s, Communist activists fiercely defended women's right to work and women's economic independence, which "alone could permit them to play a social and political role in the ranks of the proletariat as part of a revolutionary force." The problem was not that women had entered industrial produc-

---

67. Pedersen, *Family, Dependence,* p. 376.

68. Although employers attempted to continue to use the family allowance as an arm of wage policy in the 1930s and did retain a powerful influence over the family allowance system (ibid., pp. 282–83), the establishment of state control over the system ultimately separated wage negotiations from the family. The Matignon Accords in 1936, indeed, suggested as much.

69. See, e.g., F. Van Goethem, *Enquête internationale sur le travail salarié de la femme mariée* (Lyon, 1930); Eve Badouin, *La Mère au travail et le retour au foyer* (Paris, 1931); Union Féminine Civique et Social, *Le Travail de la mère et le foyer ouvrier. Documents d'Etude. Extraits du Congrès international, Juin 1933* (Paris, 1933); "Union international d'études sociales," *Chronique Sociale de France,* January 1933, pp. 19–33; Andrée Butillard et al., *Le Travail de la mère hors de son foyer et sa répercussion sur la natalité* (Paris, 1933). See also Pedersen, *Family, Dependence,* pp. 393–401.

70. Maria Vérone, president of the Ligue Française pour le Droit des Femmes, and Cécile Brunschwicg, president of the Union Française pour le Suffrage des Femmes, also reacted strongly against these proposals. See, e.g., *La Française,* 1931–36.

tion, but rather that they had joined the ranks of the exploited. As Jeanne Rougé wrote in 1933, "The return of the woman to the home . . . would mean shutting her up in . . . the family, to keeping her in domestic slavery. After all, didn't the word *familia* for the Romans refer to the slaves belonging to a man?"[71] The noncommunist CGT, on the other hand, had been more pro-family and pro-natalist than the Communist CGTU throughout the 1920s and early 1930s.[72] The CGT women's organizer Jeanne Chevenard, in a 1933 resolution that reflected the dominant position of the CGT some thirty-five years earlier, proposed that women choose between wage work and maternity, and called for "an obligatory family allowance payment calculated at a rate sufficiently high to relieve mothers from seeking a supplemental wage."[73] This resolution, which passed unanimously, came surprisingly close to Catholic appeals for an unwaged mothers' allowance. By September 1935 however, as the CGT and CGTU took the first steps toward reunification, the CGT shifted its position and called upon all workers to resist the unwaged mother's allowance and defend women's right to work.[74]

CONCLUSION

Before World War I, no consensus united French workingmen on the family wage ideal. For some workers the family wage simultaneously represented a form of resistance to capitalism and a defense of male privilege—and men's right to work—in certain trades; for these men the two were inseparable. Defense of "class" interests also meant defense of gender interests, the interests and privileges of skilled working-class men. But it is precisely this elision that throws into question unitary or universalistic notions of class and demonstrates how class was inflected, if not divided, by gender. Workingmen perceived their right to provide for their families—the mark of honest workingmen—as fundamentally

71. Jeanne Rougé, "Le Retour de la femme au foyer," *Cahiers du Bolchévisme* 10 (March 1, 1933): 296, 297.
72. Laura L. Frader, "Working Women and Working Mothers: Gendered Identities at Work and in the French Labor Movement in the 1920s," paper presented at the Sixteenth Annual Conference of the Social Science History Association, New Orleans, November 1–3, 1991. Not until 1935 did the French Communist Party adopt a more overtly pronatalist stance, partly in response to the shift in policy in the Soviet Union.
73. CGT, *Congrès confédéral national, 1933: Compte rendu sténographique des débats, XVIIIᵉ congrès national corporatif (XXIIᵉ de la CGT), 26–29 septembre 1933* (Paris, 1934), pp. 48, 308–9. See also Jeanne Chevenard, "A propos du travail de la femme mariée: L'Opinion d'une travailleuse," *La Française*, March 23, 1935.
74. CGT, *Congrès confédéral de Paris: Compte rendu sténographique des debats du XXIXᵉ congrès national corporatif (XXIIIᵉ de la CGT), 24–27 septembre 1935* (Paris, 1936), p. 271.

linked to their resistance to changes in the labor process, the introduction of new technologies, and employers' attempts to cut costs by hiring boy apprentices and women. But skilled workingmen's defense of their privileged position at work, in public, also involved preservation of their economically dominant position in the family. They could maintain this position only in the face of a broad social consensus about women's secondary—if not illegitimate—status as economic actors and simultaneously in the face of the realistic possibility that male wages would be equitably redistributed within the family. Even before World War I, however, what little agreement existed on these issues began to break down. The passage of a married women's property law in 1907 gave legal recognition to married women's economic independence, effectively acknowledged that male wages were not always equitably redistributed within the family, and provided a solution to the real problem of men's inability to support their families on their wages alone. This was in some sense the state's first step in questioning the myth of the male breadwinner.[75]

What needs explanation is why, in the pro-natalist climate of the 1920s and 1930s, the family wage did not prevail as a demand among workingmen. There are several possibilities. First, after the war, women's right to work became a part of official labor movement discourse, albeit with different meanings for Communist and noncommunist branches of the movement. The family wage ideal ran counter to the interests of both Communist and noncommunist wings of the labor movement, both of which actively competed for new recruits. For the Communists especially, defense of women's right to work and the recruitment of women to both the unions and the party were fundamental components of the Profintern's and the French Communist Party's strategy of building a mass-based and class-based party. Demands for the return of women to the home ran counter to the Communist ideal of the "modern" egalitarian household prevalent during the 1920s and early 1930s. Second, in the inflationary climate of the 1920s, working-class families could not easily survive without the income of a second wage earner, whence the fairly consistent high labor force participation of French women and especially of married women throughout the 1920s and early 1930s. Finally, in the 1920s and 1930s, in the context of concerns about the low French birth

75. See, e.g., Raoul de La Grasserie, *Le Libre Salaire de la femme et la contribution des époux aux charges de la famille: Loi du 13 juillet 1907* (Paris, 1907); André Veaux, *Le Libre Salaire de la femme mariée et la contribution des époux aux charges du ménage: Loi du 13 juillet complété par les lois des 19 mars 1919 et 8 juin 1923* (Rennes, 1925); Albert Damez, *Le Libre Salaire de la femme mariée* (Paris, 1912); M. Alibstur and D. Armgathe, *Histoire du féminisme français* (Paris, 1977), p. 397. British social investigators adopted a similar position by the end of the nineteenth century. See Lewis, *Women of England*, pp. 46–47.

rate, reproduction (or, more broadly, social reproduction) was given a social value and subjected to a new remunerative calculus. Employer (and later, state) support for childbearing in the interests of entrepreneurial and national policies provided precisely the kind of support for families that was the foundation of earlier family wage discourse. Workingmen could no longer argue for a family wage when employers had taken on the role of family providers, especially once family allowances were disaggregated from wages.

The family wage incorporated a set of beliefs about how sexual difference determines who can be considered workers and nonworkers in the public and private realms. Those beliefs came into the open in labor movement discourse at moments of change and challenge to male privilege. But the family wage was not a consistent or regular part of the discourse of French workers, nor was it the only way sexual difference was articulated in the shaping of labor or social policy. Ultimately, it was the Catholic right and after it Vichy, not the majority of working men and women, that maintained this idealized view of the relationship between gender, work, the family, and the wage in twentieth-century France.

6

Women "of a Very Low Type": Crossing Racial Boundaries in Imperial Britain

Laura Tabili

Taboos on sexual activity have been fundamental to state formation and to social stratification.[1] In the 1920s, '30s, and '40s, at the height of Britain's imperial power, interracial marriage was deplored as a threat to racial boundaries and as a catalyst for racial conflict. White women who consorted with Black workingmen were denounced in gendered and class-specific terms as disruptive, deficient, "of a very low type."[2] Inves-

I thank Helen Jones for providing me with a copy of the Fletcher report, and Sonya Rose for encouraging me to pursue this project. Quotations from Crown copyright documents in Oriental and India Office Collections of the British Library appear by permission of the Controller of Her Majesty's Stationery Office.

1. Frederick Engels, *The Origin of the Family, Private Property and the State* (New York, 1972); Gayle Rubin, "The Traffic in Women: Notes on the 'Political Economy' of Sex," in *Toward an Anthropology of Women*, ed. Rayna R. Reiter (New York, 1975); Hermann Rebel, "Peasants against the State in the Body of Anna Maria Wagner: An Infanticide in Rural Austria in 1832," *Journal of Historical Sociology* 6 (March 1993): 15–27.

2. Although all "racial" terminologies are fictive, thus provisional, I use the term "Black" because it was used in the historical sources and because it is the term of choice both among current British scholars and within Britain's contemporary Black movement. The anachronism "coloured" sometimes offends, while the typologized and reified dichotomy between "Asians" and other people of color is an artifact of late twentieth-century politics, meaningless in the period examined here. I capitalize "Black" to stress its categorical rather than descriptive function, while I refrain from capitalizing "white" because the term describes an equally diverse population whose composition has yet to be

tigating the conditions of Black and white women's lives in Britain's interracial neighborhoods not only shows how imperial race, class, and gender imperatives converged to constrain them but suggests that by transgressing racial boundaries women could strengthen as easily as fragment social solidarities, belying the rhetoric that defamed them. It also illustrates the interdependence of racism, classism, and sexism in upholding the imperial system, and the genuine threat these women posed by refusing to conform.

Early twentieth-century observers frequently attributed racial conflict to sexual competition—competition among Black and white men for white women. The *Daily Mail* of June 13, 1919, under the headline "Black Men and White Girls," reported a "race feud in Cardiff between the white population and the blacks" caused by "hostility towards the blacks mainly because of their association with white girls and women."[3] The *Western Mail* titillated readers with images of race and gender disorder, alleging the recently paid-off Black seaman ashore would "proceed to spend money freely in arraying himself in the 'swankiest' garb he could obtain. Then, with a flashily dressed white girl, it was his delight to parade the streets and visit houses of entertainment."[4] But in the eyes of the press, police, and other observers, Black men were less culpable than imprudent white women—"the Dulcineas of Liverpool and Cardiff," who exacerbated "primordial" "racial antipathy." Scolded *Reynolds Newspaper*, "A foolish woman and a Negro may easily cause a serious riot, for the white man will not put up with it."[5]

Such responses reflected a common view of women and of racial or

---

satisfactorily established. Although racial differences can be attributed at least in part to the Manichean dichotomies ubiquitous in modern Western culture, it is insufficient to say that "Black" is merely "nonwhite" and that "white" is merely "nonblack." On efforts to define "white" as a racial or ethnic category, see Ann L. Stoler, "Carnal Knowledge and Imperial Power: Gender, Race, and Morality in Colonial Asia," in *Gender at the Crossroads of Knowledge: Feminist Anthropology in the Postmodern Era*, ed. Micaela di Leonardo (Berkeley, 1991), esp. pp. 52–53; Paul Gilroy, "*There Ain't No Black in the Union Jack": The Cultural Politics of Race and Nation* (Chicago, 1991), pp. 122–23.

3. Clipping in Public Record Office (PRO), London, Home Office file HO45/11017/377969. Pending thorough historical treatment, the most suggestive discussion of the 1919 "race" riots that prompted these remarks is Roy May and Robin Cohen, "The Interaction between Race and Colonialism: A Case Study of the Liverpool Race Riots of 1919," *Race and Class* 14, no. 2 (1974): 111–26. Also see Peter Fryer, *Staying Power: The History of Black People in Britain* (London, 1984), pp. 299–316; Jacqueline Jenkinson, "The 1919 Riots," in *Racial Violence in Britain, 1840–1950*, ed. Panikos Panayi (Leicester, 1993), pp. 92–111; and the relevant Home Office file, cited above.

4. Clipping, June 13, 1919, PRO, HO45/11017/377969.

5. *Syren and Shipping* (maritime journal), June 18, 1919, p. 1055; Chief Constable of Liverpool to Home Office, June 1919; *Reynolds Newspaper*, June 22, 1919, both clippings in PRO, HO45/11017/377969.

cultural "others" as disruptive to the solidarity of an otherwise homogeneous and unproblematically unified society. Journalists, social workers, employers, and civil authorities denounced white women who married Black workingmen as deviant, overlooked Black women, and deprecated interracial children as a social menace. Women in interracial neighborhoods were defamed as sources of racial and sexual disorder defined in class and gendered terms. In much of the literature on British race relations, similarly, if women have appeared at all, it has been as objects of contention who, when not entirely passive, acted only to aggravate "primordial" hostility between men of two mutually exclusive and ineluctably hostile racial groups.[6] Such interpretations leave unchallenged a normative view of class and national identity as uniformly white and male, in relation to which racial and gender differences appear anomalous and divisive.[7]

Reading through these hostile sources to reconstruct the daily lives of white and Black women in Britain's racially diverse seaport neighborhoods reveals that gender, race, and class identities were actually fluid and complex. Racial groups were fissured by class, gender, and age, while boundaries between racial categories were shifting, permeable, unstable, and cross-cut by gender relations and family ties. In addition, racial distinctions imported from Britain's overseas colonies reacted in unpredictable ways with domestic class and gender processes.

In Britain as in the colonies, the groups called "Black" and "white" were far from internally homogeneous, mutually exclusive, or mutually hostile. The epithet "black," or the polite term "coloured," described Africans and West Indians, South Asians, Arabs, and other colonized

6. Michael Banton described them as women "who have failed to find a satisfying role in English society," in *The Coloured Quarter: Negro Immigrants in an English City* (London, 1955), p. 13; also pp. 150–51, 170–71, 185, 228; Banton, "The Changing Position of the Negro in Britain," *Phylon* 14, no. 1 (1953): 81; James Walvin, *Black and White: The Negro in English Society, 1555–1945* (London, 1973), 206–15. Also see Fryer, *Staying Power*, pp. 302–3, 310–11; and, for a different view, Fernando Henriques, *Children of Conflict: A Study of Interracial Sex and Marriage* (New York, 1975); Sydney Collins, *Coloured Minorities in Britain: Studies in British Race Relations Based on African, West Indian and Asian Immigrants* (London, 1957). Collins's field research was completed in 1952.

7. The only recent scholar to devote much attention to interracial marriages has neglected this gendered dimension. See Paul Rich, *Race and Empire in British Politics* (Cambridge, 1986), pp. 11, 133, 135, 201–3. Instead, Rich depicts hostility to interracial children as bearers of a "half-caste pathology" as a "nakedly racist" posture anomalous within an otherwise "broad consensus" "within the governing class" characterized by "paternalism and benevolence" toward Black people in the colonies. On "the essential worker" as male and "English," see Beatrix Campbell, *Wigan Pier Revisited: Poverty and Politics in the 80s* (London, 1984), esp. pp. 3–5, 97–101; as white and male, see Michael Omi and Howard Winant, "By the Rivers of Babylon: Race in the United States," *Socialist Review* 71 (September–October 1983): 31–65.

people.[8] This diverse population shared neither physiognomy nor culture; they were united by a political and historical relationship of colonial subordination. Thus "Black" was a political status rather than a physical description: the boundary between Black and white was structured not simply by natural attributes but by power relations, changing over time and continually contested. In the course of several decades this flexible category shifted and broadened to encompass new groups.[9] Racial definitions were further complicated by racially mixed children. Examining Black and white women's experiences in Britain's interracial neighborhoods can thus enhance our understanding of how global processes of class, race, and gender formation were negotiated in the everyday lives of ordinary people.

Imperial processes both shaped the Black presence in Britain and rendered it problematic. Most Black working people in interwar Britain were to be found in seaport settlements, formed in the late nineteenth century as the merchant shipping industry began to recruit cheaper labor in the colonies.[10] A single industry but an economically, politically, and culturally critical one, the merchant navy was deeply implicated in Britain's rise to and fall from global dominance, and in the reconstitution in Britain of imperial racial hierarchies.[11]

The pejorative images of women who transgressed racial boundaries

8. For contemporary usage, see Immigration Officer S. A. Wilkes, Cardiff, to Home Office, April 1921, PRO, HO45/11897/332087/24; E. N. Cooper to Home Office, February 17, 1921, HO45/11897/332087/20; David Caradog Jones, *The Economic Status of Coloured Families in the Port of Liverpool* (Liverpool, 1940), p. 11; Reverend St. John B. Groser et al., "Conditions of Life of the Coloured Population of Stepney," PRO, Board of Trade Papers, MT9/3952, pp. 1–2. Also Satya P. Mohanty, "Drawing the Color Line: Kipling and the Culture of Colonial Rule," in *The Bounds of Race: Perspectives on Hegemony and Resistance*, ed. Dominick LaCapra (Ithaca, 1991); Tony Lane, *Grey Dawn Breaking: British Merchant Seafarers in the Late Twentieth Century* (Dover, N.H., 1986), p. 18; David Byrne, "The 1930 'Arab Riot' in South Shields: A Race Riot That Never Was," *Race and Class* 18 (1977): 265.

9. See esp. Sidney Mintz, "Groups, Group Boundaries, and the Perception of 'Race,'" *Comparative Studies in Society and History* 13 (October 1971): 437–50; Virginia Dominguez, *White by Definition: Social Classification in Creole Louisiana* (New Brunswick, N.J., 1986); Laura Tabili, "The Construction of Racial Difference in Twentieth-Century Britain: The Special Restriction (Coloured Alien Seamen) Order, 1925," *Journal of British Studies* 33 (January 1994): 54–98.

10. On the formation of Britain's Black port settlements, see esp. Kenneth Little, *Negroes in Britain: A Study of Racial Relations in English Society* (1948; London, 1972); Banton, *Coloured Quarter*; Walvin, *Black and White*; Edward Scobie, *Black Britannia: The History of Blacks in Britain* (Chicago, 1972), pp. 155–63; Fryer, *Staying Power*; Ron Ramdin, *The Making of the Black Working Class in Britain* (London, 1987).

11. On the importance of merchant shipping in the preindustrial era, see Marcus Rediker, *Between the Devil and the Deep Blue Sea: Merchant Seamen, Pirates, and the Anglo-American Maritime World, 1700–1750* (Cambridge, 1987). After industrialization the British merchant fleet continued to constitute a critical infrastructure of empire.

accompanied a maritime division of labor that reproduced colonized people's subordination aboard ship. The wage structure and the labor market in British merchant shipping were designed to take advantage of the pay differentials between Britain and the colonies. Employers hired tens of thousands of colonized seamen—approximately one-fourth of their workforce—on long-term contracts beginning and terminating in colonial ports, paying one-third to one-fifth as much as white and Black seamen who operated in the relatively free European labor market. Employers reserved the better jobs for white workers, another colonial practice. Borrowing racialized gender representation from the colonies, employers demeaned Black seamen as less than men—"natives" or "boys," physically inferior, emotionally unstable, bestially hyper-sexual—to deny them men's wages as well as masculine prerogatives such as autonomy and authority. The British state and the National Union of Seamen, Britain's major maritime union, supported these racial hierarchies through legal and contractual mechanisms such as the National Maritime Board, immigration regulation, and ruthless policing.[12]

In spite of or perhaps because of these structural inequalities and impediments, in the early decades of the twentieth century, thousands of men left ships in British ports to seek jobs under union-mandated conditions, with improved working conditions, wages, rations, shipboard quarters, and chances of surviving a voyage. Apart from the illegality of jumping ship in mid-contract, as British colonial subjects they were fully entitled to live and work in Britain. Settling in dockside neighborhoods, they formed social networks, established religious, political, and fraternal organizations and institutions, and married into local families. The largest interracial settlement, numbering several thousand, was Bute Town in Cardiff, notorious worldwide as Tiger Bay, but settlements numbering in the hundreds existed in several other ports, including Toxteth in Liverpool; Holborn in South Shields; Salford, the port of Manchester; Kingston-upon-Hull; Limehouse, Stepney, and Poplar in London; and Newport and Barry on the Bristol Channel.

Among Black as well as white seamen, seafaring was a kin- and community-based occupation.[13] In Britain's dockland neighborhoods, colonized men clustered in geographically specific enclaves, linked or

12. See, for details, Laura Tabili, *"We Ask for British Justice": Workers and Racial Difference in Late Imperial Britain* (Ithaca, 1994); for examples of relative wages see *Parliamentary Debates*, Commons, 5th ser., vol. 218 (1928), cols. 1131–32. On the widespread use of indentured and contract labor in the British colonial system, see Hugh Tinker, *A New System of Slavery: The Export of Indian Labour Overseas, 1830–1920* (London, 1974).

13. In 1932 David Caradog Jones noted that "the highest proportion of sons remaining in their father's trade [25%] is found among seamen": *The Social Survey of Merseyside* (Liverpool, 1932), 2:44.

defined by kinship, language, religion, or other bonds, and analogous to
the Little Italies or Chinatowns found in American cities. In 1932, for
example, the social investigator David Caradog Jones identified several
"racial colonies" in Liverpool's cosmopolitan dockside postal district 8,
also known as Toxteth. These included "Chinese in Pitt Street" and larger
enclaves of "negroes" in Pitt Street and Upper Canning Street; local
settlement workers reported that "Arabs and [Indian] Lascars" also lived
nearby. Social life was supported by shops, cafés, clubs, and boardinghouses run by fellow countrymen. But because Black women were scarce,
most men were compelled to seek wives among the local white population. Of 285 West African and West Indian men surveyed in Liverpool in
1919, for example, forty were married, eight to Black women. Of these
eight Black or "coloured" women, only three lived in Liverpool.[14]

Far from disruptive, Black women in small numbers and white women
in larger numbers sustained Britain's interracial settlements. The practical support of wives and families ashore was critical to men absent at sea,
and their importance was reflected in women's inclusion as nonvoting
members in the National African Firemen's and Sailors' Union, a short-
lived labor organization.[15] Wives, more likely literate in English and
conversant with British institutions and cultural practices, might assist
their husbands in public sphere activities usually reserved to men. An
example was Mrs. Mary Fazel, who wrote to the India Office on her
husband's behalf in 1925. In 1935 a defense committee composed of
"Malays, Arabs, Somalies, West Indians and Africans," formed to resist
the British Shipping Assistance Act, which effectively barred Black seamen from state-subsidized ships, boasted of "the unanimous support of
the women as well as the men." Women were also active in the ethnic
service sector, assisting in cafés, acting as shills or informal agents for
boardinghouses, and operating cafés, brothels, and other businesses.
In the 1940s Stepney's "West Indian club" was managed by a white
woman.[16]

14. Ibid., 1:82; Constance M. King and Harold King, *The Two Nations: The Life and
Work of Liverpool University Settlement and Its Associated Institutions, 1906–1937*
(London, 1938), p. 17. Also see Hoskin of the Board of Trade to Turner of the India Office,
July 23, 1923, British Library, Oriental and India Office Collections (IOC), L/E/7/1152;
Ministry of Information press release by Miss E. M. Booker, December 1941, IOC, L/I/840
462/33g; PRO, Home Office file, HO45/11017/377969.

15. See Lisa Norling, "Captain Ahab Had a Wife: Women and the Whaling Industry,
1820–1870," in Margaret Creighton and Lisa Norling, *Iron Men, Wooden Women: Gender
and Anglo-American Seafaring, 1700–1918* (Baltimore, 1995). Also see papers of the
National African Sailors' and Firemen's Union, Register of Friendly Societies, PRO, FS11/
266(1800T).

16. See letter from Mrs. Mary Fazel, September 7, 1925, IOC, L/E/9/953, f297; Collins,
Coloured Minorities in Britain, pp. 24, 54–56, 139; George W. Brown, "Investigation of
Coloured Colonial Seamen in Cardiff, April 15th–20th, 1935," *The Keys: Official Organ of
the League of Coloured Peoples* 3 (October–December 1935): 20; Groser et al., "Coloured
Population of Stepney," pp. 13, 23–24, 26.

But marriage itself brought concrete and direct benefits. Although the emotional and practical rewards of marriage were no doubt the principal incentive, marriage or cohabitation with either a Black or a white woman incidentally thwarted official efforts to preserve the geographical and economic disparities between colonizer and colonized by returning a man to the colonies. In spite of their presumptive British nationality, the authorities treated single Black men as transients, refusing to relieve them, and instead viewing applications for relief as opportunities to deport them. Some even called unmarried or undocumented Black sailors "removable men."[17]

But a man who founded a household established domicile in the United Kingdom. Households' eligibility for relief and other social services rendered him less vulnerable to employers' and immigration authorities' control. He was freed to seek work either ashore or at sea, and to bargain over the price of his labor in the same market as white seamen. In Britain he could also claim other rights, such as union membership, restricted in the colonies. Householders' implied responsibility for and control over dependents signified respectable manhood, as it legitimated claims on the state. The authorities, moreover, were reluctant to deport married men, less out of respect for the conjugal bond than out of fear that, deprived of their breadwinners, wives and children would require relief. An employer's efforts to keep West African crewmen "under control," for example, were frustrated by "the disinclination of the Home Office to insist upon the removal of men who, though without British passports, have married white women in Liverpool, or are living with white women and have children by them."[18] Marriage might also integrate a man into a local family, giving him resources when unemployed and eroding the social barriers reinforcing racial divisions at work. The investigator Nancie Hare (née Sharpe) reported to Britain's League of Coloured Peoples in 1937 that "most of the men have married women from the dock areas, people whose families have lived there for some time and usually the children of docks."[19]

17. P. N. Davies to Home Office, report of a visit to Liverpool, January 11, 1933, p. 4, PRO, MT9/2735 M.3580.
18. Quote is in Home Office to Board of Trade, January 11, 1933, PRO, MT9/2735 M.15067. Nancie Hare (née Sharpe), "The Prospects for Coloured Children in England," Keys 5 (July–September 1937): 11; Groser et al., "Coloured Population of Stepney," pp. 6, 9; Board of Trade minutes, PRO, MT9/2735 M.8521. On the British state and colonial labor movements, see Partha Sarathi Gupta, Imperialism and the British Labour Movement, 1914–1964 (New York, 1975); and comments by Sir Ernest Holderness in a meeting September 10, 1935, PRO, MT9/2735 M.15067. On the politics of state provision see Michael Savage, The Dynamics of Working Class Politics: The Labour Movement in Preston, 1880–1940 (Cambridge, 1987); T. H. Marshall, "Citizenship and Social Class," in Class, Citizenship, and Social Development: Essays by T. H. Marshall (Garden City, N.Y., 1969), esp. pp. 111–12, 117. On the correspondence among householder status, citizenship, and manhood, see Arthur Marwick, The Deluge: British Society and the First World War

Interracial settlements thus threatened to undermine the very imperial processes of racial subordination and exploitation that had formed them. Interracial couples' depiction as a problem or "pathology" reflected their subversion of the racially hierarchized labor system that underpinned the shipping industry's profitability—indeed, the imperial system. Held together by bonds of kinship and personal obligation, interracial families and settlements proved relatively impermeable by employers, the union, and the state. British maritime employers frankly pursued race segregation ashore to dampen militancy aboard ship. In the words of Captain Brett of the Shipping Federation, an employers' cartel, "The more [Black seamen] mix with Europeans, the more ambitious they become to obtain European wages and European conditions."[20] Although nearly all seafarers were men, employers and their allies recognized women in port populations as threats to shipboard racial inequalities. Since marriage with either a Black or a white woman conferred relative immunity to official actions, the authorities not surprisingly frowned on Black men's relations with local women. In 1933 the immigration officer P. N. Davies commented in frustration: "Unless the men are held in prison, several would set about establishing domicile by formal and informal marriages." Officials reinforced overt constraints with gendered and racialized imagery stressing the perils of interracial marriage. In January 1926, for example, the Liverpool immigration officer E. N. Cooper reported that his colleague "Mr. Fudge, who has now acquired a very intimate knowledge of the native mind [sic], assures me that the height of ambition of the native West African is to get a white woman, preferably with children, to live with him and to qualify for the dole. These women are generally prostitutes of a very low type."[21] As references to

(Boston, 1965), pp. 26, 97, 100; Jenny Gould, "Women's Military Services in First World War Britain," in Margaret Randolph Higonnet, Jane Jenson, Sonya Michel, and Margaret Collins Weitz, eds., *Behind the Lines: Gender and the Two World Wars* (New Haven, 1987), pp. 114–25.

19. Hare, "Prospects for Coloured Children," pp. 11–12, 25–27. On workplace hierarchies and wider social relations, see Gary S. Cross, *Immigrant Workers in Industrial France: The Making of a New Laboring Class* (Philadelphia, 1983), pp. 42–43, 224–25; Stephen Castles and Godula Kosack, *Immigrant Workers and Class Structure in Western Europe* (Oxford, 1973).

20. Captain Brett's remark recorded in minutes of a conference of shipowners' representatives at the India Office, February 22, 1923, IOC, L/E/7/1152. On joint state-employer segregation schemes, see "Lascar Accommodation in the UK," IOC, L/E/7/1152; and "Elder Dempster, 1925–1935," PRO, MT9/2735.

21. Immigration Officer P.N. Davies to Home Office, report of a visit to Liverpool, January 11, 1933, p. 4, PRO, MT9/2735 M.3580; E. N. Cooper to Home Office, January 4, 1926, HO45/12314/476761/63. On the dole vs. wages in 1937, see Jane Lewis, "Dealing with Dependency: State Practices and Social Realities, 1870–1945," in *Women's Welfare, Women's Rights*, ed. Lewis (London, 1983), p. 22.

"the native mind" suggest, hostility to interracial couples reflected not only the imperatives of imperial profitmaking but the interdependence of colonial and metropolitan race, class, and gender practices and representations.[22]

For metropolitan social relations themselves were shaped by imperial ambitions. Turn-of-the-century efforts to rehabilitate the working class by regimenting youth and exerting pronatalist pressure on women were intended to facilitate the reproduction of an "imperial race."[23] Less obviously, definitions of gender, race, and class were reconstructed in relation to one another. A redefinition of masculinity—"imperial manhood"— was grasped as the remedy for British decline, and infused with racist, jingoistic, and class-specific content. Working-class men's imputed "loafing," "irregular habits," and "hooliganism" were seen as symptoms of insufficient manhood. From the late nineteenth century through the 1940s, families were defined as "rough" rather than "respectable" if they failed to meet class-specific expectations that wives remain in the home, dependent on a skilled breadwinning husband.[24] This "rough" stereotype

22. On this interdependence, see Douglas Lorimer, *Colour, Class and the Victorians: English Attitudes to the Negro in the Mid–Nineteenth Century* (Leicester, 1978); Leonore Davidoff, "Class and Gender in Victorian England: The Diaries of Arthur J. Munby and Hannah Cullwick," *Feminist Studies* 5 (Spring 1979): 87–141; Patrick Brantlinger, "Africans and Victorians: The Geneology of the Myth of the Dark Continent," in *Race, Writing, and Difference,* ed. Henry Louis Gates Jr. (Chicago, 1987), p. 201; Joanna De Groot, " 'Sex' and 'Race': The Construction of Language and Image in the Nineteenth Century," in *Sexuality and Subordination: Interdisciplinary Studies of Gender in the Nineteenth Century,* ed. Susan Mendus and Jane Rendall (London, 1989); Frederick Cooper and Ann L. Stoler, "Tensions of Empire: Colonial Control and Visions of Rule," *American Ethnologist* 16 (November 1989): 609–21; Catherine Hall, "In the Name of Which Father?" *International Labor and Working Class History* 41 (Spring 1991): 23–28; Stoler, "Carnal Knowledge," p. 86.

23. Anna Davin, "Imperialism and Motherhood," *History Workshop Journal* 5 (Spring 1978): 9–66; John Springhall, "Building Character in the British Boy: The Attempt to Extend Christian Manliness to Working-Class Adolescents, 1880-1914," in *Manliness and Morality: Middle-Class Masculinity in Britain and America, 1800–1940,* ed. J. A. Mangan and James Walvin (Manchester, 1986), pp. 52–74; John R. Gillis, *Youth and History: Tradition and Change in European Age Relations, 1770–Present* (New York, 1974), esp. pp. 102–15; Mohanty, "Drawing the Color Line." On the Contagious Diseases Acts as a means to a "healthy imperial race" and as "imperialist compulsions turned inward toward the colonization of the poor," see Judith R. Walkowitz and Daniel J. Walkowitz, " 'We Are Not Beasts of the Field': Prostitution and the Poor in Plymouth and Southampton under the Contagious Diseases Act," in *Cleo's Consciousness Raised: New Perspectives in the History of Women,* ed. Mary Hartman and Lois Banner (New York, 1974), p. 194.

24. Michael Roper and John Tosh, eds., Introduction to *Manful Assertions: Masculinities in Britain since 1800* (London, 1991), pp. 13–14. On "imperial manhood," see Catherine Hall, "The Economy of Intellectual Prestige: Thomas Carlyle, John Stuart Mill, and the Case of Governor Eyre," *Cultural Critique* 12 (Spring 1989): 192–95; John Mackenzie, "The Imperial Pioneer and Hunter and the British Masculine Stereotype in Late Victorian and Edwardian Times," in Mangan and Walvin, *Manliness and Morality,* pp. 177, 180–82, 186; J. A. Mangan, "The Grit of Our Forefathers: Invented Traditions,

of woman as a "carnal magdalen" resonated with a longstanding albeit evolving tradition, in which all women, together with colonized and working people generally, as well as animals and the natural world, were sexualized, feared, and repressed as sources of disorder, sensuality, and pollution.[25] Conversely, colonized men were defamed as unfit for political or economic power by denial of their manhood, even their humanity, in gendered as well as racial terms: "effete," "unmanly," "sedentary . . . delicate . . . languid," "children," "savages."[26] Thus class differences themselves carried racial connotations, and were gender-specific. Interracial settlements and interracial couples, by transgressing these boundaries and inverting the hierarchies, problematized and threatened the multiple inequalities on which the imperial system rested.

In the 1920s and 1930s social observers, social workers, and state officials continued to depict interracial couples as a menace. Another scholar has noted that interracial families were disparaged in the 1930s in eugenic language, in the 1940s in the language of social deviance.[27] Yet this language of pathology was also gendered. White women who married or lived with Black workingmen were denounced as unwomanly—unfit

---

Propaganda and Imperialism," in *Imperialism and Popular Culture*, ed. John Mackenzie (Manchester, 1986), esp. pp. 115, 120, 122; Mohanty, "Drawing the Color Line," pp. 335–36. On "hooliganism," see Springhall, "Building Character," pp. 54–55, 58. On "respectability," see Jane Lewis, "Sexual Divisions: Women's Work in Late Nineteenth-Century England," in *Retrieving Women's History: Changing Perceptions of the Role of Women in Politics and Society*, ed. Jay S. Kleinberg (Oxford, 1988), p. 157; Jane Lewis, "The Working-Class Wife and Mother and State Intervention, 1870–1918," in *Labour of Love: Women's Experience in Home and Family, 1850–1940*, ed. Lewis (Oxford, 1985), esp. pp. 100–101; Sonya O. Rose, *Limited Livelihoods: Gender and Class in Nineteenth-Century England* (Berkeley, 1992), esp. pp. 126–53; Elizabeth Roberts, *A Woman's Place: An Oral History of Working-Class Women, 1890–1940* (London, 1984), p. 201.

25. Davidoff, "Class and Gender"; De Groot, "'Sex' and 'Race.'" On women, sex, and nature, see Carolyn Merchant, *The Death of Nature: Women, Ecology, and the Scientific Revolution* (San Francisco, 1980); and Sherry B. Ortner, "Is Female to Male as Nature Is to Culture?" in *Woman, Culture, and Society*, ed. Michelle Rosaldo and Louise Lamphere (Stanford, 1974). On women as dangerous and carnal, see Judith Walkowitz, *Prostitution and Victorian Society: Women, Class and the State* (Cambridge, 1980), p. 128.

26. On the feminization of colonized men, see Mrinalini Sinha, "Gender and Imperialism: Colonial Policy and the Ideology of Moral Imperialism in Late Nineteenth Century Bengal," in *Changing Men: New Directions in Research on Men and Masculinity*, ed. Michael Kimmel (Beverly Hills, 1987), pp. 217–31; John Roselli, "The Self-Image of Effeteness: Physical Education and Nationalism in Nineteenth-Century Bengal," *Past and Present* 86 (February 1980): 122–23, 138–39; Patrick Brantlinger, *Rule of Darkness: British Literature and Imperialism, 1830–1914* (Ithaca, 1988), esp. pp. 181–82; Uma Chakravarti, "Whatever Happened to the Vedic *Dasi*? Orientalism, Nationalism, and a Script for the Past," in *Recasting Women: Essays in Indian Colonial History*, ed. Kumkum Sangari and Sudesh Vaid (New Brunswick, N.J., 1990), pp. 47, 49; Hall, "Economy of Intellectual Prestige," pp. 179–80, 188–89.

27. Rich, *Race and Empire*, pp. 120–44.

mothers and wanton wives—while their husbands were deprecated as less than men. These gendered images were infused with assumptions about race and class derived from colonial and metropolitan practices alike.

For in addition to jeopardizing workplace racial inequalities, white women who married Black workingmen fell afoul of dominant expectations about sexual conduct and feminine respectability. In addition to sexual probity, the promoters of an "imperial race" enjoined "maternalism" and "respectability" on women in the metropole. Definitions of "respectability" were themselves gendered and class-specific. The class-based ideal of a breadwinning husband and dependent wife and children was simply economically unfeasible for most working people. Because many workingmen earned less than an adequate wage, the conditions of working-class women's lives demanded work outside the home and other public-sphere activities, such as neighborliness, which were incompatible with middle-class definitions of respectability. Prescribed standards of proper maternal care demanded adequate nourishing food, good-quality clothing, abundant water, fuel, and soap, and other resources beyond the reach of most poor women. Observers denounced women unable to meet these unrealistic demands as "ignorant," responsible for their families' poverty; deficiencies in their maternal qualities, indeed, were blamed for the deterioration of the British racial stock, imperiling the empire.[28]

The pejorative view of interracial couples assumed the absence of

28. Davin, "Imperialism and Motherhood"; Ellen Ross, " 'Not the Sort to Sit on the Doorstep': Respectability in Pre–World War I London Neighborhoods," *International Labor and Working Class History* 27 (Spring 1985): 41; Lewis, "Working-Class Wife," pp. 100–101, 109; Walkowitz and Walkowitz, " 'Beasts of the Field,' " p. 194; Lewis, "Sexual Divisions," p. 157; Roberts, *Woman's Place*, p. 201; Rose, *Limited Livelihoods*, pp. 149–52; Maude Pember Reeves, *Round About a Pound a Week* (1913; London, 1979). In 1921 less than half of working-class families were actually subsisting on one wage. See Lewis, "Dealing with Dependency," pp. 21–23. On neighborliness, see Ellen Ross, "Fierce Questions and Taunts: Married Life in Working-Class London, 1870–1914," in *Metropolis London: Histories and Representations*, ed. David Feldman and Gareth Stedman Jones (London, 1989), pp. 245–71; Ellen Ross, "Survival Strategies: Women's Neighborhood Sharing in London before the First World War," *History Workshop Journal* 15 (Spring 1983): 4–27. As late as 1939 Margery Spring Rice deplored what she viewed as widespread maternal "ignorance": *Working-Class Wives: Their Health and Conditions* (1939; London, 1981), pp. 203–4. On European imperialism and motherhood in another context, see Gisela Bock, "Racism and Sexism in Nazi Germany: Motherhood, Compulsory Sterilization, and the State," in *When Biology Became Destiny: Women in Weimar and Nazi Germany*, ed. Renate Bridenthal, Atina Grossman, and Marion Kaplan (New York, 1984), pp. 271–96. On class-conditioned views of motherhood in other class-stratified industrial societies, see Christine Stansell, "Women, Children, and the Uses of the Streets: Class and Gender Conflicts in New York City, 1850–1860," *Feminist Studies* 8 (Summer 1982): 309–35; Linda Gordon, "Be Careful about Father . . . ," in her *Heroes of Their Own Lives: The Politics and History of Family Violence, Boston, 1880–1960* (New York, 1988).

respectable women and manly men. Black men might be seen as un-manly because they earned less than a living wage and might depend on women in other ways to negotiate the treacherous terrain of life ashore. Black men's frequent underemployment and underpayment and the lack of job prospects for interracial children were the source of interracial families' exceptional poverty. Many Black men earned even less than white workingmen, impugning their masculinity and thereby their wives' respectability, as women were compelled into waged labor and even into casual prostitution to supplement household incomes. Wives' exceptional public visibility and their families' "low standard of life" were thus due to race discrimination. Yet to many outsiders they simply constituted evidence that these women were not womanly: they were negligent mothers and wanton wives. A 1930 report on "the colour problem in Liverpool" depicted white women who went with Black men as "unreliable and of a poor type"; women "of a somewhat better type" were redeemed only if they expressed remorse for having "brought these coloured children into the world handicapped by their colour." A report on wartime Stepney depicted white women who married Black men as amoral, stupid slatterns whose fecklessness accounted for their families' problems.[29]

Even Nancie Hare, an otherwise sympathetic observer for the London-based League of Coloured Peoples, criticized white mothers for keeping their children out of school to work. "Coloured men have not the judg-ment of Englishmen concerning the white women they meet, so that a coloured man may marry a woman . . . whom he afterwards finds to have lower standards of cleanliness, general attainments, and ambitions for the children than he himself has." Yet poor white parents too often removed children from school because they needed their wages desper-ately. Hare acknowledged that since working-class wives were most often in charge of family budgets, of which their husbands remained blissfully ignorant, and also in charge of "speaking for" children with employers, this painful decision was usually theirs.[30] If there were indeed

29. M. E. Fletcher, *Report on an Investigation into the Colour Problem in Liverpool and Other Ports* (Liverpool, 1930), pp. 19–21, 23, 26, 33, 50, 53; Groser et al., "Coloured Population of Stepney." Fletcher's evidence supports conclusions different from her own. Although such investigators as Fletcher and Nancie Hare focused on the African and Afro-Caribbean population, their rhetoric and findings were consistent with the broader litera-ture, which focused on other groups as well.

30. Hare, "Prospects for Coloured Children," p. 12; Nancie Sharpe, "Cardiff's Coloured Population," *Keys* 1 (January–March 1934): 44–45, 61. Also see Laura Oren, "The Welfare of Women in Laboring Families: England, 1860–1950," in Hartman and Banner, *Clio's Consciousness Raised*, pp. 226–44; Ross, "Fierce Questions"; Sally Alexander, "Becoming a Woman in London in the 1920s and 1930s," in Feldman and Stedman Jones, *Metropolis London*, pp. 245–71.

disagreements about children's education, they may have reflected differences in orientation between upwardly mobile migrant men and their proletarian wives, "the children of docks." Mothers' fears that ambitious children might be rejected suggest their own experiences with British class relations.

An aggravating factor was the distinctive pattern of gender relations in maritime districts, which elite observers found particularly abhorrent. In the late nineteenth century "the loose sex relationships of sailor-town" had included de facto polygamy—"'sailors' women' who maintained stable relations with a series of seamen and lived with them periodically when they came into port." Vestiges of this pattern apparently persisted in some ports in the 1930s: some wives of Black men, reported the social worker Muriel Fletcher, "go to other men's houses while their own husbands are at sea." In her view, many were not professional prostitutes, but had turned to casual prostitution "in order to eke out their scanty income . . . because of the fact that they are living with a coloured man"—that is, because Black men's wages were inadequate and unreliable, and their claims on British rights and resources tenuous. But in addition, the epithet "prostitute" was often invoked spuriously to control, intimidate, or disparage women who deviated from prescribed norms—through public activity such as work outside the home, through having multiple partners, or, in this instance, simply through marrying or living with particular men.[31] When such arrangements transgressed racial boundaries, they were especially disturbing, for in Britain as in the colonies, the dominant "norm" of racial endogamy was rooted in power relations.

In the colonies, control of white women and their sexuality had become a means to enforce racial boundaries, ensuring the perpetuation of a substratum of disfranchised and superexploitable workers with no claims of kinship or solidarity on European colonizers. White women in interwar British ports too were made responsible for maintaining racial endogamy and other sexual norms, thereby safeguarding both maritime profits and imperial hierarchies.[32]

31. Walkowitz, *Prostitution in Victorian Society*, pp. 197, 199, 200, 204; Walkowitz and Walkowitz, " 'Beasts of the Field,' " pp. 193, 202, 212; Sharpe, "Cardiff's Coloured Population," p. 44; Fletcher, *Colour Problem*, pp. 19–20, 23; also Collins, *Coloured Minorities*, p. 61; Linda Mahood, "The Magdalene's Friend: Prostitution and Social Control in Glasgow, 1864–1890," *Women's Studies International Forum* 13, nos. 1–2 (1990): 49–61; Ross, "Fierce Questions." Also see Hugh Tinker, *Separate and Unequal: India and the Indians in the British Commonwealth, 1920–1950* (London, 1976), p. 261. These patterns were not confined to seafaring people. See, e.g., Lewis, "Working-Class Wife," p. 108.

32. On colonial sexual taboos, see Stoler, "Carnal Knowledge"; Amirah Inglis, *The White Women's Protection Ordinance: Sexual Anxiety and Politics in Papua* (New York, 1975); Persis Charles, "The Name of the Father: Women, Paternity, and British Rule in Nineteenth-Century Jamaica," *International Labor and Working-Class History* 41 (Spring

Perhaps this explains observers' preoccupation with interracial sexuality, reflected in views of colonized people and working-class women as pathologically hypersexual. Muriel Fletcher asserted that women became involved in interracial unions because they were already demoralized and devalued through sexual misconduct: if not prostitutes or former prostitutes, they were disgraced by illegitimate children. The men, conversely, unrestrained in the British context by "tribal discipline," became promiscuous, brutal, and "contemptuous" of women: "able to speak but little English," they shared "little but the physical bond" with their consorts. Like the Liverpool Committee for the Protection of Half-Caste Children, Fletcher stressed the at once narcotic and insatiable quality of Black men's sexual passion, which rendered white women "unable to break away," and the chief constable of Cardiff reported with disapproval that "certain women court the favour of the coloured races." A 1942 report on Stepney alleged that "the vast majority" of the white women there "have come into the district with the deliberate intention of trading on the coloured men; . . . women who, having failed to achieve real satisfaction in life, have tried to find it through sex and the easy acquisition of material things." These women were deficient in the inward and outward attributes of respectability and civility: "They have gradually lost all moral sense. Almost all of these women are below normal intelligence, and, according to officials who have dealt with them, oversexed."[33]

Thus the rhetoric that defamed women in Britain's interracial neighborhoods incorporated elements from discourses of class, race, gender, and sexuality derived from the domestic as well as the colonial experience. Mistrust of poor and working women as unreliable upholders of racial or national solidarities perhaps reflected the recognition that their stake in the imperial order was diminished by their subordinate position within it.[34] From the late nineteenth century onward, working-class women had been denounced for subverting the imperial project through their failure to attain the gendered ideals of dependent wife and domes-

---

1992): 4–22; Kenneth Ballhatchet, *Race, Sex and Class under the Raj: Imperial Attitudes and Policies and Their Critics, 1793–1905* (London, 1980); Henriques, *Children of Conflict*; Davidoff, "Class and Gender"; Sander L. Gilman, "Black Bodies, White Bodies: Toward an Iconography of Female Sexuality in Late Nineteenth-Century Art, Medicine, and Literature," in Gates, *Race, Writing, and Difference*, pp. 223–61.

33. Fletcher, *Colour Problem*, pp. 19–23, 25, 52–53; Banton, "Changing Position of the Negro"; Chief Constable Williams to Home Office, June 13, 1919, PRO, HO45/11017/377969; Groser et al., "Coloured Population of Stepney."

34. On this pattern in other contexts, see Cherrie Moraga, "From a Long Line of Vendidas: Chicanas and Feminism," in *Feminist Studies, Critical Studies*, ed. Teresa De Lauretis (Bloomington, 1986), pp. 173–90.

ticated mother, thus to bring forth an "imperial race."[35] To disrupt the racial stratification on which the empire rested, to assist colonized men in attaining the prerogatives of British manhood—the role of breadwinner and householder—and to problematize racial categories by bringing forth children who did not fit within them to place claims on the state and on British resources was to compound this failure.

Distasteful as much of this material is, it supports the prevalent view that interracial families were viewed with intense hostility and defamed in the familiar language of race, class, gender, and sexual repression. But whose view this was demands careful specification. Undermining the notion of either an endemically racist "tradition of intolerance" or a racially enlightened consensus in British society, investigation suggests there was no consensus, hostile or otherwise, toward interracial families; we find, rather, a variety of voices.[36]

Privileged white women as well as white men defamed interracial couples in class-based terms reminiscent of sometimes embittered relations between the middle-class home visitor—the much-resented "lady from the West End come to do good"—and beleaguered working-class wives and mothers. The eugenically minded Liverpool Association for the Welfare of Half-Caste Children, for example, was founded by Miss Rachel Fleming of University College Aberystwyth, and commissioned the hostile and now notorious report by Miss Muriel E. Fletcher.[37] Women were also prominent among authors of the Stepney survey, as were two Black clergymen: the Reverend E. A. Ejesa-Osora, assistant priest of St. Mary-le-Bow, and Imam S. D. Khan, Jamiab-ul-Muslimin, suggesting that racial affinities, when cross-cut by class or status difference, were no more durable than gender affinities.

Some of these investigators seemed at the same time to identify with the white wives; perhaps that is why they ignored Black women. Fletcher described them as "hopeless and embittered, resentful of approach, yet anxious to confide in someone once their confidence had been won." Yet class-specific definitions of womanly respectability prompted harsh judgments of these "fallen women." Some idea of relations between them

---

35. Davin, "Imperialism and Motherhood."

36. Paul Rich argues for an antiracist consensus "operational on the level of social attitudes" in *Race and Empire*, esp. pp. 2, 5; phenomenological cataloguing of racist practices and incidents informs the apparent "racist consensus" interpretation in Tony Kushner and Kenneth Lunn, eds., *Traditions of Intolerance: Historical Perspectives on Fascism and Race Discourse in Britain* (Manchester, 1989); and Panayi, *Racial Violence in Britain*. As Catherine Hall more convincingly asserts, "There was never one colonial discourse in England": "In the Name of Which Father?" p. 24.

37. King and King, *Two Nations*, pp. 128–29; Fletcher, *Colour Problem*. On home visitors and working-class women, see Lewis, "Working-Class Wife," pp. 111–12; Pember Reeves, *Round About a Pound a Week*, pp. 15–17.

may be gleaned from this exchange between Miss Taylor, matron of the Liverpool Settlement clinic, and a client: "A mother asked us one day for some pink wool to knit some socks so we asked how old the baby was. 'Oh no,' she said, 'they're not for my baby but for my husband.' 'Well,' we said, 'your husband won't wear pink socks; no one but a nigger would wear them.' Imagine our dismay when she said, 'He is a nigger, nurse.'" Yet even social workers and investigators, of whom we might expect homogeneity of opinion, were far from unanimous. True, Constance King of the Liverpool Settlement shared the view of "the early founders of the Settlement movement" that poverty was the result of personal defects: "essential poverty of mind, body, and spirit." But David Caradog Jones attributed poverty in Liverpool to "economic conditions and . . . the failure of nations."[38]

Greater familiarity with interracial settlements and more systematic investigation yielded more optimistic though still bleak findings. Both Nancie Hare and Caradog Jones revised their originally negative assessments after a second round of investigation. Both attributed interracial families' poverty to race discrimination against their fathers rather than deviation from prescribed gender norms. Hare attributed children's undernourishment to fathers' unemployment and "the inability of women who have been taught nothing of food value and who live in conditions that make house-keeping difficult to lay out the money they have to the best advantage." Caradog Jones reported families of Liverpool's West African firemen and greasers likely candidates for relief because the low wages and "heavy manual work" made men more likely both to "die young" and to desert.[39]

Interracial couples themselves reported that their problems stemmed not from individual race or gender pathology but from socioeconomic deprivation common to their working-class neighbors, compounded by race discrimination in the market and by the state. Black and interracial couples did face real obstacles in interwar Britain. Largely ghettoized in historically disreputable dockside neighborhoods, they paid more than white couples for cramped, inferior housing. Husbands suffered longer periods of unemployment. Their children were disadvantaged at school and in the job market. Fletcher found most Black-headed families in Liverpool living "below the poverty line," in part because the largest

38. Fletcher, *Colour Problem*, p. 23; King and King, *Two Nations*, pp. 19, 43; Caradog Jones, *Social Survey of Merseyside*, 2:381. Even Fletcher reported conflicting testimony from different local officials (pp. 47, 49).

39. Compare Caradog Jones's *Social Survey of Merseyside*, 1:75, 205; 2:102–3, 202–3, with his *Economic Status of Coloured Families*, pp. 7–8, 13–14. Hare's observation in "Prospects for Coloured Children," p. 12, echoed Pember Reeves's on Lambeth housewives two decades before, in *Round About a Pound a Week*.

employer of West Africans, the Elder Dempster Steamship Lines, systematically underpaid African seamen with state and union sanction. Cardiff authorities paid reduced relief to Black-headed households: "The excuse is made that the needs of coloured men are less."[40]

Yet these social and economic penalties were insufficient to deter intermarriage, which continued throughout the twentieth century. In contrast to lurid reports by Fletcher and the Stepney team, Nancie Hare reported interracial marriages "often quite as happy as is marriage between British people of the same standard of life." Black husbands and fathers compared favorably with white men of the same class, occupation, and district, reputedly spending more time and money on their wives and children and less in the pubs. "Race" riots in 1919 were allegedly provoked in part by consorts of Black men "boasting to the other women of the superior qualities of the negroes as compared with those of the white men." One of Hare's informants amused her by exclaiming, "I wouldn't change my husband for fifty white men!" The flexibility of racial identities, indeed, was reflected in Hare's report that many white wives identified with their husbands' social networks: "They take sides with them; they include themselves in the category 'coloured' and talk of 'we,'" and they joined social organizations such as the "Universal Negro Movement Association."[41]

Other evidence challenges expectations that interracial couples were universally shunned. The recollections of Harriet Vincent, daughter of an interracial couple who kept a seamen's boardinghouse in Edwardian Bute Town, indicate her parents were leaders and role models in Cardiff's interracial community. In the interwar years, while some interracial couples met social ostracism, others were accepted in seaport communities, living in the same houses with the wives' families, a common working-class residential pattern. Even the notoriously racist National Union of Seamen was by no means uniformly hostile to interracial marriages: in the autumn of 1930 the union's newspaper commented somewhat defensively on "the attitude . . . of toleration, and in many instances kindness" shown by "the people of South Shields towards the

40. Caradog Jones, *Economic Status of Coloured Families*, pp. 15–19; Hare, "Prospects for Coloured Children"; Sharpe, "Cardiff's Coloured Population," 44–45, 61; Fletcher, *Colour Problem*, pp. 13–15, 21, 24–25, 38–39, 48. On Elder Dempster see Laura Tabili, "Keeping the Natives under Control: The Elder Dempster Agreements and the Domestic Dimensions of Empire, 1920–1939," *International Labor and Working Class History* 44 (Fall 1993): 64–78.

41. Chief Constable of Liverpool to Home Office, June 1919, PRO, HO45/11017/377969; Hare, "Prospects for Coloured Children." The organization referred to would probably be Marcus Garvey's Universal Negro Improvement Association. Collins reported similar sentiments among Tyneside women in the 1950s, in *Coloured Minorities*, pp. 23, 54–55, 61.

Arabs," adding grudgingly that "the Arabs now resident in the district are good fathers and providers."[42]

The discrepancies among these various accounts suggest that the view of interracial couples as pathological and of white wives as women "of a very low type" was far from universal. Maritime communities formulated their own definitions of the "elusive and shifting" divide between "rough" and "respectable," only partly coincident with those of middle-class outsiders. Working people may well have had norms of sexual propriety and of race and gender order that differed from those elites promoted. In the terms of the working class as we understand them, it would be invalid categorically to apply the label "rough" to interracial families. If they were defined as "rough," we would expect to see strong links within the neighborhood, for "less respectable survival strategies were more heavily neighborhood based." Conversely, families defined as "rough" should have provoked complaints about "pub visits and public drunkenness," "apronless women," undisciplined children running "wild," and other infringements of "respectable" codes. True, Fletcher reported, "other women in the house take it in turns to look after the children on the nights on which the mother is absent." Yet schoolteachers and other observers reported children of Black fathers more warmly dressed than other local children, and Caradog Jones commented on harmonious if distant relations with white neighbors.[43]

Interracial settlements apparently applied norms similar to those found in the larger working-class community. In postwar Tyneside a woman's status in the interracial community was elevated by her "ability to organize and manage her home, and . . . the control and training of her children," and damaged by "intimacy with another man during her husband's absence, or . . . frequent visits to public houses." Mothers vetted prospective sons-in-law not merely on the basis of their race but on their relative status in the locality and community.[44] Thus there is little evidence to support elite assumptions that wives of Black men were uniformly women "of a very low type," or were so defined by

42. Paul Thompson, *The Edwardians: The Remaking of British Society* (Chicago, 1985), pp. 122–29; Hare, "Prospects for Coloured Children," pp. 11–12, 25–27; *Seaman*, October 22, 1930. On working-class residential patterns, see Ross, "'Not the Sort,'" p. 57n; Michael Anderson, *Family Structure in Nineteenth-Century Lancashire* (London, 1971); Michael Young and Peter Wilmott, *Family and Kinship in East London* (1957; London, 1977).

43. Ross, "'Not the Sort,'" pp. 39, 43, 49, 52–53; Ross, "Survival Strategies," pp. 4, 14, 18; Walkowitz, *Prostitution in Victorian Society*, pp. 192, 197, 199, 204; Fletcher, *Colour Problem*, pp. 20, 28; Caradog Jones, *Economic Status of Coloured Families*, pp. 7–8; Sharpe, "Cardiff's Coloured Population," pp. 44–45, 61.

44. Collins, *Coloured Minorities*, pp. 54, 58. On late nineteenth-century working-class community norms, see Walkowitz, *Prostitution in Victorian Society*.

their neighbors. Instead they were apparently little different from other women in these maritime neighborhoods, many of whom might have failed to attain prescribed standards of womanly respectability.

Thus the evidence suggests that white women promoted cohesion rather than division in interracial neighborhoods. In contrast to common images of disorder and pathology, women and interracial families were sources of order and stability, bridging and thereby blurring the racial boundaries dividing white and Black working people. Outsiders may have disparaged them precisely because, in offering colonized working-men the prerogatives of British manhood, they destabilized the racial inequalities supporting imperial power. Indeed, the hostile rhetoric suggests that interracial couples undermined more than racial hierarchies, for it drew on existing discourses of class, gender, and sexuality, both domestic and colonial, to impugn their manliness and womanliness. In transgressing racial boundaries, interracial couples threatened to disarrange class and gender hierarchies as well, destabilizing the multiple structures of inequality sustaining imperial power. Yet this defamation and the hostility it expressed were not universal. Rather, critics of interracial marriages may have borrowed from received race, class, and gender discourses in an effort to build a racially exclusive consensus that did not yet exist in the 1920s and 1930s, if it ever did.

But not all the women in these neighborhoods were white.[45] Outsiders focused on racially mixed couples because they threatened the race and gender barriers upholding British imperial power. For this reason, information about Black women is fragmentary and obscure. Yet Black women lived in these settlements, and, as in other racially mixed societies, Black and white men also married them when they were present. Recovering their story is critical to an accurate understanding of racial and social dynamics in Britain and in the empire.

Black women's importance to this reconstructed narrative did not inhere in their numbers, which were undoubtedly small. Their erasure from popular consciousness and historical memory, however, went hand in hand with white wives' depiction as sociopaths. Ignoring the fact that Black men also married Black or interracial women when they were available reinforced the view that interracial unions were the products of a pathological attraction between white women and Black men, rather than of the more mundane desire to establish a home and family. Restoring Black women to the historical record, then, repudiates the stress on Black and white men competing only for white women, racist in its view of Black women as less desirable and of Black men as sexually inconti-

---

45. It is not even clear that all of the foregoing applied only to white women—on this point some sources are ambiguous.

nent, and sexist in its view of white women either as agents of disruption or as passive objects of male contention.

What we discover supports the hypothesis that Black women in Britain lived out their lives subject to the triple oppressions of race, class, and gender. They shared a disadvantaged and exploited class position with their white neighbors; they shared race oppression with their families and communities; and both of these disadvantages were compounded by sex and race discrimination in the labor market, and race bias in the marriage market, to which working-class women turned to supplement their inadequate wages. These women's experiences also suggest that the boundary between Black and white could shift from generation to generation, and that Black and white working people could be as bound together by kinship as divided by race.

Women of color in interwar Britain were as ethnically disparate as their menfolk. In 1919, a partial census of African and West Indian seafarers and their families included a Jamaican and a Liverpool-born Black wife. Fletcher found many adult women who were daughters of mixed couples, and David Caradog Jones found six British-born "half-caste" women over forty-five years of age in his 1939 survey. In Stepney in 1942 the survey team enumerated twelve "coloured" women, including Malays, West Africans, and two of mixed race, including a "half-caste Indian."[46] Indeed, the most visible and well-documented women of color were the racially ambiguous daughters of interracial couples.

Like interracial marriages themselves, these children embodied a blurring of racial categories that threatened the interdependent hierarchies sustaining British imperial power. Because interwar Britain lacked the codified racial categories of the Jim Crow American South or of Nazi Germany, children who were neither Black nor white provoked disquiet. They did not fit—a prima facie problem reflected in the pejorative term "half-caste." Only in the course of growing from children to adults did their position become clear.

Social workers and other observers had difficulty locating children of interracial couples in Britain's racial hierarchy. Nancie Hare reported, "In appearance they vary from completely white to almost completely coloured. Usually the mixture of blood is obvious and noone would think most of the children were either pure Negro or pure white." Fletcher distinguished between "half-caste" women and children and "negro" women, of whom, she reported incorrectly, there were none in Liverpool. In 1939 Caradog Jones somewhat tentatively defined "coloured families" as "the families of West Africans or West Indians who marry white

46. PRO, HO45/11017/377969; Caradog Jones, *Economic Status of Coloured Families,* pp. 11, 13; Fletcher, *Colour Problem,* p. 21; Groser et al., "Coloured Population of Stepney," pp. 3, 27. Also see minutes of a conference, February 22, 1923, IOC, L/E/7/1152.

women." The Stepney report described all of the 136 children in their survey, including the 116 with white mothers, as "coloured" or "Colonial children."[47]

Observers were far from unanimous in deploring a "half-caste pathology." The Liverpool Settlement worker Constance King, to be sure, drew on eugenic and on class and race discourses, concluding, "Their mixed parentage is in the modern industrial world a handicap comparable to physical deformity." Fathers with "a lower standard of civilization" and mothers "often of a poor type," King reported, produced children "as a rule of poor stamina, physically and morally." Miss Rachel Fleming, founder of the Liverpool Association, bemoaned "adverse factors of their heredity," including "not only disharmony of physical traits but disharmony of mental characteristics."[48]

But Nancie Sharpe reported, "Children of a coloured father are usually well dressed for the area they live in." She reported, in contrast to Fletcher, that all but a small "minority" of white wives appeared genuinely fond of both their husbands and their children. The Stepney team, while denouncing white mothers as negligent harlots, acknowledged that the typical Black father "instinctively [*sic*] loves children, will spoil them . . . and do his best for them in every way." Caradog Jones found in 1939 that the mean child mortality rate for interracial families was substantially lower (at 0.2 deaths per family) than among whites (at 1.3). Caradog Jones, Hare, and Fletcher found the children bright and popular in school: several had won scholarships to "central and technical schools." Nancie Hare reported them "little different" from other neighborhood children: "They go to the same schools, their mothers are English and their upbringing is little different . . . they are gay and witty . . . often popular at school . . . and of course, in many cases, the coloured children are related to the white." The Stepney team concurred: "The years they spend at school are probably among the happiest of their lives. They have not yet become really conscious of their colour."[49]

Yet as they matured, teenagers began to meet discrimination. Scholarship students in secondary schools were snubbed by white children unaccustomed to the racial diversity common in dockland schools. Nonetheless, one Black boy became captain of his school's football squad. But, like their neighbors, few interracial couples could afford to

47. Hare, "Prospects for Coloured Children," p. 12; Fletcher, *Colour Problem*, p. 19; Caradog Jones, *Economic Status of Coloured Families*, p. 7; Groser et al., "Coloured Population of Stepney," pp. 1, 26–27. Also see King and King, *Two Nations*, pp. 128–29.

48. King and King, *Two Nations*, p. 132.

49. Sharpe, "Cardiff's Coloured Population," pp. 44–45, 61; Caradog Jones, *Economic Status of Coloured Families*, pp. 7–8, 13–14; Hare, "Prospects for Coloured Children," p. 12; Fletcher, *Colour Problem*, p. 29; Groser et al., "Coloured Population of Stepney," pp. 28–30.

keep their children in school beyond the minimum leaving age, and "once in the labour market they have to face the prejudice against colour."[50]

Caradog Jones, echoing Fletcher, asserted in 1932 that "the Anglo-negroid when grown up do not easily get work or mix with the ordinary population." George Brown, visiting Cardiff in 1935 on behalf of the League of Coloured Peoples, found "the responsible grooves of the general social order" barred to them: "Secondary education and industrial employment are practically closed to them . . . no coloured boy or girl can procure a job in any office no matter how qualified he or she may be. . . . No engineering works will employ them and apart from shipping they have no other outlet." Yet in 1934 the Liverpool Education Committee and the Juvenile Employment Bureau had concluded that "the employment position of half-castes, while . . . considerably worse than that of white children . . . was not entirely hopeless." Nancie Hare's 1937 report was also optimistic: "When they leave school . . . there is not much more immediate difficulty in finding work than among white people. Some far-sighted parents have already arranged for apprenticeship." Boys found work at sea or in other unskilled occupations, with "the additional outlet of the entertainment industry."[51]

But as gender differences intensified in the teen years, disabilities attached to womanhood compounded those of class and race in both the labor market and the marriage market, the latter so critical to working-class women's economic survival.[52] The Liverpool Association for the Welfare of Half-Caste Children reported that "the majority of Anglo-negroid girls" were unable "to secure work either in domestic service or in factories," and so perpetuated imputed social pathology and sexual disorder, evidenced in "the number of prostitutes and the number of illegitimate children, born with a definitely bad heredity and exposed to a definitely bad environment." George Brown reported that in Cardiff,

50. Hare, "Prospects for Coloured Children," pp. 12, 25; Groser et al., "Coloured Population of Stepney," p. 31; Fletcher, Colour Problem, p. 31.

51. Caradog Jones, Social Survey of Merseyside, 1:75; Brown, "Investigation," pp. 21, 23–24; King and King, Two Nations, pp. 131–32; Hare, "Prospects for Coloured Children," pp. 25–27.

52. On economic motives for working-class marriage see Sallie Westwood, All Day, Every Day: Family and Factory in the Making of Women's Lives (Urbana, 1985), pp. 103–4. For the debate about whether colonized, enslaved, or dominated Black men can exercise patriarchal power, see Hazel Carby, "White Woman, Listen!" in The Empire Strikes Back: Race and Racism in 70s Britain (London, 1982); Jacquelyn Jones, " 'My Mother Was Much of a Woman': Black Women, Work, and the Family under Slavery," Feminist Studies 8 (Summer 1982): 235–69; Suzann Lebsock, "Free Black Women and the Question of Matriarchy: Petersburg, Virginia, 1784–1820," Feminist Studies 8 (Summer 1982): 271–92; Susan A. Mann, "Slavery, Sharecropping, and Sexual Inequality," Signs 14, no. 4 (1989): 774–98.

"opposition to receiving the girls as menials in domestic service, forces them to positions where they are physically and financially exploited." Hare corroborated his observation: "There is very little work even for white girls and coloured girls find it almost impossible." While most found work in local cafés and lodging houses, a few worked as servants or in ships, and two girls were distinguished by their success in obtaining work in a local cigar factory. In wartime Stepney, too, the color bar in employment allegedly enhanced girls' "temptation to . . . drift into promiscuous living with coloured men."[53] These young women were thus handicapped not by imagined eugenic deficiencies but by the disadvantages of their class position compounded by those attached to racial difference and to womanhood.

The dearth of "respectable" work for the girls may have caused them problems in the marriage market, although on this issue the sources are wildly at odds. Although investigators in both Liverpool and Tyneside reported cases of young "half-caste" women who married white men, Sharpe reported: "Coloured girls especially are in difficulties, as . . . when the time for 'walking-out' comes, the boys of the neighbourhood will not marry them. . . . The boys have not the same difficulty, as there does not seem to be such an objection to them on the part of the white girls, and there is a bigger choice of occupation for them." Yet both Fletcher and a postwar survey found these women married very young. Fletcher attributed this finding to their poor job prospects, but Sidney Collins reported that "Anglo-coloured" wives were in high demand because of their relative scarcity, especially within the Islamic community.[54]

This discussion has been meant to suggest that considering women's position challenges the notion of race and gender as inevitably divisive of otherwise unproblematic class and national solidarities. Not simply aggravating conflicts among working men, white and Black women were integral to the survival of Britain's interracial seaport settlements. Black men in Britain were not transients, as outsiders portrayed them, for they had wives and kin ashore in Britain. Black men married Black women when they were available, countering colonialist myths about their lustful threats to white womanhood. Interracial neighborhoods were not enclaves of isolated socially deviant mixed couples, but were sustained by interracial kin networks in which Black and white women played a critical role.

53. King and King, *Two Nations*, p. 129; Brown, "Investigation," p. 21; Fletcher, *Colour Problem*, pp. 32–33; Hare, "Prospects for Coloured Children," p. 27; Sharpe, "Cardiff's Coloured Population," p. 44; also Caradog Jones, *Economic Status of Coloured Families*, pp. 19–20; Collins, *Coloured Minorities*, pp. 82–83; Groser et al., "Coloured Population of Stepney," p. 31.

54. Sharpe, "Cardiff's Coloured Population," p. 45; Fletcher, *Colour Problem*, p. 21; Collins, *Coloured Minorities*, pp. 25, 27, 58.

These settlements took shape in a structural context of labor market stratification and central and local state hostility, both shaped in turn by imperial imperatives. The attack on women and children in Britain's interracial neighborhoods appears to have been an effort to control and recolonize Black men, specifically the labor force of a strategic and powerful industry, by discrediting and marginalizing their families. Interracial families and settlements threatened to subvert the economic hierarchies that made imperialism profitable for influential sections of the British elite.[55] The ample material reasons for opposing interracial marriage were reinforced by notions of racial inferiority adapted from the colonial experience and by fears of physical degeneracy and gender disorder derived from British class relations. The defamation of white women and the erasure of Black women, however spurious, acknowledged women's critical role in the survival of Britain's interracial settlements. The intensity of outsiders' hostility was a measure of the threat interracial marriages posed to a particular vision and practice of domestic and imperial order.

For hostility to interracial sex relations in British seaports was far from isolated: a similar and explicitly gendered discourse of pathology appeared in European colonies during the same decades.[56] Black men's status as householders implied not only patriarchal control over white women and their sexuality but other prerogatives of British "manhood," threatening imperial race and gender hierarchies that defined colonized men as feminized, childlike, and bestial—less than men.[57] White women who married or lived with Black men were denounced as gender outlaws, contributing to imperial decline through their failure to maintain racial boundaries as well as their deviation from class-based norms of womanly respectability: they were defamed in gendered terms as bad mothers and unchaste wives. Norms of respectable manhood and womanhood were racially contingent, less because "whiteness" was a constitutive element in a static and monolithic definition of class identity—or of

55. On elite manipulation of women's availability for sexual services or other "domestic" labor, see Claudia Koonz, *Mothers in the Fatherland: Women, the Family, and Nazi Politics* (New York, 1987); Luise White, "A Colonial State and an African Petty-Bourgeoisie: Prostitution, Property, and Class Struggle in Nairobi, 1936–1940," in *Struggle for the City: Migrant Labor, Capital, and the State in Urban Africa*, ed. Frederick Cooper (London, 1983), pp. 167–194; Cynthia Enloe, *Does Khaki Become You? The Militarization of Women's Lives* (Boston, 1983). On the question of who profited from imperialism, see P. J. Cain and A. G. Hopkins, "Gentlemanly Capitalism and British Expansion Overseas," pt. 2: "The New Imperialism, 1850–1945," *Economic History Review*, 2d ser., 40, no. 1 (1987): 1–26; Lance E. Davis and Robert A. Huttenback, *Mammon and the Pursuit of Empire: The Economics of British Imperialism* (Cambridge, 1988), after J. A. Hobson, *Imperialism: A Study* (Ann Arbor, 1965).

56. Stoler, "Carnal Knowledge"; and see n. 23 above.

57. See n. 26 above.

"Britishness"—than because employers, by denying Black men a man's wage and by refusing employment to "half-caste" children, forced their wives and daughters to transgress class-based norms of womanhood by engaging in waged labor outside the home and even in casual prostitution. Slippage among discourses of womanliness, racial purity, and respectability suggests an effort to construct a rationale for racial exclusivity out of received class and gender assumptions. In addition, it reflected the recognition, in the words of Sidney Collins, that "the coloured immigrant and the prostitute [or, simply, the "unrespectable" working-class wife] share the common experience of marginality to the society."[58]

For class, race, and gender divisions and sexual control were mutually reinforcing facets of the same oppressive hierarchy. The dominant vision of race and gender order was class-specific: among their working-class families and neighbors such women found a measure of acceptance and support. Yet neither Black nor white women nor their racially mixed daughters could escape the disabilities attached to race, class, and gender that permeated interracial neighborhoods as they permeated the larger society and indeed the imperial system in which these settlements were embedded. Britain's "colour problem" was not an isolated anomaly confined to the ports: the hostile rhetoric as well as the material practices that disadvantaged interracial families and communities were shaped by intertwined race, class, and gender processes that were not marginal but integral to British society, indeed to the imperial project. Still, British race relations did not simply mirror colonial ones, but were refracted by domestic class and gender relations.

Although stigmatized as sites of gender and sexual disorder and of racial conflict, interracial families and dockside schools and neighborhoods provided temporary shelter to children of mixed race. As the experiences of British girls and women of mixed race demonstrate, kin ties could cut across racial boundaries from generation to generation, confounding reified definitions of racial difference and their attendant disabilities. Racial positioning could shift in an individual's life course, shaped by age, gender, family, and economic relations. Black and white women were critical agents in this destabilizing process. Understanding the British working class as plural, fluid, and global rather than monolithic, static, and parochial should prompt rethinking of essentialist explanations for racial conflict and disadvantage.

In the subsequent half century, as women as well as men have migrated from Britain's colonies and former colonies, gender anxiety has been displaced onto the more numerous and visible Black women in

58. Collins, *Coloured Minorities*, p. 62.

Britain. Black and interracial families and neighborhoods are still depicted as deviant, their deviance now attributed to cultural practices. The focus of gender and sexual repression has shifted, too: harassment of women who join their menfolk in Britain has taken the form of callous and humiliating "virginity testing" and more recently DNA testing. This practice, along with such others as forcing Islamic schoolgirls to bare their legs for physical training classes, suggests lingering prurience about Black families and their cultural and sexual practices.[59] The still insufficiently documented story of white and Black women in Britain's interracial neighborhoods reveals that the disabilities attached to race were not biological, hereditary, eugenic, or cultural, but instead economic, political, historical, imperial, and gendered.

59. Although heavily criticized, "culturalist" interpretations remain influential. For an early critique, see Jenny Bourne, "Cheerleaders and Ombudsmen: The Sociology of Race Relations in Britain," *Race and Class* 21, no. 4 (1980): 331–33; for a more recent one, see Gilroy, *"There Ain't No Black in the Union Jack."* On Black women, see Amrit Wilson, *Finding a Voice: Asian Women in Britain* (London, 1978), pp. 74–75; Ambalavaner Sivanandan, *A Different Hunger: Writings on Black Resistance* (London, 1982); Elspeth Huxley, *Back Street New World: A New Look at Immigrants in Britain* (London, 1964), pp. 90, 94.

III

GENDER, CLASS,
AND THE STATE

7

Protective Labor Legislation in Nineteenth-Century Britain: Gender, Class, and the Liberal State

Sonya O. Rose

Factory reform in England was a multifaceted and contentious subject of public debate that began in the second decade of the nineteenth century and continued into the twentieth.[1] At issue for Parliament was the conflict between the political economy and its doctrines of a "self-regulating economy" and "free agency," on the one hand, and an Evangelical-inspired mission to tend to the physical and moral needs of dependent persons, important to middle-class identity, on the other hand. Working people were simultaneously concerned with gaining some measure of control over their working conditions, especially their hours of labor, and staking claims on the state for social rights. Working women and children were at the center of the maelstrom of discourses about state regulation of factory labor, and legislators

An earlier version of this chapter was presented at a conference on gender and labor legislation at University of Paris VIII, June 1993, and appears in a publication of the proceedings of the conference edited by Leora Auslander and Michelle Zancarini-Fournel, *Différence des sexes et protection sociale, XIXᵉ–XXᵉ siècles* (Paris, 1995).

1. For a discussion of the complexities in one portion of this period see Robert Gray, "The Languages of Factory Reform, 1830–1850," in *The Historical Meanings of Work,* ed. Patrick Joyce (Cambridge, 1989), pp. 143–79. Gray and other historians see the debates about factory reform in the period 1830–50 as part of a larger set of discourses about the "condition of England." See, e.g., E. H. Hunt, *British Labour History, 1815–1914* (London, 1981), p. 12.

identified them as the only appropriate subjects of protective labor legislation.

Debates about proposals for factory legislation in Parliament raised general questions about the relationship of the emerging liberal state to the capitalist economy. Legislators limited the answer to such questions by focusing on the relationship between the state and working women and children. By restricting regulation to women's and children's hours of labor, the state maintained the illusion that it would not "interfere" in contractual relations while both the debates and the resulting policies positioned it in a patriarchal relationship to working women and to the working-class family. In effect the state reinforced the idea that freedom of contract rather than state regulation or collectivist principles should govern economic relations, while both its actions and the debates about factory legislation expressed the idea that not all individuals were capable of governing themselves. The discourses intended to legitimate protective labor legislation constructed women as special kinds of workers and legal subjects. Rather than being free economic agents and autonomous legal subjects, they were defined by their sexuality and fitness for domesticity, by their maternal roles, and finally by their maternal bodies. The extent to which free-market and liberal political ideals were actually put into practice in Victorian law and social policy, then, seems quite limited.[2]

There were three periods in the history of protective labor legislation. The first began in 1802 and lasted until about 1830. During this time elites concerned with the welfare of children working in factories initiated legislation. Although operatives sometimes supported these initiatives by petitioning or by staging demonstrations, they were not organized into a mass movement, and elite humanitarians pressed the issue of factory legislation. The first bill that regulated the conditions of labor in textile factories was the Health and Morals of Apprentices Act, passed in 1802. The act was intended to protect Poor Law apprentices who had been sent (largely from London) to work in the northern, rural water-powered spinning mills to relieve their local parishes of the burden of supporting them. Contemporaries considered this bill an extention of

2. For the thesis that freedom of contract and classical political economy had replaced earlier understandings of the relationship between state and economy, see Phillip S. Atiyah, *The Rise and Fall of Freedom of Contract* (Oxford, 1979). For critiques see Karen Orren, *Labor, the Law, and Liberal Development in the United States* (New York, 1991); Paul Johnson, "Class Law in Victorian England," *Past and Present* 141 (November 1993): 147–69; Richard Soderland, "The Master and Servants Acts in Mid-Victorian England," paper presented to the North American Labor History Conference, Detroit, October 1993. As Orren points out for the United States and Soderland shows for Britain, the master-and-servant laws that made workers "unfree" once they entered a contract persisted well into the period of the "liberal state" and beyond.

the Poor Law rather than an act that imposed regulations on industry, although both the impetus for the act and some of its provisions fore-shadowed later measures. Parliament passed the first factory act proper in 1819 when it set a minimum age at which children could be hired and regulated their hours of labor. A provision that would have provided for inspection of factories was deleted from the bill before it became law, and in spite of halfhearted attempts by Parliament in 1825 and 1830 to strengthen the measure, it was totally ineffective. Discussion during this period focused almost exclusively on children, and although the majority of factory workers in the early mills were female, their gender was not a particularly significant subject of contention.[3]

The second period started with the rise of the ten-hours movement, which began a concerted drive for factory reform in 1830 and ended in 1853, when the Ten Hours Bill, passed in 1847, because effective. Factory operatives championed by radical reformers and supported in Parliament by humanitarian legislators agitated for a reduction in children's hours of labor. The aim of the textile operatives, however, was to shorten the work day of everyone who worked in a textile factory, for employers kept the machines running up to sixteen hours a day. As early as 1816 a petition from operatives in a Carlisle spinning mill complained of the long hours of children's labor, but requested that Parliament "restrict the labour of children and others in the cotton mills."[4] The Lancashire cotton spinners were more direct in 1818, when they petitioned Parliament for a univer-sal ten-and-a-half-hour day, of which nine hours would be for work. Until 1841, significant voices in the campaign for shorter hours advocated restricting the hours that machinery could be worked in order to secure an enforceable reduction in the hours of labor—a measure that would certainly have reduced the hours for adult workers as well as children.[5]

Until 1841, however, the rhetoric of the ten-hours movement focused on the need to regulate *children's* factory hours. Because the labor of men, women, and children was interdependent in the textile factories, if Parliament limited children's hours, there would be de facto limits on the hours of adult workers as well.

Under intense pressure, Parliament reluctantly responded in 1833 with an ineffective measure that limited the working hours of children and young persons. As a consequence the ten-hours movement increased its

3. See the evidence of a Glasgow employer in 1816 indicating that approximately 78% of the workers were females, the majority over the age of 18: House of Commons, *Sessional Papers, 1816*, vol. 3, p. 8; and the evidence from the company of Henry and Charles Hollins of the East Midlands, where approximately 61.5% of the employees were females, the majority under the age of 18: ibid., p. 422.
4. *Hansard Parliamentary Debates*, 1st ser., vol. 34 (April 26, 1816), cols. 1–2.
5. B. L. Hutchins and Anna Harrison, *A History of Factory Legislation* (London, 1907), pp. 43–44, 67.

agitation for genuine factory reform. In 1844 women's hours of work in factories were limited to the twelve hours that young persons were permitted to labor. Finally in 1847 a Ten Hours Bill for women and children was enacted, and by making it effective in 1853, Parliament established a de facto standard ten-hour day for all workers in the textile factories. Even though women were not made subject to the factory acts until the mid-1840s, gender distinctions were crucial in the reformers' rhetoric throughout the debates.

The third period began in the early 1870s, when a new movement was organized to press Parliament for a legislated nine-hour day in textile factories. After a lengthy strike by the Newcastle engineers, male workers in a host of trades secured a nine-hour day by trade union negotiation. The cotton operatives, however, were unsuccessful in their negotiations for a reduction in their hours, and so they appealed to Parliament for a legislated nine-hour day for women and children. Parliament passed a bill reducing the work week for women and children to $56\frac{1}{2}$ hours in 1874.[6] Rhetoric about motherhood was central in the 1870s debates, and when new protective measures were debated in the 1880s and 1890s, women's maternal bodies became the focus of concern.

Throughout the century employers, members of Parliament, and even some reformers remained convinced that economic actors were and should be "free agents." "Free agency" was central to the tenets of laissez-faire political economy. The idea was that workers should be free to enter into contracts with employers. Underpinning this concept was the liberal notion of the rational, autonomous individual who was capable of freely negotiating the terms under which he or she would work. Parish apprentices, whose conditions of labor in factories were the first to be regulated by legislation, were by definition not free labor. Rather they were bound to their employers, their indentures having been arranged by Poor Law administrators. Bound parish apprentices, like slaves, epitomized the contemporary understanding of workers who lacked free agency. The symbolic opposition between slavery and free labor was to remain central to debates on factory reform throughout the century.[7]

6. For a more detailed discussion of the debates concerning the nine-hour day see Sonya O. Rose, " 'From Behind the Women's Petticoats': The English Factory Act of 1874 as a Cultural Production," *Journal of Historical Sociology* 4 (March 1991): 32–51; and Sonya O. Rose, *Limited Livelihoods: Gender and Class in Nineteenth-Century England* (Berkeley, 1992), chap. 3.

7. For a discussion of the question of "freedom" as a major source of controversy in the "condition of England" debates, see Catherine Gallagher, *The Industrial Reformation of English Fiction, 1832–1867* (Chicago, 1985), pp. 3–110. For a stunning analysis of the significance of free labor to the ending of slavery in Jamaica, see Thomas C. Holt, *The Problem of Freedom: Race, Labor, and Politics in Jamaica and Britain, 1832–1838* (Baltimore and London, 1992).

The principle that adult labor should be free from government interference was continually reaffirmed in debates over factory reform. In
fact, discussions about reducing the hours of labor were preoccupied
with questions about which workers were and which were not free to
enter into labor contracts, and why. In other words, the subject of free
agency was the ground on which debates over factory reform in Parliament were conducted. Reformers had to convince legislators that women
and children, unlike men, were not free labor; they did not have free
agency.

Legislators who claimed that the state should regulate everyone's
hours, thus challenging the principle that adult male workers were
free agents, were rare.[8] The elder Sir Robert Peel, who in 1815 introduced
a measure in Parliament to limit the workday for children, reassured
his fellow legislators that "he was still an advocate of free labour,
and he wished that the principle should not be infringed on. He could
not think that little children, who had not a will of their own, could
be called free labourers. They were either under the control of a
master or a parent." Peel proposed 16 as the age at which children would
become free agents.[9] Some legislators argued that the principle of
free agency could not be abrogated, even in the case of children, because
legislation for children would be only the first step in state intervention into economic relations.[10] In the debates that led to the Factory
Act of 1819, then, legislators established what was to be fundamental to
future debates about factory reform: only if subjects could be considered
unfree or not free agents would the state protect them in economic
transactions.

One of the most powerful arguments that persuaded legislators to
abandon this principle was the issue of morality, especially sexual morality. Even before female workers became central to factory reform rhetoric—before the 1830s, that is—elite reformers who were concerned about
children working in factories focused on this issue in addition to the
children's physical health and development. Morality was a primary
consideration in the 1802 Health and Morals of Apprentices Act, as its
title suggests. Along with limiting apprentices' labor to a twelve hour day
and abolishing nightwork, it stipulated that the apprentices be given
rudimentary education and be required to attend church at least once a
month. Moreover, it mandated that employers provide the apprentices
with sexually segregated sleeping quarters.

Factory work, in fact, was singled out for state regulation in this act,
even though parish apprentices were known to be abused in other work

8. Quoted in Hutchins and Harrison, *History of Factory Legislation*, p. 110.
9. *Hansard*, 1st ser., vol. 37 (February 23, 1818), cols. 581, 582.
10. See, e.g., Lord Lascelles, ibid. (February 19, 1818), col. 560.

settings.[11] What captured humanitarian concern was the fact that
Poor Law apprentices had been sent from their places of origin and
from their families.[12] They were working in settings that lay outside of
the "natural" control and protection that was assumed to reside in
families. Employers could not always be counted upon to act in loco
parentis by providing the apprentices with religious and secular education, and with such restraints on immorality as sexually segregated living
quarters. By passing the 1802 law, the state symbolically inserted itself in
the position of father or head of the family to the apprentices, for in
liberal political theory, the family was imagined to be both patriarchal
and the source of "natural" moral order.[13] The state would assume this
position with regard to working women for related reasons some forty
years later.[14]

Women who worked in factories and mines came under scrutiny as
elite apprehensions about their immorality mounted along with developments accompanying the growth of industrial capitalism in the 1830s
and 1840s. With the rapid expansion of the factory system in the textile
industries, especially with the spread of steam-powered weaving sheds in
the cotton industry, women increasingly were employed in factories and
were paid as individuals; thus they were subject to the same relations of
production as men. In the declining domestic industries, in contrast,
women and children worked as members of their families, under the
control of their husbands and fathers. Furthermore, factory employers'
practice of hiring whole families, though never as widespread as some
scholars have maintained, had declined.[15]

Women's free agency in the economic realm, theoretically governed by
the abstract laws of the market, therefore, contradicted and threatened
the deeply entrenched view that women belonged in the "natural" realm
of the family, governed by the hierarchies of sex and age. This was the

11. See Ivy Pinchbeck and Margaret Hewitt, *Children in English Society* (London,
1969), 1:253–55.

12. E. H. Hunt, *British Labour History, 1815–1914* (London, 1981), pp. 11–12.

13. For a discussion of the family in Locke's theories, e.g., see Carole Pateman, "Feminist Critiques of the Public/Private Dichotomy," in *The Disorder of Women: Democracy,
Feminism, and Political Theory* (Stanford, 1989), pp. 118–40.

14. Victorian thought reworked this idea of the family as the source of natural moral
order by making women's domesticity the key to its functioning. Rigid sexual distinction
and women's attachment to and full engagement in the domestic sphere were central
tenets of Victorian understandings of social order. This concept of social order coexisted
with the very contradictory notions of free-market individualism.

15. The decline of family employment was a major theme of Neil Smelser's *Social
Change and the Industrial Revolution* (Chicago, 1959). Michael Anderson criticized
Smelser's ideas on the grounds that the practice of family employment in factories was
never very extensive. See Michael Anderson, "Sociological History and the Working-Class
Family: Smelser Revisited," *Social History* 3 (October 1976): 317–34, esp. 324–25.

view of women that was fundamental to Enlightenment political theory and the one that was also encoded in the common law of coverture, which had long prohibited a married woman from entering into a contract, owning property, and serving as a court witness unless she had the consent of her husband. Blackstone, who codified these principles in 1765, wrote, "Even the disabilities which the wife lies under, are for the most part intended for her protection and benefit. So great a favourite is the female sex of the laws of England."[16] The development of industrial capitalism, therefore, produced the possibility of discrepant definitions of adult women workers as legal subjects.

In addition, industrialism brought women along with men into factories to work for capitalist employers, and thus made it possible for women and men to compete for jobs. This development challenged the presumption of sexual difference, which was a cornerstone of bourgeois society and a linchpin of nineteenth-century ideas of social order.[17] Capitalist industry depended on the labor of women while at the same time it created the potential for a new female subject, one that contradicted the female subject at the heart of nineteenth-century gender ideology. Women workers, then, were anathema to laissez-faire political economy.

The specter of women living and working outside of the confines of their families stimulated deeply entrenched fears of women's unrestrained sexuality. These fears were exacerbated by the explosive growth of factory towns and cities.[18] Numerous urban and public health reformers, as well as those writing about the factory system, focused on the real or imagined autonomy of the working-class woman in conjunction with the "promiscuous mingling of the sexes" as both a social problem and a metaphor for social disorder.[19]

16. Quoted in Mary Poovey, *Uneven Developments: The Ideological Work of Gender in Mid-Victorian England* (Chicago, 1988), p. 71.

17. Mary Poovey's important analyses reveal how ideas about women's sexuality and desire were linked to beliefs about the source of social order, making sexual difference rather than class difference key to Victorian society. See esp. her analysis of W. R. Greg's tract on prostitution in "Speaking of the Body: Mid-Victorian Constructions of Female Desire," in *Body/Politics: Women and the Discourses of Science*, ed. Mary Jacobus, Evelyn Fox Keller, and Sally Shuttleworth (New York, 1990), pp. 29–46.

18. For a discussion see Elizabeth Wilson, *The Sphinx in the City: Urban Life, the Control of Disorder, and Women* (Berkeley, 1991), pp. 26–46.

19. See, e.g., James Phillips Kay Shuttleworth, *The Moral and Physical Condition of the Working Classes Employed in the Cotton Manufacture in Manchester* (1832; London, 1970); P. Gaskell, *The Manufacturing Population of England, Its Moral, Social, and Physical Conditions, and the Changes Which Have Arisen from the Use of Steam Machinery* (1833; New York, 1972); Edward Baines, *The Social, Educational, and Religious State of the Manufacturing Districts* (London, 1843); Edwin Chadwick, *Report on the Sanitary Condition of the Labouring Population of Great Britain*, ed. M. W. Flinn

The debates about factory reform in Parliament in the 1830s and 1840s were conducted in an atmosphere of intensifying social and political crisis. In 1830, spurred by Radical reformers, the operatives' ten-hours movement began to agitate in earnest for a reduction in the hours children could work in the textile factories. They continued to demand a ten-hour workday after the disappointing 1833 Factory Act was made law. Working-class men participated in tumultuous demonstrations for the suffrage in 1831 and 1832. Their purposeful exclusion from the 1832 Reform Bill, which gave property-owning, middle-class men the franchise, contributed substantially to their discontent. Fuel was added to the fires of class antagonism with the 1834 Poor Law Amendment Act, which promised draconian treatment along with poor relief for unemployed male workers. A severe economic downturn created massive unemployment, and some textile employers attempted both to deskill the work of skilled factory operatives and to hire lower-paid women to do "men's work." Chartism, the most significant mass movement of the nineteenth century, took root and flourished in this troubled climate.

As Robert Gray has suggested, anxieties about these developments created a public for the social knowledge produced in the debate on factory reform.[20] Legislators and reformers particularly homed in on the topic of sexual immorality, linking it to the adverse physical consequences of long hours of factory labor and female workers' failure to learn and practice the skills of domesticity.[21] They portrayed women's unregulated sexuality as a concern in its own right, constructing it as the cause of the social disorder sweeping the country.[22]

Although gender difference was not a stated focus of the debates in the early 1830s, both proponents and opponents of state limitation of children's working hours were preoccupied by a concern about the "peculiar" physical susceptibilities of young girls, their morals, and their fitness to be wives and mothers.[23] In hearings held by the committee that

---

(1842; London, 1965). See also Mary Poovey's analysis of writings by Chadwick in her "Domesticity and Class Formation: Chadwick's 1842 *Sanitary Report*," in *Subject to History: Ideology, Class, Gender,* ed. David Simpson (Ithaca, 1990), pp. 65–83; and her analysis of Kay Shuttleworth's pamphlet, "Curing the 'Social Body' in 1832: James Phillips Kay and the Irish in Manchester," *Gender & History* 5 (Summer 1993): 196–211.

20. Gray, "Languages of Factory Reform," p. 170.

21. For a discussion of the rhetoric of domesticity, see Marianna Valverde, "'Giving the Female a Domestic Turn': The Social, Legal, and Moral Regulation of Women's Work in British Cotton Mills, 1820–1850," *Journal of Social History* 21 (June 1988): 619–34.

22. See Joan Scott's discussion of the images of sexual disorder and the descriptions of working women by French political economists: "'L'Ouvrière! Mot impie, sordide . . . ,'" in Joyce, *Historical Meanings of Work,* pp. 119–42, esp. 128–32.

23. Gray, "Languages of Factory Reform," p. 152.

Member of Parliament Michael Sadler had formed to provide evidence to support his proposed legislation, physicians were asked specifically about and commented on girls' "particular susceptibility to injury" at the age of puberty.[24] Notably questions that Sadler asked physicians and their answers often linked the effects of factory labor on women's health to female sexuality. In response to a question Sadler posed to the physician T. H. Green concerning the phenomenon of "premature puberty" and the likelihood that "females sooner arrive at the period at which they are likely to become mothers than they otherwise would," Green responded that "the animal propensities are early developed in the mills, and very frequently before the development of those moral feelings which would restrain their indulgence." Green portrayed the mills as incubators of vice, declaring that the "reason for illicit sexual relations is the early development of the animal propensities from the high temperature of the factories, which is not sufficiently checked by the moral and religious education of the children."[25] By stressing the heat of the mills, "early puberty," and "animal propensities," Green metaphorically contrasted cool, "civilized" England and sexual order with tropical heat, savagery, and sexual licentiousness. Orators used such racialized images to stimulate sentiments of national pride.[26]

Reformers focused not only on girls' sexual morality but also on their fitness for domesticity. When Sadler asked the operative James Carpenter what he believed to be the effect "upon the morals of the females" of long hours of factory labor, Carpenter replied that "many of them have worked so very long and very hard, they turn out to be very ill in the end and the end is very awful; they have no time to learn any domestic affairs and . . . instead of being useful as a female . . . they turn out to be nothing

24. See Robert Gray, "Medical Men, Industrial Labour, and the State in Britain, 1830–50," *Social History* 26 (January 1991): 19–43. Also see the interesting assessment of medical views on women and factory legislation by Barbara Harrison, "Women's Health or Social Control? The Role of the Medical Profession in Relation to Factory Legislation in Late Nineteenth-Century Britain," *Sociology of Health and Illness* 13, no. 4 (1991): 469–91. For primary evidence see, e.g., the testimony of the surgeons Anthony Carlisle, William Blizard, and Joseph Henry Green in House of Commons, *Sessional Papers, 1831–32*, vol. 15, pp. 562, 574, 588.

25. House of Commons, *Sessional Papers, 1831–32*, vol. 15, pp. 523, 524.

26. There are numerous examples of the significance of race and national identity in the construction of social problems during this period. In arguing his case for restricting women's factory hours in 1844, for example, Lord Ashley quoted a contemporary's observation that with the increase in women's factory employment, "the county of Lancaster will speedily become a province of pigmies." Ashley added that "the toil of the females has hitherto been considered the characteristic of savage life; but we in the height of our refinement, impose on the wives and daughters of England, a burthen from which, at least during pregnancy, they would be exempted even in slave-holding states, and among the Indians of America": *Hansard*, 3d ser., vol. 78 (March 18, 1844), cols. 1099–1100. Also see Poovey, "Curing the 'Social Body' in 1832."

worth, and in consequence of that, to be worse than worth nothing."[27] The operative's suggestion that they become "ill in the end" connected the failure of factory girls to learn domestic skills with both prostitution and bodily disorder.

The cause of the ten-hours movement was aided in 1841 by a commission specifically focused on women and children who worked in the coal mines, which drew public attention to the subject of working women. Most of the witnesses were queried as to whether the men took "liberties" with the women in the pits, about the women's clothing, and about their chastity.[28] The commission's findings emphasized accounts of immorality.

Parliamentary advocates of legislation to remove women and children from the mines ignored those witnesses who countered the accusations of immorality. They made very little of the backbreaking labor assigned to collier women, and showed little concern for the fact that they continued to work through their pregnancies and often miscarried or gave birth to stillborn infants. Instead, they exploited the sensationalism in the reports to excite the moral outrage of fellow legislators. These discussions paved a path for legislation to limit women's hours in factories by providing the discursive context in which legislators could contest the notion that women were free agents and economic actors on a par with men. Legislators who pressed for government intervention in the mines and factories were aided as well by those ten-hours advocates who began to demand that women should be barred from employment altogether because they were replacing men at their work. As one Short-Time Committee member put it, this was "an inversion of the order of nature and providence—a return to the state of barbarism, in which the woman does the work while the man looks idly on."[29] Legislators' increasing fascination with working women's sexuality and their fears about gender-role reversal were provoked more by the growing social crisis during which they were debating factory and mine regulation than by the actual conditions under which women labored in the mines and factories, the conditions that legislation presumably addressed.

The years 1841 and 1842 were economically disastrous and there was massive unemployment in the factory districts. Chartist agitation and the economic duress experienced by the working classes led to strikes and disturbances that culminated in pitched battles between strikers and troops in the summer of 1842. The next year the government introduced

27. House of Commons, *Sessional Papers, 1831–32*, vol. 15, p. 152.

28. For discussions see Angela V. John, *By the Sweat of Their Brow: Women Workers at Victorian Coal Mines* (London, 1984), chaps. 1 and 2.

29. *The Ten Hours' Question: A Report Addressed to the Short-Time Committees of the West Riding of Yorkshire* (London, 1842), pp. 6–7.

a measure that became law in 1844, limiting women to a twelve-hour day, barred them from working at night, and defining them, like children, as unfree agents in the labor market. Lord Ashley, the parliamentary standard-bearer for the Ten Hours Bill, alluded to the insurrections of 1842 when he called the lawmakers' attention to the "ferocity of conduct exhibited . . . in the manufacturing towns in the disturbances . . . and the 'share born by girls and women.'" He quoted a Manchester police superintendent who said that factory women

> lose the station ordained them by Providence . . . wearing the garb of women, but actuated by the worst passions of men. The women are the leaders and exciters of the young men to violence in every riot and outbreak in the manufacturing districts, and the language they indulge in is of a horrid description. While they are themselves demoralised, they contaminate all that comes within their reach.

Social chaos, in Ashley's view, was caused by gender disorder; women were demoralized by becoming men, and they, not hunger and the absence of political rights, caused the turmoil. In his speech advocating regulation of women's hours of labor in 1844, Ashley asked the House rhetorically what possibilities for domestic life existed if women, especially married women, worked in factories. "What about the wife or mother and if she can't accomplish that which Providence has assigned her, what must be the effect on the whole surface of society?"[30] The solution to both the social problems and the social unrest sweeping the country, Ashley was implying, lay in women's domesticity. For Ashley, as well as for numerous social commentators during the period, women's domesticity was the symbolic key to "natural" social order.[31]

By passing the Ten Hours Bill in 1847, Parliament helped to diffuse class antagonisms, which had reached a peak in the early 1840s. The debates about factory reform and the significant role that the contradictory images of women played in the discourses about the factory question contributed in important ways to the fragile social harmony that was to prevail in Britain during the mid-Victorian period.

By protecting women workers, legislators resolved the tension between images of women workers implied by the silence about them in statutory labor law and images of women in the common law. At mid-century both married women and women workers were "protected" from entering contracts and were defined as nonautonomous or dependent individuals. By including working women with children under the protection of the state, legislators, attempting to dampen fears concerning

30. *Hansard*, 3d ser., vol. 78 (March 18, 1844), cols. 1097, 1092.
31. Poovey, "Domesticity and Class Formation."

both women's unregulated sexuality and general social disorder, placed the state in the position of paterfamilias vis-à-vis women in factories.

While "disordered" gender relations and sexual promiscuity seized public imagination in the debates about factory legislation in the 1830s and 1840s, the subject of women's maternal bodies was discussed but not stressed. Some debate participants remarked that women's anatomy and physiology made them particularly susceptible to injury as a result of overwork, but pregnancy, childbirth, and women's lactating bodies were not a primary focus of the rhetoric of factory reform. It took a changed social and political climate, as well as new discourses about infant health and working-class families, to make maternity per se a focus of public discussion.

The last major round of debate about hours legislation in the nineteenth century occurred when cotton textile operatives sought a legislated nine-hour day in the early 1870s. Like their forebears in the 1840s, the Factory Acts Reform Association requested a bill for the protection of women and children, knowing that their own hours also would be limited. A. J. Mundella, a member of Parliament with known sympathies for the trade union movement, introduced a nine-hour bill that was debated in 1872 and 1873. In 1874 the Tory government under Benjamin Disraeli introduced the "Factories (Health of Women etc.) Bill." It became law and restricted the working hours of women, children, and young persons employed in textile factories to $56\frac{1}{2}$ hours a week.

Supporters of these measures, like the earlier reformers, had to make the argument for reform specific to women. Legislators would not consider a bill that regulated men's hours because of the principle of free agency. Unlike their counterparts in the 1840s, legislators focused not on women generally but on married women and especially mothers. Rather than stressing women's sexual immorality, they stressed infant mortality.

Physicians had been prominent authorities in earlier commission hearings about factory legislation, and when attention to public health and sanitation increased after mid-century they assumed an even more commanding position.[32] After mid-century health officials began to detail the rates of infant mortality in working-class communities, defining infant mortality as a social problem and precipitating attention to its causes and consequences. Social science and medical journals featured articles by medical officers and other public health workers on the issue of infant deaths.[33] In 1870 the subject spilled from the pages of scientific journals

32. For an interesting discussion of the role of physicians in debates about factory reform, see Gray, "Medical Men, Industrial Labor."

33. Articles appeared in the *Transactions of the National Association for the Promotion of Social Science*, the *Journal of the Statistical Society*, and such medical journals as *Lancet*. See Mary Lyndon Shanley, *Feminism, Marriage, and the Law in Victorian England* (Princeton, 1989), p. 88.

to the popular press as coroners' inquiries became causes célèbres. Public pressure for government intervention mounted, and in 1871 Parliament debated bills aimed at curbing infant deaths, specifically identifying those women who cared for other women's babies as a major cause of infant deaths.[34] In 1872, after two years of debate, Parliament passed the Infant Life Protection Act, an ineffective measure requiring women who took in more than one child to keep a register of the children under their care.

In the same year, in response to new initiatives for factory legislation, the government appointed two physicians to investigate the effects of factory life on women and children. Drawing on and contributing to the discourse that linked working-class women and infant mortality, their report focused on the high rates of infant mortality in the factory districts, which they argued were caused by the employment of mothers. Legislators and industrialists interpreted these findings as portents of a decline in the quality of the English working population. Public concern with motherhood was increasingly linked to concerns about the quality of the race.[35] In the last quarter of the nineteenth century, motherhood became a duty that women owed not simply to their individual families but to the nation. Again women were linked to the national interest, but now the focus was not on women as sexual rebels but rather on women as mothers.

Complex and interconnected factors made women themselves the focus of the heightened attention to infant mortality, and account for the shift from morality to motherhood in these debates. Increasingly in the nineteenth century, women were identified in popular thought with their procreative capacity. As Mary Poovey has argued, this notion was fundamental to the binary opposition of sexual difference that was at the heart of Victorian society. Understandings about women's nature as being identical with their reproductive function were legitimated and widely disseminated by physicians and scientists. Women's roles as reproducers "defined their character, position and value."[36] Any activities that jeopardized that maternal identity also threatened the fundamental distinction between male and female. As Susan Kent has written, "So exclusively were women represented as 'the Sex' in the nineteenth century that any behavior on their part that deviated from the functions

34. For a discussion of this bill and the debates about infant mortality more generally see Shanley, *Feminism, Marriage, and the Law*, pp. 87–93.

35. Jane Lewis, "The Working-Class Wife and Mother and State Intervention, 1870–1918," in *Labour of Love: Women's Experience of Home and Family, 1850–1940*, ed. Lewis (London, 1986), pp. 99–120.

36. Poovey, *Uneven Developments*, p. 37. See also Susan Kingsley Kent, *Sex and Suffrage in Britain, 1860–1914* (Princeton, 1987), pp. 24–59; Ludmilla Jordanova, *Sexual Visions: Images of Gender in Science and Medicine between the Eighteenth and Twentieth Centuries* (Hemel Hempstead, 1989).

of the woman as wife and mother was denounced as 'unsexed.'"[37] Whereas women as sexual beings were perceived as threatening and represented disorder, women as mothers, defined by their domesticated bodies, conveyed safety and moral order.[38]

From mid-century on, increasingly overt challenges to coverture threatened to unhinge the symbolic equation between sexual order and social order. They began in the 1850s with the debates over both divorce law (the Matrimonial Causes Act) and married women's property.[39] Feminist challenges to women's place as it had been defined by Victorian society, as well as in the law, intensified in the 1860s and 1870s with the movement to repeal the Contagious Diseases Acts and appeals for woman suffrage. (John Stuart Mill made his famous speech to Parliament advocating the suffrage in 1867.) The first Married Woman's Property Act was passed in 1870. Bourgeois women were demanding access to higher education and to the professions. Women's rights advocates such as Millicent Fawcett, extending liberal political theory to women, argued that because women and men were fundamentally alike, women should have the same rights under the law that men had.[40] Women, in other words, were free agents. These challenges to all forms of protective legislation contributed to an increasing sensitivity on the part of legislators and others to the threat of women's autonomy.

Working-class women, meanwhile, continued to earn wages in the factories as individuals, prompting continuing expressions of concern about the propriety of their behavior. Middle-class observers delighted in remarking on "working girls'" spending habits and their love of finery, using imagery that linked them to prostitution, as Marianna Valverde has noted.[41] If they were married, they were subject to special disapprobation. Family respectability in working-class communities, as well as in the eyes of elite observers, came increasingly to be determined by whether or not a husband earned sufficient wages so that his wife could "stop at home." As Barbara Taylor has written, "The wage-earning wife, once seen as the norm in every working-class household, had become a symbol and symbol of masculine degradation."[42] Married working-

---

37. Kent, *Sex and Suffrage*, p. 41.

38. This point is made in Scott, "'L' Ouvrière!'" p. 133. Also see Kent, *Sex and Suffrage*, p. 46.

39. For discussions see Poovey, *Uneven Developments*, pp. 51–88; Shanley, *Feminism, Marriage, and the Law*, pp. 22–78.

40. For a discussion of feminist appropriation of liberal political theory see Shanley, *Feminism, Marriage, and the Law*, pp. 10–12.

41. Marianna Valverde, "The Love of Finery: Fashion and the Fallen Woman in Nineteenth-Century Discourse," *Victorian Studies* 32 (Winter 1989): 169–88.

42. Barbara Taylor, *Eve and the New Jerusalem: Socialism and Feminism in the Nineteenth Century* (London, 1983), p. 111.

class women whose husbands did not earn enough to support them, therefore, threatened the image of womanhood that equated them with their procreative capacities. Their class position, in other words, conflicted with their "natural" position. Legislators, however, consistently and systematically neglected to entertain the idea that they might alter the economic inequities that both led women to work and increased infant mortality. Instead, they blamed working-class husbands for married women's employment and argued that ultimately infant mortality was the fault of inadequate mothering and irresponsible men. A lawmaker who favored the bill said that "as far as he was concerned, he hoped and believed that the time was not far distant when working men would be ashamed to allow their wives to work in factories at all. The sooner that time arrived the better it would be for England; but until then he thought we ought to legislate in such a way as to render the evil of the present system as small as possible."[43] In this legislator's eyes, husbands controlled wives, but until they could be trusted to control them properly, the state would act in their stead to protect the women and their newborn children. Since in the view of Parliament, legitimated by scientists, married women's work in factories was the proximate cause of infant mortality, the state could be seen as taking action to fix the problem by reducing the hours of all women who worked in factories.[44]

The idea that working-class husbands were at fault was reinforced by bourgeois feminist opponents of factory legislation, especially by the Vigilance Association for the Defense of Personal Rights and for the Amendment of the Law in Points Wherein It Is Injurious to Women, which was formed in 1871 to fight the Contagious Diseases Act.[45] To many of these middle-class activists and commentators, women were responsible for domesticity, but it was men who were to blame if women could not do their motherly duties.[46]

Significant political developments also fostered this line of argument. The 1867 Reform Bill gave taxpaying working-class male householders

---

43. *Hansard*, 3d ser., vol. 221 (August 1874), col. 1547.

44. In a thoughtful essay, Barbara Harrison and Helen Mockett point out that the measures that Parliament enacted for women's health and safety were usually woefully inadequate and that factory legislation was an effort to control women while not disturbing capitalist relations of production. See their "Women in the Factory: The State and Factory Legislation in Nineteenth-Century Britain," in *The State, Private Life, and Political Change*, ed. Lynn Jamieson and Helen Corr (New York, 1990).

45. Some members of this group also were involved in campaigns against the Protection of Infants Acts. The Committee to Amend the Law in Points Wherein It Is Injurious to Women blamed infant mortality on feckless husbands, and attempted to exonerate both mothers and nurses. See Shanley, *Feminism, Marriage, and the Law*, p. 90.

46. Jane Lewis, *The Politics of Motherhood* (London, 1980), p. 100.

the suffrage. Respectability, based in important ways on a conception of manhood as equated with the role of family provider, was key to the arguments made about why certain working-class men earned the right to the vote.[47] Trade unions, headed by "respectable men" who consistently espoused the mutual interests of capital and labor, and advocated that workingmen should see that their wives "stopped at home," achieved important legislative recognition. As a consequence of these new political alignments, there was a reconfiguration of the opposition, fundamental to state formation, between "subjects—those people considered able to determine and act on their own interests, hence capable of binding themselves by contract—and nonsubjects, who were not considered responsible."[48] By blaming working-class husbands for their fecklessness and working-class women for their failure as mothers, legislators debating the Nine Hours Bill and the Health of Women etc. Bill reinforced the significance of these new divisions. By implication, they figured respectable working-class men as citizens while they extended state protection to women as mothers and their disapprobation to the husbands who could not support them. In this way the state both reasserted a patriarchal relationship with working women and maintained a paternalist relationship with their families while by implication denying any responsibility for the jeopardies of class inequality.

During the 1880s, as Angela John has detailed, proponents of restrictive legislation for women pushed to remove women even from jobs at the surface of coal mines.[49] Although they were unsuccessful in excluding women from this work, the debates about the legislation elaborated ideas about motherhood and continued to legitimate women workers' special legal status. Proponents focused on a host of issues concerning the gender boundaries that their work appeared to threaten.[50] Despite the fact that only a very small percentage of the pit brow women were married, proponents of the legislation focused on the physical effects of the work on women's procreative capacity. Whereas earlier in the century debates had focused on women's sexuality and their fitness for domestic life, and in the 1870s discourses of protection were concerned with infant mortality and women's maternal roles, during the 1880s and 1890s debates began to focus on women's responsibility for bearing future generations. Some people argued, for example, that the pit

47. For a more lengthy discussion see Sonya O. Rose, "Respectable Men, Disorderly Others: The Language of Gender and the Lancashire Weavers' Strike of 1878," *Gender & History* 5 (Autumn 1993): 382–97.

48. Poovey, *Uneven Developments*, p. 75.

49. John, *By the Sweat of Her Brow*.

50. Judy Lown, *Women and Industrialization: Gender at Work in Nineteenth-Century England* (Cambridge, 1990), p. 195.

women's constitutions would be so damaged that "puny weaklings will be the result for the succeeding generation."[51] Public concern about motherhood was increasingly being linked to concern about "the quality of the race," which fed into eugenicist concerns and the notion of imperial motherhood that developed at the turn of the century.[52]

Thus at the end of the nineteenth century, the discourse on work and motherhood focused both on women's abilities as mothers of infants and increasingly on their biological capacity to bear healthy children. These themes were elaborated in initiatives in the 1890s. A new factory act passed in 1891 included a provision that barred women from returning to work for four weeks after childbirth. This measure had been discussed before the enactment of the 1874 Factory Act but rejected as unenforceable. The clause providing for (unpaid) maternity leave was passed as a consequence of Britain's participation in the Berlin Conference of 1890, organized by the German government to create uniform laws regulating factory labor in an effort to deal with international competition. Supporters of the measure in Parliament expressed their view that the provision was not just for the sake of women but, as Lord de Ramsey put it, "for the sake of those yet unborn."[53]

Finally, debates about legislation passed in the 1890s restricting all women from working in dangerous trades focused on the effects on the babies of pregnant women who did this work.[54] Thus discussions about work and motherhood that began at the end of the nineteenth century may be seen as foreshadowing the current discourses that "disembody women," to use Barbara Duden's imagery, and instead privilege the fetus.[55]

Throughout the nineteenth century the issue of factory reform marked the boundary between incompatible ideologies: between "family values" on the one hand and market values on the other; between women as dependent, sexual, domestic, and maternal beings and women as workers and economic actors; between womanhood and class standing.[56] As Robert Gray has put it, "factory reform was . . . an important site for renegotiating some of the inherent contradictions of liberal

51. *Women Worker*, June 12, 1908, as quoted in John, *By the Sweat of Her Brow*, p. 194.

52. Jane Lewis, *Women in England, 1870–1950* (Bloomington, 1984), p. 32. On imperial motherhood, see Anna Davin, "Imperialism and Motherhood," *History Workshop* 5 (Spring 1978): 9–65.

53. *Hansard*, 3d ser., vol. 351 (July 23, 1891), col. 82.

54. Adelaide Anderson, *Women in the Factory: An Administrative Adventure, 1893–1921* (New York, 1922), p. 124.

55. See Barbara Duden, *Disembodying Women* (Cambridge, Mass., 1993). And for an excellent discussion of fetal rights and women's citizenship in the United States, see Cynthia Daniels, *At Women's Expense* (Cambridge, Mass., 1993).

56. Poovey, *Uneven Developments*, p. 12.

ideology."[57] Working women were key figures at the center of both the contradictions and their renegotiation.

Protective labor legislation for women circumscribed the purview of orthodox political economy, while at the same time the debates surrounding the legislation reinforced its primacy. These moves were crucial to the developing state because together they articulated government's limited role in ameliorating the injuries of class. Additionally, the legislation *legitimated* women's employment in factories, at the same time that it constructed men and women as different and unequal workers.[58] Finally, legislators, enhancing the nation's image of itself, constructed the state as a moral institution, portraying Britain as a land governed by bourgeois and elite humanitarians.

57. Gray, "Languages of Factory Reform," p. 178.

58. In an insightful article that focuses on some of these issues, Philippa Levine reads protective labor legislation for women and the regulation of prostitution as stemming from the same impulse to confine women to the private sphere. What united these two areas of law, she suggests, was that they defined men's difference through women's similarity. Operating with a somewhat different analytical scheme from the one employed here, she reaches a conclusion consistent with mine, that "contractarianism which underlay the laudatory evocation of the free market economy—the central pillar of economic and legal order—... breaks down when gender considerations are applied": Philippa Levine, "Consistent Contradictions: Prostitution and Protective Labour Legislation in Nineteenth-Century England," *Social History* 19 (January 1994): 17–18.

8

Social Policy, Body Politics: Recasting the Social Question in Germany, 1875–1900

Kathleen Canning

For a prolonged moment in German history the intricate links between social and sexual order, in the guise of female factory labor, became the object of national public debate for the first time. As Germany underwent its rapid second wave of industrialization during the last two decades of the nineteenth century, women's work outside of the home, especially married women's factory work and its long-term effects on the working-class family, came to constitute a new social question.

Within the expansive body of literature on the history of European welfare states, protective labor legislation has remained relatively unexamined, submerged between the dichotomized male and female streams or strands of the welfare state—the maternal and child welfare strand of poor relief and public assistance and the male stream of social insurance. Social insurance (old-age, health, disability), instituted in Germany by Bismarck during the 1880s, is generally regarded as the linchpin of the German welfare state. In seeking to solve one aspect of the social question—economic security for skilled male workers, who posed the greatest political challenge to the Bismarckian state—social insurance legislation also demarcated a male stream of welfare that extended a new kind of social citizenship to skilled male workers.[1]

---

1. See, e.g., Florian Tennstedt, *Sozialgeschichte der Sozialpolitik in Deutschland vom 18. Jahrhundert bis zum Ersten Weltkrieg* (Göttingen, 1981), pp. 139–92; Gerhard A.

Feminist historians have pointed out that the social insurance system constructed an ideal of the male breadwinner earning a family wage, thus implicitly fostering the dependence of women and children. Moreover, they point out, the systems of poor relief and public assistance served to reinforce and institutionalize women's dependent status.[2] Feminist scholars have delivered even more compelling evidence regarding the bifurcation between the male and female streams of the welfare state, analyzing the maternal/child welfare stream as the result of maternalists' interventions on behalf of women's and children's "needs," while viewing the male stream as the outcome of workers' mobilizations for expanded political rights. Protective labor laws, however, fit only uneasily into either strand of the dichotomized welfare state. As a social policy aimed almost exclusively at protecting female and underage workers at work, labor legislation disrupts the dichotomy between the two streams, for it implicitly erases the boundary between them.

Similarly, the important expansion of welfare state scholarship to encompass and compare the crucial contributions of maternalist visionaries, female social workers, and female clients as a "social and political force which demanded, brought about, influenced, and introduced" reforms has done little to interrogate or defuse the dichotomies between the streams.[3] Path-breaking comparative studies of the role of women in the rise of European welfare states, for example, have produced models and paradigms that measure the level of bourgeois women's maternalist activism against "the range and generosity of state welfare benefits for women and children." Yet this comparative exploration of the role of female agency in shaping the welfare state has led to some quite contradictory conclusions, suggesting, for example, that there was little correlation between female activism and the implementation of comprehensive social welfare programs for women. Indeed, Seth Koven and

Ritter, *Social Welfare in Germany and Britain: Origins and Development*, trans. Kim Traynor (New York, 1986), esp. chaps. 1 and 2; Heide Gerstenberger, "The Poor and the Respectable Worker: On the Introduction of Social Insurance in Germany," *Labour History* 48 (May 1985): 69–70.

2. Linda Gordon, "Social Insurance and Public Assistance: The Influence of Gender in Welfare Thought in the United States, 1890–1935," *American Historical Review* 97 (February 1992): 20–21; Linda Gordon, "The New Feminist Scholarship on the Welfare State," in *Women, the State, and Welfare*, ed. Gordon (Madison, Wis., 1990), pp. 20–22. Also see Barbara Hobson, "Feminist Strategies and Gendered Discourses in Welfare States: Married Women's Right to Work in the United States and Sweden," in *Mothers of a New World: Maternalist Politics and the Origins of Welfare States*, ed. Seth Koven and Sonya Michel (New York, 1993), p. 396.

3. Gisela Bock and Pat Thane, eds., *Maternity and Gender Policies: Women and the Rise of the European Welfare States, 1880s–1950s* (New York, 1991), p. 6; Koven and Michel, *Mothers of a New World*, "Introduction: 'Mother Worlds.'"

Sonya Michel argue convincingly that in the strongest states, defined as those with well-developed bureaucracies and long traditions of government intervention, such as Germany, women's restricted access to political space prevented them from formulating and effecting visions and programs of social welfare. Furthermore, they contend, women's movements were more likely to be effective when their causes "were taken up by male political actors pursuing other goals, such as pro-natalism or control of the labor force."[4]

The history of labor legislation in Germany between 1878 and 1914 suggests, however, that even where women lacked "bureaucratic and political power" (in France and Germany, but not in the United States, according to Koven and Michel), ideologies of gender shaped the definitions and practices of welfare and were in turn recast by state interventions and anchored by state authority.[5] In fact, the history of labor legislation and the welfare state offers an excellent illustration of how the analytical categories of women and gender might shape two distinct kinds of inquiry, of how different aspects of the welfare state become visible and are highlighted, depending on which of those categories serves as a lens. Put in the simplest terms, social policy, in which the family historically figured as the key site of intervention, sought to fix gender roles, to align the sexual division of labor with the social order, and to regulate the social body by policing female bodies, even where bourgeois feminist-maternalists were unsuccessful or inactive.

A similar critique might also apply to those feminist studies that analyze protective labor legislation in terms of its positive and negative effects on women workers, revealing, for example, that protective labor legislation adversely affected women workers across Europe by "barring them from employment without compensatory benefits."[6] Mary Lynn Stewart for example, deems "perverse" both the failure of the French state to discern the needs of women workers for labor protection and its tendency to regulate female factory labor only to prop up women's housewifely role in the patriarchal family. While it may be valid to label protective labor laws "perverse," "paternalistic," or "patriarchal," Stewart's placement of them within a fixed "paternalist tutelary complex" seems to preclude serious inquiry into the ways in which labor protection also figured as a site of contest and negotiation among and between women and men, workers and the state, the outcomes of which

4. Seth Koven and Sonya Michel, "Womanly Duties: Maternalist Politics and the Origins of Welfare States in France, Germany, Great Britain, and the U.S., 1880–1920," *American Historical Review* 95 (October 1990): 1079–80; Koven and Michel, *Mothers of a New World*, pp. 26–27.

5. Ibid., Koven and Michel, *Mothers of a New World*, p. 26.

6. Koven and Michel, "Womanly Duties," pp. 1091–92.

were contingent rather than always fixed and predictable.[7] In the work of Sonya Rose and Robert Gray on factory reform and of Mary Poovey on "the sanitary idea," for example, social reform and factory legislation figure as important sites "for renegotiating some of the inherent contradictions of liberal ideology."[8] These authors also explore the particular social publics and social knowledges produced by the discourses of factory reform in England, in particular by reformers' debates about sexual immorality and declining domesticity. In fact, in the German case, the mobilization and intervention of social reform publics mark a key difference between labor legislation on the one hand and the streams of social insurance and poor relief on the other. Unlike the social insurance laws of the 1880s, which Bismarck initiated in the absence of genuine popular demand and in collaboration with employers' associations, protective labor legislation represented the outcome of intense discursive and social mobilization around the social question of female factory labor.[9]

Finally, explicating the ways in which the female body served as a new object of intervention for both the regulatory and tutelary regimes of state social policy and industrial paternalism in Germany helps to forge intriguing links between and among the histories of the body, labor legislation, the welfare state, and the social identities of class and citizenship. Though the medicalization of state welfare formulated and legitimated individual and collective visions of *Körperlichkeit* (embodiment), most of the literature on medicalization and the welfare state has focused on social insurance as the locus of the late nineteenth-century *Homo hygienicus* or has emphasized the ways in which the system of poor relief and public assistance "coloniz[ed] and assimilat[ed] marginalized classes" through attempts to discipline the body.[10] Protective labor legis-

7. Mary Lynn Stewart, *Women, Work, and the French State: Labour Protection and Social Patriarchy, 1879–1919* (London, 1989), pp. 5–6, 12–13. For an interesting contrast to Stewart's view, see Jane Jenson, "Representations of Gender: Policies to 'Protect' Women Workers and Infants in France and the United States before 1914," in Gordon, *Women, the State, and Welfare*, pp. 152–77.

8. See Sonya O. Rose's chap. 7 in this volume; Robert Gray, "Medical Men, Industrial Labour and the State in Britain, 1830–1850," *Social History* 16 (January 1991): 19–43, and "The Languages of Factory Reform in Britain, 1830–1850," in *The Historical Meanings of Work*, ed. Patrick Joyce (Cambridge, 1989), pp. 143–79; Mary Poovey, "Domesticity and Class Formation: Chadwick's 1842 *Sanitary Report*," in *Subject to History: Ideology, Class, Gender*, ed. David Simpson (Ithaca, 1991), pp. 65–81.

9. Rüdiger Baron, "Weder Zuckerbrot noch Peitsche: Historische Konstitutionsbedingungen des Sozialstaats in Deutschland," in *Gesellschaft: Beiträge zur Marxschen Theorie* 12 (Frankfurt am Main, 1979): 15–18; Monika Breger, *Die Haltung der industriellen Unternehmer zur staatlichen Sozialpolitik in den Jahren 1878–1891* (Frankfurt am Main, 1982), pp. 37, 124, 156, 212.

10. Alfons Labisch and Reinhard Spree, eds., *Medizinische Deutungsmacht im sozialen Wandel des 19. und frühen 20. Jahrhunderts* (Bonn, 1989), p. 13; Alfons Labisch, "Gesundheitskonzepte und Medizin im Prozeß der Zivilisation," ibid., pp. 25–26.

lation has, perplexingly enough, escaped the gaze of Foucauldian critics of the welfare state, although uncovering and explicating its focus on the female body might well render it emblematic of a Foucauldian kind of "bio-politics."[11] During the late 1870s, for example, the "female organism" became the object of both moral and hygienic concern in Germany, as some reformers relied on statistics or medical diagnostics, while others recounted sensational stories of seduction and sexual abandon in the carnal underworld of the factory.[12] State legislators went to considerable lengths to ensure that protective measures would not apply to male workers, even inadvertently (say, by virtue of their employment in the same shop as women whose work was restructured by protective codes). For in their view, male breadwinners, by definition, were able to assert and defend their own interests through political association, whereas women and children, deprived of the same political rights, required the protection of the state. Indeed, as Mary Nolan argued some years ago, the incipient German welfare state, in identifying workers as objects of reform or legislation, had a crucial part in demarcating the boundaries of the working class. Specifically, protective labor legislation fixed women's place in production and anchored both class and citizenship in a particular vision of the female body, which became centrally implicated in and representative of the ills of the social body.[13]

Let us explore these links by examining labor legislation across three historical periods. After the "hungry 1840s," the social question of pauperism was gradually supplanted by the *Arbeiterfrage* (worker question) as factories began to transform urban and rural landscapes. Workers launched their first protests against factory regimes during the 1850s and 1860s. Female factory employment became an important topic in social reform circles during the 1870s, one that was discussed and debated mainly among policy makers at the level of government or in social

11. Martin Hewitt, "Bio-politics and Social Policy: Foucault's Account of Welfare," *Theory, Culture and Society* 2 no. 1 (1983): 67–84.

12. The vocabulary of "female organism" typified the discussion of women's factory labor across the political spectrum. See, e.g., Ludwig Hirt, *Die gewerbliche Thätigkeit der Frauen vom hygienischen Standpunkt aus* (Breslau, 1873), pp. 5–6; Heinrich Herkner, "Zur Kritik und Reform der deutschen Arbeiterschutzgesetzgebung," *Archiv für Soziale Gesetzgebung und Statistik*, March 1890, pp. 226–27; Johannes Wenzel, *Arbeiterschutz und Centrum mit Berücksichtigung der übrigen Parteien* (Berlin, 1893), p. 86; August Bebel, *Women under Socialism*, trans. Daniel De Leon (New York, 1971), pp. 89–90, 123–24; Clara Zetkin's article in *Die Gleichheit*, July 1897, pp. 128, 137–38. Stewart finds a similar emphasis on the female organism in French social reform: *Women, Work, and the French State*, pp. 3, 61–62.

13. Mary Nolan, "Economic Crisis, State Policy, and Working-Class Formation in Germany 1870–1900," in *Working-Class Formation: Nineteenth-Century Patterns in Western Europe and the United States*, ed. Ira Katznelson and Aristide Zolberg (Princeton, 1986), pp. 360–61.

reform associations. During the second phase, from the mid-1880s through the turn of the century, the social question of women's work exploded into a volatile public controversy for the first time in German history as reformers issued strident calls for a legal ban on married women's factory employment, prompting the emergence of new ideologies and social policies toward female factory labor. The third phase, from 1900 through 1914, was marked by attempts to resolve the debates of the 1890s as the expanded German welfare state, in its guise as mediator and regulator of labor and gender relations, assigned a new legitimacy to women's work outside the home.

THE SOCIAL QUESTION, 1848–1880

Between 1848 and 1914 the social question constituted a discursive site at which the relationship between public and private, production and reproduction, factory and family was defined, contested, and reimagined periodically. From the founding of the first social policy organization, the Central Association for the Welfare of the Working Classes, in 1844, reformers focused their attention on the family as they sought to prevent the "impending dissolution of society into two opposing and hostile classes."[14] When Wilhelm Heinrich Riehl made his ethnographic foray into "The natural history of the *Volk* as the foundation of German social policy" during the 1850s, he lamented the loss of "family consciousness" and family bonds.[15] In 1864 Gustav Schmoller, a founding member of the Verein für Sozialpolitik (Association for Social Policy) and renowned professor of politics and government, framed the "worker question" as a *sittliche Kulturfrage*, a social problem embedded in issues of morality, culture, and family, rather than one defined mainly in terms of wage inequities or working conditions.[16] Middle-class social reformers such as Schmoller, along with such Catholic reformers as Bishop Ketteler, sought to achieve not only a more equitable distribution of goods in the new

14. Rüdiger vom Bruch, "Bürgerliche Sozialreform im deutschen Kaiserreich," in *Weder Kommunismus noch Kapitalismus: Bürgerliche Sozialreform in Deutschland vom Vormärz bis zur Ära Adenauer,* ed. vom Bruch (Munich, 1985), p. 3.

15. Wilhelm Heinrich Riehl's four-volume study, *Die Naturgeschichte des Volkes als Grundlage einer deutschen Social-Politik,* was published between 1853 and 1869. Vol. 3 is on the natural history of the family.

16. Gustav Schmoller, "Die Arbeiterfrage," in *Preussische Jahrbücher* 14 (1864): 393–424, 523–47; 15 (1865): 32–63. On the meanings of *sittliche Kulturfrage,* see vom Bruch, "Bürgerliche Sozialreform," p. 67; Hans Gehrig, *Die Begründung des Prinzips der Sozialreform: Eine Literarisch-historische Untersuchung über Manchestertum und Kathedersozialismus* (Jena, 1914), pp. 140–41; Albert Müssiggang, *Die soziale Frage in der historischen Schule der deutschen Nationalökonomie* (Tübingen, 1968), pp. 133–34.

nation-state but also to repair the moral and cultural fabric of family and community, rent by industrial and urban growth, through the intervention of a *Kulturstaat* (cultural state).

The combined efforts of middle-class social reformers, the Catholic Center Party, and the Social Democratic Reichstag delegation introduced the issue of women's factory employment and protective labor legislation into the arena of high politics between 1870 and 1885. In 1875, under pressure from the Center Party and social reformers to "tell the German people about workers' conditions," the upper house of the German legislature requested that factory inspectors conduct a survey of factory working conditions to ascertain the dangers they posed to teenage and female workers' health and morality. Although this was not yet an issue of public debate, inspectors undertook a systematic inquiry of employers, local chambers of commerce, doctors, and workers themselves about the desirability and feasibility of restrictions on women's factory employment. This survey, the first official state inquiry into the conditions and effects of women's factory work, was informed by the social scientists of the Association for Social Policy. When their findings were published in 1878, the inspectors indicated that they had found no overwhelming evidence that women's work outside the home was necessarily detrimental to their families' health and welfare. The Düsseldorf inspector even asserted that working-class families were healthier then than they had been during the era of domestic textile production, because the additional earnings of wife and teenagers provided the family with better nourishment, housing, and clothing. Finally, few of the people interviewed, notably members of several workers' associations, advocated restrictions on the employment of married women in factories. The authors of the survey concluded that there was no compelling need for the state to intervene to stem the growth of the female factory workforce. Rather, the inspectors found a general consensus that the harmful effects of women's factory work could best be remedied by the renovation of factory buildings and other technical improvements, not by the imposition of legal limits on women's labor.[17] Thus in the 1870s, as Jean Quataert has pointed out, most factory inspectors and state bureaucrats "still accepted the notion that lower-class women had to work, even if this meant outside the home in factories."[18] Social reformers, however, were not so easily convinced: as a result of their continued demands for

17. Reichskanzler-Amt, *Ergebnisse der über die Frauen- und Kinderarbeit in den Fabriken auf Beschluss des Bundesraths angestellten Erhebungen, zusammengestellt im Reichskanzler-Amt* (Berlin, 1878), pp. 42, 67.

18. Jean Quataert, "A Source Analysis in German Women's History: Factory Inspectors' Reports and the Shaping of Working-Class Lives, 1878–1914," *Central European History* 16 (June 1983): 108.

government intervention, the labor code of 1878 extended legal protection to women workers for the first time, prohibiting female labor in mines and providing for three weeks of maternity leave after childbirth.[19] Even more important, perhaps, the new code reorganized the factory inspectorate and widened the scope of its surveillance to include regular inspection of all shops with more than ten employees.[20] Furthermore, working women's bodies, as carriers of the next generation, were at the center of the parliamentary debates about the revision of the labor code during the mid-1870s, as reformers decried the declining health of working women and called for urgent and expansive protection of pregnant workers.[21] At this juncture the female body came to figure as a powerful marker of the dichotomy between independent worker-citizens and workers who required protection by the state.

Although the legislative reforms of 1878 were rather modest, the first wave of protective labor legislation in Germany represents a formative moment in the history of "the social." If the social is understood in George Steinmetz's terms, as "an arena of conflicts over the reproduction of labor," which was located between the state and the "realm of markets and property relations,"[22] and if the family was at the heart of the social and the woman the heart of the family, then it is important to consider how gender inscribed the social, how women were aligned with the social, how they came under the public gaze that constituted the social and were assigned certain tasks within it from its inception.[23] Lujo Brentano's address to the Association for Social Policy in 1872 on German factory legislation suggests that this articulation of sexual difference was crucial in the formation of "the social." First, Brentano sought to differentiate between "those who genuinely require[d] protection"—women and children, who lacked the political rights to assert and defend their own needs—and male breadwinners, who were able to assert and defend their own interests through political associations. By contrast to

19. "Die Frauenarbeit als Gegenstand der Fabrikgesetzgebung, von einem Sachverständigen," *Jahrbuch für Gesetzgebung, Verwaltung und Volkswirtschaft im Deutschen Reich* (hereafter *Schmollers Jahrbuch*) 9, no. 2 (1885): 95.

20. Quataert, "Source Analysis," pp. 100–101; Franz Hitze, "Zur Vorgeschichte der deutschen Arbeiterschutzgesetzgebung," *Schmollers Jahrbuch* 22, no. 2 (1898): 377. According to Quataert, it was growing interest in lower-class women who were entering industrial and craft occupations that prompted the government to refurbish the factory inspectorate.

21. See, e.g., Hirt, *Die gewerbliche Thätigkeit der Frauen*, pp. 11–12.

22. George Steinmetz, "Workers and the Welfare State in Imperial Germany," *International Labor and Working-Class History* 40 (Fall 1991): 20–21. See also George Steinmetz, *Regulating the Social: The Welfare State and Local Politics in Imperial Germany* (Princeton, 1993), esp. chap. 3.

23. Denise Riley, *"Am I That Name?" Feminism and the Category of "Women" in History* (Minneapolis, 1988), pp. 50–51.

his laudatory view of male workers' associations, Brentano contended that women had little "capability for building coalitions." Elaborating his "ethical" objections to female unions or clubs, Brentano argued that a woman could wage successful struggle against her employer only at the price of a "hardened character." By this transformation of her character, however, she would "sacrifice the very qualities that make women a significant force in society, that foster women's moralizing influence on male workers." Ultimately, he concluded, "it would mean poisoning family and society at their very source."[24] The social, then, became a key site for the articulation of sexual difference, for the formulation of ideologies of gender that would eventually recast state social policy. Intrinsic to but not yet distinct from the broader worker question, female factory labor was defined as a social problem at the level of high politics during the 1870s. The social investigations, scholarly debates, and legislative initiatives that produced the labor code of 1878 shaped the social knowledges and the mental landscape of the social reform milieu, furnishing it with rhetorical and legislative strategies that it would continue to deploy in the reform campaigns of the 1880s.

DEBATES ABOUT FEMALE FACTORY LABOR DURING THE 1880S AND 1890S

Female factory employment and its long-term effects on the working-class family came to constitute a new social question during the last two decades of the nineteenth century, as Germany underwent its rapid second wave of industrialization. The campaigns of academic social reformers, often waged invisibly through bureaucratic channels, and the persistence of the Catholic Center Party, which had bombarded the Reichstag and the government with numerous motions concerning women and industrial working conditions during the 1880s, culminated in impassioned calls for a legal ban on married women's work outside the home during the late 1880s and early 1890s. The immediate cause of the heightened interest in and concern with the female factory worker was likely the steady and perceptible expansion of the female factory

---

24. Brentano's speech is quoted in Else Conrad, "Der Verein für Sozialpolitik und seine Wirksamkeit auf dem Gebiet der gewerblichen Arbeiterfrage" (Phil. diss., Universität Zürich, 1906), pp. 86, 88. Dieter Lindenlaub, *Richtungskämpfe im Verein für Sozialpolitik: Wissenschaft und Sozialpolitik im Kaiserreich vornehmlich vom Beginn des "Neuen Kurses" bis zum Ausbruch des Ersten Weltkrieges (1890–1914)* (Wiesbaden, 1967), p. 6; James J. Sheehan, *The Career of Lujo Brentano: A Study of Liberalism and Social Reform in Imperial Germany* (Chicago, 1966); pp. 35–44. For his views on male trade unions, see Lujo Brentano, *Die Arbeitergilden der Gegenwart* (Leipzig, 1871/72).

workforce during the last quarter of the century. As the economy boomed at the end of the century, employers faced a continuous labor shortage in nearly all industrial sectors, including the so-called women's industries—textiles, garments, cigars. Accompanying the steady influx of female workers into factories was the specter of "displacement" of male workers by women or of lowered wages and "feminization" of the factories.

The visible expansion of female factory labor had begun to challenge established definitions of masculinity and femininity and the dichotomies of male and female spheres in new and persistent ways.[25] Along with growing anxieties about Social Democracy, social discord, and imperial expansion during the 1880s and 1890s came fears about the working-class family, endangered by the expansion of the female factory workforce—children left to fend for themselves, men driven into the pubs by dirty, inhospitable living quarters in the absence of wife and mother. Reformers sought to preserve the working-class family as an anchor in a rapidly changing world, a bulwark against poverty, disorder, and decay, some by "regulating" and "protecting" women workers, others by banning them altogether from factories. The textile industry, first to mechanize and the largest factory employer of women, figured prominently in the representations of men "transformed into maidens," of women "abducted" from home and family, and of a morally dissolute and physically declining workers' estate.[26]

This new social question erupted during the late 1880s into a controversy in which the "public," both bourgeois and working class, was intricately involved. The sites of discussion and debate about the new social question spanned the arenas of high and low politics, encompassing both the sphere of governing—the Reichstag and the Prussian Ministry for Industry and Trade, for example—and that of public opinion, from the associational networks that constituted the bourgeois public sphere to the weavers' grievance committees and union locals in textile towns and mill villages across the Rhineland and Westphalia.[27] The narratives

25. Karin Hausen, "Family and Role-Division: The Polarisation of Sexual Stereotypes in the Nineteenth Century—An Aspect of the Dissociation of Work and Family Life," in *The German Family*, ed. Richard J. Evans and W. R. Lee (London, 1981), pp. 57–58. See also Claudia Honegger, *Die Ordnung der Geschlechter: Die Wissenschaften vom Menschen und das Weib* (Frankfurt, 1991).

26. Rudolf Martin, "Die Ausschliessung der verheirateten Frauen aus der Fabrik: Eine Studie an der Textilindustrie," *Zeitschrift für die gesamte Staatswissenschaft* 52 (1896): 399–400. The implication of the word "maiden" here is also that of "handmaiden" to a machine. See Robert Wilbrandt, *Die Weber in der Gegenwart: Sozialpolitische Wanderungen durch die Hausweberei und die Webfabrik* (Jena, 1906), p. 31.

27. On discourse as a social relation in a new kind of public arena see Richard Terdiman, *Discourse/Counter-Discourse: The Theory and Practice of Symbolic Resistance in Nineteenth-Century France* (Ithaca, 1985), pp. 44–46.

of danger about female factory labor were constituted across a range of statements, texts, signs, and practices: from academic lectures and scientific surveys, state inquiries and parliamentary resolutions to union brochures and feminist tracts, employers' sanctions, and even calls for strikes against the hiring of women workers.[28] They encompassed both scholarly treatises on "sexual characteristics" and scandalous revelations about the effects of women's work that stimulated popular interest in the problem: women's bodies ravaged by machines and long hours of labor, infant mortality, filth and squalor in workers' living quarters. These narratives evoked dramatic visions of social dissolution that were replete with analogies between the destruction of the social body, the body of the family, and the physical bodies of women workers and the children they bore.

Some participants spoke with a purported scientific expertise, others as victims who decried the feminization of the factory workforce and the displacement of male workers by women. Amidst the din of voices were not only prominent politicians and officials of state but also Germany's leading social thinkers and social scientists—Gustav Schmoller, Lujo Brentano, Max Weber, and Ferdinand Tönnies, to name a few—who sought, many under the auspices of the Association for Social Policy, later others through the Gesellschaft für Soziale Reform (Society for Social Reform), both to formulate pragmatic suggestions and to conduct academic, "scientific" inquiries into the social impact of industrialization.[29] However disparate their political contexts and political languages, the discourses of social reform were linked not only by "webs of cross-references" but also by a common appeal to the German state as mediator of social and industrial relations.[30] Agitation at the various "sites" formed a groundswell of social pressure that ultimately prompted the state to sanction a resolution in the form of protective labor legislation in 1890–91 and an official inquiry into married women's factory employment in 1898–99. Both were key in the articulation of a new ideology of women's work which left a lasting imprint on the policies and programs of state, employers, and labor unions.

The fact that the new social question of female factory labor came to preoccupy the public imagination between 1884 and 1894 should also be viewed as part of a growing discontent among factory inspectors, government administrators, legislators, medical doctors, and trade unions with

28. On the dispersed sites of discourse, see Judith R. Walkowitz, *City of Dreadful Delight: Narratives of Sexual Danger in Late Victorian London* (Chicago, 1992), p. 6; Peter Stallybrass and Allon White, *The Politics and Poetics of Transgression* (Ithaca, 1986), p. 194.

29. See vom Bruch, *Weder Kommunismus*, pp. 13–15, 66–71.

30. The term "webs of cross-references" is Denise Riley's, as quoted in Joan Scott, *Gender and the Politics of History* (New York, 1988), p. 141.

Bismarckian social policy. Widely admired for its unprecedented (in Europe at the time) social insurance legislation, the Bismarckian welfare state refused to intervene in or regulate the "pathogenic" aspects of the industrial workplace. A source of constant friction between chancellor and Reichstag, the parliamentary contests over labor protection reached their pinnacle between 1884 and 1890 as a majority in the Reichstag came to favor state regulation of female factory labor while Bismarck remained stubbornly impervious to the shifting groundswell of parliamentary and public opinion on the issue. By 1887, the Reichstag had assembled a large majority to pass a bill expanding protection for female and teenage workers. Despite the overwhelming consensus in the Reichstag, the upper house of the legislature rejected the bill, and its leading authority, Chancellor Otto von Bismarck, asserted that expanded protection would negatively affect both the living conditions of the workers and the profitability of German industry.[31]

Heretofore a domain of social reform expertise, debates about the worker question spilled over into the sphere of public opinion in 1889–90. In the spring of 1889 some 150,000 coal miners in the Rhine and Ruhr regions walked off their jobs after a dispute with mine owners over wages, work time, health, and safety. As the strike quickly spread to the Saar, Saxony, and Silesia, it brought to a head the growing dissension over social policy between Reichstag and government and fueled the tensions between Bismarck and the young Kaiser Wilhelm II, prompting the shift in state social policy known as the "new course" of the early 1890s.[32] The strike revealed the shortcomings of Bismarckian social policy, dramatizing its failure to ameliorate dire working conditions or to forge a bond of

31. Hans-Jörg von Berlepsch, *"Neuer Kurs" im Kaiserreich? Die Arbeiterpolitik des Freiherrn von Berlepsch 1890 bis 1896* (Bonn, 1987), pp. 13, 51–52, 143, 152, 161, 182–84. According to Berlepsch, pp. 134–37, 272–77, Bismarckian social policy remained tailored to the needs of industry. Also see Lothar Machtan and Hans-Jörg von Berlepsch, "Vorsorge oder Ausgleich—oder beides? Prinzipienfragen staatlichen Sozialpolitik im Deutschen Kaiserreich," *Zeitschrift für Sozialreform* 32 (May 1986): 266; Karl-Erich Born, *Staat und Sozialpolitik seit Bismarcks Sturz: Ein Beitrag zur Geschichte der innenpolitischen Entwicklung des deutschen Reiches, 1890–1914* (Wiesbaden, 1957), pp. 71–98; Alfred Weber, "Die Entwickelung der deutschen Arbeiterschutzgesetzgebung seit 1890," *Schmollers Jahrbuch* 21 (1897): 1145–46. On the electoral shifts between 1884 and 1887, see James J. Sheehan, *German Liberalism in the Nineteenth Century* (Chicago, 1978), pp. 214–16.

32. On the Strike, see Tennstedt, *Sozialgeschichte der Sozialpolitik*, p. 194; Jürgen Reulecke, "Stadtbürgertum und bürgerliche Sozialreform im 19. Jahrhundert in Preussen," in *Stadt und Bürgertum im 19. Jahrhundert*, ed. Lothar Gall, special issue of *Historischen Zeitschrift* 12: (1990) 194; Otto Pflanze, *Bismarck and the Development of Germany*, vol. 3: *The Period of Fortification, 1880–1898* (Princeton, 1990), pp. 327–45; Vernon L. Lidtke, *The Outlawed Party: Social Democracy in Germany, 1878–1890* (Princeton, 1966), pp. 294–95.

genuine loyalty between workers and the state.[33] The largest mass walk-out in the history of the *Kaiserreich* thus far, the strike engaged both working-class and bourgeois public opinion and left a deep impression on the young emperor, who expressed horror at the idea that the beginning of his reign might be stained "with the blood of [his] subjects."[34]

Within a few months Wilhelm and his advisers formulated a new vision of the relationship between the state and the working class: they sought to implement the paternalist, rather than repressive, apparatus of state in order to confront the social problems that had led to the massive strike. The welfare state was reshaped as Wilhelm, responding to pres-sure from the labor movement and social reform circles, placed an emi-nent social reformer, Hans Freiherr von Berlepsch, at the head of the Ministry for Industry and Trade; paved the way for lifting the ban on the Social Democratic Party; issued (the February) edicts outlining the pro-tective measures to be incorporated in the revised labor code; and called an international congress on protective measures for workers most en-dangered by industrial work, which was held in Berlin in March 1890.[35] These policy shifts marked the beginning of the "new course" in social policy, which would last until Berlepsch's firing in 1896. The Kaiser's edicts and the call to the Berlin Congress mapped out a new role for the German state as mediator of labor relations, a task that Bismarck had resolutely resisted throughout the 1880s as harmful to the competi-tive vitality of German industry in an increasingly complex world market.

The miners' strike had galvanized public opinion around social reform, drawing attention to the poor conditions of work in the mines, to the unruliness of youth and the militance of adult men, which many people linked to the alleged erosion of working women's skills as housewives and mothers. Thus, even though the strikers were overwhelmingly male, the Reichstag debates and the legislative consensus of the late 1880s about the regulation and restriction of female and youth labor framed the response of the state and of social reformers to the climate of crisis surrounding the strike.[36] Extending the purview of the German welfare state to encompass the welfare of German workers and their families, the February edicts laid the groundwork for the revision of the labor code in

33. Berlepsch, *"Neuer Kurs,"* pp. 13, 432–33. See also Rüdiger vom Bruch, "Streiks und Konfliktregelung im Urteil bürgerlicher Sozialreformer, 1872–1914," in *Streik: Zur Geschichte des Arbeitskampfes in Deutschland während der Industrialisierung,* ed. Klaus Tenfelde and Heinrich Volkmann (Munich, 1981), p. 257.

34. Kaiser Wilhelm II's speech is quoted in Berlepsch, *"Neuer Kurs,"* p. 25; Pflanze, *Bismarck,* 3: 358. See also Lidtke, *Outlawed Party,* pp. 294–95.

35. "Zur Erinnerung: Die beiden Erlässe Kaiser Wilhelm II vom 4. Februar 1890," *Soziale Praxis* 7 (October 7, 1897): 7.

36. Weber, "Die Entwickelung," pp. 1152–55.

1891 and for its further expansion in 1908. From the restoration of the German family envisioned by the Kaiser's February edicts to the consensus underpinning the programmatic demands of the international congress of March 1890, the protection of female and youth labor was the principal aim of the reforms of the new course.

While extending the scope of protection significantly beyond that of 1878, the revised labor code of 1891—one of the key outcomes of the new course—excluded women from nightwork, mandated an eleven-hour day for women workers, and expanded maternity leave from three to six weeks with the provision that women would be permitted to return to work after four weeks with a doctor's permission. Despite the long-term campaign of the Catholic Center to ban married women from factory work, the code differentiated married women and mothers from single women workers only with respect to the extra half-hour midday break "for those with households to tend to." Responding to popular sentiment that the factory had become "the source of moral ruin" for female and teenage workers, paragraph 120 prescribed the separation of the sexes at work wherever possible: on the shop floor, in cafeterias, courtyards, and washrooms.[37] As in the case of youth, the revised code sought to determine more than the mere conditions of work in the mills, drawing the household into the regulatory complex and mapping out the paths women workers traversed between the two. By extending the daily lunch break and curtailing working hours on Saturdays so women could shop and clean, the new legislation aimed not to banish women from factories but, as Jean Quataert has argued, "to give the gainfully employed woman more time in the day to learn and perform her crucial household tasks."[38] The new laws also widened the offical denotation of "trade schools" and "skill training" to include housekeeping schools for young female workers. Skill training was to provide young workers with the qualities of "order, discipline, and mental stimulation." However, while young women were to complete courses in "female handiwork and housework," young men were to receive instruction in reading, writing, arithmetic, drawing, and trade-specific subjects, such as textile weaves and mechanics.[39] In all of these respects the revised code represented a negotiated compromise between the alarmist visions of social decay conjured

37. Nordrhein-Westfälisches Hauptstaatsarchiv Düsseldorf (herafter HStAD), Landratsamt Mönchen-Gladbach 710, "Bericht des Gewerbeaufsichtsbeamten Mönchen-Gladbach vom 14.12.1874," p. 108. On para. 120 see HStAD, Jahresberichte der Königlich Preussischen Gewerberäte (hereafter JBdKPG) 1891: Düsseldorf, p. 290, and Quataert, "Source Analysis," p. 107.

38. Quataert, "Source Analysis," pp. 111–12; HStAD, JBdKPG 1892: Düsseldorf, pp. 328–30.

39. Kreisarchiv Viersen, Gemeindeamt Grefrath 1154, "Gewerbliche Fortbildungsschule, 1864–1912." Also see Marie Elisabeth Lüders, Die Fortbildung und Ausbildung der im Gewerbe tätigen weiblichen Personen und deren rechtliche Grundlage (Leipzig,

up by the rhetoric of social reform and the growing demand of mill owners, particularly in textiles, for female workers during the late 1880s and 1890s.

While the revised code of 1891 was widely touted as reform "in the interests of the community, i.e. for the health and the well-being of the whole nation," in fact it defined the social identities of class and citizen in highly gendered terms.[40] The new laws delimited the political rights of men at work, restricting some (right to quit, right to strike), augmenting others (elected workers' committees in each factory), and generally excluding men from protective measures such as restricted work hours. Thus from the social policy debates of the late 1880s, the mass strikes of 1889–90, and the legislative innovation of 1891 had emerged two distinct social questions and two different categories of citizenship: on the one hand, the state expanded protection of women, adolescents, and children at work, thereby undertaking a thorough reform of family life through intervention on their behalf in the workplace; on the other hand, it established new organs of representation through which adult male workers could assert their claims to economic and civic equality, their rights of representation, association, and expression.

After the revision of the labor code in 1891, the numbers of married women working outside the home continued to expand; they nearly doubled between 1882 and 1907, and the percentage of married women among adult female factory workers increased from 21 to 29 percent in the four years between 1895 and 1899.[41] And the calls for greater state

---

1912), pp. 22–23; Berlepsch, *"Neuer Kurs,"* pp. 243–47, Heinrich Herkner, "Der Entwurf eines Gesetzes betr. die Abänderung der Gewerbeordnung," *Archiv für Soziale Gesetzgebung und Statistik,* March 1890, p. 575. Attendance at the Fortbildungsschulen, operated by district or city governments, was voluntary until 1891, when it became mandatory in several German states for men and for both sexes in Baden, Württemberg, and Bavaria.

40. Alice Salomon, *Labour Laws for Women in Germany* (London, 1907), p. 11. Alfred Weber also pointed out that "it is the interest of the *nation* to protect the health and morality of women in particular": "Die Entwickelung," p. 1149. Also see Herkner, "Zur Kritik und zur Reform," p. 229, and *Handwörterbuch der Staatswissenschaften, 1890–94,* s.v. "Arbeiter," "Arbeiterfrage," p. 389; Gerhard A. Ritter, *Staat, Arbeiterschaft und Arbeiterbewegung in Deutschland: Vom Vormärz bis zum Ende der Weimarer Republik* (Berlin, 1980), p. 68.

41. "Married women" here includes the widowed, divorced, and separated. Between 1882 and 1907 the married female workforce grew by 90%, the single female workforce by 78%. The figures cited here are based on Stefan Bajohr, *Die Hälfte der Fabrik: Geschichte der Frauenarbeit in Deutschland* (Marburg, 1979), p. 25; Hanns Dorn, "Die Frauenerwerbsarbeit und ihre Aufgaben für die Gesetzgebung," *Archiv für Rechts- und Wirtschaftsphilosophie* 5 (1911/12): 86–87; Rose Otto, *Über die Fabrikarbeit verheirateter Frauen* (Stuttgart, 1910), p. 10; Helene Simon, *Der Anteil der Frau an der deutschen Industrie* (Jena, 1910), p. 7; Ludwig Pohle, "Die Erhebungen der Gewerbeaufsichtsbeamten über die Fabrikarbeit verheirateter Frauen," *Jahrbuch für Gesetzgebung, Verwaltung, und Volkswirtschaft* 25 (1901): 158–61.

intervention and social disciplining grew more vociferous during the 1890s, as opponents of female factory labor, inspired by the restrictions on women's labor of 1891 and by the newly awakened interest of the public in this issue, launched a renewed and more vigorous campaign for a legal ban on married women's factory employment. Fueling their campaign was the impressive array of empirical studies that reformers had conducted and compiled on household budgets, nutrition, illness, and infant mortality, which purportedly demonstrated the impact of female factory labor on working-class family life. The experts' research furnished opponents of women's factory employment with hard "scientific" evidence to back their heretofore idealistic appeals. For example, H. Mehner's article of 1886 on working-class family budgets, published in *Schmollers Jahrbuch*, calculated carefully that a married woman contributed more to the family income by staying home and managing her household efficiently than by working at a factory job.[42] According to Jean Quataert, Mehner's piece signaled a "transition" in public opinion about married women's factory employment, for it laid poverty at the doorstep of working-class wives.[43] A study conducted in the mid-1880s by Arthur Geissler, a medical doctor and government official in Saxony, determined that the infant mortality rates in textile towns, where a large percentage of married women worked in factories, exceeded those in all other Saxon districts.[44] Geissler's findings, as well as subsequent research on other textile regions, contributed to a growing sense of urgency among opponents of female factory labor that women workers must be enlightened as to the grave consequences of their double burden.

In addition to the perceptible ills of dismal living conditions and poor infant care in working-class families, opponents also associated the widespread employment of women in factories with a fundamental disintegration of social, cultural, and moral order. A highly respected economist and member of the Association for Social Policy, Heinrich Herkner, articulated this sense of disorder in his popular book *The Worker Question*, first published in 1890. Herkner first summoned visions of moral decay inside the factory itself. Citing Alfons Thun's classic study of the textile industry in the Lower Rhine, he described male and female bodies, sweaty and scantily clad, working side by side in the mills, where "during the work day the way was paved for the excesses of the night." Then

42. H. Mehner, "Der Haushalt und die Lebenshaltung einer Leipziger Arbeiterfamilie," *Schmollers Jahrbuch*, 1886, reprinted in *Seminar: Familie und Gesellschaftsstruktur*, ed. Heidi Rosenbaum (Frankfurt am Main, 1982), pp. 309–33. See also Quataert, "Source Analysis," p. 112. Certainly the publication of Mehner's piece in such a respected academic journal as *Schmollers Jahrbuch* increased its circulation and its legitimacy.

43. Quataert, "Source Analysis," pp. 112–13.

44. Geissler's apparently unpublished study is quoted in Martin, "Die Ausschliessung," pt. 2, p. 404.

Herkner addressed the implications of women's factory work for family and community, pointing to the example of England, where rising income among male workers had enabled many married women to return to the household. He aimed to show that the era of expanding married women's factory employment had left its indelible mark on English working-class family life. Here he drew upon an eyewitness report titled "How the English Worker Lives," by a German miner who had lived and worked for several years in England. Implicitly warning his readers about the consequences of the expansion of married women's work in Germany, Herkner evoked a vision of domesticity turned upside down:

> English workers' wives are often not capable of preparing an ordinary meal. What they do understand, however, is how to drink whiskey. ... It is certain that more women than men are addicted to drink. The factory workers' wives are usually drunkards. As far as morality goes, one can only imagine. Married women offer themselves for sale when they are drunk. ... Most workers' wives are too lazy to sew, even though every young girl must learn how to sew at school. An outsider, who is not familiar with the conditions and who wanders through a working-class quarter at 9 or 10 A.M., would be astonished to see that two-thirds of the women have fastened their clothes together with pins, are unwashed and uncombed.[45]

Replete with such shocking revelations and rooted firmly in scholarly methods and discourse, social reformers' accounts of working-class life stimulated popular interest in the problem of female factory labor. Others elevated the new social question to the more abstract level of women's "true nature," portraying female factory labor as irreconcilable with and destructive of the feminine character, and ultimately of the social order. In his classic *Gemeinschaft und Gesellschaft*, Ferdinand Tönnies, sociologist and member of the Association for Social Policy, gave female factory labor a leading part in his analysis of the dissolution of the *Gemeinschaft* (community) and the formation of modern *Gesellschaft* (society). Tönnies argued that "the home and not the market, their own or friend's dwelling, and not the street, is the natural seat of [women's] activity." Factory work was inherently incompatible with women's nature:

> As woman enters into the struggle of earning a living, it is evident that trading and the freedom and independence of the female factory worker

45. Heinrich Herkner, *Die Arbeiterfrage: Eine Einführung*, 4th ed. (Berlin, 1905), pp. 27, 38–40. Herkner cites Alfons Thun, *Die Industrie am Niederrhein und ihre Arbeiter* (Leipzig, 1879), 1:174, and Ernst Dückershoff, *Wie der englische Arbeiter lebt?* (Dresden, 1898), pp. 19, 32–33.

as contracting party and possessor of money will develop her rational will, enabling her to think in a calculating way, even though, in the case of factory work, the tasks themselves may not lead in this direction. The woman becomes enlightened, cold-hearted, and conscious. Nothing is more foreign and terrible to her original inborn nature, in spite of all later modifications. Possibly nothing is more characteristic and important in the process of formation of the *Gesellschaft and the destruction of Gemeinschaft*. Through this development, the 'individualism' which is the prerequisite of Gesellschaft comes into its own.[46]

Tönnies may not have intended to enter into a discourse about women's nature and women's work, but his views reappeared in the arguments of at least one key opponent of female factory labor. In 1892, Rudolf Martin, junior barrister at the district court in Crimmitschau, Saxony, undertook an independent investigation of factory and family life among married female textile workers in his vicinity, which was published in the 1896 edition of the *Zeitschrift für die gesamte Staatswissenschaft*. Martin was the first social reformer to link empirical evidence from factories and working-class neighborhoods with theoretical constructs about women's nature. His article represents a critical juncture in the history of the discourse on women's work, for it shifted the emphasis from protective measures for women workers toward consideration of a legal ban on married women's factory employment. Following Tönnies, Martin asserted that in the course of their "abduction" from the home and domestic workshop, women had become emancipated. But he rendered even more dramatic images of social dissolution than Tönnies when he claimed that women's work would ultimately "ravage the social body." Martin drew a parallel between the destruction of the social body, the body of the family, and the physical bodies of women workers and the children they bore. Women who worked in factories, he argued, harmed the social body in two ways: first through what they did not do—that is, through neglect of their homes, husbands, and children—and second through the mechanical work they performed in the mills. In his view, women's negligence was "one main cause of the mortality rates among children, especially among infants . . . it spoils the human material and damages the labor power of the nation."[47] Here Martin held working women responsible not only for poverty but also for the moral degeneration of the workers' estate and the physical decline of the human (raw) "material." In posing the fundamental question as to

46. Ferdinand Tönnies, *Community and Association* (1887; London, 1974), pp. 186, 191.
47. Martin, "Die Ausschliessung," pp. 105, 399–400.

why women went to work in factories, Rudolf Martin broke with previous assumptions, such as those that permeated the inspectors' report of 1878, that women had always worked, whether at home or in a factory, and that their employment was compatible with housework and child rearing.[48]

Rudolf Martin's study, which was widely read, furnished the framework for the debate on women's work—the key questions and controversial solutions—which engaged social reformers during the next decade, as the "new course" in social policy was overshadowed and then dismantled during the mid-1890s, not least by the Kaiser's growing desire for an expanded German empire. It inspired numerous subsequent studies and commentaries by social reformers of diverse political persuasions, including Heinrich Herkner, Ludwig Pohle, and Robert Wilbrandt of the Association for Social Policy and the feminist social reformers Henriette Fürth and Alice Salomon.[49] Fürth, writing in 1902, pointed out that since the publication of Martin's article, "this question [of married women's factory employment], the critical importance of which is recognized by all sides, has not ceased to engage the world of social policy."[50] A new constituency—middle-class feminists—stepped forward during the 1890s to defend the right of women to work outside the home. Banned by the Prussian Law of Association from official participation in most of the social reform associations, educated women, many of whom were students or protégées of the eminent political economists and reformers, perceived many parallels between their own lack of political, social, and economic rights and the plight of working-class wives and mothers. Forging links between the middle-class "woman question" and the "worker question," they challenged the images of working women that filled the texts of conservative social reformers.

48. According to Quataert, "Source Analysis," p. 115: "To ask . . . why married women worked in factories implied that ideally married women ought not to work, a new assumption . . . that accompanied the industrial age."

49. See Herkner, *Die Arbeiterfrage*, pp. 36–40; Ludwig Pohle, *Frauenfabrikarbeit und Frauenfrage: Eine Prinzipielle Antwort auf die Frage der Ausschliessung der verheirateten Frauen aus der Fabrik* (Leipzig, 1900), pp. 47–48, 113; Wilbrandt, *Die Weber*, pp. 146–47; Henriette Fürth, *Die Fabrikarbeit verheirateter Frauen* (Frankfurt am Main, 1902), pp. 9–11, 16; Alice Salomon, "Frauen-Fabrikarbeit und Frauenfrage," *Die Frau* 8 (January 1901): 196–97.

50. Fürth, *Die Fabrikarbeit*, pp. 9–10. See, e.g., Henriette Fürth, "Die Ehefrage und der Beruf: Sozialistische Betrachtungen," *Die Frau* 4 (September 1897), pp. 710–18; Salomon, "Frauen-Fabrikarbeit und Frauenfrage"; and Alice Salomon, "Fabrikarbeit und Mutterschaft," *Die Frau* 13 (1905–6), pp. 365–69.

THE EMBODIMENT OF THE FEMALE WORKER

As the social question of female factory labor was debated fervently within the Social Democratic and Catholic labor movements and in the milieu of bourgeois social reform, it also continued to engage the Reichstag during the 1890s. The Catholic Center Party, encouraged by the concessions of 1891 regarding the protection of women and minors, and propelled into motion by the growing popularity of the SPD among working-class voters, intensified its campaign for restriction of married women's employment soon after the new code became law. Asserting that state social policy had thus far been grounded in a deficient grasp of the workers' conditions, and presuming that social investigation would advance and expand protective legislation, the Center introduced a motion in the Reichstag in 1894 requesting a formal state inquiry, complete with statistical compilations, into the effects of married women's factory work on their families' physical and moral well-being.[51] Although the measure failed in 1894, by the late 1890s the debate and agitation around the issue formed a groundswell of social pressure on the German state to investigate further the conditions of female factory labor and their effects on working-class families.

Thus in 1898 the chancellor authorized an official state inquiry into married women's factory employment, and the next year in each government district of Germany factory inspectors set out to determine precisely how many married women worked outside the home and why they sought waged work, thereby reiterating the question that Rudolf Martin had raised a few years earlier. On the basis of a study far more extensive than the inspectors' report of 1878, including interviews with workers' and employers' associations, local chambers of commerce, health insurance boards, priests, teachers, doctors, midwives, married women, and male workers, inspectors were to determine the necessity of restrictions on the employment of married women.[52] Furthermore, the government inquired about the consequences of eventual restrictions: How would the loss of women's earnings affect the working-class standard of living? How would it influence male workers and their propensity to marry if their future wives were not allowed to work? Would restrictions harm

51. Otto, *Über die Fabrikarbeit*, p. 177; Pohle, "Die Erhebungen," p. 149; Berlepsch, "*Neuer Kurs*," pp. 431–32; Herkner, "Zur Kritik und Reform," pp. 243–44.

52. According to Pohle, "Die Erhebungen," p. 150, the inspectors employed disparate methods to obtain information and the reports from the various districts were not necessarily comparable. Some, for example, interviewed women workers directly, whereas others asked them to complete questionnaires.

German industry and would employers be able to replace married women with single women or male workers?[53]

With this inquiry—drafted by the Reichstag, approved by the chancellor, and conducted by factory inspectors—the German state officially recognized the new social question of female factory labor and lent its authority to its resolution. At the same time, the state entered into the discourse about women's factory employment and joined social reformers in the task of delineating male and female spheres of work, of defining a sexual division of labor. According to the feminist social reformer Alice Salomon, the inquiry marked the peak of the campaign for exclusion of married women from factories and in one sense attested to its success. At the same time, the inspectors' final report, published by the Ministry of the Interior in 1901, discounted many of the campaign's main tenets and dampened its often inflammatory and ideological overtones; it banished, in Salomon's words, "the threatening phantom" that had "persecuted women struggling for economic independence and social equality." With the intervention of the state and the carefully crafted inquiry, "the ship found safe harbor," Salomon contended. For "women would be certain to find greater understanding for their economic needs and difficulties among these men of the practical world" than in the realm of high politics, which remained remote from what it sought to protect: women workers and their families.[54]

Indeed, Salomon's prediction was accurate in several respects: the inspectors' report of 1901 underscored the economic necessity of female factory labor and imparted to women's factory work a new legitimacy. While acknowledging that a legal ban would, in many respects, be beneficial to women and their families, all but one inspector rejected them as impracticable.[55] These "men of the practical world" viewed married women's factory work as an "irreversible consequence of the material reality among the workers," notably of the failure of wages to keep pace with the rising cost of living.[56] The inspectors feared that loss of women's earnings would force many families to turn to the public relief system.[57] Furthermore, employers had stressed the inflexibility of the labor market and the impossibility of wide-scale replacement of married women with men or single women. Employers delineated a sphere of "women's work,

53. Reichsamt des Innern, *Die Beschäftigung verheirateter Frauen in Fabriken, nach den Jahresberichten der Gewerbeaufsichtsbeamten für das Jahr 1899, bearbeitet im Reichsamt des Innern* (Berlin, 1901), pp. 1–2.

54. Salomon, "Frauen-Fabrikarbeit," pp. 193–99.

55. Reichsamt des Innern, *Die Beschäftigung*, p. 149.

56. Otto, *Über die Fabrikarbeit*, p. 125.

57. HStAD, JBdKPG 1899; Düsseldorf, p. 521. Reichsamt des Innern, *Die Beschäftigung*, pp. 150–52, 217–19.

which men regard as such as beneath their dignity." Women workers, they argued, were more suited than men for many jobs, especially those requiring the dexterity of "female hands."[58]

In defining spheres of male and female labor, the inspectors tacitly sought to legitimate married women's factory employment in the eyes of its opponents. In addition, they proposed a practical alternative to prohibition. Implying that a legal ban would be of little benefit to the many families whose female members were unable to keep house properly, the inspectors recommended that the state institute obligatory housekeeping schools for female factory workers, where young women could learn to cook, sew, and care for infants.[59] In the promotion of *Häuslichkeit* (domesticity), the inspectors defined the social problem of women's factory work in new terms and shifted its solution from the factory to the home.

After the publication of the factory inspectors' findings in 1901, only a few reformers continued to advocate a legal ban on married women's factory employment; most renewed efforts to expand protective legislation.[60] The Catholic Center Party, which still favored a legal ban in principle, settled on a campaign for a reduction of the workday for married women to six hours.[61] Unable to banish married women to the home, social reformers now sought to import the home into the workplace, to instill domestic skills in female factory workers and to supplant the imagery of disorder, the specter of feminization and disintegration of gender roles, with a new order founded on the division between the male breadwinner and the female "secondary" earner. Underpinning this new order was a consensus among reformers, inspectors, industrialists, and male workers' organizations about the natural basis of this division and about the rightful claim of male breadwinners to higher earnings, skill, and status.

Even as the inspectors' reports mapped out a resolution to the social question of female factory labor at the turn of the century, their survey also compiled new and compelling information regarding the dangers factory work presented to pregnant women; namely, the extraordinarily high rates of miscarriage, premature birth, and infant mortality among female textile workers reported by medical doctors,

58. Rheinisch-Westfälisches Wirtschaftsarchiv, Handelskammer Duisburg 20: 43/6 (Gewerbe und Industrie, vol. 1): Verband der Textilindustriellen von Chemnitz und Umgebung, "Schreiben an das Hohe Reichskanzleramt zu Berlin von 9. Dezember, 1899."

59. HStAD, JBdKPG 1899: Aachen, p. 607; Reichsamt des Innern, *Die Beschäftigung*, pp. 251–52; and Pohle, *Frauenfabrikarbeit*, p. 110.

60. Otto, *Über die Fabrikarbeit*, p. 179.

61. See Franz Hitze, *Die Arbeiterfrage und die Bestrebungen zu ihrer Lösung* (Berlin, 1900), p. 80.

health insurance officials, and employers.[62] In specifying the site of intervention as the maternal body, they began to widen the scope of the social question from the factory to the nation, to link more explicitly the conditions of work to the conditions of (national) reproduction and the national birth rate.[63] In the course of formulating solutions to the new social question of female factory labor, social reformers also staked out a domain of sexuality, one that was constructed in direct relation to themes of danger, disease, filth, and depravity, thus laying the groundwork for the even more explicit medicalized intervention in women's bodies from the late 1890s until World War I. As Germany launched its quest for empire after 1890, the growing alarm regarding the birth rate placed women's bodies at the center of a hygienicist, natalist enterprise of identifying and eradicating social pathologies, which by now included not only alcoholism, tuberculosis, venereal disease, and infant mortality but also female factory labor. Interestingly, all of these pathologies could be located directly or indirectly in the moral or bodily deficiencies of women who worked outside the home. Thus, during the first decade of the twentieth century, women's embodiment became a more explicit focus of the social question as it was understood not only by employers and trade unionists but also by the welfare state and the popular hygienicist associations (the various leagues to combat tuberculosis, venereal disease, alcoholism, and infant mortality) which mobilized within the expanded civic sphere during the first decade of the twentieth century.[64] At the same time the emergent psychophysics of work and other productivist visions of the body as a "human motor" began to inscribe female bodies with a new kind of disruptive potential that required new interventions aimed more explicitly to improve the productivity and economic utility of bodies at work.[65]

---

62. HStAD, JBdKPG 1899: Düsseldorf, pp. 518–20, and Münster, p. 372. The Barmen inspector reported that the rate of illness was 15% higher and the average duration of an illness 70% longer among married women than among unmarried women. See also Reichsamt des Innern, *Die Beschäftigung*, p. 96.

63. Reichsamt des Innern, *Die Beschäftigung*, pp. 97–99, 210; HStAD, JBdKPG 1899: Aachen, p. 609.

64. Paul Weindling, *Health, Race and German Politics between National Unification and Nazism, 1870–1945* (New York, 1989), p. 175.

65. On the psychophysics of work, see Anson Rabinbach, "The European Science of Work: The Economy of the Body at the End of the Nineteenth Century," in *Work in France: Representations, Meaning, Organization, and Practice*, ed. Steven L. Kaplan and Cynthia J. Koepp (Ithaca, 1986), pp. 475–513, and *The Human Motor: Energy, Fatigue, and the Origins of Modernity* (Berkeley, 1992); Josefa Ioteyko, *The Science of Labour and Its Organization* (London, 1919); Max Weber, "Zur Psychophysik der industriellen Arbeit," *Archiv für Sozialwissenschaft und Sozialgeschichte* 28 (1909): 219–77, 719–61; 29 (1909): 513–42.

CONCLUSIONS

The crises that accompanied Germany's transition from an agrarian to
an industrial state were understood by contemporaries in highly
gendered terms. The discourses about women's work, which both constituted and attempted to resolve the new social question of female factory
labor, are crucial in understanding the expansion of the German welfare
state during the "new course" of the early 1890s. Galvanized by agitation
in both the bourgeois and working-class public spheres, policy makers
drafted inquiries and proposed legislation to counteract the perceived or
threatened dissolution of the social order, an order anchored in sexual
difference. The German welfare state was structured centrally and explicitly around a gender program not only because women and children
became objects of maternalist welfare policies, or because female social
reformers emerged on the scene and articulated in a new and powerful
fashion the needs of women and children, as much scholarship on the
welfare state would have it.[66] The central task of labor legislation was to
reorder the relations between the sexes, which had gone awry during the
rapid wave of industrialization at the close of the century. The revised
labor code of 1891 and the factory inspectors' inquiry about married
women's work of 1898 codified a sexual division of labor as one means of
reordering those relations.

While a purported crisis of the family appears to have preoccupied
reformers across industrialized Europe during the 1890s, this particular
confluence of concerns in the context of expanding bourgeois and working-class public spheres marks one of the more intriguing "peculiarities
of German history."[67] Another peculiarity—and the immediate cause of
the heightened interest in and concern with the female factory worker—
was the steady and perceptible expansion of the female industrial labor
market, which occurred as the pace of industrial growth intensified and
industrial employers confronted a continuous labor shortage in nearly all
sectors, including the so-called women's industries of textiles, garments,
and cigars, during the late 1880s and 1890s. In particular after 1890, the
recurrent labor shortages in industrial regions such as the Rhineland and

66. See Koven and Michel, "Womanly Duties."
67. David Blackbourn and Geoff Eley, *The Peculiarities of German History: Bourgeois
Society and Politics in Nineteenth-Century Germany* (New York, 1984). On the crisis of
the family during the 1890s, see Eve Rosenhaft and W. R. Lee, "State and Society in
Modern Germany: Beamtenstaat, Klassenstaat, Wohlfahrtsstaat," in *The State and Social
Change in Germany, 1880–1980*, ed. Rosenhaft and Lee (New York, 1990), pp. 27–29. For
an interesting comparison with France, see Judith Coffin, "Social Science Meets Sweated
Labor: Reinterpreting Women's Work in Late Nineteenth-Century France," *Journal of
Modern History* 63, no. 2 (1991): 230–70; and Jacques Donzelot, *The Policing of Families*
(New York, 1979).

Westphalia drew married women into the workforce in large numbers, whereas in England the percentages of married women with jobs had been on the decline for at least a decade. Despite the rapid pace of industrial and social change in Germany, closer study of specific regional and local conditions indicates that the sense of crisis associated with the transition from domestic to factory industry lingered well into the early 1890s. Thus the welfare state took shape at a time when a sense of dislocation and disorder were still acutely felt and passionately articulated in both popular demands on the German state and the social-scientific languages of social reform.[68]

The discourse about female factory labor also raises some interesting questions about the German state at the end of the nineteenth century. Some scholars have taken the existence of a vital welfare state as a basis for a critique of the authoritarian model of political rule in German social-science history.[69] The agitation around the social question of female factory labor during the 1880s and 1890s, for example, reveals the German state to be a "permeable arena in which contending social and political forces interact[ed]," "a space for struggle and negotiation, rather than an incorporative machine."[70] Read in this light, protective labor legislation becomes an integral part of "the reshaping of the political nation" which occurred during the Wilhelmine period as new structures of public communication changed "the very terms on which political life took place." Labor legislation becomes a prime site for analyzing how "opposing publics maneuvered for space" within an expanding public sphere, especially during the 1890s, when the social reform nexus, a cross-section of liberal academics, Catholics, Social Democrats, feminists, and intellectuals, succeeded in dislodging the social question from the sphere of high politics and locating it in the widening sphere of public opinion.[71] Their debates about female factory labor, about the changing relationship between women and family, between family and state, were crucially important parts of the discursive and social mobilizations that transformed the relationship between civil society and the state and that

68. Jean Quataert, "Woman's Work and the Early Welfare State in Germany: Legislators, Bureaucrats, and Clients before the First World War," in Koven and Michel, *Mothers of a New World*, p. 166.

69. Berlepsch, *"Neuer Kurs"*; Rüdiger vom Bruch, *Wissenschaft, Politik und öffentliche Meinung: Gelehrtenpolitik im Wihelminischen Deutschland (1890–1914)* (Husum, 1980); Geoff Eley, "German History and the Contradictions of Modernity," in *Society, Culture, and the State in Germany, 1870–1930*, ed. Eley (Ann Arbor, 1996).

70. Eley, "German History," p. 94; Gray, "Languages of Factory Reform," p. 172.

71. Geoff Eley, "Introduction I: Is There a History of the Kaiserreich?" in Eley, *Society, Culture, and the State*, p. 11; and idem, "Nations, Publics, and Political Cultures: Placing Habermas in the Nineteenth Century," in *Habermas and the Public Sphere*, ed. Craig Calhoun (Cambridge, Mass., 1992), p. 325.

challenged and ultimately widened the scope of the German welfare state and reconstituted "the social."[72] Granting labor legislation a more central place in the historical narratives of the welfare state also raises a question about the profoundly different ways in which the various parts of the welfare state were made, with labor legislation embedded in the public sphere and the public imagination, while social insurance remained confined to the bureaucratic imagination.

Thus the example of labor legislation affirms not only the permeability of the welfare state but also the importance of discursive struggle as a particular means of recasting it. The debates about women's work analyzed here occurred at a "classic" historical moment of the nineteenth century, when, as Richard Terdiman notes, "the techniques for assuring discursive penetration," as well as those of "symbolic subversion"—newspapers, new disciplines and bodies of knowledge such as statistics and management—"solidified themselves." As social discourses became the locus of "increasingly conscious struggle," Terdiman argues, they also brought into existence a newly influential category of citizens able to use and administer the new mechanisms.[73] Finally, this history of the discursive terrain of labor legislation also complicates the functionalist view of the German welfare state, which explains its origins and outcomes in terms of its ability to legitimate and secure the conditions of capitalist reproduction, by uncovering the diverse coalitions, the claims of professionalism and expertise, the assertion of scientific knowledge, and the contests about gender that shaped state social policy during the 1890s.[74] For the German welfare state sought to anchor that legitimation not merely in the sphere of labor-capital relations but also and perhaps even primarily in the spheres of family and reproduction, while at the same time seeking to align these two spheres with each other.[75]

Although the expansion of the German welfare state can be viewed as one of the discernible outcomes of the discourses of social reform, the implications of the shifts in state social policy of the 1890s and the emergence of a new ideology of women's work reached far beyond

72. On the significance of the 1890s in German history, see Geoff Eley, *Reshaping the German Right: Radical Nationalism and Political Change after Bismarck* (1980; Ann Arbor, 1991); Eley, "Introduction I: Is There a History of the Kaiserreich?" pp. 11–15.

73. Terdiman, *Discourse/Counter-Discourse*, pp. 44, 66, 74.

74. For an analysis of the ways in which the German welfare state legitimated and secured capitalist reproduction, see Geoff Eley, "Social Imperialism in Germany: Reformist Synthesis or Reactionary Sleight of Hand?" in Eley, *From Unification to Nazism: Reinterpreting the German Past* (Boston, 1986), p. 161, and Rosenhaft and Lee, "State and Society in Modern Germany," pp. 24, 29–30. For further reflection on this issue, see Michael Hanagan's review of Stewart, *Women, Work, and the French State,* in *Interational Labor and Working-Class History* 39 (Spring 1991): 98–100.

75. Eley, "German History," p. 96.

the realm of governing. For both were central in shaping class and citizenship as social concepts and political identities. This is particularly true of the 1890s, when the transformation of the public sphere—the emergence of Social Democracy as a mass party, the popular mobilizations of right-wing nationalists, feminists, and liberal social reformers—changed the meanings of both class and citizenship in Germany. While state social policy reinforced the identities of male workers as breadwinners, women workers' relations to class politics were mediated by the discursive and legislative emphasis on their maternal duties and identities. Under the gaze of male mill owners, trade unionists, factory inspectors, medical doctors, and parliamentary legislators, female workers were always embodied. Entwined in these debates about women's work and the protective legislation they produced were concerns about both the health and moral integrity of women's bodies: the advent of maternity leave in 1878 and its expansion and the eleven-hour limit placed on women's workday in 1891 were necessitated by concerns about high rates of infant mortality and the health not only of pregnant women and new mothers but also of young girls as future mothers. Protective labor codes fixed women's place in production and hence in class, as it was popularly understood in the German Social Democratic milieu. Labor legislation inscribed class and citizenship with sexual difference in its explicit distinction between women and children, on the one hand, who lacked the political rights to assert and defend their own interests and whom the state was compelled to protect, and male citizens on the other, who enjoyed civil equality with employers, including the right to form political coalitions against them. Finally, rethinking the welfare state from the perspective of labor legislation and reading labor legislation against the grain to find the body may illuminate how the dichotomies of public/private, work/nonwork, and production/reproduction underwrote both middle class and working class as concepts and as particular visions of male citizenship.

9

Republican Ideology, Gender and Class: France, 1860s–1914

Judith F. Stone

Jenny d'Héricourt, writing in 1860, warned French republican men, and the romantic historian Jules Michelet in particular, that republicanism was in danger of negating itself by excluding women.

> Take care gentlemen! Our rights have the same foundation as yours: in denying the former, you deny the latter in principle.
>
> A word more to you, pretended disciples of the doctrines of 89, and we have done. Do you know why so many women took part with our Revolution, armed the men, and rocked their children to the song of the *Marseillaise*! It was because they thought they saw under the Declaration of the rights of men and citizens, the declaration of the rights of women and female citizens.
>
> When the Assembly took it upon itself to undeceive them, by lacking logic with respect to them, and closing their meetings, they abandoned the Revolution, and you know what ensued.[1]

Research for this chapter was made possible by awards from the Burnham-Macmillan Research Fund, Department of History, Western Michigan University, and the Faculty Research and Creative Activities Support Fund, Western Michigan University.

1. Jenny d'Héricourt, *A Woman's Philosophy of Woman, or Woman Affranchised: An Answer to Michelet, Proudhon, Girardin, Legouvé, Comte, and Other Modern Innovators* (New York, 1864), quoted in Susan Groag Bell and Karen M. Offen, *Women, the Family, and Freedom: The Debate in Documents* (Stanford, 1983), 1:347.

Michelet pursued the polemic and the same year published an expanded version of his views on women, *La Femme*. Héricourt's demand to be recognized as a *citoyenne* with full rights was dismissed out of hand. Not only were women banished from the public political realm, but in Michelet's view they ought to be excluded from the economic world of wage labor. Claiming to protect and cherish the essence of woman, Michelet declared the very existence of women workers an affront against nature. "*L'ouvrière*! impious, sordid word that no language has ever known, that no age ever understood before this age of iron, and that holds in the balance all our supposed progress!"[2] French republicanism had no place for women either as citizens or as workers; their exclusive role was to be that of republican mother. While apparently marginalizing women, republican ideology was profoundly shaped by great anxieties about family, gender, and class.

ALL REPUBLICANS of the nineteenth century identified themselves with the Great Revolution. Since 1789 family and gender had always played a critical role in republican ideology. The Revolution had asserted the sovereignty of citizens and deposed the traditional authority of patriarchal monarchy. By 1793 the Jacobins had aggressively imposed an exclusively male identity on the essential category of citizen which remained unquestioned by most republicans until the second half of the nineteenth century.[3] Deeply influenced by Jean-Jacques Rousseau, French republicans promoted egalitarianism and universality, but they insisted that these qualities could be applied only to men, who alone were "naturally" citizens. The influential theories on education which Rousseau promoted in *Emile* and *Julie, ou La Nouvelle Héloïse* specifically required sharply divergent training for boys and girls, whose social roles were to remain fundamentally different.[4] In Rousseauean theory and Jacobin practice women were assigned the domestic sphere, given the responsibility to rear republican citizens, and were expected to defer to male

2. Jules Michelet, *La Femme*, 3d ed. (Paris, 1860), p. 29.

3. There has been an increasing number of excellent studies that explore gender and citizenship during the Revolution. See Joan Landes, *Women and the Public Sphere in the Age of the French Revolution* (Ithaca 1988); William H. Sewell Jr., "Le Citoyen/La Citoyenne: Activity, Passivity, and the Revolutionary Concept of Citizenship," in *The Political Culture of the French Revolution*, ed. Colin Lucas (New York, 1988); Carole Pateman, "The Fraternal Social Contract," in *The Disorder of Women: Democracy, Feminism, and Political Theory* (Stanford, 1989); Lynn Hunt, *The Family Romance of the French Revolution* (Berkeley, 1992).

4. Carol Blum has persuasively demonstrated Rousseau's insistence on the subordination of women to men and how his new educational models reinforced that subordination: *Rousseau and the Republic of Virtue: The Language of Politics in the French Revolution* (Ithaca, 1986), pp. 122–23.

authority.[5] Public virtue and clear gender identities would be possible only as long as separate spheres for men and women were maintained.[6]

Republican egalitarianism embraced equality before the law, equality of political participation for citizens, and equality of opportunities. While the Code Civil guaranteed citizens legal equality, it relegated married women to the status of minors, barring them from participation in legal actions. Great wealth and unrestrained capitalism remained suspect, but personal property was highly valued. Without it republicans could not imagine authentic individualism and citizenship. In the absence of personal property, independence seemed impossible, and without independence an authentic individual identity could not exist. Individual identity and personal independence formed the basis of citizens' actions and their right to exert political sovereignty. It was precisely their condition of being without property that made industrial workers in the second half of the nineteenth century so threatening to republicans and led republicans to search for means by which workers might gain access to property. Cooperatives, unions, inexpensive housing, state-backed social insurance programs were all viewed as possible alternatives that would provide new forms of property for workers. But the object of this concern was unquestionably the male worker, whom republicans hoped to transform into a full citizen by eliminating his condition of being propertyless. Along with the political and moral significance they bestowed on property, most republicans endorsed the legal restrictions that made it impossible for married women of any class to control property and in effect to function as fully independent individuals with political rights. Such restrictions made it clear that the public political world and the domestic familial would were never regarded as equal. From its origins, then, modern republicanism associated male political equality with a hierarchical family. The apparently universal principles of the public realm depended on the exclusion and subordination of women. Men were individuals and citizens, active in the state; women were mothers, producing and nurturing future citizens.

By the mid–nineteenth century, pressured by both revolutionary attempts to reorganize the state and the family and by conservative versions of domesticity, republicans devoted considerable attention to the "woman question." The declining birth rate, the increasing number of women working for wages, and reported discontent within bourgeois marriages all brought renewed attention to the "condition of women." In addition, while gender segregation and masculine dominance appeared to

5. Pateman, *Disorder of Women*, pp. 19–21.
6. Rousseau's clearly expressed his fear of feminization in his *Discours sur les sciences et les arts*. Hunt offers an insightful and provocative exploration of anxieties about gender identity during the most radical phase of the Revolution: *Family Romance*, pp. 115–23.

be a central and secure element of republican ideology, a persistent unease about how to reconcile claims for equality with the defense of the hierarchical family could not be entirely silenced, as the protests of Jenny d'Héricourt demonstrated. Some republicans began to wonder if the idealized domestic woman, *la femme au foyer*, could actually fulfill her civic functions of republican mother. Separate spheres and the republican principle of equality did not fit seamlessly together. Others reasserted the critical role that the hierarchical family had to play in a future republican state and society.

The influential romantic historian Jules Michelet produced several tracts during the Second Empire focusing on "issues of secular morality." He examined women's conditions, their relations with men, class relations, and the reform of both gender and class relations. One of his most popular publications was the 1860 *La Femme*, essentially a marriage manual addressed to the young men of France and especially to the circle of Left Bank students who avidly followed his courses and his publications. Near the end of the manual Michelet depicted his vision of perfect familial, social, and political harmony. It is a a cold, snowy winter Sunday; the family cozily gathers around the "flaming hearth, where supper is warming." There is almost no sound and "he, the man, takes advantage of this day to do what he likes. . . . [He reads.] He knows that she is behind him. She makes almost no noise, but does all that is necessary with a soft, undulating movement." She instructs the children with lessons drawn from nature; robins arriving on this winter day offer excellent examples of fraternity. In fact, one doesn't even have to listen to her exact words, simply her presence instructs. At the end of the day the children delight their father by singing the "Marseillaise" and a hymn to God. And she blesses the family and this patriotic apotheosis .[7]

Throughout his works Michelet often identified women with the working class, or focused on relations between bourgeois men and working-class women. Michelet's observation that working-class women were doubly exploited increased his concern and his desire for these women, whom he regarded as more malleable and in greater need of salvation. He admonished his young male readers, "The woman you ought to marry . . . should be simple and loving, without any final definition. . . . I like her best poor, alone, with few family ties. Her educational level is a very secondary issue." Bourgeois women had acquired too great a taste for luxury, artifice, and religion, thus threatening men with corruption and the loss of masculinity. The condition of the working-class woman, *l'ouvrière*, called out for salvation, but she could in turn be a savior, reinvigorating the bourgeoisie and promoting national unity

---

7. Michelet, *La Femme*, pp. 359–63.

without threatening bourgeois masculine leadership. Ideally, a similar exchange of "natural" vitality and superior leadership ought to occur between the working class and the bourgeoisie, ultimately consolidating the unity of "the people." But the union of the men of the two classes was difficult and perhaps threatening to imagine. Working-class men were too obviously associated with violence and disorder. Women's "natural" subordination was proposed as a model to be followed by the entire working class. In fact, Michelet observed that "women of the people (who are not nearly as vulgar as the men . . .) listen to men [socially] above them. . . . [They express the] touching confidence of the people." This was the appropriate relation between men and women, bourgeois and workers, and the "natural" one between bourgeois men and working-class women. In Michelet's powerful vision, the seemingly insurmountable nineteenth-century problems of class and gender might all be resolved if women, and especially working-class women, followed their proper biological destiny and allowed themselves to be defined by republican men. Woman would then be the "Sunday of man . . . his joy, his freedom, his celebration."[8]

Only two years after the publication of Michelet's *La Femme*, Victor Hugo's monumental novel, *Les Misérables*, appeared. Its sale in imperial France was a major political and literary event.[9] Stories were told of Parisian artisans and students forming associations to purchase a copy to read aloud in their *cercles d'amitié*. The novel's circulation contributed to the electoral victories of the republican opposition in 1863, which marked a further relaxing of the repressive Second Empire. *Les Misérables* was a "modern epic," intended to prepare a new future. In its pages Hugo pronounced his magnificent, sonorous, and endless words on the social question, republicanism, revolution, gender relations, the family, and the future of France. Two central and interrelated themes dominated this massive fiction: the horror and pointlessness of class war and the urgent need to construct loving, healthy, "intact" families.

Hugo dramatically expressed an important shift in republicanism after 1851: class conflict, civil war, and armed insurrection on the barricades were increasingly seen as the greatest threat to emancipatory politics and republicanism. On one level, Hugo's solution was to offer what was already becoming by the 1860s the social program of advanced republi-

---

8. Ibid., pp. 68–69, 23, 209, 356–57.
9. Hugo had been working on the manuscript since the 1840s and the essential narrative had been completed before his exile, but important and lengthy passages were added during the 1850s. See Camille Pelletan, *Victor Hugo: L'Homme politique* (Paris: 1907), pp. 270, 284; Camille Pelletan, "Mémoires inédites," in Paul Baquiast, "Camille Pelletan (1846–1915): Esquisse de biographie" (mémoire de maîtrise d'histoire, Université de Paris IV, 1986), p. 266.

cans. "Encourage the rich and protect the poor. . . . end the unjust exploitation of the weak by the strong . . . adjust workers' wages . . . introduce
free and obligatory education . . . democratize property, not by abolishing
it but by universalizing it, so that every citizen without exception is a
property owner."[10] Yet the novelist never assumed that such practical
reforms to alleviate economic "misery" would alone be adequate.

The essential problems of French society lay in the painful experiences
of separation, dehumanization, and isolation created by the complex
tensions of class, gender, ideology, and individual identity. The family
might be the means to overcome such multiple despair. Such a family,
centered on the *femme simple* described by Michelet, would be the
source of harmony, unity, and solidarity. Again the "natural," procreative, loving subordination of wives to husbands was to be a model for all
social relations and would also produce individuals capable of entering
such relations. And once again the authentic *femme simple* would instruct bourgeois men in the deeper values of life which lay outside the
market and politics. In the concluding epiphany of the novel the ideal
woman, Cosette—illegitimate daughter of the ultimate *ouvrière*, an exploited seamstress and prostitute—describes her future family. She pictures a gathering set in a beautiful flowering garden where her husband
and her guardian eat strawberries that she has cultivated. "[And there]
we'll all live in a republic where everyone will say *tu*." Cosette is the
ideal wife, instinctively able to enlighten her husband without abandoning her subordinate role.[11] In *Les Misérables* Hugo, like Michelet, identified the success of the future republic as dependent on affinities among
the political, social, and domestic realms. Class conflict, which posed
one of the greatest dangers to a nascent republic, would be eliminated as
class relations followed the new family model. Division would be transformed into a new harmony in which hierarchies would be accepted as
reasonable and natural.

The rhetoric and images of Michelet and Hugo shaped the republican
political culture of the 1860s. Numerous lesser-known writers, journalists, and politicians disseminated this culture. A representative member
of this group was Eugène Pelletan, a widely read journalist, lecturer, and
politician with personal ties to both Michelet and Hugo. He was a
respected member of the anti-Bonapartist republican opposition. Com-
plementing the images of domesticity powerfully evoked by Michelet
and Hugo, Pelletan emphasized the role of the mother as educator and
transmitter of a particular moral vision. This perspective combined republicanism, liberal Protestantism, romantic sentiment, anticlericalism,

10. Victor Hugo, *Les Misérables* (1862; Paris, 1972), 2: 407–8.
11. Ibid., 3:528, 468–70, 525–26.

an unshakable belief in progress, and support for the social order. The family was the linchpin of this morality and central to the success of a republic, but it must be a reformed family, transformed by a new cooperative marriage. Like Michelet and Hugo, Pelletan was profoundly disturbed by what he observed as the failure of bourgeois marriages. More than other republicans Pelletan explored the tensions created by the demand that women's exclusive role be that of the republican mother. Could women who were barred from the public sphere and exhorted to remain within the limits of domesticity ever adequately contribute to the formation of responsible citizens?

In the 1860s he was convinced that the "decline" of the family was linked to the public and private decadence of the authoritarian Second Empire.[12] In 1864 he wrote *La Charte au foyer*, selecting a political metaphor for his title. Pelletan proposed a new set of relations between husband and wife to include respect for mothers and an emphasis on secular education for women. While subscribing to the dominant ideology of domesticity, he attempted to redefine the governing of the home and simultaneously to endorse a new political regime. "As for woman, her place is at home, directing, administering the house, and above all constantly forming those young souls that Providence has confided to her, making them one day citizens worthy of their country. Thus, if I had to define marriage ... I would call it a constitutional government. The husband minister of foreign affairs, the wife minister of the interior, and all household questions decided by the council of ministers."[13] Women had to have access to all forms of knowledge if they were to succeed in their "natural" duties as wives and mothers. This republican model of family organization was inherently unstable; subordination and equality uneasily coexisted without any clear indication of how authority was legitimated. In addition, although class was never mentioned, it was clear that this constitutional family was necessarily bourgeois. Pelletan

12. This was the central theme of Eugène Pelletan, *La Nouvelle Babylone* (Paris, 1862).

13. Eugène Pelletan, *La Femme au dix-neuvième siècle* (Paris, 1869), p. 29. This passage supports Carole Pateman's incisive analysis demonstrating the shift from traditional patriarchal theories of the state and family to those of the contract theorists. Locke and Rousseau dissociated paternal authority in the family and political rule of the state, making political rule the exclusive creation of the fraternal contract. See esp. her "Fraternal Social Contract," p. 36. Since Pateman's main concern in *Disorder of Women* is to demonstrate the patriarchal character of liberalism, she devotes less attention to the increasing dissatisfaction with liberal theory after 1850. Pelletan's metaphor indicates that many nineteenth-century social commentators were no longer content with the sharp distinction between domestic and public realms. See also Pateman's "'The Disorder of Women': Women, Love, and the Sense of Justice" and "Feminist Critiques of the Public/ Private Dichotomy," both in *Disorder of Women*. See also Hunt, *Family Romance*, pp. 201–4.

ignored the problems workers might have in establishing this new republican family.

The following year Pelletan produced a survey of women's history. Throughout this study, *La Famille: La Mère*, he struggled to reconcile his belief in progress with the historical evidence of women's continuing subordination. Contradictions were especially numerous in the final, difficult chapter on "women as citizens." Pelletan insisted that women shared with men the essential quality of humanness, and therefore they must have all the same inherent natural rights and liberties. Yet he resisted the thought of women active in any aspect of the public sphere. Significantly, the possibilities and consequences of women's productive activities presented him with the greatest dilemmas. He never thought to examine the actual conditions of contemporary working women. Rather he speculated that women could never truly have a profession; they could only master an *état*, a trade, something he described as comparable to weaving in classical antiquity. A few pages later, however, he admitted that once women worked for wages, they must be recognized as citizens. Implicit in this conclusion was the recognition that an exclusively domestic existence barred one from public life, and that labor, even for women, ought to confer access to the public realm. But that public realm was also in need of major reform. With a rather audacious blurring of the public/private distinction, he stated that "the problem with politics is that it has been masculine. . . . There is a need for women's sentiments." While apparently promoting marriages in which wives and husbands would be genuine companions, nonetheless Pelletan seemed uncertain about the consequences of such a restructuring of the domestic order. He ended his history of women ambiguously, calling for the education of women in order that "women may be what they ought to be."[14] Despite his uncertainties about a solution to the "woman question," Pelletan claimed that a transformed woman would promote compatibility between husband and wife and a more tranquil, more moral, and happier family. Such families in turn would support the reform efforts toward a new, parliamentary republican regime, which in turn would lend support to harmonious domestic and social relations.

THESE MID-CENTURY IDEOLOGUES emphasized certain strains within the republican traditions of the Great Revolution. They repeatedly questioned how a future republic ought to address the issues of the family, republican mothers, the working class, and working-class women. Concerns (sometimes obsessions) about women and class intersected with one another, and often stood in complex relations to the positive repub-

14. Eugène Pelletan, *La Famille: La Mère* (Paris, 1865), pp. 312, 315, 327, 335.

lican categories of citizen and nation. This ideology gained new stature when in September 1870, for the third time in less than one hundred years, France was proclaimed a republic. Few expected such an experimental regime to survive. Surprisingly it did, continuing well into the twentieth century. The Third Republic, however, was not established as the republican opposition to the Second Empire had imagined. It was tentatively declared during the fall and spring of 1870–71, in the midst of military defeat, invasion, and civil war. Its actual political and institutional foundation was protracted and precarious, not being complete till the early 1880s. At least until 1905, most committed republicans retained a permanent sense of insecurity, perhaps paranoia, about the republic's survival, despite their electoral and parliamentary victories. They feared the strength of clerical, authoritarian, and traditionalist forces, whose supporters were by no means insignificant. This new regime, the only major European republic, faced several additional challenges. First, the French economy and society were continuing to experience a profound transformation: a relative decline of the agricultural sector, nationwide growth of industrialization, and expansion of the market. This transformation was accompanied by a relatively high participation of women in the labor force and a continuing decline in the birth rate. Second, though republicanism achieved the position of the dominant, official ideology by 1900, it confronted a well-organized and growing socialist opposition. The socialists presented themselves as the authentic heirs to the revolutionary tradition of 1789, which—they claimed—republican politicians had abandoned. Finally, beginning in the 1880s feminist organizations, which primarily identified themselves as part of the larger republican movement, demanded increased civil rights and, after 1900, the vote.

The first generation of Third Republic politicians who reached maturity in the 1880s and 1890s not only had imbibed the masculine mid-century republican ideology but had come of age during a period of ever more rigid social segregation between bourgeois men and women.[15] Political success inevitably reinforced such segregation in these republicans' personal and social lives. Excluded from the world of politics, women remained outside all the formative experiences of republican men. The politicians' education was shaped by the lycée and the male members of their families. For the typical republican the masculinism of this early social formation was reinforced by university training, occasional forays into bohemian circles, the practice of journalism, Masonic lodges, electoral campaigns, and the Chamber of Deputies—all exclu-

15. Bonnie G. Smith's rich and intriguing *Ladies of the Leisure Class: The Bourgeoises of Northern France in the Nineteenth century* (Princeton, 1981) demonstrates this development irrefutably for the Nord and suggests the same for all of France.

sively male environments.[16] During the first half of the Third Republic these politicians lived in a world in which most social intercourse occurred exclusively among men. For some this exclusivity led to a bemused incomprehension and reduced interest in the woman question, for others to a deep antipathy toward women.

By the 1890s, however, these republican politicians could not avoid addressing a new set of political and social problems connected with women's actual experiences. With continuing electoral successes, these men were called on to construct and implement republican legislation affecting the lives of French women and men. It had been relatively easy to use woman and the family as part of a rhetorical repertoire portraying the benefits of a future harmonious republic; now, in the Third Republic, republican politicians had to respond to concrete issues of women's reproductive, productive, and civic lives. Three related conditions— women working outside the home, male industrial workers, and women's demands for civil and political rights—revealed the tensions, contradictions, and limits of republican ideology. These conditions pressured republican politicians to formulate effective policies. Republicans were forced to ask: What should be the appropriate relation between the state and women workers, who in reality were not citizens? Could men whose working situations permitted few options to secure property and assert individual independence really function as citizens? Could women and men whose lives were regulated by the factory ever establish republican families? Were working mothers the cause of the decline in the French birth rate? If working women could be biological mothers, could they be republican ones? Could women be citizens? Could the muchvaunted republican commitment to universal suffrage be genuinely universal?

These questions created considerable uneasiness among the most ardent supporters of republicanism, the Radical republicans. They were dedicated to the defense of the regime, to the creation of a more egalitarian state and society that would ensure permanence as well as authenticity to the state. Popular and national sovereignty resting on the inviolability of independent citizens constituted their first principle. Radicals led the most vociferous attacks against the power and influence of the Catholic Church, which they identified as a major obstacle to authentic individual independence. Until 1893 they constituted a small but growing number of parliamentary representatives who sat on the

---

16. Camille Pelletan, prominent Radical leader and son of Eugène, was typical in this regard. Although a member of the Chamber's Groupe Parlementaire de Défense des Droits de la Femme from its founding in 1895 and despite apparently happy relations with a companion of thirty years and a wife, Pelletan could not imagine any interest in women other than a "conquering physical passion." See Pelletan, "Mémoires inédites," p. 332.

extreme left of the Chamber of Deputies. After 1893 they entered electoral and parliamentary alliances with socialists in support of reform
programs. They organized a formal Radical Party in 1901 and in the first
years of the twentieth century made impressive electoral gains. Five
years later they were the largest party in the Chamber of Deputies and
had a considerable contingent in the upper house, the Senate.

The Radicals were key actors in the process of restructuring the relations of the state to both female and male workers, to women as a group,
and to the family. They are the critical group of politicians in our analysis
of republican ideology, not simply because of their numbers in parliament but also because they insisted that they alone were authentic
republicans. They claimed to represent "the people" and the nation, as
well as to defend the essential legitimacy of a regime based on popular
sovereignty. But, as we have seen, such republican claims to universality
explicitly excluded women, and while male workers were certainly
counted among "the people," Radicals voiced concern about how workers could exercise their rights as citizens. The Radicals' dedication to this
highly gendered ideology led them to a series of impasses. There was a
certain strain between a commitment to individual rights and the need to
enforce social responsibilities, obligations to the larger republican community, the nation. Even more serious were the assumptions about the
individual which the Radicals inherited. It was difficult to imagine the
republican individual as anything other than male, the head of a family,
and the possessor of property. These dissonances intruded in all areas of
social policy, but they were especially acute when Radicals sought to
respond to the circumstances of working women.

The Radicals' response to the dilemmas of working-class women was
articulated through ideological assumptions that linked economic and
sexual exploitation and identified *l'ouvrière* with subordination, which
they found abhorrent and yet natural. Furthermore, the question of how
the republican state should react to women who worked outside the
home, particularly in factories, became entangled with two other major
late nineteenth-century issues—the decline in the birth rate and state
intervention in the economy. Earlier concerns about a slowing population growth had grown to a crescendo of alarm as the French birth rate
continued to fall.[17] Fertility rates declined throughout the population, but

17. Karen Offen, "Depopulation, Nationalism, and Feminism in Fin-de-Siècle France,"
American Historical Review 89 (June 1984): 648–76. This important article demonstrates
the increasing significance of this issue for feminists and antifeminists during the Third
Republic. In the late nineteenth century France's population growth was one of the
slowest in Europe, and the small increase depended on immigration rather than fertility.
To contemporaries this situation was especially alarming in view of the continuing rapid
expansion of population in the new German Empire.

the drop was often more precipitous in certain urban areas. The underlying cause for declining fertility rates was the ever more widespread acceptance of family limitation, a practice already well established in the late eighteenth century. Nonetheless, in the second half of the nineteenth century these demographic shifts were linked to the continuing high rate of female participation in the labor force, which rose from 24 percent in 1866 to 38 percent in 1911. The majority of these women were employed in the large but slowly contracting agricultural sector; however, what drew greater attention was women's presence in non-agricultural work, which doubled between 1856 and 1906. Women were highly visible in the textile industry, the garment trades, and the new white-collar occupations.[18] For decades observers had voiced concern about the consequences of factory work on childbirth. Statistics on rates of infant mortality in heavily industrialized communities certainly seemed to justify this concern. A study of textile and metallurgy workers in the southern town of Saint Chamond corroborates the conclusions of nineteenth-century commentators. Infant mortality increased from 122 deaths per 1,000 births in the first half of the century to 200 deaths per 1,000 in the period 1861–98, the decades of rapid industrialization. Maternal mortality also doubled during the nineteenth century in this industrial town, a statistic that drew less attention from contemporaries.[19] Ideology, demography, and the structure of the labor force made it impossible to separate women's participation in production from their role in the reproductive process.

Politicians of both the right and the left called on the state to act in defense of this most fundamental "national resource." Motherhood distinguished women workers from male workers and from all citizens. It legitimated state intervention, but in such a way that the principles of individual independence were not violated. One of the Third Republic's earliest regulations of labor limited the work day for women in factories, primarily in the textile industry. Passed in 1892, after almost a decade of debate, it excluded women from nightwork and restricted their work day to eleven hours. In response to liberal critics of such intervention, one Radical social theorist argued in effect that women need not be consid-

18. Michael Hanagan, "Population Trends," and Karen Offen, "Women in the Labor Force," both in *Historical Dictionary of the Third French Republic, 1870–1940*, ed. Patrick H. Hutton (Westport, Conn., 1986), pp. 793–96, 1072–74.

19. Elinor Accampo, *Industrialization, Family Life, and Class Relations: Saint Chamond, 1815–1914* (Berkeley, 1989), pp. 125–29. The figures cited were for deaths between birth and one year. For infants aged 1–5 mortality also increased, from 95 per 1,000 in 1816–45 to 130 per 1,000 in 1861–98. Accampo accounts for the general fertility decline by a combination of increased infant and maternal mortality rates, resulting from the new industrial organization of work, *and* increased use of birth control in response to the new demands of factory work, especially as they affected women.

ered individuals, because they were mothers or potential mothers. The state had an obligation to protect the future of the nation. "If women who worked to excess would injure only themselves, it might be permissible to argue that the legislator should not intervene; but this is not the case. The woman injures the child she might produce. Without regulation of female labor, society will soon be menaced by a bastardization of the race."[20] Reformers also stressed that because women were considered legal minors, the state had a responsibility to care for their welfare.[21] This argument was especially apt in the case of the 1892 law, which clarified earlier regulation of child labor. Children and women were thus identified as distinct categories deserving special consideration because of their status as minors without full rights, and, in the case of women, because of their reproductive role. Not surprisingly, feminists increasingly voiced opposition to such gender-specific legislation. After 1900 organizations for women's rights adopted the socialist demand for a universal eight-hour work day.[22]

Radical politicians, however, easily endorsed the gender arguments. They shared the general concern about population decline; they were extremely uncomfortable with women as *ouvrières*; and they were uncertain about what place the hierarchical factory organization should have in a republican society. To some extent Radicals promoted gender-specific labor legislation because it was the most likely of all their reform efforts to be enacted into law. The rhetoric of domesticity and natalism could not easily be ignored by any legislator. Such regulation intensified the gender segregation of the labor market by creating distinct work schedules for men and women, and by excluding women from certain types of work.[23] Many deputies viewed this as a positive step. Most important for many liberal and conservative politicians, as well as for employers outside the textile industry, these gender-specific laws excluded men from regulation. Ultimately such arguments legitimated a series of gender-specific laws that not only regulated women's working conditions but also intervened in circumstances surrounding pregnancy, birth, and child care.[24]

Some reformers promoted gender-specific legislation in part because it

20. Paul Pic, *Traité élémentaire de législation industrielle: Les Lois ouvrières*, 2d ed. (Paris, 1903), p. 503.

21. Paul Deschanel, "Les Conditions du travail et le collectivisme," *Revue Politique et Parlementaire* 10 (1896): 7.

22. Mary Lynn Stewart, *Women, Work, and the French State: Labour Protection and Social Patriarchy, 1879–1919* (Montreal, 1989), pp. 56–57.

23. Ibid., pp. 98, 196–97.

24. Mary Lynn Stewart, "Protecting Infants: The French Campaign for Maternity Leaves, 1890's–1913," *French Historical Studies* 13 (Spring 1983), and her important *Women, Work, and the French State.*

seemed a strategy to avoid a more acrimonious debate over universal labor regulation. Some liberal theorists and powerful politicians viewed any form of state intervention as a threat to laissez-faire principles. And some reformers supported gender-specific legislation as a means to establish the legitimacy of the principle of state intervention, no matter how limited. These politicians dared to extend the argument of the state's obligation to protect the weak to cover male workers as well. This debate between reformers and liberals over the implications of regulating women's work linked gender-specific legislation to the issue of the extent to which the state could legitimately intervene in labor conditions. By the late nineteenth century the Radical response to classical laissez-faire was expressed in the theory of *solidarité*, most closely associated with Léon Bourgeois, one of the founders of the Radical Party. Bourgeois, who identified himself as a moderate and conciliatory Radical, participated regularly in the parliamentary committee work that constructed reform legislation. He intended his theory of *solidarité* to provide a new set of principles that would, enable Radicals to transcend liberal individualism *and* refute socialist class conflict. All members of society were tied by bonds of reciprocal indebtedness; the republican state was to guarantee that this reciprocity would be acknowledged. In practice Bourgeois's theory endorsed a mild slate of social insurance programs.

It is not surprising that at the heart of Bourgeois's theory was once again an image of the family. The family was both a metaphor for the state as envisaged by the solidarists and the original network of mutual relations of dependence. Without following its full implications, Bourgeois came very close to revealing the gender bias of liberal individualism and liberal contract theory. Behind the sacrosanct individual of both liberal and republican theories stood others who had been neglected and excluded from political consideration, the members of the individual's family, the women and the children.[25] In 1897 Bourgeois proclaimed, "Solitary man does not exist; man in the state of nature is already associated with another.... The origins of *solidarité* are the family and the fatherland." Bourgeois, however, had little interest in pursuing theoretical issues concerning the ideological construction of the individual. He viewed *solidarité* in practical political terms as the means to legitimate social reform legislation, not as a critique of republican individualism. As might be expected, Bourgeois was prominent among those politicians who identified the declining birth rate as one of France's most serious problems. Labor legislation, even universal regulation of the work day, had "the higher goal to ensure the vigor

25. Pateman, "Fraternal Social Contract," pp. 36, 43.

and the future of the race, by organizing social hygiene."[26] Bourgeois campaigned for both gender-specific and universal labor reforms principally as a means to protect the working-class family and by extension the "fatherland."

When Bourgeois was not equating himself with the healing physician, his favorite metaphor was *le bon père de famille*. As minister of labor in 1912, Bourgeois reminded the Senate, "We are the guardians of our nation's finances, but we are also the guardians of social peace. We are required to administer the national fortune wisely, like good fathers of the family . . . , but we are also required like good fathers of the family we head to see that no child can say that it doesn't have its fair share."[27] In Bourgeois's view a "fair share" for French working women was a series of insurance and protective laws that would help them to fulfill their obligations as mothers and wives. *Solidarité* could reduce the consequences of unjust social inequalities, but it was not intended to disturb what Bourgeois regarded as natural inequalities. Sex, first on his list of such "natural" differences, was followed by "age, race, physical force, intelligence, and will."[28] *Solidarité* was never the most consistent or rigorous theory. Its emphasis on domesticity, social hygiene, and gender inequality often undermined calls for universal protective labor legislation. All the same, its critique of the "natural" masculine individual made it more difficult for liberals to defend the "liberty" of the male worker against the intervention of the state.

Rejecting the ambiguities of *solidarité*, more militant Radical politicians continued to link gender-specific protective labor legislation with legislation covering all adult workers. A few of these Radicals were willing to admit that, despite the existence of the republican state, working-class men, like women, were denied meaningful equality. Since the mid–nineteenth century the growing number of propertyless male workers had alarmed republicans, who feared that such proletarians would not be able to exercise the rights and responsibilities of citizens. From this viewpoint male workers, being propertyless, were de facto excluded from an essential republican condition of citizenship. Some Radicals insisted that the state could rectify this situation through universal labor legislation, and in fact must do so in order to defend the Republic. Protective labor legislation was necessary so that *men* might have greater economic security and therefore be better able to fulfill their

---

26. Léon Bourgeois, "Réunion sur l'éducation sociale" (May 1897) and speech in the Chamber of Deputies (1912), both in *La Politique de la prévoyance sociale: La Doctrine et la méthode* (Paris, 1914), 1:68, 244. See also his "Discours de l'Alliance d'hygiène" (October 1910), ibid., pp. 96–97.

27. Bourgeois speech in the Senate (1912), ibid., pp. 240–41, 378.

28. Léon Bourgeois, *Solidarité*, 2d ed. (Paris, 1897), p. 109.

responsibilities as citizens.[29] Such a view was beginning to alter the nineteenth-century republican assumptions about individuals, citizens, and the state. Most Radicals, however, were alarmed by this departure from conventional beliefs. Not a few came to fear that by enacting such universal labor legislation they would be admitting what the Marxist leader Jules Guesde had proclaimed: "To vote a protective labor law is to recognize social classes. . . . You will affirm that there is an oppressed and exploited class."[30] Rather than risk a legal recognition of class and an admission of inequality among citizens, those Radicals committed to improving workers' conditions preferred gender-specific legislation. They found it easier to recognize the subordination of working women and extend some legal protection to mothers than to acknowledge that neither men nor women of the working class could easily exercise their freedoms. Radical politicians were reluctant to view women in the same way as men, or to view both as members of the workforce, whose natural freedoms were limited equally by their economic insecurity. Women remained above all mothers: their physiology required protection not for their individual benefit but for the good of their children and the nation.

Labor legislation was finally enacted for a variety of motives and relied on sometimes contradictory arguments. The ten-hour bill passed in 1900 is a case in point. Many supporters and opponents of the law viewed it as a step toward a ten-hour work day for all French workers. Its principal architects, the independent socialists Alexandre Millerand and Pierre Colliard, spoke of its potential to enable workers to function more fully as citizens.[31] The parliamentary debates on the length of the work day implicitly recognized the importance of the revolutionary demand for an eight-hour day, which the Socialist International and the French labor movement had put forward since 1890. Catholic supporters of the bill regarded it as a means to strengthen the family.[32] Liberal opponents of the legislation denounced it as a coercive attempt to impose uniformity on naturally diverse social categories and predicted economic ruin.[33] While these ideological debates raged, the actual legislation functioned to make the gender-specific legislation of 1892 more efficient. The passage of the law reflected a general consensus that the earlier regulation of women's hours had created serious problems for management as well as for labor

---

29. Report of the Chamber's Committee on Labor on ten-hour legislation, Assemblée Nationale, Chambre des Députés, Documents, session extraordinaire, December 11, 1899, p. 341. (Hereafter cited as Chambre des Députés.)

30. Chambre des Députés, Débats, June 15, 1896, p. 254.

31. Alexandre Millerand, Chambre des Députés, November 21, 1902, p. 458.

32. Abbé Lemire, Chambre des Députés, December 21, 1899, p. 598.

33. Edouard Aynard, Chambre des Députés, June 24, 1896, p. 421.

in the textile industry. Only under the threat of stringent application of the 1892 law did the Parliament finally pass the 1900 reform. The new legislation stipulated that men, women, and children who worked together would be subject to the same regulations. In an effort to effect a compromise between the Senate and Chamber versions, as well as to placate those who feared the disruption of reduced hours, the law introduced the ten-hour work day over a four-year period—eleven hours in 1900, ten and a half in 1902, and finally ten in 1904. Like all labor legislation, this bill permitted numerous specific exemptions.

Reflecting the considerable confusion with which republicans viewed labor regulation, the 1900 ten-hour bill was both an effort to protect "minors" and an attempt to promote the independence of male workers. In practice it did not significantly improve working conditions for either men or women in the textile industry. Especially in the heavily industrialized north of France, strikes occurred at each phase of the new hours regulation. Men and women defended their wages against employers' attempts to reduce them along with their hours.[34] To avoid compliance with the law, employers sometimes dismissed women, or more commonly reorganized the workplace in order to separate men and women. The courts then accepted this arrangement as one in which the law no longer applied.[35] In the end, however, and despite the variety of motives and consequences, the ten-hour day became the norm in the textile industry.

Republican rhetoric, which had long associated the republic with a harmonious but hierarchical family centered on the nurturing *femme simple*, made it difficult for Radical politicians to view working women as anything other than mothers. Many Radicals, never the most cohesive of political groups, simply continued to use whatever argument and rhetoric seemed least controversial to enact reforms that might serve as valuable assets in electoral campaigns. They voted for the gender-specific legislation, and their often vacillating support for universal legislation was usually couched in the rhetoric of social peace and natalism. By this strategy they avoided dealing with difficult ideological issues, such as genuine equality, which might require them to consider the working conditions of both men and women. The debates on labor legislation immediately before World War I raised—but could not resolve—the issues of the relations between gender, class, and citizen. Certainly the republican rhetoric forged during the second half of the nineteenth century could not easily provide answers to such questions.

34. Judith F. Stone, *The Search for Social Peace: Reform Legislation in France, 1890–1914* (Albany, 1985), pp. 123–34; Stewart, *Women, Work, and the French State*, p. 119.
35. Stewart, *Women, Work, and the French State*, p. 103.

AT THE SAME TIME that politicians succeeded in securing some gender-specific labor legislation by arguing the special case of women as mothers, a vital national resource, or as persons with limited legal protection, the growing French women's movement was demanding greater civic equality. This movement, in presenting women's claims to full citizenship, appealed to republican ideology. Since the beginning of the Third Republic middle-class republican women had been organizing to demand the extension of civil and political rights. They were deeply committed to the Republic and assumed that its establishment would necessarily increase the participation of women in public and political life.[36] This was not the case; greater civil rights were won only slowly over several decades and suffrage was denied women for the entire history of the Third Republic.[37] Resistance to the expansion of equality suggests the strength of gender differences in republican ideology, the diversity of republican politicians' responses to women's emancipation, and the range of women's attitudes toward the Republic.

Educational reform, like labor reform, was an area in which republican and Radical politicians held out the promise of greater opportunities for women while maintaining, if not reinforcing, women's subordinate status. The Ferry laws of 1881 and 1882 made free, secular primary education obligatory for both boys and girls; public secondary education was established for girls in 1880. The republican politicians who promoted this expansion were very explicit, however, that the goal of educating girls was to prepare a new generation of "republican mothers." The state-authorized primary curricula differed sharply for the two sexes, and girls' secondary schools did not prepare their students for the baccalaureate exam necessary for admission to the university.[38] The republican educational reforms closely mirrored the ideological commitment to both equality and gender hierarchy, but they did create new careers that made upward social mobility possible for women.[39] Yet republican and Radical politicians and administrators continued to view female teachers as civic versions of "republican mothers." At the same time, however, the educa-

---

36. Claire Moses, *French Feminism in the Nineteenth Century* (Albany, 1984), pp. 197–200.

37. Some gains were made: divorce became legal in 1884, although not by mutual consent; in 1893 single and separated women were accorded full legal status; women could be witnesses in law courts after 1897; and in 1907 married women gained control over their own wages.

38. Linda Clark, *Schooling the Daughters of Marianne: Textbooks and Socialization of Girls in the Modern French Primary Schools* (Albany, 1984).

39. Between 1876 and 1906 the number of women in education quadrupled, increasing from 14,000 to 57,000. In 1906 women accounted for 92.5% of all primary teachers. See Steven C. Hause and Anne R. Kenney, *Women's Suffrage and Social Politics in the French Third Republic* (Princeton, 1984), p. 18.

tion bureaucracy refused to recognize that women teachers with families might have particular needs that male teachers did not.[40]

The expansion of state-organized education, and especially female education, was central to the conflict between the Third Republic and the Catholic Church. A major motive in creating state secondary schools for girls was to reduce the number of convent-educated bourgeois women. Female education was an aspect of the clerical question in which women and their deepest allegiances were constantly being examined. It is hardly surprising that the discussion of women's political attitudes should in turn become part of the debate surrounding women's suffrage. Influential parliamentary leaders as well as sections of the Radical Party's rank and file remained adamant opponents of women's suffrage. The ostensible reason that most Radicals offered for postponing or denying full political equality was defense of the Republic against the onslaught of clerically controlled women. This was hardly a logical argument for those who were dedicated to "the sovereignty of universal suffrage," but the reality of many women's continued commitment to the Catholic Church and the prominent position of women in stridently clerical and antirepublican organizations supplied justifications for the Radicals' hesitation and resistance. This purported republican defense was tied to the Radicals' fear that any change in the system might threaten their recently established prominence. Many among them recognized no distinction between their own electoral victories and the survival of the Republic. Defense against the clerical danger also rationalized some Radicals' deeper misogyny. They could not imagine women acting in the public arena. Republican men had always claimed that women must be emancipated from the priests, but they had not imagined women as citizens.

Republican feminist organizations, which had adopted the right to vote as their central demand by 1900, called on the Radical Party to make its commitment to universal suffrage a reality. They petitioned Radical congresses beginning with the first in 1901. Each year the Congress, which excluded women from participation, easily defeated motions to endorse woman suffrage. Not until 1907 did the party program include a statement on women. Then at the height of their political power the Radical Party pledged to endorse "the gradual extension of the rights of women, who ought to be legally protected in all the circumstances of their lives. Communal, departmental, and national assistance ought to be provided for pregnant and poor women; the legislated leave of six weeks before and after giving birth should include women in small

40. Leslie Page Moch, "Government Policy and Women's Experience: The Case of Teachers in France," *Feminist Studies* 14 (Summer 1988).

workshops, stores, and offices."[41] Gender-specific protection for working mothers was easier to promise than the vote to an entirely new category of citizens. With thunderous silence the Radicals ignored the question of votes for women.

Antifeminists, however, did not constitute the entire party; it also included leading parliamentary spokesmen for suffrage, such as Ferdinand Buisson. A prominent Radical, member of the important Chamber Committee on Universal Suffrage, Buisson was a staunch supporter of women's struggle for political equality. He had been a leader in republican educational reforms, served as president of the Ligue des Droits de l'Homme, and was a highly respected member of the liberal Protestant community. In 1906 the bill on the municipal vote for women was sent to the Committee on Universal Suffrage; finally after three years Buisson reported favorably to the committee; in 1911 his report was published as *Le Vote des femmes* and widely read. Despite this support, the Chamber failed to debate the bill during the 1910–14 session.[42]

Buisson's argument in support of women's suffrage reflected the difficulties encountered when republican ideology was used to promote the political emancipation of women. In *Le Vote des femmes* Buisson sought to present women's suffrage as another inevitable step in the march of human progress, fulfilling the rationalist vision of "the natural rights of all human beings." Examining the historical record, however, Buisson had to concede that the Jacobin revolutionaries treated women who claimed their rights with "extreme harshness and a most unjust disdain."[43] This confrontation between women's early demands for political equality, and the Jacobins' exclusionary practice placed the origins of the modern women's movement and the origins of French republicanism in conflict. Buisson's argument for evolutionary, inevitable progress lost much of its persuasiveness. Despite all his goodwill and commitment to women's suffrage, Buisson could not easily incorporate the struggle for women's rights into the heritage of the Revolution and the nineteenth-century republican formulation of equality and progress.

THROUGHOUT THE NINETEENTH CENTURY perceptive observers recognized the tension between the ideal of political equality extended to all citizens and the demand that women must occupy a separate domestic sphere.

41. *Compte rendu du septième congrès annuel du parti Radical et Radical-socialiste* (Nancy, 1907), "Programme du parti."

42. This was the third bill addressing women's suffrage that had been sent to the committee and the only one reported on in committee. While the Radicals had promised the suffrage organizations support, they had explained that no general debate could occur until after the difficult issue of proportional representation was decided. See Steven C. Hause, *Hubertine Auclert: The French Suffragette* (New Haven, 1987), pp. 172–76, 190.

43. Ferdinand Buisson, *Le Vote des femmes* (Paris, 1911), pp. 19, 15.

Even those republican men most sympathetic to women imperiously relegated them to the home, denying the reality of their growing presence in the labor force. Despite all the talk of separate but equal spheres, there could be no question that in the republican vision the domestic world was subordinate, although vitally necessary, to the public realm of politics. Not a few republicans were uncomfortable with an ideology that attempted to encompass both male political equality and a subordinate female domesticity. Some feared that such contradictions might endanger the legitimacy of republicanism itself. The ideological dissonance became especially pronounced as republicans confronted concrete issues that dealt with working women's lives and as they had to respond to women's demands for political rights.

Yet their belief system offered few possibilities for fundamental adjustment. Radicals, such as Léon Bourgeois, employed a rhetoric that presented the state as a benevolent patriarch, protecting mothers and their children. This emphasis on the enforcement of social responsibility proved a successful method to enact gender-specific legislation. The state would regulate working women's lives as a result of fathers' and husbands' absence or inadequacy. In effect these solidarist Radicals denied working-class women any independent identity. Bourgeois's image of the Radical politician as *bon père de famille* carried distant echoes of the patriarchal royal state. But there were limits to such paternalism; political equality and individual liberty were the essence of republicanism and had to remain paramount in its ideology and rhetoric.

When the largely middle-class suffrage organizations demanded these rights for women, however, they were rejected. Education was extended to all women, but its intention was to emancipate them from the priests so that they might function as more companionable wives and better republican mothers. One might say that republicans never went far enough to make their cult of domesticity competitive with the Catholic version. Despite all the republicans' quasi-mythical references to fecundity, spirituality, and nature, they never matched the appeal of the much older and more internally consistent Catholic cult of mother and child. Republicans had clearly intended that their domestic idyll would dethrone the power of the church in favor of the republican husband's authority. For many women, however, the secularized myth had little appeal.

Before World War I, French women gained a few advances in the area of civil rights. Here, too, even the limited gains were problematic, for from its inception the republican meaning of individual and citizen had always meant man, and there has never been any systematic attempt to alter this essential assumption. Some of the many working women received protection through gender-specific labor legislation. There is evidence, however, that many working women resented these laws and that they did little to improve their lives.[44] Although this contradictory republican ideology offered relatively few improvements in response to women's political, social, and economic needs, it did function as a means to legitimate the state and society of the Third Republic. Politicians' universal acceptance of separate spheres contributed to the functioning of the masculine world of the state administration and the National Assembly. The republican cult of domesticity provided rhetoric and symbols through which erstwhile political opponents could communicate and agree on fundamental social institutions.[45] The idealization of wife and especially mother offered an intriguing point of consensus and competition between republicans and clericals.

Most important, the central tension between political equality and a gendered hierarchy provided a dramatic illustration of the "inevitable" coexistence of equality and inequality. It demonstrated the "natural" impossibility of full equality. In the powerful writings of Michelet and Hugo gender and class constantly reflected and stood for each other. The organization of harmonious gender relations in the family was to be a model for class relations and vice versa. When republicans considered the state, the family, and society, they found the hierarchical ordering of gender the most accessible and powerful medium to express their desire for harmony, security, and an end to conflict. At the same time, however, republicans, and particularly Radicals, were never entirely satisfied with defending the political or social status quo; to do so would undermine their identity as republicans. Their desire for stability, including the stability of traditional gender relations, was constantly disrupted by their continuing allegiance to political equality. These disruptions created a perpetual dissonance in their ideology, particularly as women adopted republican rhetoric and demanded citizenship and equality.

44. Stewart, *Women, Work, and the French State*, pp. 156–57, 201–2.
45. Karen Offen discusses the impact of domesticity on feminism and argues persuasively for the existence of a familial feminism in France: "Depopulation, Nationalism, and Feminism," and "Ernest Legouvé and the Doctrine of 'Equality in Difference' for Women: A Case Study of Male Feminism in Nineteenth-Century French Thought," *Journal of Modern History* 58 (June 1986): 479–81.

IV

GENDER,
POLITICS,
AND
CITIZENSHIP

10

Manhood, Womanhood, and the Politics of Class in Britain, 1790–1845

Anna Clark

Many British historians have begun to abandon the Marxist analysis of class, realizing that early nineteenth-century working people did not share a common experience of the mode of production and did not espouse a socialist program. Instead, some historians have taken the "linguistic turn": they find that working people borrowed radical republican and constitutionalist rhetorics from earlier traditions originated by men of a higher social rank. Instead of espousing a class analysis, working men spoke in terms of "the People."[1] But who were the People? Elite late eighteenth-century reformers excluded laboring men from their concept of the People, and by 1832 the First Reform Act hardened the class line by enfranchising middle-class men, demarcating the working class as undeserving of the vote. In response, early nineteenth-century radicals often declared that working men *were* the

Thanks to Sonya Rose for her helpful comments on this chapter. Fragments of it appear in a different form in my book *The Struggle for the Breeches: Gender and the Making of the British Working Class* (Berkeley: University of California Press, 1995).

1. Most notably Gareth Stedman Jones, "Rethinking Chartism," in his *Languages of Class: Studies in English Working-Class History, 1832–1982* (Cambridge, 1983), pp. 90–95. See also Patrick Joyce, *Visions of the People: Industrial England and the Question of Class, 1840–1914* (Cambridge, 1991), p. 27; James Vernon, *Politics and the People* (Cambridge, 1993), p. 310.

People; as James Epstein and others point out, they also defined class through politics.[2]

But does a political definition of class further marginalize women in working-class history? When working-class politics is placed in a tradition of civic humanism and republicanism that defines the public world as necessarily separate from the private, domestic one, the danger is that women and their concerns will be seen as politically irrelevant. Ruth Smith and Deborah Valenze have argued that eighteenth-century plebeian political action, which often took the form of riots and crowd agitation, allowed women to defend their own community values. When radicals began to focus on formal organization and individual rights, women could find no place in politics.[3] Several feminist historians have also pointed out that the language of class defined the working-class citizen as male and excluded women from politics; furthermore, Joan Scott argues that women acceded to their own exclusion by defining themselves in domestic terms.[4]

An examination of political language, however, must problematize masculinity as well as femininity. The traditions of civic humanism and classical republicanism often excluded working men as well as women, for they simply could not aspire to the propertied manhood of the gentleman. In response, plebeian radicals drew upon more inclusive political philosophies, such as that of Tom Paine, and redefined political manhood to suit themselves. The universalist promise of a politics based on liberty, reason, and equality, however, could also provide avenues for a few women to assert their political rights. Conversely, many plebeian men as well as women were more concerned with issues of community survival than with abstract constitutional issues.

Second, we must not only see how political *language* can be under-

2. For the argument that Chartism was a working-class movement, see James Epstein, "Rethinking the Categories of Working-Class History," *Labour/Le Travailleur* 18 (Fall 1986): 202; Marc W. Steinberg, "The Re-making of the English Working Class?" *Theory and Society* 20, no. 2 (1991): 173–97; Neville Kirk, "In Defense of Class: A Critique of Gareth Stedman Jones," *International Raview of Social History* 32, no. 1 (1987): 5; John C. Belchem, "Radical Language and Ideology in Early Nineteenth-Century England: The Challenge of the Platform," *Albion* 20, no. 2 (1988): 258.

3. Ruth L. Smith and Deborah Valenze, "Mutuality and Marginality: Liberal Moral Theory of Working-Class Women in Nineteenth-Century England," *Signs* 13, no. 2 (1988): 289.

4. Sally Alexander, "Women, Class, and Sexual Difference in the 1830s and 1840s: Some Reflections on the Writing of a Feminist History," *History Workshop Journal* 17 (Spring 1984): 125–49; Joan Scott, "On Language, Gender, and Working-Class History," in her *Gender and the Politics of History* (New York, 1988), p. 53; Catherine Hall, "The Tale of Samuel and Jemima: Gender and Working-Class Culture in Early Nineteenth-Century England," in her *White, Male, and Middle Class: Explorations in Feminism and History* (Cambridge, 1992), p. 131.

stood in gendered terms; by integrating women into the People, we can also integrate language with practice and widen our notion of the political. What people do is as important as what they say. Political rhetoric could acquire real power only if radicals could incite working people to action. Since radical rhetoric did not have the power of the vote or state authority behind it, working people had to draw on the power of numbers; they had to mobilize women as well as men to exploit the potential of whole communities. To appeal to plebeian men *and* women, radicals sometimes refused to accept a politics of the People restricted to constitutional and parliamentary concerns; for them, political issues included food and families, and political practice went beyond the expression of public opinion to mass organization. As Dorothy Thompson has shown, women responded, becoming extremely active in most radical movements during the first half of the nineteenth century.[5] Their experience of activism then enabled some women to transform their concepts of themselves as political actors.

By examining the changing interaction between radical language and organizational practice, first in the period 1790–1820, the initial wave of popular radicalism, and then in the period 1832–1842, when Chartism was the working people's response to the 1832 Reform Act, we shall see how notions of the People changed along gendered lines.

THE ORIGINS OF CITIZENSHIP

Before 1832, not only almost all workingmen but many men of property were excluded from the privilege of voting for members of Parliament. For eighteenth-century reformers, too, the meaning of citizenship did not encompass working men, let alone women. Their ideology, known as civic humanism, was influenced by ancient Greek republicanism, Machiavelli, and seventeenth-century republicans such as James Harrington.[6] In this tradition, only free male householders were citizens, certainly not women, servants, slaves, or mechanics, who were regarded as inferior beings.[7] As Carole Pateman has pointed out, the equality of the male citizen in relation to other men depended on his ability

---

5. Dorothy Thompson, "Women and Radical Politics: A Lost Dimension," in *The Rights and Wrongs of Women*, ed. Juliet Mitchell and Ann Oakley (Harmondsworth, 1976), p. 115.

6. John Robertson, "The Scottish Enlightenment and the Civil Tradition," and J. G. A. Pocock, "Cambridge Paradigms and Scotch Philosophers," both in *Wealth and Virtue: The Shaping of Political Economy in the Scottish Enlightenment*, ed. Istvan Hont and Michael Ignatieff (Cambridge, 1983), pp. 138, 235.

7. Susan M. Okin, *Women in Western Political Thought* (Princeton, 1979), p. 91.

to control and dominate women, children, and servants in his own household.[8]

Masculinity therefore defined citizenship—but the definition of masculinity was historically mutable. The civic humanists built on the tradition of classical republicanism to argue that the prerequisite for citizenship was independence, which enabled a man to exercise civic virtue—in Latin, *virtus*. *Virtus* connoted masculinity, austerity, force, strength, and autonomy, all qualities that enabled the citizen to put public concerns above private interests.[9] Eighteenth-century thinkers who opposed the ruling party used these ideas to denounce the aristocratic oligarchy as effeminate, degenerate, and corrupted by luxury.[10] The ideal citizen was therefore the benevolent country gentleman, who looked after society's interests rather than being bought off by the government.

This oppositional ideology, however, was based on landholding rather than trade, the foundation of the growing middle class's wealth and power. Civic humanists had often attacked commerce, the source of their wealth, as leading to luxury and effeminacy.[11] To transform civic humanism into an ideology that could justify their own claims to political power, middle-class reformers began to develop the notion of separate spheres. They modified the old stoicism of civic virtue in favor of a civilized domesticity, in which the middle-class male's status as head of household countered any suspicion of effeminacy. They also developed a new "public sphere" of associations, debating clubs, and local government, defining this arena by excluding women and working men.[12] Middle-class men thus began to define themselves as "citizens," both in

8. Carole Pateman, *The Disorder of Women: Democratic Feminism and Political Theory* (Stanford, 1989), p. 6.

9. Hanna Pitkin, *Fortune Was a Woman: Gender in the Political Thought of Niccolò Machiavelli* (Berkeley, 1984), p. 25.

10. Caroline Robbins, *The Eighteenth-Century Commonwealthman* (Cambridge, Mass., 1959), pp. 43, 49, 182, 201. This trope was borrowed by American revolutionaries. See Linda K. Kerber, "The Paradox of Women's Citizenship in the Early Republic," *American Historical Review* 97 (1992): 354.

11. As John Dwyer points out in *Virtuous Discourse: Sensibility and Community in Late Eighteenth-Century Scotland* (Edinburgh, 1987), p. 38, this tradition persisted in eighteenth-century Scotland along with Enlightenment thinking. See also J. G. A. Pocock, *Virtue, Commerce, and History* (New York, 1985), p. 235; G. J. Barker-Benfield, *The Culture of Sensibility: Sex and Society in Eighteenth-Century Britain* (Chicago, 1992), pp. 104–53.

12. John Seed, "From 'Middling Sort' to Middle Class in Late Eighteenth- and Early Nineteenth-Century England," in *Social Orders and Social Classes in Europe since 1500: Studies in Social Stratification*, ed. M. L. Bush (New York, 1992), p. 131; Jürgen Habermas, *The Structural Transformation of the Public Sphere*, trans. Thomas Burger (1962; Cambridge, Mass., 1989), p. 73. For the exclusion of women, see Catherine Hall, "Gender, Class, and Politics, 1780–1850," in her *White, Male, and Middle Class*, p. 159; for exclusion of workingmen, see John Smail, *The Origins of Middle-class Culture: Halifax, Yorkshire, 1660–1780* (Ithaca, 1994), chap. 5.

common usage, as citizens of a city ("burghers"), and as those whose
status as property-owning, taxpaying heads of households made them
most deserving of political participation.[13] Noted Lord Cockburn, "The
public was the word for the middle ranks, and all below this was the
populace or the *mob.*"[14] They did not think that plebeian men,
unendowed with property, had the independence that would give them a
political will of their own.[15] During the era of the French Revolution, for
instance, the middle-class Society for Constitutional Information believed the vote should be given only to men whose property made them
independent.[16] Middle-class reformers, therefore, did not see working
men as deserving the full privileges of masculinity.

Inspired by the French Revolution, plebeian radicals nonetheless
formed their own political organization, the London Corresponding Society (L.C.S.), with provincial branches. Not surprisingly, at the first meeting of the L.C.S. its members had to struggle against the disbelief of some
that "mere tradesmen, shopkeepers and mechanics had a right to seek
Parliamentary reform."[17] Plebeian radicals could not simply adopt whole-
heartedly the tradition of civic humanism by counterposing the austere
virtue of the male householder with the corruption of the effeminate
aristocrat, for plebeian men often could not live up to this ideal themselves. In fact, their ability to attain the autonomy of mastership and
marriage had steadily eroded over the course of the eighteenth century as
capitalist competition and proletarianization increased. Many artisans
were forced to remain journeymen all their lives and could not afford to
marry. To gain solidarity against the masters, they bonded together
through drinking and socializing in workshops and pubs, forming a lively
journeyman culture. Many members of the London Corresponding Society were bachelors who based their notion of citizenship on the fraternal
bonding they experienced as they discussed politics in pubs, rather than
on the status of the individual male householder and property owner.[18]

13. For citizens as burghers or burgesses of a city, see *Oxford English Dictionary* S.V.
"citizen." See also Penelope J. Corfield, "Class in Eighteenth-Century Britain," in *Language, History, and Class,* ed. Corfield (Oxford, 1991), pp. 117, 122.

14. Lord Henry Cockburn, *An Examination of the Trials for Sedition Which Have
Hitherto Occurred in Scotland* (1888; New York, 1970), p. 248.

15. Carl B. Cone, *The English Jacobins: Reformers in Late Eighteenth-Century England*
(New York, 1968), p. 16.

16. Albert Goodwin, *The Friends of Liberty: The English Democratic Movement in the
Age of the French Revolution* (London, 1979), p. 211.

17. Ibid., p. 192. In Glasgow the main organization was the Associated Friends of the
Constitution and the People, which was somewhat less republican than the L.C.S.,
corresponding with the London Friends of the People, but it had a wider membership than
the London group, being dominated by weavers, tradesmen, and shopkeepers. See Henry
W. Meikle, *Scotland and the French Revolution* (Glasgow, 1912), p. 92.

18. British Library (BL), Add. Ms. 27, 814, f. 238, in *Selections from the Papers of the
London Corresponding Society, 1792–1799,* ed. Mary Thale (Cambridge, 1982), p. 8.

Thomas Paine gave such men the political philosophy to justify their claims. Paine cut across the old assumptions of civic humanism by arguing that all men deserved political representation because as humans they had access to reason. All men were born equal, declared Paine, created equal by God. Although Paine did not explicitly extend these rights to women, his philosophy, unlike civic humanism, did not rely on sexual difference, because it was not essentially dependent on the association of masculinity with the power of the head of household.[19] He rejected organic models that depicted society as a body, complete with the natural subordination of hands and heart to head; instead, he proclaimed, a nation "is like a body contained within a circle, having a common centre in which every radius meets; and that centre is formed by representation."[20]

Mary Wollstonecraft took up Paine's ideas to argue that because women could reason, they deserved citizenship as well. In her *Vindication of the Rights of Woman* she argued that women should be industrious so that they could be independent citizens, rather than dependent parasites like the aristocracy. Women deserved citizenship, she pointed out, for as rational mothers they contributed to civic virtue. Her interpretation of the tradition of civic humanism thus detached the idea of independence from masculine power over a household.[21] Unlike her contemporaries, who linked women with emotion and men with reason,[22] Wollstonecraft did not see women as opposite to and utterly different from men, nor did she see them as the same as men. For her, "humanity" required the breaking down of rigid gender differentiations: women should acquire "manly virtues" and men should become "chaste and modest."[23] This strategy allowed her to claim citizenship for women without denying women's experiences.

Paine and other radical theorists, however, had to acknowledge sexual difference in order to assert their own humanity against conservatives such as Edmund Burke, who denounced the French Revolution for destroying rank and therefore reducing people to the level of animals. "On

19. Unlike Locke's philosophy. See Okin, *Women in Western Political Thought*, pp. 200–201.

20. Tom Paine, *The Rights of Man* (1791) (London, 1921), p. 178.

21. See George Barker-Benfield, "Mary Wollstonecraft: Eighteenth-Century Commonwealthwoman," *Journal of the History of Ideas* 50, no. 1 (1989): 95–115, for another discussion of these ideas.

22. Barker-Benfield, *Culture of Sensibility*, pp. 24, 384.

23. Mary Wollstonecraft, *A Vindication of the Rights of Woman* (1792), ed. Miriam Kramnick (Harmondsworth, 1978), pp. 80, 84. Catherine Macaulay, who wished to educate "a woman into a careless, modest beauty, grave, manly, noble, full of strength and majesty," believed there was "no characteristic Difference in Sex." See her "Letters on Education," excerpted in *First Feminists: British Women Writers, 1578–1799*, ed. Moira Ferguson (Bloomington, 1985), pp. 402, 410.

this scheme of things," he lamented, "a king is but a man; a queen is but a woman; a woman is but an animal; and an animal not of the highest order." For Burke, a binary understanding of gender was horrifyingly crude. To put Marie Antoinette in the same category as a fishwife was to offend his sensibilities. For him, in fact, only the upper class was gendered, as "gentlemen and ladies"; he scorned plebeians as an ungendered "swinish multitude."[24]

In response, Paine asserted, "It is time that Nations should be rational, and not be governed like animals, for the pleasure of their riders."[25] The common people, Paine and other radicals declared, were "men," not animals or children, as Burke had depicted them. Radicals asserted their humanity against Burke's attacks by defending the rights of families as well as men. Mary Wollstonecraft, for instance, accused Burke of "reserving" his "tears . . . for the downfall of queens, whose rank . . . throws a graceful veil over vices that degrade humanity; whilst the distress of many industrious mothers . . . were vulgar sorrows that could not move your commiseration."[26] Beginning in the 1790s, radicals articulated this wider vision as a concern for "humanity." "Humanity" meant an empathy, derived from one's own hardships, for the sufferings of others, rather than the condescending pity of bourgeois humanitarian philanthropists.[27] In the face of the civic humanists' assumption that only the concerns of individual males were relevant to politics, Paine's politics potentially appealed to women because of its concern for the welfare of families. Paine advocated government payments to women at childbirth, for instance, among other social benefits.[28] By 1795, the L.C.S. initiated mass meetings that addressed "a range of more urgent popular grievances" such as food shortages and high taxes, appealing to the family concerns of working people, most of whom were apathetic about constitutional affairs.[29]

24. Edmund Burke, "Reflections on the Revolution in France," excerpted in Marilyn Butler, *Burke, Paine, Godwin, and the Revolution Controversy* (Cambridge, 1984), pp. 44–45.

25. Paine, *Rights of Man*, pp. 242, 169. See also *The Trial of Thomas Muir . . . for Sedition* (London, 1793), p. 63, quoting *The Patriot*, a radical tract that Muir was accused of giving to a Kirkintilloch weaver. Similar language is found in a broadsheet, "London, Executive Committee, Sitting of Thursday, March 23, 1797," BL, Place Collection, volume on L.C.S., f. 32.

26. Mary Wollstonecraft, "A Vindication of the Rights of Man" (1790), in Butler, *Burke, Paine, Godwin*, p. 74. The "vices that degrade humanity" probably referred to rumors of Marie Antoinette's heterosexual and lesbian affairs circulated by ultraradicals at the beginning of the French Revolution, according to Iain McCalman in a talk at the Eighteenth-Century History Seminar of John Brewer, May 1992, Victoria and Albert Museum, London.

27. Raymond Williams, *Keywords* (New York, 1976), pp. 121–23.

28. Paine, *Rights of Man*, pp. 42, 253.

29. Goodwin, *Friends of Liberty*, p. 360.

For radicals, claiming the rights of fatherhood and motherhood was a way of asserting their humanity. They complained that governmental corruption and oppression prevented them from marrying and raising children. These complaints reflected both the personal concerns of bachelor journeymen, who were not paid enough to support a family, and the political problem that as lodgers rather than householders they were not considered to be independent citizens.[30] *Pigott's Political Dictionary* defined "wedlock . . . as that happy and enviable state, which but few can enjoy in wicked and unprincipled governments."[31]

The London Corresponding Society tried to appeal to workingmen as husbands and fathers. Trying to encourage flagging activity in 1797, the L.C.S. asked delinquent members if they stopped attending meetings because "the pittance of the Labourer well provides him with Food, comfortable clothes, and fills his little Cot with cir'cling pleasure?"[32] They must respond, it claimed, to "the voice of reason, and the tears of suffering humanity . . . in the name of . . . your famished wives and weeping children, to rally around the standard of liberty," and prove, "by your virtuous, peaceable and manly conduct, that you are worthy of being free."[33] Similarly, the militant pamphlet *The Happy Reign of George the Last* told men, "If you love your wives and children, or yourselves, you will not always consent to have needless and enormous contributions raised upon you."[34]

When radical groups began to address the specific issues of dearth, unemployment, and war, plebeian women as well as men expressed an interest in politics. In 1793, when rumors circulated at an open-air L.C.S. meeting that the society's aim was to "lower the price of provisions," women in the large curious crowd cried, "God bless them."[35] By 1795, the L.C.S. responded to this enthusiasm, and to food shortages and repression, with mass meetings that addressed "a range of more urgent popular grievances."[36] Food riots, in which women had always participated vigor-

---

30. Thomas Bentley, *A Short View of Some of the Evils and Grievances Which Oppress the British Empire* (London, 1792), in Greates London Council Record Office, Middlesex Sessions Roll 3553, Indictment 46, December 1792; *A Proposal on Behalf of the Married Poor* (London, 1801). This topic persisted in later radicalism. See "Remonstrance of the Journeymen Carpenters and Joiners," January 27, 1816, BL, Place Collection, Add. Ms. 27,799, f. 124. *Black Dwarf*, May 28, 1817, argued that soldiers should be allowed to marry.

31. *The Rights of Man, consisting of Extracts from Pigott's Political Dictionary* (London, 1794?), p. 7.

32. John Bone, secretary of L.C.S., "Fellow Citizen," 1797, in BL, Place Collection, Set 38.

33. "London, Executive Committee, sitting of Thurs. March 23, 1797," ibid., f. 32.

34. Anon., *The Happy Reign of George the Last: An Address to the Little Tradesmen, and the Labouring Poor of England* (London, 1795), p. 2.

35. Thale, *Papers of the L.C.S.*, p. 87.

36. Goodwin, *Friends of Liberty*, p. 360.

ously, sometimes acquired a radical context. Women dominated food riots in Manchester, for instance, and "bitterly" defied troops.[37]

Male reformers, however, persisted in defining the People as male, instead of representing whole communities including women and children. Indeed, they often wished to detach themselves from women, whom they associated with riots rather than rationality.[38] To assert their manhood, many radicals reinterpreted the old tradition of civic humanism to create a new vision of masculine citizenship. Grafting Paine's ideas onto civic humanism and the allied theory of the ancient constitution, they claimed that in the distant past manhood suffrage was an English right.[39] They borrowed civic humanism's critique of effeminacy and luxury to attack the upper class, counterposing their own virile masculinity to the femininity of aristocratic corruption and decadence. Even Paine pointed out that a title "reduces man into the diminutive of man in things which are great, and the counterfeit of woman in things which are little. It talks about its fine *blue ribbon* like a girl, and shows its new *garter* like a child."[40] William Godwin complained, "The dissipation and luxury that reign uncontrolled have spread effeminacy and irresolution everywhere."[41] This trope, of course, stemmed from a long tradition of civic humanism, but radicals used it in a new way to assert their own manliness at the expense of the upper class. Radicals even argued that noble Whiggish reformers had abandoned the masculine virtues of their revolutionary seventeenth-century ancestors. *Pigott's Political Dictionary*, for instance, declared that "effeminacy is now perfectly well described in Fop's Alley, at our Opera House, . . . by the descendents of Hampden, Sidney, Russell," and other seventeenth-century radicals.[42]

The dark years of repression during the Napoleonic Wars caused a divergence in notions of masculine citizenship. Many reformers retreated to conventional domesticity, and Mary Wollstonecraft's adventurous life seemed disreputable in the newly repressive atmosphere, tainting all other feminists as well. More plebeian activists, however, concealed their political agitation in a libertine subculture of

---

37. John Bohstedt, "Gender, Household, and Community Politics: Women in English Riots, 1790–1810," *Past and Present* 120 (1988): 110.

38. Hall, "Tale of Samuel and Jemima," p. 131.

39. Goodwin, *Friends of Liberty*, p. 21; James A. Epstein, "The Constitutional Idiom: Radical Reasoning, Rhetoric, and Action in Early Nineteenth-Century England," *Journal of Social History* 23, no. 3 (1990): 555.

40. Paine, *Rights of Man*, p. 59.

41. William Godwin, *A Defense of the Rockingham Party*, in *Four Early Pamphlets*, ed. Burton R. Pollin (1783; Gainesville, Fla., 1966), p. 2.

42. *The Rights of Nobles, consisting of Extracts from Pigott's Political Dictionary* (London, 1794?), p. 3.

London artisanry.[43] These ultraradicals emphasized a virile, heterosexual manhood as superior to that of the sober, punctilious middle-class man or the effeminate aristocrat. Plebeian men had long sought in a bachelor subculture consolations for the inability to attain the status of mastership and marriage. They celebrated their freedom in ribald songs, bragging of seducing girls and then saying no to marriage; if they married, they still spent most of their time and money at the pub.[44] As Iain McCalman notes, these artisans could regard themselves as rational, independent, and respectable even as they indulged in wine, women, song, and brawls. At the beginning of the nineteenth century various of the ultraradical leaders were indicted for rape and brothelkeeping.[45] Yet they went on the offensive by attacking supporters of the government and soldiers as effeminate dandies of uncertain gender.

This retreat into libertinism further closed off possibilities for women's involvement in politics, for it could easily descend into misogyny. Radicals who satirized "dandies" as examples of aristocratic corruption and decadence also undermined the nascent feminism of female activists.[46] In the periodical The Black Dwarf, "Roderick Random" advised "sweet revolutionary termagants" to expose dandies as unmanly instead of making ridiculous demands for political rights.[47]

But in the radical revival immediately after the Napoleonic Wars, activists began to reject the old libertine misogyny in favor of a wider vision of political mobilization that appealed to women. Even ultraradicals began to reform their heavy-drinking, bawdy ways to espouse a new, more respectable masculinity. Radicals began to augment the notion of plebeian citizenship as based on fraternal bonding around constitutional concerns to revive a wider conception of citizenship based on the needs of families and the mobilization of entire communities.

As a result, women's participation in politics increased, especially in the Lancashire and Glasgow textile districts. London artisans could immerse themselves in the fraternal solidarity of workshop and pub and view wives and children as distracting burdens, but northern male textile workers needed women's auxiliary labor in cottages and factories. They

43. J. Ann Hone, For the Cause of Truth: Radicalism in London, 1796–1821 (Oxford, 1982), p. 87; Iain McCalman, Radical Underworld: Prophets, Revolutionaries, and Pornographers in London, 1796–1840 (Cambridge, 1988), p. 45; McCalman, "Ultra-Radicalism and Convivial Debating Clubs," English Historical Review 102, no. 403 (1987): 311.

44. For a discussion of this subculture, see also Clark, Struggle for the Breeches, chap. 3.

45. Iain McCalman, Radical Underworld, pp. 28, 45, 187, 192.

46. Ellen Moers, The Dandy: Brummell to Beerbohm (London, 1960), p. 33; Leonore Davidoff and Catherine Hall, Family Fortunes: Men and Women of the English Middle Class, 1780–1850 (London, 1987), pp. 410–15.

47. Black Dwarf 2 (1818): 592, 704.

focused their organizations on networks of kin, neighborhood, and community, drawing women into strikes.[48] Northern women's experience in friendly societies and radical religion also prepared them to enter politics. The northern weaver Samuel Bamford, for instance, welcomed women's political participation and initiated a move to allow them to vote at meetings.[49] By 1818, a few women had begun to assert their right to participate in politics, emulating Mary Wollstonecraft by claiming their capacity to reason.[50]

At radical meetings around 1819, women commonly organized themselves into political unions and presented beautifully embroidered "caps of liberty" to male leaders. On one hand, male radicals were clearly using women as symbols of purity and virtue to counterbalance aristocratic corruption. On the other hand, as James Epstein notes, radical women often described themselves in modest, self-effacing terms even as their actions contradicted their rhetoric.[51] Such women's radical activity also enabled them to begin to modify the old association of femaleness with effeminacy and weakness and replace it with a new notion of radical virtue. This stress on virtue vaguely resembled the separate sphere to which middle-class doctrine consigned women, but radical womanhood differed from it in important ways. By appearing on public platforms, radical women violated the middle-class principle that female purity required domestic seclusion. Instead, radical women asserted that good mothers became political activists. Echoing Thomas Spence, they declared they were forced to enter politics because "our oppressors and tyrannical rulers" had withheld their natural rights to feed their children.[52] And women earned their place in radical politics at the Peterloo Massacre in 1819, when the cavalry attacked a Manchester working-class meeting and wounded one hundred women and girls.[53]

By 1820, therefore, plebeian radicals had created a new form of politics; they were able to mobilize large numbers of women as well as plebeian men by revealing to them the connections between their exclusion from the constitution and their suffering through war, unemployment, and dearth. In the process of appealing to women, plebeian activists also changed their notions of masculinity, moving away from the libertine virility of ultraradicalism toward a chivalrous manhood, especially in

48. As Maxine Berg suggests in *The Age of Manufactures* (London, 1985), p. 161. This point is developed in depth in Clark, *Struggle for the Breeches.*

49. Thompson, "Women and Radical Politics," p. 115; Samuel Bamford, *Passages in the Life of a Radical* (1844; Oxford, 1984), p. 123.

50. *Black Dwarf* 2 (1818): 655.

51. James Epstein, "Understanding the Cap of Liberty: Symbolic Practice and Social Conflict in Early Nineteenth-Century England," *Past and Present* 122 (1989): 103.

52. *Black Dwarf* 3 (1818): 510, 452.

53. Thompson, "Women and Radical Politics," p. 116.

defense of the vilified Queen Caroline when the profligate George IV tried to divorce her.[54] Yet this new chivalrous manhood provided common ground with middle-class reformers, and radicals still defined "the people" as the productive classes, including factory owners as well as artisans.[55]

THE CREATION OF A MASCULINE
WORKING-CLASS CONSCIOUSNESS

Events of the 1830s, however, rudely disrupted the potential acceptance of the wider notion of "the people." Most middle-class reformers rejected this alliance, denying the manhood of working-class men by excluding them from the 1832 Reform Act, which enfranchised only the middle class. In the process, a coherent definition of the working class was created—but a negative one.[56] Gendered notions of virtue, expressed in the ideologies of separate spheres, Malthusianism, and political economy, defined working people as undeserving of the privileges of participating in the state. In their separate sphere, middle-class men proved their public probity by the private virtue of their wives and daughters. Malthusianism and political economy depicted working class men as drunken louts who had not earned citizenship, the breadwinner wage, or even the right to procreate.[57] The newly reformed Parliament promptly acted upon these ideologies by refusing to pass effective legislation to limit the hours children worked in factories, and by enacting the New Poor Law, which confined the poor in prisonlike workhouses where husbands and wives were separated for Malthusian reasons.[58]

In response, working-class radicals needed to create a positive class identity for themselves. But they had inherited two disparate notions of the political from earlier radicals. Did class consciousness involve the actions of whole communities in the streets in defense of the interests of families? Or should class consciousness be defined as defending in Parlia-

54. Anna Clark, "Queen Caroline and the Sexual Politics of Popular Culture in London, 1820," *Representations* 31 (Summer 1990): 47–68.

55. *The People*, 1817, pp. 1–10; in Goldsmith's Library, University of London.

56. Stedman Jones, *Languages of Class*, pp. 90–95. For the ways in which language creates class, see Ernesto Laclau and Chantal Mouffe, *Hegemony and Socialist Strategy: Toward a Radical Democratic Politics* (London, 1985), p. 88; see also Pierre Bourdieu, "What Makes a Social Class," *Berkeley Journal of Sociology* 32 (1987): 13.

57. "The Chartists and Universal Suffrage," *Blackwood's Edinburgh Magazine* 187, no. 46 (1839): 296–97.

58. For a fuller discussion, see Clark, *Struggle for the Breeches*, chaps. 9 and 10, also Pat Thane, "Women and the Poor Law in Victorian and Edwardian England," *History Workshop Journal* 6 (Fall 1978): 28; Karl Polanyi, *The Great Transformation* (London, 1944), pp. 123–25.

ment the interests of working men? Especially in the early years of
Chartism, between 1838 and 1842, the first vision of politics promised to
predominate. Chartism, the working-class movement for the vote, grew
out of the movements against the New Poor Law and for the factory acts,
so it appealed to persons concerned with family issues even more than
the earlier movements.

As a result, women enthusiastically participated in the early years of
Chartism. Indeed, Chartists needed their help in mass demonstrations, in
gathering signatures for petitions, in strikes, and in exclusive dealing—
that is, boycotting shopkeepers who refused to support Chartists. To
draw women in, they tried to reshape the old masculine plebeian public
of beershops and workshops into a more integrated, disciplined, orderly
public sphere. As an alternative to the pub, they had tea parties, soirees,
and processions attended by whole families.[59]

Extending their activist cooperative traditions from textile communities into Chartism, women formed more than 150 flourishing female
Chartist associations in England and at least 23 in Scotland.[60] Chartist
women fashioned a political identity for themselves as mothers, workers,
and activists which differed in important ways both from the middle-
class ideal of domesticity and from male Chartists' notions of women's
role.[61] Chartist women developed what I call a militant domesticity,
justifying their actions in stepping outside the home by defining the
responsibilities of motherhood not just as nurturing children in the home
but as laboring to feed them and organizing to better their lives.[62] "We
have a right," the female Chartists of Manchester maintained, "to
struggle to gain for ourselves, our husbands, brothers and children, suitable houses, proper clothing and good food."[63]

The process of participating in Chartist activity enabled some women

59. James Epstein, "Some Organisational and Cultural Aspects of the Chartist Movement in Nottingham," in *The Chartist Experience: Studies in Working-Class Radicalism
and Culture, 1830–1860,* ed. James Epstein and Dorothy Thompson (London, 1982), pp.
221–68; James D. Young, *The Rousing of the Scottish Working Class* (London, 1979), p. 73.

60. Jutta Schwarzkopf, *Women in the Chartist Movement* (London, 1991), p. 199;
Alexander Wilson, *The Chartist Movement in Scotland* (New York, 1970), p. 273, lists
twenty in Scotland, but we know of three more: Barrhead and Paisley (*Scottish Patriot,*
July 27, 1839); Campsie (*Scots Times,* January 27, 1841); and Dundee (*True Scotsman,*
February 8, 1840). See also David Jones, "Women and Chartism," *History* 68, no. 1 (1983):
1–21; Jutta Schwarzkopf, "The Sexual Division in the Chartist Family," *British Society for
the Study of Labor History Bulletin* 54, no. 1 (1989): 12–14.

61. Hall, "Tale of Samuel and Jemima."

62. Similar to "republican motherhood" of the American Revolution. See Linda K.
Kerber, *Women of the Republic: Intellect and Ideology in Revolutionary America* (Chapel
Hill, 1980).

63. *Northern Star,* July 24, 1841, quoted in *Political Women, 1800–1850,* ed. Ruth Frow
and Edmund Frow (London, 1989), pp. 199–200.

to change their conceptions of themselves as political actors. The Scottish Chartist women of Glasgow initially spoke with great hesitance and modesty (in large part because of vitriolic attacks on them by local dignitaries and newspapers), but soon developed a more militant stance by defining themselves as heroines and not just as victims to be rescued.[64] The women of Dunfermline, Scotland, defended themselves against criticism for organizing a meeting by declaring that "until woman becomes an independent creature, not the subservient slave of man, but a fit companion and assistant in all his undertakings," the constitution could never be reformed.[65]

The Chartist notion of citizenship also potentially included women. Like the Paineites of the 1790s, the Chartists believed that citizenship was a "universal political right of every human being" rather than a privilege of property.[66] Although they demanded manhood suffrage, the logic of their assumptions could always be extended to female enfranchisement. A few women demanded the vote for themselves on the basis of natural rights, and a few men supported them.[67] A "plain working woman" of Glasgow, a weaver, argued in 1838 that women could reason as well as men and therefore deserved the vote.[68] After all, according to Chartist logic, there was no reason women should not have the vote. The *National Association Gazette* accused opponents of female suffrage of hypocrisy for "contradicting the Chartist profession of universal justice."[69]

But female suffrage was difficult to reconcile with the domestic and patriarchal ideals Chartists upheld to combat Malthusianism and political economy.[70] R. J. Richardson, for instance, used a Paineite language of rights and citizenship to show that women should participate in political affairs because they were subjected to the laws of the state, paid taxes, and worked. Yet Richardson also proclaimed that women were formed to

64. *Scots Times*, May 1, 1840; November 18, 1840; December 30, 1840.
65. *True Scotsman*, December 22, 1838.
66. "Petition Adopted at the Crown and Anchor Meeting," 1838, in *The Early Chartists*, ed. Dorothy Thompson (Columbia, S.C., 1971), p. 62; Epstein, "Constitutionalist Idiom," p. 565.
67. Jones, "Women and Chartism," pp. 2–3; Dorothy Thompson, *The Chartists: Popular Politics in the Industrial Revolution* (Aldershot, 1986), p. 126; Schwarzkopf, *Women in the Chartist Movement*, p. 59.
68. *Northern Star*, June 23, 1838.
69. Schwarzkopf, *Women in the Chartist Movement*, p. 62; also Thompson, *Chartists*, p. 124.
70. For further development of these ideas, see Clark, *Struggle for the Breeches* and "The Rhetoric of Chartist Domesticity," *Journal of British Studies* 31 (January 1992): 62–88.

"temper man," and should "return to [their] domestic circles and culti-
vate [their] finer feelings for the benefit of their offspring."[71]

Chartist men turned away from the Paineite notion of citizenship
toward a constitutionalist one in order to accommodate their vision of
masculinity.[72] They simply replaced property in a household, land, or
business with property in labor as the basis for citizenship and suffrage.
However, there remained many tensions over evolving definitions of
citizenship within Chartism, which reflected both differences over political strategy and varying visions of masculinity.

Some Chartist men followed a strict "moral force" line, denouncing the
"physical force" of demonstrations or even insurrections as dangerous.
The moral-force Chartists never gained many adherents, partly because in
an effort to gain middle-class support they treated suffrage not as a right
but as something that had to be earned by moral virtue. The moral-force
London Working Men's Association admitted as members only those
men who "possess the attributes and characters of *men*; and little worthy
of the name are those who . . . forgetful of their duties as fathers, husbands, and brothers . . . drown their intellect amid the drunken revelry of
the pot house."[73] William Lovett's vision was closer to the middle-class
sentimental ideal of domesticity, for he blamed working people for their
own familial misery. His notion of masculinity was middle class as well,
centered on rationality and self-control rather than the "pugilistic skill"
on which many working-class men still based their honor.[74]

Many other Chartists rejected Lovett's moralism, instead espousing a
fierce commitment to change by any means necessary, including, as a
last resort, physical force. One of their journals, the *London Democrat*,
often referred to the "manly virtues" of working men and opposed the
Charter newspaper because its "dandy cockney politician" editor did
"not represent the straightforward, manly political sentiments of the
working men of this country."[75] Yet this belligerent physical-force masculinity differed from the libertine ultraradicalism of earlier years, for
these men asserted a chivalrous motivation: they were determined to
protect their families. Their favorite slogan was "For child and wife we
will war to the knife!"[76]

71. R. J. Richardson, *The Rights of Woman* (1840) in Thompson, *Early Chartists*, pp.
115–27; Barbara Taylor, *Eve and the New Jerusalem: Socialism and Feminism in the
Nineteenth Century* (New York, 1982), p. 269.

72. For this tradition, see Epstein, "Constitutionalist Idiom," p. 565.

73. *Address and Rules of the Working Men's Association, for Benefitting Politicly,
Socially, and Morally the Useful Classes* (London, 1836), p. 2.

74. William Lovett, *Social and Political Morality* (London, 1853), p. 83.

75. *London Democrat*, May 11, 1839.

76. *Northern Star*, May 18, 1839.

Although physical-force Chartists differed from moral-force Chartists on the political strategy they should follow—confrontation or conciliation of the middle class—they fundamentally shared a notion of manhood based on the status of a respectable workingman earning a breadwinner wage. Chartist men claimed they needed the vote to protect their wives and children from the dangers of the factory. By manipulating the middle-class ideology of domesticity, Chartists insisted that the class-based privileges of separate spheres—citizenship for men, domestic motherhood for women—become universalized markers of gender. In the short run, manipulating the notion of domesticity was a powerful tool to pry concessions from the government, and indeed Parliament passed acts limiting the work of women and children in factories and mines in the 1840s.

Chartism's focus on respectable, chivalrous manhood, however, also narrowed the scope of working-class consciousness. Chartist politics retreated from the streets into the meeting room, moving away from a populist community base toward more "rational," nationally based forms of organization.[77] By the mid-1840s, as Dorothy Thompson notes, Chartism's more formal organization discouraged women's political participation.[78] Indeed, male Chartists actively pushed women out of the movement. As Jutta Schwarzkopf points out, in 1843 the Chartist delegates used the word "'males' instead of 'persons' in the rules" of the National Chartist Association, making clear that Chartism defined only men as political agents. A woman using the pseudonym Vita wrote to protest that women might as well "withdraw from a movement from which an improvement of their status was not to be expected."[79]

Though the chivalrous manhood of the workingman provided common ground with middle-class men, as in early periods, Parliament persisted in delaying universal suffrage for decades, and the eventual masculine bias of Chartist working-class consciousness must share some of the blame. Although workingmen continued to demand the vote as a natural right, they also claimed they deserved it as respectable patriarchs. In response, middle-class reformers would attempt to enfranchise only those men they judged had attained that status, relegating most workingmen to the "residuum.'[80]

77. Wilson, *Chartist Movement in Scotland*, p. 172; *Northern Star*, October 1, 1842; Tony Dickson, *Scottish Capitalism* (London, 1960), p. 211; Fiona Ann Montgomery, "Glasgow Radicalism, 1830–1848" (Ph.D. diss., University of Glasgow, 1974), p. 226; Donald Read, "Chartism in Manchester," in *Chartist Studies*, ed. Asa Briggs (London, 1967), p. 60.

78. Thompson, "Women and Radical Politics," p. 122.

79. Schwarzkopf, *Women in the Chartist Movement*, p. 249.

80. For further discussion of this question, see Keith McClelland's "Rational and Respectable Men," chapter 11 in this volume; and Anna Clark, "Gender, Class, and the

CONCLUSION

As I hope to have demonstrated, a gendered analysis helps us understand the relation of class to politics in the early nineteenth century. Initially, elite notions of the People excluded workingmen, who could not live up to the patriarchal notions of manhood inherent in civic humanism. The people were considered to consist only of men of property, whose public opinion Parliament had to respect. Radicals redefined this notion of the people to include working men and women, and transformed their notion of the political to encompass issues of food, family, and employment, not just abstract constitutionalist concerns. By the 1830s, they developed a class consciousness, linking workingmen's exclusion from Parliament with the perceived attacks on working people's families and communities through the New Poor Law and the factory system. By the late 1840s and 1850s, however, working-class radicals drew away from these wider concerns to focus on the political interests of skilled men. When the People included just men, the possibility of class consciousness faded; by the second Reform Act, the thought that workers and gentlemen could share an ideal of masculinity and both participate in politics transcended class lines but rigidified those of gender. The People could be understood again not as male and female working people organized in communities but as respectable *men* united in the national interest. In the process, radicals lost a wider notion of class and returned to a narrower definition of politics.

Nation: Franchise Reform in England in the Long Nineteenth Century," in *Rereading the Constitution*, ed. James Vernon (Cambridge, forthcoming).

11

Rational and Respectable Men: Gender, the Working Class, and Citizenship in Britain, 1850–1867

Keith McClelland

The passing of the 1867 Reform Act in Britain entailed a new phase in the relationship between the working class and the state, and at the same time it legitimated a new figure, the working-class citizen. Interpretations of the origins, nature, and significance of the act are various and attended by controversies.[1] But two points may be made which will be uncontroversial: first, that the reform fundamentally modified the system by which property ownership was virtually the sole qualification for the franchise. The lowering of the franchise in the boroughs to merely household suffrage—the voter had to be the head of a household and in occupation of it for a minimum of twelve months—represented a compromise between property as the criterion and "manhood suffrage." Second, perhaps 35 to 40 percent of the adult male urban working class were enfranchised, although the exact percentage varied a great deal over the constituencies.

How and in what terms were these new male working-class citizens constructed? There is already a substantial literature dealing with the

I am particularly grateful to Laura Frader and Sonya Rose—not least for their patience—and to Catherine Hall and Jane Rendall for their comments and encouragement. Footnotes have been kept to a minimum.

1. A brief introductory guide to the debates is John K. Walton, *The Second Reform Act* (London, 1987).

class side of the issue (and the discussion is hardly over yet); but the issue of sexual difference, the plain fact that men continued to be the only people with voting rights, is an issue that has scarcely been broached. The fact has simply been taken for granted. Yet an understanding of the ways in which the citizen was constructed in terms of gender as well as class is indispensable to comprehending who that person was thought to be.[2]

Since the demise of Chartism as a mass movement by the end of the 1840s, popular social and political action had been organizationally splintered, and very many people effectively dropped out of politics altogether. The renewed agitation for parliamentary reform, evident from 1857–58 but really getting up steam in 1866–67, once again brought together many thousands of workingmen.[3] Trade unionists, members of co-operative and friendly societies, and activists in a variety of small minority causes (internationalism, republicanism, secularism) were fused once again by the reform movement and its organizations, including the (national) Reform League and such bodies as the Northern Reform League in the northeast of England, and by their opponents' calumnies that they were not fit to be trusted to exercise political rights effectively, rationally, or in any respect other than narrow "class interest."[4] Those who spoke at the many public meetings in favor of the vote and the tone in which they did so may be exemplified here by simply two of them. Speaking in Newcastle in January 1867 at a meeting attended by perhaps 60,000, William Hunter, a chainmaker at Armstrong's engine and ordnance works, and a man who once described himself as "only an obscure artisan," said that "in intelligence, respectability, and earnestness the working classes were worthy of having a fair share in the representation of the country."[5] At the same meeting, Robert Warden, a brass founder at Stephenson's locomotive works, said that

2. Much of the detail of the argument is drawn from the northeast of England, an area notable for the vibrancy of its popular radicalism from the late 1850s to the early 1870s and more generally for the tenacious hold of liberalism between 1832 and 1914. Whatever the distinctive qualities of the area and its politics, however, the general arguments I am proposing transcend the particularities of the region.

3. Among the many works dealing with the reform movement, see esp. F. E. Gillespie, *Labor and Politics in England, 1850–1867* (1927; London, 1966); Royden Harrison, *Before the Socialists: Studies in Labour and Politics, 1861–1881* (London, 1965); Eugenio F. Biagini, *Liberty, Retrenchment and Reform: Popular Liberalism in the Age of Gladstone, 1860–1880* (Cambridge, 1992).

4. The most notable opponent who helped to effect the fusing of the reformers was Robert Lowe. See, among others, Biagini, *Liberty, Retrenchment and Reform*, pp. 259–61; Patrick Joyce, *Visions of the People: Industrial England and the Question of Class, 1848–1914* (Cambridge, 1991), esp. pp. 52–53.

5. For Hunter see Cowen Collection, Tyne and Wear County Record Office, Newcastle-upon-Tyne (hereafter CC), A247; letter to John Bright, CC, C312; *Newcastle Weekly Chronicle*, January 19, 1867.

in their various occupations, the working classes had shown great energy, intelligence, and perseverance, which proved them to be worthy of being admitted to the franchise. (Cheers.) They were able to build leviathan ships to carry the commerce of the world across the mighty oceans; they were able to construct mighty iron warps to connect two distant continents together; but the opponents of Reform did not consider that those same artizans were able to choose their representatives in Parliament. (Cheers.) The large meetings and demonstrations that were being held in all the large towns throughout the country . . . must before long convince their opponents that the working classes were neither indifferent to their political rights, nor yet unable to exercise them. (Cheers.)[6]

The terms in which Hunter and Warden articulated the claim for the vote were typical of many speeches being made up and down the country in 1866–67. Four points should be emphasised at this stage about what Hunter and Warden said. First, the demand for the vote was claimed as a right—what kind of right is something I shall return to in a moment—as against the notion that the vote was merely something to be entrusted with, the characteristic view of such men as Gladstone. Second, the appeal was to certain moral qualities—"intelligence" and the like—which made workingmen "worthy" of the vote. Third, however, those moral qualities were attached to certain kinds of economic characteristics; that is, these men made such things as ships, and these qualities ought to be recognized, given the high esteem in which work and labor were held in the society. Fourth, it was assumed that working men and the working class(es) were synonymous.

These characteristics underpinned the specific claims that such men made. The popular reform movement as a whole varied in its demands. Some men, and many in the northeast of England, continued to adhere to the old radical and Chartist demand for "universal manhood suffrage." Others claimed a narrower franchise, commonly household suffrage qualified by rating and residential requirements, which is to say that the head of the household should get the vote subject to paying poor rates and being in continuous residence of the household for at least six months. But if the claims varied, there was more general agreement about who should be excluded: paupers, criminals, lunatics, and, not least, women. Thus, even organizations and individuals who were sympathetic to the demands for women's suffrage generally rejected them as being "too early": "Get the vote for men first" was a common argument.[7]

6. *Newcastle Weekly Chronicle*, suppl., February 2, 1867.
7. For example, the Northern Reform Union (NRU), founded in 1858 and the forerunner of the Northern Reform League, rejected women's appeals that the claim to the vote be extended to universal suffrage: see letters in CC from Caroline Ashurst Biggs (of

What was being asserted in these claims and exclusions? Quite central here was the notion of (qualified) equality, an idea that was central, of course, to both radicalism and a broader liberalism. This idea may be linked to two related ones: the object of radical antagonism and the moral arguments deployed. The object of the radical critique of the existing political system continued to be in many important ways the persistent power (real or assumed) of the aristocracy, that Old Corruption of the landed and moneyed oligarchy which ruled everything "without seeming to do so." The oligarchy's control over taxation (particularly indirect), complained the Northern Reform Union, "was the trunk of the tree of misgovernment, whence spring innumerable branches, the unwholesome fruits of which have poisoned the body-politic of England; have impoverished the blood, debilitated the limbs, degraded the features, and deprived . . . almost every natural function of what should be a free and healthy State."[8]

Workingmen's votes would bring to the political system moral purity, "manly virtues" rather than the "effeminacy" of a debased aristocracy, and a disinterestedness as opposed to corruption, virtues that informed the strong adherence of the radicals to the secret ballot (granted, in fact, in 1872). Entitlement to the vote was grounded in a notion of equal rights. The franchise for the working class would bring political equality and ought to be based on an already existent equality of men, which itself may be broken down into three main components.

First, men were equal as men. In essence this was a natural rights contention, a type of argument that certainly did not disappear after Chartism. Further, while religious argument was of diminishing importance in radical politics, for many men their equality was derived from God, was sanctioned by the Bible and Christianity, and existed regardless of any power or quality emanating from the possession of property. Thus when Richard Bagnall Reed, chainmaker and from January 1858 the full-time secretary of the Northern Reform Union, addressed a meeting in the village of Swalwell, he put the case in terms that had been common among Chartists (not least in this area, where Primitive Methodism was a vibrant force). He quoted "several texts from the New Testament to prove that it advocated the equality of men in the sight of God, high and

Tunbridge, Kent), August 4 and 12, 1858, C139 and C146; Frances Gill (Shrewsbury), August 1858, C147 and C150; and Jeanette Nasham (London), August 23, 1858, C157. At the same time, some men, among them Richard Bagnall Reed, secretary of both the NRU and the Northern Reform League, were personally sympathetic to the claim.

8. NRU, *To the People of Great Britain and Ireland* (4 pages; Newcastle, March 1, 1858), copy in NRU Scrapbook 1 in CC; also reprinted in *Newcastle Chronicle*, March 12, 1858.

low, rich and poor. The philosophy of Christianity was that men should not be honoured because they possessed wealth, yet our legislature refused to allow a man to vote without he had a pecuniary or property qualification."[9]

Second, to the natural rights argument was joined argument from "historically constituted rights." It was widely believed that there was a moment—sometimes before the Reformation, sometimes before 1066—when universal manhood suffrage had existed. In the 1850s many Chartists, disparate radicals, the followers of the bizarre Russophobe David Urquhart, and others delved into historical records in a search for precedents of forms of election and government before the existing systems, a search that buttressed the desire to restore "lost rights."[10] The third argument for equality stemmed from the conditions and obligations imposed on men by a requirement to pay taxes (most important, of an indirect kind), to obey law, and to participate in the defense of the nation. "No taxation without representation"—perhaps the only old Whig maxim that these radicals might admit to—continued to be a widely voiced slogan.[11] Moreover, to require men to agree to such conditions and obligations without being able to participate actively in the creation of such conditions and obligations was to produce not consent to government but, as W. E. Adams put it, "mere passive obedience."[12]

I SUGGESTED a little earlier that these arguments for equality were qualified. Clearly this was the case in a formal sense in that the exclusion of women as well as paupers, criminals, and lunatics entailed the notion that only some people, some men, were equal and deserving of the vote. Moreover, the argument that the franchise might be limited by rating and residential requirements to heads of households was necessarily to restrict the vote to adult male heads (thus excluding, as was the case after 1867, those young unmarried men who lived in the households of others but did not qualify under the extremely parsimonious lodger franchise enacted by Derby and Disraeli).[13] What was being asserted here was, as

9. *Newcastle Daily Chronicle*, October 12, 1859; cf. Eileen Yeo, "Christianity in Chartist Struggle, 1838–1842," *Past and Present* 91 (1981).

10. A persistent element of radical analysis was the tradition of the Norman Yoke (for which see Christopher Hill, "The Norman Yoke," in his *Puritanism and Revolution* [London, 1968], chap. 3). For the search for historical precedents in the 1850s, see Olive Anderson, *A Liberal State at War* (London, 1967), pp. 139–43. For a typical expression of such arguments see the widely circulated *Hand-Book for Reformers* (Newcastle-upon-Tyne, 1859), by James Paul Cobbett and Thomas Doubleday.

11. It was used, for example, as the motto of the *Northern Reform Record* (12 issues, July 1858–1859), organ of the NRU.

12. W. E. Adams, *An Argument for Complete Suffrage* (16 pages; London, 1860).

13. In 1869 only some 12,000 electors out of about 2.5 million were in on the lodger franchise. According to Thomas Wright, those excluded were especially the young unmarried men who were "taken in and done for" without renting apartments. See Biagini,

has often been noted, the politics of the "respectable" and "independent" worker, lauded by many liberal politicians—the man who was "fixed" in place by 1867 as a legitimate political subject.

If one examines the changing social and economic landscape of the working class in the period from the late 1840s, one finds a variety of conditions that made possible the emergence of the "respectable and independent worker." The gender gap widened significantly in spheres of employment as women became further concentrated in distinctive areas of paid labor (notably domestic service, textiles, and the clothing trades) and consequently were excluded from others, and as men were increasingly concentrated in jobs separated from the household. These tendencies, long evident in modern capitalism, were powerfully reinforced by the long boom of (roughly) 1850–73. The expansion in this era of industries such as engineering, metalworking, shipbuilding, and mining (sectors from which the popular radicals of 1866–67 in the northeast and elsewhere were overwhelmingly drawn) strengthened the gap between men's and women's skills and earnings and also the division between a male-centered world of work and a female-centered world of the home, the street, and the neighborhood.[14]

"Work," in the sense of a job, and the work group were prime sources of a sense of self, of individual and collective identity for men. Thus getting into a trade as an adolescent not only was the route to a hoped-for degree of security in an extremely unstable economic world—even in times of boom—but also was seen to be a kind of liminal state in the passage from boyhood to manhood. Once it was completed, the competent man would have become "free and independent." Yet what did this mean? The notion of independence, like that of respectability, was always uncertain in its boundaries. Much has been made of the "languages" of social classification. Whatever else may be said about them, every single one of the terms commonly used to describe the working class must defy simple and fixed classification. Not least is this true of "independence." Thus, "independent artisan" frequently breaks down when one examines particular cases.[15]

But the core of "independence" consisted of a number of related notions generally held. It was not to be a slave. This was meant literally.

Liberty, Retrenchment and Reform, pp. 309–10; Thomas Wright, *The Great Unwashed* (London, 1868), p. 74.

14. This discussion draws on Keith McClelland, "Masculinity and the 'Representative Artisan' in Britain, 1850–80," in *Manful Assertions: Masculinities in Britain since 1800*, ed. Michael Roper and John Tosh (London, 1991), esp. p. 76.

15. This and the following four paragraphs are drawn largely from two previous articles of mine: "Masculinity and the "Representative Artisan'" and "Time to Work, Time to Live: Some Aspects of Work and the Re-formation of Class in Britain, 1850–1880," in *The Historical Meanings of Work*, ed. Patrick Joyce (Cambridge, 1987).

The long-standing sympathy of working-class radicals and others for the antislavery cause in the British Empire and the United States was commonly enunciated in terms of what was taken to be its antinomy: it was the "virtue" of Englishness that England was the home of the "free-born." However, the notion of slavery was less literal too. The attacks on the "slavery" of the factory and wage system, most powerfully articulated by "Tory radicals" and popular ones in the 1830s and 1840s in Lancashire and the West Riding of Yorkshire, could still be heard in the 1850s and 1860s (and, indeed, may be heard now). Counterpoised to "slavery" was a man's freedom to sell his labor: a man should be able to maintain himself without recourse to charity or the state poor law; he should have a degree of freedom in the regulation of his trade or job; and collective organization of the trade, in a formal union or otherwise, was preferable (if not always possible) to maintaining his position as a worker.[16] In short, what a man was endowed with, or might gain, was the possession of his self or, to use a phrase that resonates through popular culture from the seventeenth century, his "property in labor." Yet independence had another aspect that was becoming much more prominent in the second half of the nineteenth century: the idea that to be independent a man should be able to maintain not only himself but his dependents as well. Some historians of labor have read the evidence without noting the fact, but it seems clear that the bargaining strategies of trade unions were increasingly informed by the notion that what had to be maintained was not only the trade and its customs, its wages and conditions of work, but also the family economy of its members.[17] Defending the property of labor meant claiming what is now known as the "family wage," a wage sufficient to support a wife and children as well as the male worker.

The demarcation of the independent man (and the resources needed to sustain him) needs to be seen in relation to another element of critical importance in understanding the politics of respectable men in this period, namely, their conceptions of economic activity and of work.

From the 1840s on, workingmen held increasingly to the belief that the sphere of the economy was distinct from other arenas of the social and political; that it was subject to its own laws—above all, of the market; that class was determined by, above all, economics rather than politics; and that workingmen's interests were primarily bound up with their

16. According to Thomas Wright, "trade unions do more than any other existing institution to secure the working men 'the glorious privilege of being independent'. Trades unionists are, generally speaking, the best respected and most self-respecting of working men": Thomas Wright ("The Journeyman Engineer"), *Our New Masters* (London, 1873), p. 282.

17. Cf., e.g., E. F. Biagini, "British Trade Unions and Popular Political Economy, 1860–1880," *Historical Journal* 30, no. 4 (1987).

position as economic agents, as "laboring men." In part these assumptions reflected both the actual expansion of the economy in the period and the real gains being made by at least the best organized (and most visible) of working-class groups. They also, however, reflected the sense of the permanence of the system, of "industrialism." Historians may rightly dispute the extent to which industrialization had developed by about 1850, but it was palpably the case that by the 1850s few people believed that it would go away. Yet these changes in the emphasis of assumptions also reflected three other developments in the cultural and ideological context. First was a widespread diffusion of the "gospel of work," popularized and lauded by Thomas Carlyle; by mid-Victorian painters;[18] by that repository of simple "truths" and conventional wisdom, Samuel Smiles; by such politicians as Palmerston; and by a host of other commentators, ideologues, and priests. This gospel was complex, but I would emphasise two aspects of it: first, that work was seen to be the inevitable, compulsive, and burdensome necessity of men; and second, that it was to be celebrated as a glorious activity, the foundation of "national greatness."[19] And one should not underestimate the extent to which many workingmen felt pride in their work and derived a powerful sense of self-esteem from doing the job well. If work was seen as a source of loss, to be escaped from if possible through gaining shorter working hours and in recreations (or re-creation), it is no accident that the primary sources of public identification that men such as Robert Warden should deploy in political demonstrations and on other occasions were the images and models of what they did at work—as in their union banners and in the bearing of the tools they used in the job.

The second major development in the cultural and ideological context was the sharper demarcation between the virtues of men's and women's paid work. As Anna Clark has argued, it was widely assumed until about 1830 that working-class women should work for wages whenever possible; indeed, that it might be desirable to do so.[20] What shifted in the subsequent decades was both the increasing prevalence among working-class men of the belief that women's employment was certainly not desirable, reflected in adherence to the "family wage" and the related imbibing of the "virtues" of domesticity, and the impact of the barrage of moralizing opinion that sought to drive women out of certain kinds of

18. Perhaps most famously by Ford Madox Brown in his *Work* (1852–63) (in the Manchester City Art Gallery).

19. When the Boilermakers' Society (Tyne and Wear District) held a public demonstration in the Whitsun of 1865 in Newcastle-upon-Tyne, among the mottoes on their banners was "England's Greatness, the Working Man": *Newcastle Weekly Chronicle*, June 10, 1865 (suppl.).

20. Anna Clark, "The Rhetoric of Chartist Domesticity: Gender, Language, and Class in the 1830s and 1840s," *Journal of British Studies* 31 (1992): 62–88.

work (as by the mines legislation of 1842) or at least to restrict that work (as by the Factory Act of 1844).

The third development lay in the crisis and degradation of popular-radical economic critiques of the existing order and an assimilation of many of the dominant ideas of political economy. This is not to say that all of these ideas were unambiguously adhered to or absorbed: there was a persistent tension between the logic of the market and the moral limits of subjection to it, evident, for instance, in the necessity of hanging on to the proper standards of work and the critique of those employers who encouraged shoddy work and the like done by insufficiently trained men. Yet, at bottom, political economy was assimilated to the extent that it was assumed not only that the market should be accepted as ultimately determining labor and its rewards but also that there was, or ought to be, a "free and equal" contract between the employers and the employed. Realization of such a contract, and the removal of the fetters on its development—which might of course entail not only the removal of legal fetters but also strong action against those employers who refused to treat the men with justice and decency—would lead to further economic progress for all.[21]

IT SHOULD BE NOTED that the popular movement for parliamentary reform of 1858–67 was a much more masculine affair than earlier campaigns had generally been. The fact that the claim for the vote was made by and for workingmen was rather less novel than the fact that scarcely any women participated in the movements for it. A considerable number of women had participated in earlier movements of popular protest and politics in Britain, from eighteenth-century crowd actions over food to Chartism in the 1830s and 1840s. It is evident that as the forms of popular politics and protest shifted from the "prepolitical" to the demonstrations, organizations, and movements in favor of parliamentary reform in the earlier part of the nineteenth century, the involvement of women in the creation of a working-class "public sphere" was significant and continuing. Thus in the period 1815–20 one sees the formation of female radical societies; in the Owenite movement, the creation of the first currents of "socialist feminism"; and in Chartism, at least in its earlier phases of 1838–42, a sustained commitment to the cause of political rights among many women. It is also of course evident that powerful countervailing forces threatened to push women out of the public sphere or prevent them from transcending the boundaries between it and the private. These forces were reflected in the characteristic de-

21. See McClelland, "Time to Live, Time to Work," esp. pp. 185–89; Joyce, *Visions of the People*, chap. 4.

mands of the women themselves: when women did demand the vote, it was generally not for themselves but for their husbands, fathers, and brothers in order that the conditions of their own lives and of their families' lives might be improved. Yet what is especially striking, as Dorothy Thompson and others have argued, is the extent and rapidity of women's virtual disappearance from the working-class public sphere after 1840–42. Thus to take the Tyneside instance, a female Chartist organization had been active there in 1838–40, but by the 1850s and 1860s we catch only the occasional glimpse of women at demonstrations or at political meetings. Otherwise, silence.[22]

If one examines the content and form of the political movement from 1857, one finds that its social base consisted of a variety of political associations and then by 1866–67 the trade unions above all. This development reflected partly the transformation of the social landscape through the extension of large-scale industry, partly the increasing strength and visibility of trade unionism to the extent that it was the core of labor organization. Needless to say, these institutions were exclusively male. They brought with them to the movement, however, not merely the fact of being male but particular definitions of the nature and scope of politics and of those men who might be political subjects. The reform movement sought to mobilize and articulate a particular kind of constituency, but one that was always ambiguously categorized. Thus, for instance, while the movement clearly sought to represent itself as embodying the respectable and independent, it was bound to get caught up in the arguments of men who wrestled with the problem of where to draw the line between those who were "fit" for the vote and those who were not. Indeed, in many ways the central issue of the parliamentary debates on reform was fought out over precisely this moral terrain.[23] Was it, as Robert Lowe contended, that to admit any section of the working class was to introduce dissolution and danger into the constitution? Enfranchise "the artizan," he thought, and with him will come the "venality . . . , drunkenness, and facility for being intimidated" associated with people who are "impulsive, unreflecting,

22. See esp. three works by Dorothy Thompson: "Women and Radical Politics: A Lost Dimension," in *The Rights and Wrongs of Women*, ed. Juliet Mitchell and Ann Oakley (Harmondsworth, 1976); *The Chartists* (New York, 1984), esp. chap. 7; and "Women, Work and Politics in Nineteenth-Century England," in *Equal or Different: Women's Politics, 1800–1914*, ed. Jane Rendall (Oxford, 1987). See also Jutta Schwarzkopf, *Women in the Chartist Movement* (London, 1991). A good general survey of women and popular politics is Jane Rendall, *The Origins of Modern Feminism: Women in Britain, France and the United States, 1780–1860* (London, 1985), chap. 7.

23. As is stressed by, e.g., Stefan Collini: "Political Theory and the 'Science of Society' in Victorian Britain," *Historical Journal* 23, no. 1 (1980): 216–18, and *Public Moralists: Political Thought and Intellectual Life in Britain, 1850–1930* (Oxford, 1991), pp. 111–12.

and violent."[24] On the other hand, had "the artizans" displayed the necessary qualities in their self-help institutions and the like to be trusted, as Gladstone believed? Yet if they had, where still was the line to be drawn? In the arguments of Gladstone and men of like mind on this issue, the moral and social criteria for evaluating working-class fitness— that is, were these men respectable?—were reduced to a crass economism: a man's economic status would determined his moral possibilities. Gladstone himself proposed at one point that the vote be given to any man earning a minimum of 26 shillings a week.[25]

For some popular radicals the solution to the problem was to fuse workingmen in ways that transcended economic and social, or indeed ethnic, differences, although not sexual ones. As James Birkett, an iron molder, declared, the movement should not be restricted to, say, union men as against nonunionists, to the artisans rather than the laborers, or to Englishmen rather than Irish or Scots. On the contrary, "they recognised men as men," and that was sufficient.[26]

In this regard the movement shared some of the older radical tradition that while workingmen should be admitted to the political nation as citizens, they were excluded as a class. Indeed, a greater sense of class exclusion and antagonism was once again evident in the 1860s (and, after 1867, in the trade and political movements of the early 1870s) than had been the case between 1848 and 1864. Yet a limit on the universalism of workingmen's claim to the vote, simply as workingmen, was partly the formal boundary of the political claims. This was not the mobilization of the poor, as Gertrude Himmelfarb has characterized Chartism,[27] but the mobilization of those represented as a distinct type of working class.

Class exclusion was also buttressed by a shifting understanding of the relative place of politics and economics in the social order. The dominant tendency in pre-1850 popular politics had been a conception of the political as the overdetermining element in the social order. A change in the nature of political representation would relieve the economic and social burdens imposed by "Old Corruption." Within that tradition the major dividing lines in society were defined as originating in the political system, essentially those between the represented and the unrepresented, between the oligarchy and the people. "The people" were defined in the early nineteenth century as the "productive classes" and then, as a result of 1832, increasingly as the working class. And a critical

24. Robert Lowe in a speech in the House of Commons, *Hansard Parliamentary Debates*, 3d ser, vol. 182 (March 13, 1866), col. 150.

25. Gladstone introducing the Reform Bill, ibid. (March 1866), cols. 54–55.

26. *Newcastle Weekly Chronicle*, January 19, 1867.

27. Gertrude Himmelfarb, *The Idea of Poverty: England in the Early Industrial Age* (New York, 1984), chap. 11.

fault line within this political tradition was established by the identification of the putative subject of politics as the male citizen, endowed with the necessary potentialities of reason.[28]

Of course, there were nuances in this tradition and tensions produced by the developing ideas and practices of trade unionism, Owenism, and Chartism in the 1830s and 1840s. Aspects of these views certainly persisted after the collapse of Chartism in the late 1840s, but a decisive shift occurred in that the political was seen no longer as the prime determining force but rather as an essentially intrusive one that ought to be separated from economic and social activities. A consequence of this shift was the strengthening of what one might call—although it is an ugly term—the "masculinization" of popular politics. For if it was economic relationships that determined the positions and prospects of workingmen as workingmen, it was desirable that conditions be established under which masters and men could meet as "free" and "equal" agents within the economy and the market. Such conditions entailed a certain narrowing of the scope of political action. Continuous participation in politics was seen as essential to defend and extend the interests of labor, individually and collectively, yet the prime purpose for doing so was to defend or achieve largely instrumental gains, exemplified in the campaigns of the early 1870s to establish a secure legal place for trade unionism.

Thus the concern of popular politics because very largely the concern of the man at work. Of course, this boundary did not hermetically seal off popular politics from wider concerns, but it was to take two kinds of movements—late nineteenth-century socialism and the development of a women's suffrage movement—to offer at least the possibility, if not the realization, of moving politics into a less instrumental and less narrowly focused register.

I have suggested that the central agent of this popular politics was a man who represented himself in terms of his work, his independence, and his respectability. Yet it is necessary to say something about how this figure came to be defined not only by some economic and social forces and by his own manner of self-presentation but also by other forces. After all, to return to a very broad question, why was it that within twenty years after all popular radical claims to the vote had been

28. For contrasting discussions of the pre-1850 radical tradition see, among others, Patricia Hollis, *The Pauper Press* (Oxford, 1970), chaps. 6–7; Iorwerth Prothero, "William Benbow and the Concept of the 'General Strike,'" *Past and Present* 63 (1974): 132–171; Gareth Stedman Jones, "Rethinking Chartism," in his *Languages of Class* (Cambridge, 1983); Catherine Hall, "The Tale of Samuel and Jemima: Gender and Working-Class Culture in Nineteenth-Century England," in *E. P. Thompson: Critical Perspectives*, ed. H. J. Kaye and Keith McClelland (Oxford, 1990); Joan Wallach Scott, "On Language, Gender, and Working-Class History," in her *Gender and the Politics of History* (New York, 1988).

more or less flatly rejected it became possible for politicians to fix this figure and welcome him, though never unreservedly, into the political nation? How were the boundaries around this figure being redrawn "from above"?

I suggest that the following were the key areas of change in this respect. First were the impulses from civil society which sought to differentiate and play around the differences between the sober, respectable, and desirable male figure and his family and which situated him as a suitable object for social inclusion and even celebration. Of particular importance here were those initiatives concerned with "rational recreations" and temperance. The virtues of the sober man were continually lauded, and the temperance movement persistently stressed the sexual exploitation and domestic sufferings of women and families at the hands of intemperate and unrespectable men.[29]

Second, there were major changes within state social policies. Here I suggest that there were three particularly important areas. In the first instance, the Poor Law. Not only was the post-1834 Poor Law especially concerned with women as recipients, but the intentions of its authors had been to punish the able-bodied man who did not or would not work. In this arena the state placed a decisive emphasis on attempting to "encourage," as a matter of policy, the independent man who would be able to care for his family. (The realities were, of course, different.) This emphasis, moreover, persisted throughout the history of the Poor Law, and it was perhaps no accident that within a few years of admitting "independent artisans" to the franchise in 1867, the state tightened up the law and made it even more punitive in 1871.[30] It should also be noted that the issue of poverty was becoming both less visible and more marginalized as a distinct realm of social action in this period.[31]

In the second instance, the impulses behind sanitary reform and "environmental politics" again both differentiated the area as a realm of activity and sought to distinguish, as a matter of distinct policy and concern, the independent man who might be threatened by "degrada-

---

29. The major study of the British temperance movement, and full of insight into other moral crusades, is Brian Harrison, *Drink and the Victorians: The Temperance Question in England, 1815–1872* (London, 1971).

30. The 1871 legislation has been called "the most sustained attempt of the century to impose upon the working classes the Victorian values of providence, self-reliance, foresight, and self-discipline": H. C. G. Matthew, *Gladstone, 1809–1874* (Oxford, 1986), p. 170.

31. For the Poor Law see Pat Thane, "Women and the Poor Law in Victorian and Edwardian England," *History Workshop Journal* 6 (1978); Michael E. Rose, "The Disappearing Pauper: Victorian Attitudes to the Relief of the Poor," in *In Search of Victorian Values*, ed. E. M. Sigsworth (Manchester, 1988), and his "The Crisis of Poor Relief in England, 1860–1880," in *The Emergence of the Welfare State in Britain and Germany*, ed. W. J. Mommsen (London, 1981).

tion" and political danger within the unhealthy body—literal and meta-phorical—of the city. In Edwin Chadwick's view, disease in the city would destroy the "able-bodied" and virtuous men and leave a residuum who were, as he put it in 1845, "always young, inexperienced, ignorant, credulous, passionate, violent, and proportionately dangerous, with a perpetual tendency to moral as well as physical deterioration."[32]

The third area of state policy concerned prostitution and its regulation through the Contagious Diseases Acts of 1864–69. What was crucial here was both the demarcating of prostitution as a "problem" in ways similar to the shifts in social policy concerning the poor and the urban environment and the fixing of the female prostitute as the "pollutant" figure whom the state must punish. Against her were arrayed the respectable workingmen, evident in the participation of such men in the campaign to repeal the acts. The respectable workingman was seen, and saw himself, as the household head who was the protector of "his" wife and daughters against sexual immorality and danger.[33]

The third way in which the boundaries delimiting the independent man as potential citizen were drawn was through more obviously and specifically political conditions. It is not my intention to survey this side of the question, save to say that without important shifts in the strategies and attitudes of the parties and key political groups, the possibility of enfranchising at least some workingmen would not have been resolved in the ways it was in 1867. An important part of the story here concerns shifts in the nature of middle-class radicalism from the late 1840s—a story that may be told partly through the history of John Bright but also more widely through the history of an emergent Liberal Party and its leadership. But I suggest that such political conditions, which have been the major object of study of the question of reform and the working class, cannot be comprehended without reference to the social and cultural conditions that produced the possibility of entrusting citizenship and the vote to the "rational and respectable man."

32. Quoted in U. R. Q. Henriques, *Before the Welfare State* (London, 1979), p. 127. For two very helpful discussions of environmental politics see Frank Mort, *Dangerous Sexualities: Medico-moral Politics in England since 1830* (London, 1987), and Mary Poovey, "Domesticity and Class Formation: Chadwick's 1842 *Sanitary Report*," in *Subject to History: Ideology, Class, Gender*, ed. David Simpson (Ithaca, 1991).

33. See above all Judith R. Walkowitz, *Prostitution and Victorian Society: Women, Class, and the State* (Cambridge, 1980).

12

Class and Gender at Loggerheads in the Early Soviet State: Who Should Organize the Female Proletariat and How?

Elizabeth A. Wood

The Russian Social Democrats came to power in 1917 as an expressly Marxist party for whom the most important immediate goal was the creation of a "dictatorship of the proletariat." Class analysis and consciousness of class were two of their most important weapons in the struggle against the hated tsarist autocracy. Attention to the female members of the proletariat was secondary but not inconsequential.[1] If the Social Democrats were going to mobilize a revolutionary army powerful enough to overcome the monolith of tsarism, they would need every man, woman, and child. If they were to create a vanguard of the proletariat, they would need women to be emancipated from their "patriarchal isolation" and the "stultifying world of housework" so they could join the proletariat in its new leadership.[2]

1. Numerous sources, including especially the memoirs of Aleksandra Kollontai, attest nonetheless to the tardiness of the Bolshevik Party in addressing women workers. See A. Kollontai, "Avtobiograficheskii ocherk," *Proletarskaia revoliutsiia* 1 (1921): 261–302; *The Autobiography of a Sexually Emancipated Communist Woman* (New York, 1971), pp. 13–16. A key secondary account is Rose L. Glickman, *Russian Factory Women: Workplace and Society, 1880–1914* (Berkeley, 1984), pp. 242–80.

2. V. I. Lenin, "Razvitie kapitalizma v Rossii" (1899), in *Polnoe sobranie sochinenii* (hereafter *PSS*), 5th ed. (Moscow 1958–65), 3: 548; and "O zadachakh zhenskogo rabochego dvizheniia v Sovetskoi respublike" (1919), in *PSS*, 39: 202.

Gender issues did not mesh easily with class issues, however. Above all the Bolsheviks found they had to face the question who was to organize the female half of the proletariat. Should women workers be viewed first and foremost as women, a group to be reached through the women's section of the Communist Party? Or should they be classified first and foremost as workers, to be organized through the network of trade unions and other work-based organizations?

The historical literature has not attended to women workers in the postrevolutionary period. Though there have been monographs on workers in general, they have paid only limited attention to female workers, usually including them in a subchapter of two or three pages.[3] Work on women, by contrast, has tended to treat important issues such as the ideology of "the woman question," policies toward women and the family, and the lives of female leaders, but has not given much attention to women's involvement in the workplace and in the trade unions.[4]

Yet women workers were important to the revolutionary project, particularly in relation to the problem of class consciousness.[5] Women in the laboring classes might have held the correct class location, but they were consistently depicted as having the wrong class consciousness. They were "passive," "indifferent," "a bulwark for counterrevolutionary

3. The English-language literature on workers is by now voluminous. A few key studies of workers in the early Soviet period are Lewis H. Siegelbaum and Ronald Grigor Suny, eds., *Making Workers Soviet: Power, Class, and Identity* (Ithaca, 1994); Chris Ward, *Russia's Cotton Workers and the New Economic Policy: Shop-Floor Culture and State Policy, 1921–1929* (Cambridge, 1990); Hiroaki Kuromiya, *Stalin's Industrial Revolution: Politics and Workers, 1928–1932* (Cambridge, 1988); William J. Chase, *Workers, Society, and the Soviet State* (Urbana, 1987).

4. Wendy Z. Goldman, *Women, the State and Revolution* (Cambridge, 1993); Mary Buckley, *Women and Ideology in the Soviet Union* (Ann Arbor, 1989); Richard Stites, *The Women's Liberation Movement in Russia: Feminism, Nihilism, and Bolshevism, 1860–1930* (Princeton, 1978) and "Zhenotdel: Bolshevism and Russian Women, 1917–1930," *Russian History* 3, no. 2 (1976): 174–93; Gail Warshofsky Lapidus, *Women in Soviet Society* (Berkeley, 1978); Carol Eubanks Hayden, "Feminism and Bolshevism: The Zhenotdel and the Politics of Women's Emancipation in Russia, 1917–1930" (Ph.D. diss., University of California, Berkeley, 1979) and "The Zhenotdel and the Bolshevik Party," *Russian History* 3, no. 2 (1976): 150–71; Gregory J. Massell, *The Surrogate Proletariat: Moslem Women and Revolutionary Strategies in Soviet Central Asia, 1919–1929* (Princeton, 1974); H. Kent Geiger, *The Family in Soviet Russia* (Cambridge, 1968); Barbara Evans Clements, *Bolshevik Feminist: The Life of Aleksandra Kollontai* (Bloomington, 1979); Beatrice Brodsky Farnsworth, *Aleksandra Kollontai: Socialism, Feminism, and the Bolshevik Revolution* (Stanford, 1980).

5. A few studies include materials on the organization of women as workers: Glickman, *Russian Factory Women*; Moira Donald, "Bolshevik Activity amongst the Working Women of Petrograd in 1917," *International Review of Social History* 27, no. 2 (1982): 129–60; Anne Bobroff, "The Bolsheviks and Working Women, 1905–1920," *Soviet Studies* 26 (October 1974): 540–76.

and anti-Soviet agitation."[6] They were "the most backward and immo-
bile element," one that had served "as a brake in all previous revolutions.'[7] Above all, as Lenin supposedly told Clara Zetkin, the Russian
woman's "backwardness and lack of understanding for her husband's
revolutionary ideals act as a drag on his fighting spirit, on his determination to fight. They [women] are like tiny worms, gnawing and undermining imperceptibly, slowly but surely."[8]

In the period after 1917 the revolutionaries faced the central question
articulated some years ago by Sally Alexander: "What happens when the
visionaries become lawmakers?"[9] In fact, several problems emerged at
this point which became intertwined around that of incorporating
women workers into the new body politic. One of them (discussed in
insightful ways by Sheila Fitzpatrick) involved the apparent disappearance of the working class during the Civil War (through mobilization
into the Red Army, outmigration from the cities and return to peasant
life, and upward mobility into positions of white-collar service work).[10] In
whose name was the Party, ostensibly the vanguard of the proletariat,
then claiming to speak? And how was it claiming to speak? In other
words, what would be the key institutional forms of communication
between Party and people, and how would they function?

A second problem involved the trade unions. The trade unions had
occupied crucial positions in the struggle against the autocracy, yet now
they were part of the dictatorship of the proletariat. Were they to become
part of the government? Or were they to coordinate what was known as

6. Inessa Armand, report to the plenum of the Moscow Regional Bureau of the Russian
Social Democratic Labor Party, August 1917, quoted in P. M. Chirkov, *Reshenie
zhenskogo voprosa v SSSR (1917–1937 gg.)* (Moscow, 1978), p. 28; A. Kollontai, "Kak i dlia
chego sozvan byl pervyi Vserossiiskii s"ezd rabotnits," in *Kommunisticheskaia Partiia i
organizatsiia rabotnits* (Moscow, 1919), p. 9.

7. V. I. Lenin, "Rech' na kursakh agitatorov otdela okhrany materinstva i
mladenchestva NKSO" (1919), in *PSS*, 37: 521.

8. V. I. Lenin, "Dialogue with Clara Zetkin," in *The Lenin Anthology*, ed. Robert C.
Tucker (New York, 1975), p. 698.

9. Sally Alexander, "Women, Class, and Sexual Differences in the 1830s and 1840s:
Some Reflections on the Writing of a Feminist History," *History Workshop Journal* 17
(Spring 1984): 124–49.

10. Sheila Fitzpatrick, "The Bolsheviks' Dilemma: The Class Issue in Party Politics and
Culture," in Fitzpatrick, *The Cultural Front: Power and Culture in Revolutionary Russia*
(Ithaca, 1992), pp. 116–36. See also Fitzpatrick, "Ascribing Class: The Construction of
Social Identity in Soviet Russia," *Journal of Modern History* 65 (December 1993): 745–70.
On the important problem of deurbanization, see Daniel R. Brower, "'The City in Danger':
The Civil War and the Russian Urban Population," and Diane P. Koenker, "Urbanization
and Deurbanization in the Russian Revolution and Civil War," both in *Party, State, and
Society in the Russian Civil War*, ed. Koenker et al. (Bloomington, 1989), pp. 58–80 and
81–104.

"workers' control" from a position outside the government? And whose interests were they to defend, those of the workers or those of the state, which now, after all, was claiming to speak and act in the name of those workers?[11]

As far as women workers were concerned, what was the best way to organize them? Even in the prerevolutionary period the Bolsheviks' efforts to involve women in Party and trade union work tended to be reactive; they followed events and trends rather than anticipated them. The Bolsheviks took up women's issues in a consistent way only when women workers began to receive the vote in factory affairs in 1912 and in national affairs in 1917.[12]

Yet turning to organizing women workers raised real problems for the fledgling Communist Party. Should women workers be organized separately from men if the basic goal was to "weld" and "forge" both men and women into a united revolutionary army?[13] Should they be organized separately if women's separate, excluded status (which observers sometimes compared with the medieval practice of segregating women from public view) was itself viewed as part of the problem? And if women workers were going to receive special treatment (justified on the grounds of their backwardness, their later membership in the working class), should they be organized as female members of the new revolutionary society by the Communist Party, which was primarily responsible for "upbringing" [*vospitanie*] and the instilling of correct consciousness, or should they be organized by the trade unions, as members of the larger working class?

Bolshevik theorists stressed that the two goals in working with women workers must be to make them (a) "conscious" (i.e., cognizant of the Party's vanguard role in demonstrating to them their true interests) and (b) "organized" (i.e., enrolled in trade unions, which would help them to direct their energies in useful areas and keep them from engaging in

---

11. Diane P. Koenker, "Labor Relations in Socialist Russia: Class Values and Production Values in the Printers' Union, 1917–1921," in Siegelbaum and Suny, *Making Workers Soviet*, pp. 159–93; John Brinley Hatch, "Labor and Politics in NEP Russia: Workers, Trade Unions, and the Communist Party in Moscow, 1921–1926" (Ph.D. diss., University of California, Irvine, 1985), esp. chap. 3; Jay B. Sorenson, *The Life and Death of Soviet Trade Unionism, 1917–1928* (New York, 1969); E. H. Carr, *The Bolshevik Revolution, 1917–1923* (Harmondsworth, 1966), 2: 100–115, 219–27, 323–31; Robert Vincent Daniels, *The Conscience of the Revolution: Communist Opposition in Soviet Russia* (New York, 1960), pp. 129–35; Isaac Deutscher, *Soviet Trade Unions* (New York, 1950).

12. For more on this development see my book *From Baba to Comrade: Gender and Political Culture in Postrevolutionary Russia, 1917–1924* (Bloomington, forthcoming), chap. 2.

13. Kollontai, "Kak i dlia chego," p. 9.

"undisciplined" industrial actions that might undermine the Revolution).[14] Leading women activists in the Party seem to have assumed that these two tasks could be separated. As early as the spring of 1917 (before the Bolsheviks had even seized power), women members of the Petrograd Committee proposed the formation of a women's bureau (later renamed the women's section, or *zhenotdel*), which would conduct "only agitational work"; organizational work would be carried out in the "proletarian political and trade union institutions."[15] No independent women's organization would be countenanced; all work would be conducted in full agreement with the Party. The women's sections would be responsible for women workers' "consciousness"—that is, bringing them into the fold of the Party—while the trade unions would agitate to persuade them to become union members.

The initial focus of the women's bureaus and women's sections in the years 1917–20 was on work in the neighborhoods.[16] A commission of Party comrades would form in a given neighborhood and go around to the factories, where they would choose one or two women workers to attend neighborhood meetings. At first these meetings were small, only ten to twenty people. The organizer of the neighborhood *sektsiia* would put in an appearance at one of these meetings, chair the session, then run off to his (or more rarely her) next meeting. At the beginning, then, neighborhood work was rarely planned or coordinated. It did, however, allow the women's sections to introduce broad agitation; as one activist put it, "to touch the very bottom—housewives, soviet employees, and other categories of labor."[17]

Yet the women's sections always felt that women workers were their first priority, and from the beginning they targeted them for special conferences. Still they were careful to insist that these were not "feminist" meetings; they had no separate "women's" agenda. The very first conference of women workers, for example, in November 1917, was held in large measure to drum up support for the Bolshevik candidates to the Constituent Assembly. The organizers told the assembled women workers that they should vote for the Bolshevik slate, under no circumstances for the women's slate put forth by the liberals. "We, conscious women workers," the conference resolved, "know that we have no special women's interests, that there should be no separate women's organiza-

14. A. F. Bessonova, "K istorii izdaniia zhurnala 'Rabotnitsa,'" *Istoricheskii arkhiv* 4 (July/August 1955): 37–39.

15. Minutes of the meeting of the Executive Committee of the Petrograd Committee in *Revoliutsionnoe dvizhenie v Rossii posle sverzheniia samoderzhaviia*, ed. L. S. Gaponenko (Moscow, 1957), p. 75.

16. Ibid., pp. 55, 67.

17. Rabotnitsa Klavdiia, "Zhenskie sektsii ili delegatskie sobraniia," *Kommunistka* 1/2 (June/July 1920): 31.

tions."[18] Other conference resolutions as well stressed that women workers "do not have specifically female differences from the general task of the proletariat."[19]

The Party women's section began to pay increasing attention to women workers as the Civil War came to a close in 1920 and as the Party inaugurated a series of policies that came to be known as the New Economic Policy (NEP) in 1921. The *zhenotdely* had practical as well as ideological reasons for reaching out to defend women workers at this time, as the NEP brought enormous layoffs in the state sector of the economy plus the leasing of formerly state enterprises and more layoffs in what was now a semiprivate sector. These macroeconomic developments, together with the return of demobilized male soldiers from the front, affected female workers disproportionately, and unemployment among women soared.[20]

The women's sections moved to defend women workers and to try to protect them from unemployment, which threatened their membership in the proletariat. At the same time, the women's sections were engaged in a sustained battle with their own Party organizations (particularly those at the provincial level), which sought to eliminate them on financial grounds and on the grounds that they were no longer necessary to the Revolution.[21] In these circumstances, the women's sections found it all the more imperative to prove their revolutionary credentials by increasing their organizing work among the female proletariat.

The trade unions vigorously resisted this encroachment on their organizing turf. Their mandate extended to all areas of workers' lives and did not, they argued, permit attention to the "sectional" or "particularistic" interests of individual groups. The trade unions saw no compelling reason to distinguish female workers from male. Both were members of the proletariat and should be treated as such.

This was not the only issue that brought the trade unions and the women's sections into direct competition. Another was the question of autonomy and the defense of workers' interests. Both organizations, especially the women's sections but increasingly the trade unions as well, existed at the discretion of the Communist Party. If either organization were perceived as insufficiently vigilant in defending work-

18. K. I. Nikolaeva in *Rabotnitsa*, December 8, 1917, p. 11; Hayden, "Feminism and Bolshevism," p. 122.

19. "Rezoliutsiia po voprosu 'Zadachi rabotnits v Sovetskoi Rossii,'" in *Kommunisticheskaia partiia i organizatsiia rabotnits: Sbornik statei* (Moscow, 1919), p. 118.

20. Elizabeth A. Wood, "Gender and Politics in Soviet Russia: Working Women under the New Economic Policy, 1918–1928" (Ph.D. diss., University of Michigan, 1991), chaps. 3–4.

21. Hayden, "Feminism and Bolshevism," pp. 176–78, 190–92.

ers' needs, it could be censured or even lose crucial funding and personnel resources. The two groups thus found themselves in direct competition for the approval and material support of higher Party bodies.

The conflict began in January 1920, when the Party created special "fractions" within the trade unions (as in all nonparty organizations). Each fraction was designed to serve as a bloc of Party members, who would receive joint instructions on how to vote on matters of concern to the Party. This move gave the Party enormous leverage in union affairs.[22] Barely two weeks after the creation of the fractions had been decreed, the women's section addressed a special circular letter to the new trade union fractions asking them to name special organizers for work among women.[23] The Central Committee of the Party now directed its provincial and local committees to establish "close contact" with these trade union organizers and to hold regular meetings with them. Two and a half months later, in April 1920, the Ninth Party Congress called for "intensified work among the female proletariat" as a means for the Party "to increase its ranks with new, unused forces."[24]

The trade unions, however, rejected out of hand the notion of special organizers among women. Though they agreed in principle that it was important to educate women workers and to raise their class consciousness, they emphatically rejected any notion of "special women's groups, sections, or organizers."[25] They made it clear that they resented what they perceived as interference in their internal affairs. In defending their turf, they argued for the "sameness" of women and the lack of any need for the woman worker to be treated differently from the male worker. The woman worker, they asserted, had "no special tasks in the proletarian movement," and hence, while she should become a "conscious participant in production," she required no "special paths" to draw her into socialist work in general.[26]

In May 1920 and again in the fall of that year the trade union organizations and the central women's section appealed to the Organizational Bureau (the Orgbiuro) of the Party to find a solution to the growing

22. *KPSS v rezoliutsiiakh i resheniiakh s"ezdov, konferentsii i plenumov TsK* (Moscow, 1954), 2: 468, 492; Nicholas Timasheff, *The Great Retreat* (New York, 1946), pp. 91–92; Leonard Schapiro, *The Origin of the Communist Autocracy* (Cambridge, Mass., 1955), pp. 219–20.

23. Circular letter, *Izvestiia TsK RKP(b)* 12 (1920): 2, in Chirkov, *Reshenie Zhenskogo voprosa*, p. 72.

24. *KPSS v rezoliutsiiakh*, 2: 503.

25. "Rezoliutsii i postanovleniia Tret'ego Vscrossiiskago s"ezda profsoiuzov," in Communist Party archives, Rossiiskii Tsentr Khraneniia i Izucheniia Dokumentov Noveishei Istorii (RTsKhIDNI), f. 17, op. 10, d. 9, pp. 8–9; Anna Riazanova, *Zhenskii trud* (Moscow, 1923), pp. 283–85.

26. A. Andreev, "Rabotnitsa v professional'nom dvizhenii," *Kommunistka* 6 (November 1920): 10–11.

conflict between the women's sections and the trade unions.[27] Aleksandra Kollontai, head of the women's section, wrote to the Orgbiuro to ask for help in resolving this issue, as "impassioned discussions" had broken out and were causing "disorganization" in work among women.[28]

In December 1920 the Third National Meeting of the Women's Section listened to the views of a trade union representative, Vladimir Kossior. In no uncertain terms Kossior rejected the women's section's position. It represented "an absolutely unacceptable violation" of trade union democracy, he argued, because as nonparty organizations the trade unions should have the right to their own elections. If the Party members in the fraction were to be the ones to choose organizers for work among women without input from the rank and file, they would have a special status as "chosen people," a position Kossior rejected as untenable. Either the women's sections should go ahead and do their organizing without interfering in trade union business or the trade unions should name their own organizers without Party interference.[29] Kossior was not alone in taking this position. Only a few weeks later, on January 16, 1921, Nikolai Bukharin and other critics of Party policy published an article in *Pravda* decrying what they called "appointmentalism"; that is, the Party's practice of appointing people to union positions rather than allowing full elections by the trade union members themselves.[30]

The women's sections stuck to their guns, however, insisting that there be new organizers in the unions and that they be named exclusively from the Party fraction.[31] Otherwise, they argued, the trade unions could not be relied on to take any action whatsoever on behalf of women. That same month—December 1920—they took the issue to the Eighth Congress of Soviets, and after what Kollontai later called "no small expenditure of energy, patience, and stubbornness" they managed to obtain passage of a general resolution on the importance of drawing women workers and peasants into all economic organs.[32]

A few months later, in May 1921, the trade unions met for their fourth national congress and again rejected the idea of separate woman orga-

27. RTsKhIDNI, f. 17, op. 10, d. 36, pp. 57, 107.

28. Quoted in A. M. Itkina, *Revoliutsioner, tribun, diplomat* (Moscow, 1970), p. 201; and *Sovetskie zhenshchiny i profsoiuzy*, ed. E. E. Novikova et al. (Moscow, 1984), p. 27.

29. RTsKhIDNI, f. 17, op. 10, d. 5, pp. 8–10.

30. Schapiro, *Origin of the Communist Autocracy*, p. 286. Also see Frederick I. Kaplan, *Bolshevik Ideology and the Ethics of Soviet Labor* (New York, 1968), pp. 242–45.

31. The meeting voted almost unanimously to have organizers appointed by the Party fraction rather than by the union administrations: RTsKhIDNI, f. 17, op. 10, d. 5, pp. 11–34; also P. Vinogradskaia, "Itogi III-go Vserossiiskogo soveshchaniia zavgubotdelov po rabote sredi zhenshchin," *Kommunistka* 7 (November 1920): 3.

32. A. Kollontai, *Trud zhenshchin v evoliutsii khoziaistva* (Moscow, 1923), p. 157.

nizers, though they continued to recite general platitudes in support of work among women.[33] Again their main line of reasoning was the sameness of male and female workers: "Since women workers fulfill the same work in production, they can and must take on the same functions in the unions," they resolved.[34]

At this congress one of the leading speakers against the notion of separate organizers for women was Anna Riazanova, an important trade unionist in her own right and the wife of David Riazanov, a prominent Old Bolshevik very involved in defending trade union autonomy at this time. Taking a position against what today would be called the ghettoization of women's issues, Riazanova explicitly rejected any notions of difference between men and women, arguing that having women workers meet separately with a special organizer was tantamount to "feminism" and would "inoculate the Russian woman worker with a feminist psychology foreign to her." If women workers were to meet with a separate organizer, she argued, then others could ignore these issues as "women's matters" (bab'e delo).[35]

At the height of the trade union congress, Kollontai counterattacked in Pravda with a strongly worded criticism of the meeting for its poor showing in women representatives. Only if there were more Party involvement in the unions, not less, she argued, could the ideas of communism be spread among the female masses so they would become involved in the building of the new order.[36]

In June 1921 a new Orgbiuro commission devised a compromise resolution calling for "representatives" (rather than organizers) from the women's sections to attend Party fraction meetings in the unions in order to "become acquainted" with union work and to receive materials for carrying out their own agitation work among women. This time, however, the Orgbiuro refused to accept the resolution of its own advi-

33. Before the Trade Union Congress had even met, the women's sections had worked out what they hoped would serve as a compromise decree on the issue of organizers. When they attempted to send it out to the unions, however, the Central Council of Trade Unions directed that it was not to be recognized. See RTsKhIDNI, f. 17, op. 10, d. 11, p. 142.

34. Chetvertyi s"ezd professional'nykh soiuzov SSSR (Moscow, 1922), p. 160. At the same time the unions were directed to carry out a detailed registration of all their most capable women workers so that they could be promoted to elected positions in the unions and in other administrative organs: Gosudarstvennyi Arkhiv Rossiiskoi Federatsii (GARF), f. 5451, op. 5, d. 100, pp. 7–8, cited in Novikova et al., Sovetskie zhenshchiny i profsoiuzy, p. 14.

35. Stenograficheskii otchet IV Vserossiiskogo s"ezda profsoiuzov, bulletin 6 (Moscow, 1921), p. 22, quoted in Riazanova, Zhenskii trud, pp. 285–86. Also GARF, f. 5451, op. 2, d. 154, p. 2.

36. A. Kollontai, "Profsoiuzy i rabotnitsy," Pravda, May 22, 1921.

sory commission.[37] Party officials themselves were forced to acknowledge that the issue remained at an "impasse" throughout the fall and winter.[38]

It was only in February 1922 that a decree was finally approved and published in the central Party organ, *Izvestiia TsK RKP(b)*.[39] It was not without contradictions, however, and soon became the ground for more confusions and conflicts. It named both "instructors" from the women's sections and "organizers" from the central trade union committees to take responsibility for work among women. The women's section instructors as well as the trade union organizers were to be paid from the union budget and made full-time members of the organizational-instruction section of the union.

This was hardly a solution. In the first place, it failed to demarcate the responsibilities of "instructors" and "organizers." Second, it put the burden of fiscal and managerial responsibility on the trade unions, despite their vociferous resistance to the very notion of special efforts on behalf of women. Third, the instructors and organizers were not given release time for this new work but were expected to combine it with full-time work in the union organization sections while at the same time serving in the Party fractions and on the boards of the local women's sections.

The Eleventh Party Congress dealt another blow to trade union autonomy in April 1922 when it resolved that women workers named by the women's sections were to be introduced into all elected trade union organs.[40] This Congress also insisted that all leading trade union officials had to be long-standing Party members.[41] Even after these resolutions,

37. RTsKhIDNI, f. 17, op. 84, d. 153, p. 79; op. 10, d. 11, p. 142.

38. A. Kollontai and V. Mikhailov, "Oblastnym i gubernskim komitetam RKP, otdelam po rabote sredi zhenshchin," *Pravda*, October 16, 1921, p. 1; V. Molotov and V. Golubeva, "Tsirkuliarnoe pis'mo," *Pravda*, December 13, 1921, p. 1.

39. "Polozhenie ob organizatsionnykh vzaimootnosheniiakh zhenotdelov i soiuznykh i mezhsoiuznykh organov i sovmestnoi rabote ikh v oblasti vovlecheniia rabotnits v professional'noe dvizhenie," *Izvestiia TsK RKP(b)* 2 (38) (February 1922): 34, reprinted in *Sbornik postanovlenii i rasporiazhenii partiinykh, professional'nykh i sovetskikh organov po voprosam vovlecheniia rabotnits v professional'noe i sovetskoe stroitel'stvo v sviazi s voprosom sokhraneniia zhenskoi rabochei sily v sovremennykh usloviiakh proizvodstva* (Moscow, 1922), pp. 11–12; *Biulleten' VTsSPS* 6 (1922): 4, with discussion in Novikova et al., *Sovetskie zhenshchiny i profsoiuzy*, p. 28; quoted as well in *Odinnadtsatyi s''ezd RKP(b)* (Moscow, 1966), p. 807n. A report of the women's section on the four-month period between November 1921 and March 1922 referred to this directive as "conclusively" resolving the issue of organizing women in the trade unions: RTsKhIDNI, f. 17, op. 10, d. 20, p. 21.

40. *Odinnadtsatyi s''ezd RKP(b)* (Moscow, 1936), p. 575; reported in *Pravda*, April 5, 1922, p. 4, and reproduced in *Sbornik postanovlenii*, p. 6.

41. On the Eleventh Party Congress and the subjugation of trade union officials to "verification and renewal" by the Party, see T. H. Rigby, *Communist Party Membership in the U.S.S.R., 1917–1967* (Princeton, 1968), p. 466, and Deutscher, *Soviet Trade Unions*, p. 65.

however, the trade unions continued to refer to organizers as "representatives" of women workers and stressed that all work among women was to be carried out "in conjunction with general trade union work."[42]

Soon the issue spilled over into the press and publications for the general public. In 1923 Anna Riazanova published a long monograph, *Female Labor*, in which she endeavoured to show that European trade unions were perfectly successful in organizing women workers without separating the sexes and without naming special organizers.[43] As soon as the book appeared, Varvara Moirova, deputy director of the women's section, attacked it on the grounds that it gave the trade unions credit for organizing women workers when that credit really belonged to the women's sections. It was through separate work among women that the most effective political work could be done, Moirova argued.[44]

That same spring *Trud*, the leading trade union newspaper, ran a series of articles on the question "Are labor organizers for women necessary?" Some trade unionists rejected the notion of special organizers on the grounds that they would become alienated from general trade union work and that they were "co-opted" rather than fully elected.[45] Others, however, argued that women's "peculiarities," their "lack of culture," and their lack of initiative called for special organizers to "weaken their unhealthy instincts and encourage healthy ones."[46] Still others advocated woman organizers on the grounds that they were "specialists" (*spetsrabotniki*) and could accomplish much more than general trade union organs could.[47]

In April 1923 the Twelfth Party Congress officially sanctioned the existence of the special woman organizers. The congress resolution made it clear, however, that this was no victory for the women's sections. Rather the congress mandated special organizers as an explicit "counterweight" to alleged "feminist deviations" within the women's sections themselves. The congress criticized the women's sections for potentially mobilizing popular discontent to create "special societies," which in

42. Resolution of the Fifth National Trade Union Congress in September 1922, reported in *God raboty sredi zhenshchin: Otchetnyi doklad VTsSPS s okt. 1922–okt. 1923 gg.* (Moscow, 1924), pp. 3–4.

43. Riazanova, *Zhenskii trud*, p. 295.

44. V. Moirova, "Kniga tov. Riazanovoi, 'Zhenskii trud,'" *Kommunistka* 5 (1923): 46–47. L. Polonskaia also reviewed Riazanova's work in *Sbornik retsenzii po okhrane truda*, ed. S. Kaplun (Moscow, 1925), pp. 47–54.

45. R. Kogan, "Profsoiuzy i rabota sredi zhenshchin," *Trud*, February 24, 1923.

46. A. Mironov, "Nuzhny li organizatory po rabote sredi zhenshchin (V poriadke obsuzhdeniia)," *Trud*, April 12, 1923.

47. "Spets-rabotniki sredi zhenshchin," *Pravda*, April 13, 1923, cited in Gurvich, "K voprosu o proforganizatorakh," *Kommunistka* 5 (1923): 33.

turn would foster "the alienation of the female part of the workers from the general class struggle."[48]

By strengthening the trade union organizers and insisting that the women's sections had to work in tandem with the trade unions, the Party was clearly attempting to ensure that the two organizations would keep each other in line. The Twelfth Party Congress made it abundantly clear that both organizations existed at the sufferance of the Party and according to its will. As Stalin explained,

> In the political sphere, in order to realize the leadership of the vanguard of the class—that is, the Party—the Party must invest itself with a broad network of nonparty mass apparatuses to serve as tentacles of the Party, with whose help it will be able to transmit its will to the working class, and the working class will turn from a disparate mass into the army of the Party.[49]

In Party circles such mass apparatuses became known as "transmission belts."[50] Both the women's sections and the trade unions faced the problem that in agreeing to such an intermediary role between the Party and the masses, they diminished their own will and identity.

A year and a half later the Party Central Committee resolved that woman organizers were to be introduced onto the staffs of the factory committees, which otherwise were elected organs and in fact had originally been independent of the trade unions. By now the Party was making it clear that the main goal of organizing work was to increase its own influence. At the meeting that discussed this issue, the Party leader Grigorii Zinoviev called for "the complete inclusion and as far as possible the complete organization in one form or another of all women workers engaged in industry."[51]

The trade unions refused to give up, however. Although the delegates to the Sixth Trade Union Congress, which met in November 1924, were willing to discuss the possibility of allowing work among women at the factory level, they insisted that the union worker responsible for overseeing work among women be elected *by the union*.[52] The sponsor of this

48. *Dvenadtsatyi s"ezd RKP(b)* (Moscow, 1968), p. 724. For discussion of events around this resolution, see Hayden, "Feminism and Bolshevism," pp. 217–44.

49. *Dvenadtsatyi s"ezd RKP(b)*, p. 56.

50. At this time Stalin suggested that there should be seven such transmission belts from the Party to the working class: trade unions, cooperatives, youth leagues, conferences of women delegates, schools, the press, and the army. See Carr, *Bolshevik Revolution*, 1: 231–32.

51. O. Sokolova, "O massovoi rabote sredi rabotnits," *Kommunistka* 1 (1925): 36. In the original decision of 1922, organizers for work among women had been assigned only to the highest levels of the trade unions (the central committees of the individual unions and the Central Council of Trade Unions), not to the individual factory committees.

52. *Shestoi s"ezd professional'nykh soiuzov SSSR (11–18 noiabria 1924 g.). Plenumy i sektsii. Polnyi stenograficheskii otchet* (Moscow, 1925), pp. 571–73.

resolution argued that the organizer would then be closer to the work of the union as a whole, implicitly contrasting such a union worker to the outside workers from the women's sections, who often had no union experience and even no factory experience.[53]

Two issues became intermeshed by this point. One was the question of hierarchy and penetration; that is, at what levels should "woman organizers" operate? Should they be only at the national and regional levels or should they also work at the factory level? A second question was whether responsibility should lie with individual organizers or with the factory committees. The argument in favor of committee responsibility centered on the danger that if only one individual had responsibility, he or the rest of the committee might shirk their work in this area. A given individual organizer might also bypass the Party and the factory committee that was supposed to be supervising him or her. Yet, if the whole committee were responsible, it could adopt a purely formal approach to women's issues, merely putting issues on the agenda without any commitment to solving them, or offering to take them "under advisement," thus effectively tabling them.[54]

For many months the central women's section argued in favor of individual organizing. In May 1926 they reversed themselves, however, and decreed that the work should be done by the factory committees as a whole.[55] In their report they put forward stinging criticisms both of the factory committees and of their own women's section activists. The report lambasted the factory committees for brushing off their responsibilities onto individual committee members, who worked in an amateurish fashion without adequate supervision and without the involvement of the committee as a whole.[56] Party cell organizers came under fire for failing to report to the Party fractions of the factory committees and for concentrating all the work in their own hands, without sufficient input from either the Party or the factory committees. The report leveled equally harsh criticisms at the organizers from the women's sections for "deviations from the general directives of the Party," for failing to distinguish between their own tasks and those of the trade unions, and for calling in members of the factory committees and telling them what to

53. The women's journal *Kommunistka*, however, reported only that the Congress "gave a firm directive for deepening work among women": O. Chernysheva, "Rabota profsoiuzov sredi zhenshchin na predpriiatiiakh," *Kommunistka* 1 (1925): 38. It was only after the formal trade union meeting was over that the official resolution was drafted at a special meeting of Party and trade union representatives. By now the trade unions were limited even in the resolutions they could pass.

54. "K postanovleniiu TsK o rabote v profsoiuzakh," *Kommunistka* 6 (1926): 6–7.

55. Ibid., pp. 3–8; GARF, f. 5451, op. 10, d. 110, pp. 2–11.

56. GARF, f. 5451, op. 10, d. 110, pp. 8–9; "K postanovleniiu," pp. 5–6; Z. Divavina, "Profrabota sredi zheleznodorozhnits," *Kommunistka* 5 (1927): 31.

do. Above all, they were criticized for giving reports without the knowledge of the Party fraction.[57]

At first glance, this debate over forms of organizing might seem to be mere carping on the part of the central women's section. In fact, however, the conflict between the women's sections and the trade unions suggests that the weakness of each could be exploited to attack the other. The women's section's report directed the brunt of its attack at what it called the "vulgarization" of Party leadership. Individuals working without sufficient Party supervision, the report claimed, whether they were trade union officials or women's section organizers, might hinder Party work in the factory committees.[58] The woman organizers themselves, caught between the factory committees, the trade unions, and the women's section of the Party, became easy targets on jurisdictional matters.

As the Party became enmeshed in its own internal struggles with first the Left and then the Right Opposition in 1926–28, criticisms of both the trade unions and the women's sections grew shriller. In November 1926 the Fifteenth Party Conference roundly criticized the unions for "insufficient fulfillment of their direct obligations to defend the economic and domestic needs and interests of male and female workers, insufficient attention to their everyday domestic and economic needs and demands, insufficient vigor in defense of the workers' just and legal demands before the state and the economic organs, slowness and sometimes bureaucracy in carrying them out." The conference further criticized the insufficient ties between the factory committee leaders and the working masses, and overly bureaucractic work methods that they claimed often led to mutual lack of understanding, formalism, and frustration. Strikes occurred without the foreknowledge of the unions. The agendas of general meetings and delegate meetings were often overloaded with abstract political issues that were of no interest to workers.[59]

The degree to which various organizations were behaving correctly with respect to women's issues was now to be carefully monitored. In December 1926 the Seventh Trade Union Congress insisted that the Central Trade Union Council would judge the work of the factory committees and their attention to issues of women workers' labor and

---

57. "K postanovleniiu," pp. 6–7. Even organizers named from the Party cells in the factories were criticized for calling production conferences and general meetings of women workers without factory committee approval and for making efforts to combat women workers' illiteracy, a task that was supposed to belong to the Party, not to the factory committees. The commissions on work among women were also called onto the carpet for taking on functions of the factory committees.

58. Ibid.

59. *KPSS o profsoiuzakh* (Moscow, 1967), pp. 217–18. By "abstract political issues" they presumably meant boring speeches concerning the international situation and other issues far from workers' daily lives.

lives.[60] A leading woman official (who worked for both the trade unions and the women's section) told the women's sections they should pay close attention to the Trade Union Congress's decisions so that they could monitor the union organizations through their Party fractions and make sure they were not slackening in their work.[61] A decree of May 21, 1928, further called on the Party fractions in the Central Trade Union Council to 'verify' the work of both the factory committees and the higher-level trade union organizations in serving women workers' needs.[62]

The battles over how to organize women workers, who should do it, and under what circumstances and in what conditions it should be done continued right up until 1930, when the women's sections were "reorganized" out of existence and the trade unions were brought firmly under Party control.

What caused all this confusion over the best forms of organizing women workers? The issues were not merely ideological. The trade unions and women's sections faced genuine difficulties in seeking to organize women workers: shortages of material, financial, and personnel resources; their own lack of experience; the dispersion of women workers in occupations particularly difficult to organize (domestic service, clerical work, and such occupations as garment work and tobacco production, which had been leased to private individuals with the transition to the New Economic Policy); and the high female unemployment in this period.

Yet the debates over organizing women workers are striking for their abstraction and lack of grounding in real industrial relations. Although articles concerning specific industries appeared in trade union periodicals and in the journal of the women's section, the general discussion about organizing among women tended to focus primarily on the more abstract issues of jurisdiction, responsibility and lack thereof, autonomy versus intervention, and *kontrol'* or supervision over labor and management. A key source of the confusion clearly was the Party itself, which put enormous pressures on these two organizations which were somehow supposed to represent the interests of both their own constituencies and the new authorities. At the same time, both organizations felt enormous ambivalence and constraints over the question of Party discipline (which they had highly prized during the long years of underground opposition to

60. A. Artiukhina, "Itogi soveshchaniia zaveduiushchikh oblastnymi i kraevymi otdelami rabotnits i krest'ianok," *Kommunistka* 1 (1927): 26.

61. A. Tikhomirova, "Shto skazal VII s"ezd profsoiuzov v oblasti raboty sredi zhenshchin," *Kommunistka* 2 (1927): 57.

62. "Ob obsluzhivanii rabotnits fabzavmestkomami," TsK VKP(b), May 21, 1928, in *VKP(b) o profsoiuzakh*, 2d ed. (Moscow, 1940), pp. 339–40.

the autocracy) and independence or *samodeiatel'nost'*, the right to self-determination. Both the trade unions and the women's sections, moreover, existed entirely at the discretion of the Party, which financed them and mandated their existence. Because of this dependence on the central authorities (a dependence with both psychological and material roots), these intermediary organizations allowed themselves to be drawn into criticizing one another and competing rather than cooperating.

The new government and its representatives in the women's sections and trade unions were thus caught in force fields of competing discourses and practices concerning the organization of women workers. With the women's sections at their side, the central Party authorities judged and criticized the trade unions for the inadequacies of their work among women. At the same time, they made disparaging remarks concerning the women's sections, judging them as having insufficient class consciousness and being overly concerned with the positions of prostitutes and housewives, rather than focusing on women workers.

In the spring of 1925 Zinoviev had announced that all the parties in the Communist International would now be judged on the basis of their organizing among women workers: "Let all the Communist parties remember: in the future the Comintern will judge the level of Bolshevization on the basis of, among other things, how serious their successes have been in the mass organization of women."[63] Yet nowhere did Zinoviev or anyone else give concrete standards that would allow parties to evaluate their actual progress. Here was an area where the work of organizations could always be shown to be inadequate. If the trade unions and women's sections were insufficiently vigilant in their defense of women workers, they could be and were charged with excessive "passivity." Yet if they were overly active in defending women workers' interests, they could be charged with insubordination to the Party. By creating such a vague criterion, the central Party authorities established a Scylla and Charybdis that was difficult for individual organizations to navigate.[64]

By establishing such a difficult yardstick as "successes . . . in the mass organization of women," the Party enhanced its position as the dominant political organization and arbiter of success and failure. By having four or even five organizations (the women's sections, trade unions, factory committees, women's commissions, and Party cells) take on the task of

63. Grigorii Zinoviev, "Bol'shevizatsiia i rabota sredi zhenshchin," *Kommunistka* 3 (1925): 2.
64. For a related argument that Marxism-Leninism could be manipulated by those who claimed to be its guardians, see Rachel Walker, "Marxism-Leninism as Discourse: The Politics of the Empty Signifier and the Double Bind," *British Journal of Political Science* 19 (1989): 161–89.

organizing women, the Party (whether consciously or unconsciously) created a tight field in which boundary disputes were inevitable, especially as the initial notion of "organizing" was left vague and open to interpretation. Organization of workers may have been one of the ABCs of communism, but it pitted social organizations against one another to the detriment of cooperation among them.[65]

Women workers' marginal position made them both a prime target for a regime that sought to mobilize every citizen and also a source of ongoing conflict over jurisdiction, ideology, and control. Ultimately the issues of class and gender were not just about workers and women. Over the course of the first decade of Bolshevik rule they also became structures of signification organizing the dictatorship of the proletariat, establishing norms of discipline and control, and fostering the hegemony of a party that claimed to be the judge of "consciousness" and of "organization."

65. Historical work on Germany under the Third Reich has suggested that Nazi power rested at least in part on a similar degree of jurisdictional confusion, overlap, and chaos rather than on some kind of "totalitarian" control from above. A good summary of this work can be found in Ian Kershaw, *The Nazi Dictatorship: Problems and Perspectives of Interpretation* (London, 1985), pp. 65–70.

13

The Heroic Man and
the Ever-Changing Woman:
Gender and Politics in European
Communism, 1917–1950

Eric D. Weitz

In November 1920, the Executive Committee of the Communist International (ECCI) adopted "Guidelines for the Communist Women's Movement." Drafted by Clara Zetkin, the long-time leader of the socialist women's movement in Germany, the statement asserted the full equality of men and women, called for recognition of the "social function" of motherhood, and demanded equal pay for equal work and wide-ranging social protection measures. The Comintern called on its member parties to promote the full and active participation of women in all realms of life, and to integrate women into all levels of the "proletarian class struggle." In the "Guidelines" and in their subsequent political work, the Communist parties invariably attacked their socialist rivals for

Earlier versions of this chapter were read at the annual meeting of the Social Science History Association, October 1991, and at the North American Labor History Conference at Wayne State University, October 1994. I thank the commentators at these sessions, Elisabeth Domansky, Laura Frader, Eve Rosenhaft, Laura Tabili, and Judith Wishnia, for their very helpful criticisms, and Carol H. Weitz for her photographic skills and sensibilities. The chapter draws on and develops material contained in my book, *Communism in Germany: Worker Movement and Socialist State, 1890–1990*, copyright © 1996 by Princeton University Press, and essay "Popular Communism: Political Strategies and Social Histories in the Formation of the German, French, and Italian Communist Parties, 1919–1948," Western Societies Program Occasional Paper 31 (Cornell University Institute for European Studies, 1992).

their failure to address women's issues, for their high-flown rhetoric and lack of action, for their petit-bourgeois "family values." Ideologically, the communist movement seemed the legitimate heir of the bourgeois and socialist feminist movements of the late nineteenth and early twentieth centuries.[1]

Despite the fervent statements in support of women's emancipation and social advancement, the Communist parties were overwhelmingly masculine in character. Their memberships were composed predominantly of men, and in those countries where women had suffrage rights, the Communist parties typically had the most masculine electoral profiles.[2] Moreover, communism unquestionably drew upon—indeed, deepened—the masculinist definition of labor and politics that had become a fixed part of the socialist movements of the nineteenth century.[3] The heightened self-consciousness about ideology in the communist movement meant the reiteration and reemphasis of the Marxist and more generally materialist understanding of the sphere of production as the bedrock of social organization and the locus of class struggle. As a result,

1. The "Guidelines" were confirmed at the Third Congress of the Communist International in 1921 and served as the basis for all subsequent statements and resolutions in relation to women's issues. See Clara Zetkin, "Richtlinien für die kommunistische Frauenbewegung," *Kommunistische Internationale* 15 (1920/21): 530–55. The text is also available in Karin Bauer, *Clara Zetkin und die proletarische Frauenbewegung* (Berlin, 1978), pp. 237–66. In general on the Comintern and women, see Aurelia Camparini, *Questione femminile e Terza internazionale* (Bari, 1978).

2. For some statistics on the various parties, see Hans-Jürgen Arendt, "Weibliche Mitglieder der KPD in der Weimarer Republik: Zahlenmäßige Stärke und soziale Stellung," *Beiträge zur Geschichte der Arbeiterbewegung* 19 (1977): 654; Gabriele Bremme, *Die politische Rolle der Frau in Deutschland: Eine Untersuchung über den Einfluß der Frauen bei Wahlen und ihre Teilnahme in Partei und Parlament* (Göttingen, 1956), pp. 73–74; Annie Kriegel, "Le Parti Communiste français sous la Troisième République (1920–1939)," *Revue français de science politique* 16 (February 1966): 24–25; Victoria E. Bonnell, "The Representation of Women in Early Soviet Political Art," *Russian Review* 50 (July 1991): 282.

3. Good examples from what is now a very large literature are Harold Benenson, "The 'Family Wage' and Working Women's Consciousness in Britain, 1880–1914," *Politics and Society* 19 (March 1991): 71–108; idem, "Victorian Sexual Ideology and Marx's Theory of the Working Class," *International Labor and Working Class History* 25 (Spring 1984): 1–23; Eric Hobsbawm, "Man and Woman: Images on the Left," in his *Workers: Worlds of Labor* (New York, 1984), pp. 83–102; Ava Baron, ed., *Work Engendered: Toward a New History of American Labor* (Ithaca, 1991); Kathleen Canning, "Gender and the Culture of Work: Ideology and Identity in the World beyond the Mill Gate, 1890–1914," in *Elections, Mass Politics, and Social Change in Modern Germany: New Perspectives*, ed. Larry Eugene Jones and James Retallack (Cambridge, 1992), pp. 175–99; Sonya O. Rose, *Limited Livelihoods: Gender and Class in Nineteenth-Century England* (Berkeley, 1991); Mary Jo Maynes, *Taking the Hard Road: Life Course and Working-Class Autobiographies* (Chapel Hill, 1995); Heinz Niggemann, *Emanzipation zwischen Sozialismus und Feminismus: Die sozialdemokratische Frauenbewegung im Kaiserreich* (Wuppertal, 1981). On a later period, see Elizabeth Faue, *Community of Suffering and Struggle: Women, Men, and the Labor Movement in Minneapolis, 1915–1945* (Chapel Hill, 1991).

the imagery of muscular, determined men, whose labor provided the material riches of society and whose political activism led the way to the bright socialist future, infused communist iconography.

But to the depictions of productive men the Comintern parties added a new dimension: the militarized male revolutionary, weapon in hand, trampling over the ruins of capitalism. To be sure, such imagery had its nineteenth-century precursors—one need only think of Delacroix's *Liberty Leading the People*, in which the female figure of Liberty is followed by rifle-bearing men. But the combined impact of World War I and the Bolshevik Revolution and Civil War greatly intensified the militaristic tendencies of the labor movement, at least of its communist wing. World War I contributed to the brutalization of public life in general, and communists, of course, were not alone in idealizing political violence as the means of social progress. Revolution on the Bolshevik model came to mean a singular military assault—the legend of the storming of the Winter Palace—combined with active military defense of the seizure of state power. Thus postwar communism had a pronounced militaristic tone, and it cut across all the various party factions. It found cultural expression in the militarization of dress among the Bolshevik leaders, the continual reference to the "lessons of October," and the adoption of military metaphors for all sorts of campaigns and programs, culminating in the Stalinist forced collectivization and industrialization programs.[4]

The militaristic style signified, almost necessarily, the heightened masculinization of labor politics and culture in the communist movement. Indeed, a fixed and unchanging construction of masculinity characterized the Communist parties from the poster art of the Bolshevik Revolution to the propaganda appeals of the Communist-led antifascist resistance in Italy, France, and other countries. With only slightly varying nuances, powerful male proletarians build socialism, march in demonstrations, and fight for class, nation, and the Soviet Union. The heroic male revolutionary, hammer, weapon, and fists at the ready, lay at the epicenter of communist understandings of society and politics.

But the enormous impact of World War I was not confined to masculinity and militancy. The war also profoundly destabilized and politicized gender roles. Women, of course, assumed many jobs previously reserved for men, and took on more public and emancipated personas. Though most women were driven out of "male" occupations with demobilization, the rapid emergence of the "new woman" of the 1920s—

4. See Diane P. Koenker, William G. Rosenberg, and Ronald Grigor Suny, eds., *Party, State, and Society in the Russian Civil War: Explorations in Social History* (Bloomington, 1989), and Sheila Fitzpatrick, ed., *Cultural Revolution in Russia* (Bloomington, 1978).

active, slender, athletic, sexual, and amaternal—provoked widespread
unease that, in some quarters, took on near-hysterical, apocalyptic hues
bound up with fears of national decline. The natalist character of much
of this discourse was fueled also by the immense loss of male lives in the
war and, for those who survived, the reality and vision of debilitated
men: the virile male hero returned from the front, often in defeat, and,
even if victorious, wounded bodily and psychically. The specter of
demasculinized men and virile but amaternal women seemed the essential expression of a world gone awry, a world of chaos and social disorder
that included strikes, revolution, national disgrace, and, not least, gender
confusion. The pronatalist discourses and policies that ensued marked a
heightened level of state intervention in familial and sexual life, but were
directed primarily at controlling women's, not men's, bodies.[5]

The Communist parties, struggling to become mass movements, operated in this environment in which gender had become destabilized and
women's roles in particular subject to intense political debate. The express commitment to women's emancipation provided a core set of
beliefs—the right of women to work in the paid labor force and to engage
in politics, for example—but these beliefs could intersect in a highly
mobile fashion with all sorts of other conceptions of women. As a result,
the constructions of femininity within the communist movement varied
enormously. Oppressed mothers, joyous and loving mothers, slender and
active new women of the 1920s, harassed and exploited workers, cool and
elegant patrons of Parisian shops, partisans wielding machine guns at
the side of their proletarian brothers—the cacophony of female imagery
stands in sharp contrast to the stability of male representations. They do
not work together, collage-like, to reveal a movement that understood
the complexities of women's lives and developed a comprehensive approach to reaching them in all of their social roles. Instead, they show

5. This paragraph draws heavily on Elisabeth Domansky, "Militarization and Reproduc-
tion in World War I Germany," in *Society, Culture, and State in Germany, 1870–1930*, ed.
Geoff Eley (Ann Arbor, forthcoming); Mary Louise Roberts, *Civilization without Sexes:
Reconstructing Gender in Postwar France, 1917–1927* (Chicago, 1994); Susan Kingsley
Kent, *Making Peace: The Reconstruction of Gender in Interwar Britain* (Princeton, 1993);
Young-Sun Hong, "The Contradictions of Modernization in the German Welfare State:
Gender and the Politics of Welfare Reform in First World War Germany," *Social History*
17 (May 1992): 251–70; Cornelie Usborne, *The Politics of the Body in Weimar Germany:
Women's Reproductive Rights and Duties* (Ann Arbor, 1992); and David F. Crew, "'Eine
Elternschaft zu Dritt'—staatliche Eltern? Jugendwohlfahrt und Kontrolle der Familie in
der Weimarer Republik, 1919–1933," in *"Sicherheit" und "Wohlfahrt": Polizei,
Gesellschaft und Herrschaft im 19. und 20. Jahrhundert*, ed. Alf Lüdtke (Frankfurt am
Main, 1992), pp. 267–94. For the Soviet case, in which many of the same issues received
quite different resolutions, at least in the 1920s, see Wendy Z. Goldman, *Women, the
State, and Revolution: Soviet Family Policy and Social Life, 1917–1936* (Cambridge,
1993).

Communist parties groping unsteadily, lurching from one image to another in the search for some way to appeal to women. Moreover, the representations of women, however varied, appear far less frequently than those of men, particularly in the 1920s. They surface only intermittently in the pages of the party press, in Bolshevik political art of the 1920s, in the highly successful illustrated weeklies such as the German *Arbeiter-Illustrierte-Zeitung* (*AIZ*), as shadowy figures in proletarian novels and memoirs, as the afterthought at Party and Comintern conferences—despite all the resolutions in favor of women's equality and the organization of proletarian women.[6]

The shifting imagery of women did not, however, reflect only confusion or the instability of the larger political and social environment. It reflected also the shifting political strategies of the parties and the connections between the political spaces within which parties operated and their conceptions of gender. Indeed, the gendered character of Party strategies was not the product of a kind of free-floating discursive terrain that merely mirrored the range of existing views; it was deeply embedded in the logics of particular political spaces. The Communist parties of Germany, France and Italy became mass parties in sequential decades—the German in the 1920s, French in the 1930s, and Italian in the 1940s. Each placed the heroic, productive, and combative male proletariat at the center of its political efforts, though the nuances differed slightly. But the representations of women derived in great part from the varying combinations of spaces—streets and battlefields, households and workplaces, municipalities and national legislatures—within which each party accomplished its popular breakthrough.

The Communist Party of Germany (KPD), driven from the battlefield by the superior firepower of the state and from the workplace by rationalization, the world economic crisis, and employer repression, was forced to use the streets as the primary space of political mobilization. There it developed a politics of display and spectacle built around military-like demonstrations and street battles with the police, fascist organizations, and, occasionally, employed workers. Even more than the other parties, the KPD made the physically powerful, militaristic male proletarian the center of its politics, while women were rendered the passive objects of capitalist exploitation and (male) proletarian sympathy.

6. On the absence of women from Bolshevik imagery, see Bonnell, "Representation of Women." Clara Zetkin had to fight to give more prominence and more nuanced understandings to women's issues in the Comintern program, even though it had been drafted by her friend and political ally Nikolai Bukharin. See Ernesto Ragionieri, "Il programma dell' Internazionale comunista," *Studi storici* 13, no. 4 (1972), and 14, no. 1 (1973).

The French Communist Party (PCF) in the Popular Front dramatically broadened its presence within the political spaces of French society. Ensconced in the institutions of the nation, the PCF began to forge reform policies, especially at the municipal level, that directly addressed family and gender issues. Though men remained heroic producers committed to socialism, the militaristic imagery waned a bit as the party sought to maintain the cross-class and cross-political alliances of the Popular Front. Most critically, the PCF shifted to a pronatalist position and a highly conventional view of sexuality fully in keeping with the dominant French discourse on these matters. Far from presenting the difficulties of female proletarian life—indeed, far from presenting female proletarians at all—the Communist press in the Popular Front depicted women whose contribution to society was to be found in their elegance and their maternity.

The Italian Communist Party (PCI) came to occupy the broadest range of political space. Barred from the "normal" arenas of political activity by the Fascist monopolization of power, the party at first could establish itself only in the workplace, which, with the adjacent working-class communities, provided the security in which clandestine activity could develop. With the decision in September 1943 to launch an armed resistance, the PCI quickly became the major force of the partisan war. The very nature of resistance—the primacy placed on individual initiative and the dependence on the population for support—served to politicize virtually all the arenas of civil society. The PCI's promotion of this broad-based popular insurgency won it support not just from proletarian men but from other social groups, women and the agrarian population in particular. Engaged in war, the PCI revived the imagery of the proletariat under arms, but now included women along with men. In the political contest with Christian Democracy that soon followed the Resistance, however, the PCI largely abandoned its representations of combative, active women. Instead, it retreated to representations of the maternal and nurturing woman, depictions of women and the family that distinctly echoed those of the Christian Democratic world.

CONSTRUCTING MASCULINITY

Communist propaganda from the very beginning idealized male productive labor as the source of the material riches of society and the basis of the future socialist order. Bolshevik political art, drawing on both socialist and traditional Russian representations, depicted the blacksmith as the ideal proletarian—the powerful man forging the steel of socialist construction and imbued with near-magical powers. Occasion-

ally he has a female helper, but certainly not a female fellow blacksmith.[7]
His male comrades, wherever they are—the Soviet Union, Germany,
France, Italy—are invariably strong, determined, and skillful. They gaze
upward, heroically, into the socialist future, concentrate deeply on their
labor, or march together shoulder to shoulder (Figures 13.1–4).

Through these representations, class came to be defined in terms of
gender: productive male workers constituted the core of the proletariat;
women, if present at all, played an ancillary role. And class was inextricably entwined with struggle. In line with the classical Marxian texts,
Communists argued that in struggle the proletariat would become a class
for itself and fulfill its world historical role. Hence the language of
struggle—*der Kampf, la lutte, la lotta*—runs through all Communist
propaganda and literature, and struggle figures dramatically in the visual
representations of the parties. The striking covers of the *Arbeiter-
Illustrierte-Zeitung*, many created by John Heartfield, convey the militant sense of struggle—powerful male proletarian arms and fists, rifles
drawn, bayonets slashing upward (Figures 13.5 and 13.6).[8] *Kampf* became, quite literally, physical struggle, and the rhetoric, with its constant invocation of battles, campaigns, and weaponry, served to reinforce
the militarism of the communist movement.

Heartfield's representations in particular depict the virulence of
struggle, and struggle as a social act, almost invariably of men. But even
when the military aspects of struggle waned, as in France during the
Popular Front, militancy remained. It was conveyed through depictions
of male workers struggling in solidarity for their class, and symbolically
through the clenched fist (Figure 13.7).[9] Occasionally joyous, more often
militant, male camaraderie stood for the camaraderie and solidarity of
the proletariat in general (Figure 13.8).

With these representations, Communists built upon but also extended
an ethos of proletarian masculinity centered on toughness—of body
and will—and of political commitment. Social democrats, in contrast,
were generally depicted as soft, frightened, fat, and old, commingl-
ing with the bourgeoisie and the aristocracy in genteel circumstances,

7. Bonnell, "Representation of Women," pp. 277–80.
8. The PCI's daily, *L'unità*, May 7, 1945, conveyed the same sense at the very end of
World War II with a caricature that depicts powerful male arms holding rifles in front of
a factory, thereby welding together male productivity and male combativeness.
9. See esp. the articles by Gottfried Korff: "Bruderhand und Arbeiterfaust: Zur
politischen Metaphorik der Hand" (manuscript, 1991); "From Brotherly Handshake to
Militant Clenched Fist: On Political Metaphors for the Worker's Hand," *International
Labor and Working Class History* 42 (Fall 1992): 70–81, an abbreviated version of the
German manuscript cited above; "Rote Fahnen und geballte Faust: Zur Symbolik der
Arbeiterbewegung in der Weimarer Republik," in *Fahnen, Fäuste, Körper: Symbolik und
Kultur der Arbeiterbewegung*, ed. Dietmar Petzina (Essen, 1986), pp. 27–60.

STOSSBRIGADE
DES SOZIALISMUS

13.1. Soviet workers, the "shock brigades of socialism," gaze heroically into the future in front of the smokestacks of socialist development. (*AIZ* 16 [1930])

13.2. Heroic male labor—a riveter. (*AIZ*, April 18, 1928)

regards

GRÈVE à LIMOGES

13.3. In France also the Communist Party represents the male worker, such as this ceramic worker in Limoges, as the skilled creator of wealth. (*Regards*, June 29, 1934)

13.4. The Italian Communist Party idealizes male agricultural workers with this call for "peace and the renewal of the Mezzogiorno." (*Modern Italy*, vol. 3: *1939–1960: War, Postwar Reconstruction, Take-off* [Milan: Electa Editrice, 1984])

13.5. Class means the solidarity of powerful male proletarians. Socialists and Communists march together with clenched fists, but the KPD (symbolized by the armband) stands above the SPD. (*AIZ* 49 [1931], copyright © 1996 by Artists Rights Society, New York/VG Bild Kunst, Bonn/The Heartfield Community of Heirs)

13.6. The essence of proletarianism. Rifles drawn, bayonets at the ready, the working class defends the Soviet Union. (*AIZ* 31 [1930])

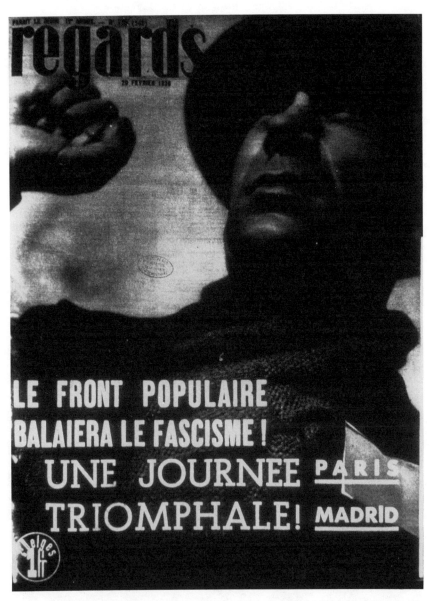

13.7. The clenched-fist salute, the symbol of male combativeness and commitment to the struggle. (*Regards*, February 20, 1936)

13.8. Working-class solidarity is defined by male camaraderie, here outside Renault's sprawling factory in the Paris suburb of Billaincourt. (*Regards*, April 13, 1934)

whereas Communists, women and men, are broad-shouldered and muscular.[10]

Though all the Communist parties emphasized male solidarity and struggle as the essence of proletarianism, the KPD developed a particularly militaristic tenor, forged in the political spaces of failed revolutionary uprisings and combative street battles. The violence of the KPD's political rhetoric and the individual and political martyrdoms endured by many of its fighters sustained the party's militaristic ethos. In the midst of one of the failed uprisings, the March Action of 1921, the *Ruhr-Echo*, the local party paper in Essen, ran a banner headline, taken from the penultimate phrase of the party program, written by Rosa Luxemburg: "Thumb in the enemy's eye, knee on his chest!"[11] The title of a short-lived KPD newspaper, *Rote Peitsche* (Red Whip), established as a four-page publication for the 1928 electoral campaign (which quickly became a supplement to the *Ruhr-Echo*), is just one other example of the rhetoric of militant violence that pervaded the KPD.[12] The party bestowed lavish attention on its paramilitary organizations, primarily the Rote Front-kämpferbund (RFB—Red Front Fighters Association), and infused its press with militaristic images.[13] The *AIZ* published photo after photo of uniformed men, banners flying, marching in disciplined military formation or standing at rallies amid seas of red flags (Figure 13.9). Only the character of the uniforms and banners enables a viewer to distinguish the RFB from the Nazi SA. One sees the same determined men—women are completely absent—in both the KPD and Nazi representations, the same emphasis on a muscular masculinity. In photos even the Communist leader Ernst Thälmann appears in jackboots and brown cap.[14] By glorifying its own militaristic culture the KPD sought to join its traditions with the Soviet invocation of the October Revolution and the victorious Civil War as *the* heroic moments of Bolshevism and of world socialism.[15]

10. See, e.g., the collection of caricatures sent out by the KPD Central Committee: "Illustrations-Vorlagen für Betriebs- und Häuserblock-Zeitungen," vols. 10–12 (Frankfurt am Main, [early 1930s]), Bundesarchiv Koblenz R45 IV 39.

11. *Ruhr Echo*, March 29, 1921.

12. "Bericht über den Wahlkampf im Bezirk Ruhrgebiet," Stiftung Archiv der Parteien und Massenorganisationen der DDR im Bundesarchiv, Zentrales Parteiarchiv 3/18–19/13, p. 124.

13. On the RFB see Kurt G. P. Schuster, *Der Rote Frontkämpferbund, 1924–1929: Beiträge zur Geschichte und Organisationsstruktur eines politischen Kampfbundes* (Düsseldorf, 1975).

14. These impressions are based on reading the *AIZ* from 1926 to 1932. Some especially revealing photos can be found in the following issues (the paper variously used volume and issue numbers, dates, and a combination of the two): 10 (1926); June 5, 1927; June 19, 1927; April 25, 1928; May 9, 1928 (the photo of Thälmann); 4 (1930); 31 (1930); 49 (1931); 24 (1932).

15. Koenker et al., *Party, State, and Society*, esp. Sheila Fitzpatrick, "The Legacy of the Civil War," pp. 385–98.

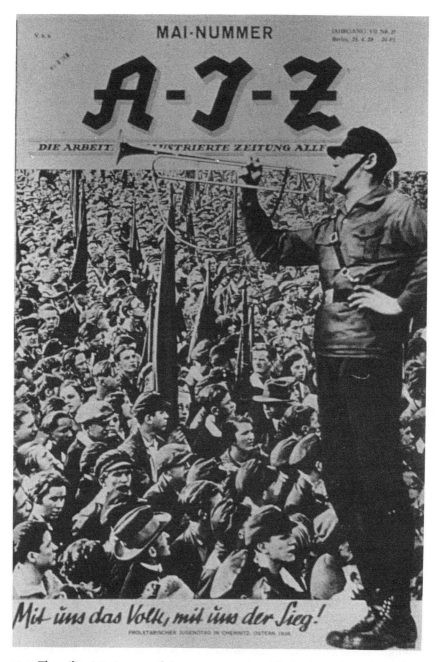

13.9. The militaristic imagery of German communism. The bugler in the uniform of the
KPD's paramilitary organization calls the masses to the struggle. (*AIZ*, April 25, 1928)

Guns carried a very particular mystique, and possession of one was a cherished symbol of commitment—and of masculinity—among Communist cadres.[16] The proletarian-in-arms, rifle at the ready or over the shoulder, was a fixed feature of the Communist press and literature. The knowledge that possession of a gun was punishable by a stiff prison sentence only heightened some men's fascination with weaponry. It made them part of a conspiratorial society, an elite of men devoted to the revolutionary cause and bonded together by their ideas and the dangers they shared. Memoirs of party functionaries such as Erich Wollenberg, active in various branches of the KPD's military units, depict a life of conspiratorial meetings, shoot-outs with the police, and constant movement to prevent capture.[17] Women appear infrequently, as shadowy figures without personality or individuality, just the wives of comrades who give Wollenberg a meal while he is on the run from the police.

Some party members and Comintern officials were aware that street fights and conspiracies were not quite the same thing as mass revolution, and that the sense of civil disorder they created might ultimately benefit the Nazis. But for a party schooled on the Luxemburgist-Leninist celebration of mass activism, and whose cadres had experienced war, armed revolution, and street battles, the specter of thousands of workers marching in military formation and small groups beating up policemen and fascists was simply too enticing. For the French and Italian parties, the real experience of combat would come later, in the antifascist resistance. For all three parties, male physical prowess constituted the essential character of revolutionary commitment, a result of both ideological intransigence and the movement of the space of labor politics from the workplace to contested streets and the battlefields of World War II.

CONSTRUCTING FEMININITY

No single image of femininity dominates Communist representations in the way the heroic and combative male proletarian provides a uniform and consistent construction of masculinity. Most often in the 1920s, representations of women entailed Käthe Kollwitz–like depictions of oppression and depression—the proletarian housewife, old before her time, overwhelmed by poverty and motherhood and unending household labor. In Germany, John Heartfield's powerful statements against paragraph 218, the law that criminalized abortions, offer examples of the melodramatic genre that predominated in relation to women in the *AIZ*

---

16. See Eve Rosenhaft, *Beating the Fascists? The German Communists and Political Violence, 1929–1933* (Cambridge, 1983).

17. Erich Wollenberg, memoirs (typescript), Hoover Institution Archives.

and other Communist media (Figure 13.10).[18] The women in these depictions are objects of sympathy and pathos, but rarely is the viewer offered representations of activist women. Presumably, women's emancipation from their dire straits would arise from the actions of their male relations and comrades.

Moreover, female labor is only rarely depicted in the heroic cast with which male labor is endowed. Women workers were depicted as oppressed by long hours and low wages, by the authoritarian relations of the office and department store, by the dirt and grime of factory labor, by barely concealed sexual exploitation. Rarely, if ever, does one see women as the skilled creators of wealth. They work in the interstices of the capitalist economy—as ticket collectors, office workers, saleswomen, home workers, and, occasionally, factory laborers (Figure 13.11). Women might work outside the home, and in increasing numbers, but it was not by their labor that the new society, with unlimited riches, would be created. Even Soviet propaganda did not begin to depict women workers until some years after the Bolshevik Revolution, and most often as helpers or otherwise in the company of male workers, rarely alone as masters of a trade.[19] In France in the 1930s, women workers on strike were represented not for their labor power but for the elegance they displayed, as with the dressmakers in Figure 13.12.

While the Communist parties constructed women's paid labor as ancillary to "true" productive labor, they also denigrated the household as a backward province of precapitalist social forms and petit-bourgeois values.[20] Individually rather than socially organized, the household was by definition a retrograde social organism, hence a site of the most backward political and social ideas—political passivity that oscillated with spontaneous, semi-anarchistic eruptions; loyalty to an unthinking socialist reformism or Catholicism; petit-bourgeois individualism; pacifism.[21] Women as a group and the household as a retrograde political space constituted the ever-present others that threatened to undermine the (male) proletarian resolve forged in the workplace and the streets. Full emancipation could emerge only from women's participation in the industrial economy. Concomitantly, household labor would be socialized in communal kitchens, nurseries, and laundries, as the Comintern's 1920 "Guidelines" stipulated.

18. See Patrice Petro, *Joyless Streets: Women and Melodramatic Representation in Weimar Germany* (Princeton, 1989), esp. pp. 94–103, 127–39.

19. Bonnell, "Representation of Women." See also Bonnell, "The Peasant Woman in Stalinist Political Art of the 1930s," *American Historical Review* 98 (February 1993): 55–82.

20. On this issue generally see Silvia Kontos, *"Die Partei kämpft wie ein Mann!": Frauenpolitik der KPD in der Weimarer Republik* (Frankfurt am Main, 1979), esp. pp. 131–41. The KPD's position here followed the Comintern's "Guidelines."

21. Kontos provides suitable quotes: ibid., pp. 173–78.

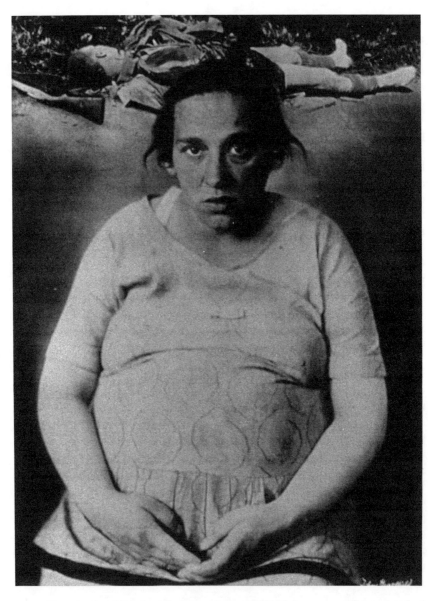

13.10. The miseries of female proletarian existence. Behind the pregnant woman is a dead soldier. The caption reads: "Forced to carry human material. Have courage! The state needs the unemployed and soldiers!" (*AIZ* 9 [1930], copyright © 1996 by Artists Rights Society, New York/VG Bild Kunst, Bonn/The Heartfield Community of Heirs)

13.11. Women, such as this subway ticket collector, work at nonproductive jobs. (*AIZ* 43 [1929])

13.12. Dressmakers on strike are depicted not at work or on a picket line but as the elegant occupants of urban space. (*Regards*, May 30, 1935)

Nonetheless, the Communist parties did make efforts to reach proletarian women in the home. The *AIZ* generally published a women's
column titled, for a few weeks in 1926–27, "Mother and Child," though
that quickly changed to "The Working Woman." Whatever its title, the
column offered women typical household advice—how to sew jackets or
knit sweaters for the family, reuse old clothing, keep food without ice.
The fashions depicted were plain and utilitarian. Women were also
shown how to bathe, carry, and breast-feed their infants.[22]

While offering "traditional" household advice, the *AIZ* at times also
promoted a proletarian version of the "new woman" of the 1920s.[23] She
not only cooked and laundered, but also repaired electrical appliances,
plastered, and painted windows.[24] In accord with other political tendencies in the Weimar Republic, the KPD advocated a "rationalized" household in which efficient work and modern technology would combine to
ease women's burdens.[25] Women in the home were advised to work while
seated and to adjust table and chairs to the proper height, to put dishes
where they would not gather dust, to arrange the work space of the
kitchen efficiently, to make use of the newest appliances. The party
almost always accompanied such advice with the caveat that most modern appliances were too expensive for the proletarian family, and household labor could be truly rationalized only in socially organized
communal kitchens, laundries, and nurseries.[26]

Like her bourgeois counterpart, the new proletarian woman was youthful, healthy, slender, athletic, erotic, and most definitely not pregnant.
Idealized Soviet women, especially Soviet athletes, often served as the
models, but the German new woman also graced the party press (Figures
13.13 and 13.14). Often she was shown juxtaposed with her precise
opposite—the old, heavy-set, haggard-looking woman who worked inef-

22. "Dein Kind—dein Kamerad!" *AIZ* 10, no. 51 (1931): 1030.
23. See Atina Grossmann, "The New Woman and the Rationalization of Sexuality
in Weimar Germany," in *Powers of Desire: The Politics of Sexuality*, ed. Ann Snitow,
Christine Stansell, and Sharon Thompson (New York, 1983), pp. 153–71; Petro, *Joyless
Streets*, pp. 104–39; Usborne, *Politics of the Body*, pp. 85–101; Ute Frevert, *Women in
German History: From Bourgeois Emancipation to Sexual Liberation* (New York, 1989),
pp. 168–204. For the Soviet peasant version of the new woman, see Bonnell, "Peasant
Woman in Stalinist Political Art."
24. "Die Frau als Elektriker," *AIZ* 9, no. 20 (1930): 386; "Die Frau als Handwerker,"
AIZ 9, no. 26 (1930): 506.
25. See, e.g., *AIZ*, April 4, 1928, p. 7. The campaign for "rationalized" households cut
through the political divisions of the Weimar period, as Mary Nolan shows (though she
does not discuss the KPD): "'Housework Made Easy': The Taylorized Housewife in
Weimar Germany's Rationalized Economy," *Feminist Studies* 16 (Fall 1990): 549–73.
26. "Die werktätige Frau," *AIZ*, June 5, 1927, p. 10; June 29, 1927, p. 10; July 20, 1927,
p. 12; "Alter und neuer Haushalt," *AIZ*, April 4, 1928, p. 7; "Um die Gesundheit der
proletarischen Hausfrau," *AIZ* 9, no. 39 (1930): 766.

Entdeckung der Neuen Welt

DIE ARBEITER

A·J·Z

JAHRGANG VII NR. 48
5. Woche November 1928
20 Pf.
15 Kon.
40 Gr.

LÄNDER

RUSSISCHE
SPORTLERIN

13.13. The female Russian athlete symbolizes the bright, youthful socialist future. (*AIZ* 48 [1928])

13.14. Young, slender, lively, and not pregnant—the ideal Communist of the 1920s. The caption reads: "... better than being bitten by the stork!" (*AIZ* 24 [1931])

ficiently and was worn down by years of backbreaking labor bent over the washtub.[27] By juxtaposing the old and the new, the KPD clearly presented itself as the party of change, of the new woman, of the future. The celebrations of youth served the same function, and come uncomfortably close to fascist representations (Figure 13.15).

Body politics and class politics often ran together. The *AIZ* claimed that the old German *Turnvereine* (gymnastics associations) promulgated tight and rigid forms of movement, in keeping with their rigid and outmoded political ideology. By implication, the revolutionary sports movement promoted new bodies and the new class, emancipation and socialism.[28] The *AIZ*, for its part, assured the proletarian housewife that she could exercise even without gymnastic equipment. All it took was "one-quarter hour every morning, goodwill, and a sturdy towel." The exercises were best done naked, "because then one has at the same time an air bath, [good] for the body, which, unfortunately, given our European morals, must languish most of its life in the constraints of clothing and coverings."[29] The weekly also advocated group gymnastics, and the pictures show women whose body movements were at one and the same time loose and free and collectively disciplined and organized.

Fashion constituted another site of the class struggle. "Bourgeois decadence" finds its expression in luxurious and impractical clothing, which involves "wasteful excesses of material, . . . extravagant lines, . . . complicated style of preparation," and makes the woman an object of masculine desire, whereas the working-class woman

> neither is the luxury creature of a man nor follows the dictates of fashion, which maintain [bourgeois] class interests in refined form. But she has a natural need to dress in a pretty fashion, to wear beautiful colors and good material that highlight her figure. . . . [She wears clothes that allow for] their clear movement around the body.[30]

The drawing that accompanies the article shows two decadent bourgeois women opposite two working women, whose clothes are plain but fashionable. They are the epitome of the proletarian new woman: slender, short hair, loose clothes that show the body form (Figure 13.16).

Especially in the realm of sexuality the KPD in particular emerged as the advocate of the new woman and staked out an emancipatory position

27. E.g., "Die werktätige Frau," *AIZ*, June 5, 1927, p. 10; "Mordparagraph 218," *AIZ*, July 13, 1927, p. 7; "Alter und neuer Haushalt," *AIZ*, April 4, 1928, p. 7.

28. "Frauengymnastik," *AIZ* 8, no. 42 (1929): 18.

29. "Die werktätige Frau," *AIZ*, April 17, 1927, p. 10. The editors, however, could not quite bring themselves to depict a naked woman. The sketches that show how to do the exercises are of a desexed child.

30. "Die Mode-Reaktion," *AIZ* 8, no. 45 (1929): 14.

DEM NEUEN JAHRE ENTGEGEN:

VORWÄRTS!
IST DIE GROSSE LOSUNG
UNSER IST DIE WELT!

13.15. Youth looking to the future, a socialist future created by the Communist Party.
The similarities to Nazi representations are obvious. (*AIZ* 52 [1930])

13.16. Class struggle on the fashion front. Overdressed bourgeois women on the left, the socialist new women on the right. (*AIZ* 45 [1929])

with wide-ranging political and social possibilities. Its defense of a woman's right to an abortion placed it squarely in opposition to prevailing legal and moral codes, and made it possible to imagine a society in which women could control reproduction. The party press published laudatory articles about Magnus Hirschfeld and other sex reformers, and occasionally the *AIZ* turned over its pages to sexologists such as the physician Max Hodann.[31] Hodann bluntly criticized the hypocrisy and inhumanity of "bourgeois" morals and the notion that sexual relations should occur only within marriage. Like other sex reformers, Hodann advocated birth control and, when necessary, legal abortion to remove the fear of unwanted pregnancy, and companionate marriages in which men and women shared in the household responsibilities.[32] Even more radically, *AIZ* published an excerpt from Otto Rühle's *Illustrierte Kultur- und Sittengeschichte des Proletariats* (Illustrated Cultural and Moral History of the Proletariat), which equated marriage and prostitution. Like Hodann, Rühle condemned the hypocrisy of the bourgeoisie, which castigated sexual relations outside of marriage, leaving many people trapped in sexually unsatisfying marriages or condemned to no sexual life at all.[33] Similarly, the party implicitly defended single women's right to a sexual life when *AIZ* ran an article that conveyed sympathy for the plight of a young woman who had to rent a room completely lacking in beauty and whose private life became subject to the rules and surveillance of the tyrannical landlord, who forbade visitors, gramophone music, and any laughter whatsoever.[34]

DURING THE Popular Front the French Communist Party promoted its own variant of the "new woman"—a maternalist vision that proved central to the incorporation of French communism into the nation. In the 1920s the party had followed the standard Comintern denigration of the household sphere. To the extent that the party addressed itself to women at all, it was to women in the paid industrial labor force, even though the workplace offered only limited possibilities for organizing women.[35] In

31. "Magnus Hirschfelds Lebenswerk: Zum 60. Geburtstag des Forschers," *AIZ*, May 23, 1928, p. 13; Max Hodann, "Sexualforschung/Gebärzwang und Massenelend," *AIZ* 7, no. 30 (1928): 3.

32. Max Hodann, "Kameradschaftsehe?" *AIZ* 8, no. 12 (1929): 4–5.

33. "Ehe und Prostitution," *AIZ* 9, no. 20 (1930): 394.

34. "Die Qualen der jungen Mieterin," *AIZ* 8, no. 9 (1929): 6.

35. See Albert Sauvy, ed., *Histoire économique de la France entre les deux guerres* (Paris, 1984), 2:35–37; Evelyne Sullerot, "Condition de la femme," ibid., 3:195–209; and Jean-Louis Robert, "Women and Work in France during the First World War," in *The Upheaval of War: Family, Work and Welfare in Europe, 1914–1918*, ed. Richard Wall and Jay Winter (Cambridge, 1989), pp. 251–66, all of which demonstrate the decline in women's participation in the paid industrial labor force throughout the interwar years coupled with the structural transformation of women's labor.

contrast to most other political tendencies in France, the PCF before 1934 espoused a neo-Malthusian approach to the population issue.[36] It viewed family limitation as an acceptable strategy adopted by working-class families to make their lives more reasonable materially and to provide them with more time to engage in the class struggle.

As part of the dramatic strategic shift of the Popular Front, the PCF abandoned the exclusive emphasis on women as workers and the belief in neo-Malthusianism. To accomplish its popular breakthrough, the PCF began to move in tandem with the dominant French discourse on gender and the family, adopting both a pronatalist position that gave primacy to women's household and maternal roles and a rather conventional view of sexuality. The new position became evident in the party daily, L'Humanité, and in the representations of women and the family in the party's popular weekly, Regards.[37]

In the winter of 1935–36, L'Humanité ran a series of articles on the family. In language evocative of a more generalized pronatalist discourse, the paper's editor, Paul Vaillant-Couturier, defined the party's task as "to make motherhood a social function of the highest order . . . because upon it depends the continuity and improvement of the species."[38] Similarly, during the 1936 strikes, the PCF leader Jacques Duclos called on "the women of France to unite for the protection of their homes" and for "the future of the race."[39] The party leader Maurice Thorez gave expression to the new PCF position at a national conference in 1937 by calling for "a national policy for the protection of children, of maternity, of the family. . . . On that depends the future of the race."[40]

In the popular weekly Regards, women workers were pictured much less frequently than either elegant or maternal women. The women's column, introduced in mid-1935, was titled "La Femme, l'Enfant, le Foyer" (Woman, Child, Hearth)—a rather stark contrast to the AIZ's "The Working Woman."[41] Though in the pre–Popular Front period the

36. On this issue generally see François Delpla, "Les Communistes français et la sexualité (1932–1938)," Mouvement social 91 (1975): 121–52; and William H. Schneider, "The Eugenics Movement in France, 1890–1940," in The Wellborn Science: Eugenics in Germany, France, Brazil, and Russia, ed. Mark B. Adams (New York, 1990), pp. 97–102. For the Soviet shift to more familial, if not quite maternalist, imagery in the mid-1930s, see Bonnell, "Peasant Woman in Stalinist Political Art."

37. Delpla, "Les Communistes français et la sexualité," is the major study on this topic, one that prompted me to look more closely at the journal. I thank my colleague Dolores Peters for the reference.

38. Quoted in Schneider, "Eugenics Movement in France," p. 99.

39. Quoted in Siân Reynolds, "Women, Men and the 1936 Strikes in France," in The French and Spanish Popular Fronts: Comparative Perspectives, ed. Martin S. Alexander and Helen Graham (Cambridge, 1989), p. 199.

40. Quoted in Delpla, "Les Communistes français et la sexualité," p. 141.

41. The first issue of Regards with the column is July 25, 1935.

PCF had dismissed the public display of sexually suggestive art and advertisements as a sign of bourgeois degeneration, now *Regards* devoted more and more space to such "feminine" topics as beauty, household economics, creams and ointments. Its standards became elevated as well, and haute coiffeure and haute couture appeared in its pages (Figure 13.17). In preparation for Christmas Eve, *Regards* advised, female readers should take a few minutes to make themselves beautiful—for themselves and for their families. The column provided extensive makeup directions, including advice to move one's head "in the manner of the stars." The holiday celebration is a success: "The fine mood that you derive from the impression of your beauty—and you would not be a woman if this left you indifferent—is communicated to all the others."[42] Even the film star Claudette Colbert came to grace the pages of this PCF magazine.[43]

In this manner, the PCF connected beauty, maternity, and health, all of which were critical to the national drive to expand the population. One issue of the women's column, for example, carried the headlines "Pour votre santé" and "Pour votre beauté," and included pictures of babies in the bath and an elegantly attired woman on skis.[44] The warm, nurturing environment that women were to provide for the family is evident in numerous images of mothers—very rarely fathers—and children in *Regards* (Figure 13.18). Many of these representations fervently linked the social achievements of the Popular Front, especially the paid vacations, with the maternalist and pronatalist ethos.[45] Significantly, when activist women were depicted, they were most often Spanish women struggling for the Republic—while French women went to the beauty shop.[46]

The PCF's revised views on gender and the family became articulated in the legislature and especially in the municipalities, the political space conquered by the party in the Popular Front. In the political sphere primarily, not in the workplace, the PCF addressed the multiple interests of women—as homemakers, mothers, spouses, and workers—and articulated its newfound support of pronatalism and high fashion. In this manner the party expressed demands for basic material improvements in the lives of workers in the pronatalist terms of French political discourse. Public health facilities, summer camps for children, community parks, even day-care centers—all were supported on the basis of providing for the health and safety of women and children, and thereby ensuring the procreation and survival of the nation. In this context, the party also

42. *Regards*, December 23, 1937, p. 21.
43. Delpla, "Les Communistes français et la sexualité," p. 146.
44. E.g., *Regards*, December 17, 1937, pp. 20–21.
45. See, e.g., *Regards*, July 29 and October 7, 1937.
46. *Regards*, September 10 and November 5, 1936.

13.17. The French Communist weekly during the Popular Front displays the elegant fashions to which proletarian women should aspire. (*Regards*, November 25, 1937)

13.18. The maternalist image promoted by the Communist Party of France during the Popular Front. (*Regards*, March 18, 1937)

connected its critique of French capitalism with pronatalism by indicting capitalism for creating the conditions that made it difficult for French parents to support large families, thereby inhibiting the development of the nation.

Similarly, the acquisition of many more parliamentary seats in the 1936 election enabled the PCF to propose legislation that won a wide hearing. Its 1936 bill for "effective protection of maternity and childhood" called for the creation of a national office to coordinate programs that supported women and children and new legislation that "'would protect mothers effectively before, during, and after pregnancy,' encourage breastfeeding, and protect all children through three years of age." In later proposals, the PCF also called for the panoply of measures designed to promote large families that had become a fixture of pronatalist demands in France, such as a state-provided bonus that increased with each additional child, subsidies, and tax breaks. Significantly, in this bill the party abandoned its earlier support of legalized abortion and easier access to contraception. Pointedly, Thorez stated that he did not want the PCF to repeat the error of the KPD, which through its advocacy of abortion rights had handed the Nazis a valuable political weapon to use against it.[47]

Thus, in the words of François Delpla, the PCF managed the "laborious construction of a pronatalist common front."[48] Though these policies had little impact on the party's membership, which remained overwhelmingly male—in 1926 only 1.7 percent of the membership was female, in 1946, by the PCF's own reckoning, only 11.2 percent[49]—they were critical in inscribing the PCF into French society, an inscription mediated through the occupation of political space in the municipalities and the Chamber of Deputies.

IN A MANNER typical of the Communist parties, the PCI initially focused its attention on working women, accepted a rather conventional notion of separate spheres that reproduced ideas of women's innate capacity to "create and render pleasant and restful intimacy, the home, the family," and denied the possibility of women's oppression within the proletarian household.[50] Yet in the Resistance the PCI moved away from the exclusive focus on working women and began to redefine its understanding of the subordination of women—a shift inspired by the convergence between the political activism of women and the party's own efforts to promote resistance through all spheres of society. In the extreme conditions of war, Fascist oppression, and German occupation, the household as political space and women as political actors became crucial components of the Italian Resistance, and thereby shaped the PCI's emergence as a mass party.

Women's extensive participation in the Resistance derived from both the intense material crisis of the war years and a relatively long-term politicization that owed a great deal to the ideology and character of Italian Fascism. The fluid and antibureaucratic nature of Resistance activity, which left so much to individual initiative or to the actions of

47. Schneider, "Eugenics Movement in France," pp. 100–102.
48. Delpla, "Les Communistes français et la sexualité," p. 142.
49. See Annie Kriegel, Les Communistes français dans leur premier demi-siècle, 1920–1970, 2d ed. (Paris, 1985), pp. 76–85, on the party's limited support among women, figs. 76–78.
50. Nadia Spano and Fiamma Camarlinghi, La questione femminile nella politica del PCI, 1921–1963 (Rome, 1972) pp. 27–29, quoting Camilla Ravera, "Il nostro femminismo." Ruggiero Grieco, who headed the party's women's section, denied the possibility of women's oppression in the proletarian household: ibid., p. 39.

small groups, facilitated the participation of women.[51] Some women fought with the armed partisan units, such as the PCI's Garibaldi Brigade and the left-liberal Giustizia e Libertà. Perhaps more significant is the fact that women lent to the Resistance their own forms of activism; their Resistance activities had, as one historian has put it, their own "physiognomy."[52] Women demonstrated for peace and bread, as on International Women's Day in 1943, 1944, and especially 1945, and their actions sparked additional protest strikes and demonstrations. They demonstrated and collected petitions against the deportation of male laborers to Germany and against massacres carried out by the Germans. Women provided crucial links between the extraordinary realm of guerrilla forces and more "normal" social arenas. They smuggled arms and food to Resistance forces; hid men as they moved from the city to the mountains to join the fighters; and provided support for families of partisans and deportees. They participated in strikes, and provided support for the many, many industrial conflicts that were themselves a part of the Resistance. Their actions were in many instances designed to ensure the survival of their own household and its various members, particularly males threatened with deportation as forced laborers or combatants, or males subject to political persecution.

The nature of Resistance activities politicized the household. Both as geographic space and as a social entity, the household became as much a part of the public realm of political contestation as the workplace and the battlefield. Hence the nature of the Resistance further intensified the politicization of women and brought gender issues to the forefront of Italian politics. At least for a brief period, PCI propaganda depicted women in activist roles, partisans bearing arms next to their male comrades (Figure 13.19).

With these kinds of representations, the PCI, more than the PCF or even the KPD, presented a far more transformative understanding of gender relations. Indeed, the Resistance activities of women pushed the PCI into a subtle but significant reevaluation of its position on women's equality. The broad-based character of women's political activity forced

51. For some indications of the forms of women's activism, see Giulietta Ascoli, "L'Udi tra emancipazione e liberazione (1943–1964)," *Problemi del socialismo* 17 (October/December 1976): 111–13; Alba Mora, "Per una storia dell' associazionismo femminile a Parma: GDD e UDI tra emancipazione e tradizione (1943–1946)," in *Comunisti a Parma: Atti del convegno tenutosi a Parma il 7 Novembre 1981*, ed. Fiorenzo Sicuri (Parma, 1986), pp. 299–307; Victoria de Grazia, *How Fascism Ruled Women: Italy, 1922–1945* (Berkeley, 1992), pp. 272–88; Spano and Camarlinghi, *La questione femminile*, pp. 87–95; Miriam Mafai, *L'apprendistato della politica: Le donne italiane nel dopoguerra* (Rome, 1979), pp. 68–92; and Ada Marchesini Gobetti, "Perchè erano tante nella Resistenza," *Rinascita* 3 (March 1961): 245–51.

52. Ascoli, "L'Udi tra emancipazione e liberazione," p. 112.

13.19. Just a few days after the end of World War II, the Communist Party of Italy depicts women as active participants in the antifascist struggle. The headline reads: "Italian women, like women all over the world, have fought." (*L'unità*, May 12, 1945)

the party to abandon its earlier economistic concentration on women as workers. Moreover, the PCI gave more explicit recognition to inequalities within the family. In a major departure from Comintern practice, the PCI leadership in 1944 decided to allow separate male and female cells at the base of the party structure, an indication of the heightened awareness of the specificity of women's subordination and of the greater politicization of women in the Resistance.[53] In the PCI-dominated Union of Italian Women (UDI), women promoted issues and demands that, according to one scholar, "contained an analysis of the subordination of women that anticipated by thirty years the proposals and debates on the reforms of the family code."[54] In addition, Palmiro Togliatti was arguing in the 1940s that the oppression of women resulted not only from economic relations but also from civil relations, which in the family created a situation of inequality and oppression. Hence the emancipation of women was an issue not only for one class but for all women, and was part and parcel of the profound social transformation that the PCI intended to implement.[55]

Yet Togliatti's notable analysis of civil society as a source of women's oppression marked the closure, not the beginning, of a trenchant reconsideration of gender relations.[56] The PCI's strategy of transforming capitalism from within—a strategy encapsulated in the terms *il partito nuovo* and *democrazia progressiva*—depended on the continuation of the national front coalition of the Resistance years and its acceptance by Britain and the United States. Under Togliatti, the PCI sought to win this toleration by a process of compromise with the other forces of Italian society, notably the middle classes and what would soon become Christian Democracy.

Maintaining the Resistance coalition required, therefore, reigning in some of the more activist elements in the spheres the party dominated, particularly during the years of reconstruction, when popular political activism remained at a very high level. The PCI-dominated trade union federation, for example, collaborated with employers in the drive to increase production and in curbing the influence of the co-management

53. Fausto Anderlini, "La cellula," in *Il Partito comunista italiano: Struttura e storia dell' organizzazione, 1921/1979*, ed. Massimo Ilardi and Aris Accornero, Fondazione Giangiacomo Feltrinelli, *Annali* 21 (1981): 207–10; and Giordano Sivini, "Le parti communiste: Struture et fonctionnement," in *Sociologie du communisme en Italie*, Cahiers de la Fondation Nationale des Sciences Politiques no. 194 (Paris, 1974), p. 88.

54. Ascoli, "L'Udi tra emancipazione e liberazione," p. 117.

55. See esp. Togliatti's speeches to the First Women's Conference of the PCI in June 1945 and to the UDI in September 1946, in Palmiro Togliatti, *L'emancipazione femminile* (Rome, 1965), pp. 21–71.

56. See Ascoli, "L'Udi tra emancipazione e liberazione," p. 128.

commissions established during the Liberation.[57] In the realm of gender the party sought to accommodate Catholic sensibilities. The representations of women as determined fighters, characteristic of the Resistance years, remained, but were soon overrun by depictions of the eternally maternal woman (Figure 13.20).[58] On abortion the party refused to challenge the church and the Christian Democrats. Women's issues in general became subordinated to the more general concerns of peace and reconstruction, and the party political conflicts of the Cold War. Increasingly the UDI became subservient to party direction, and even International Women's Day received scant attention in the party press.[59] And as the Resistance coalition broke up and Italian politics became increasingly defined by the Cold War, the PCI began to lay exclusive claim to the Resistance legacy. In the party's construction, the Resistance became an event largely of male partisan warfare and strikes; the crucial activities of women and the political space of the household were pushed to the margins of historical memory.

CONCLUSION

What, then, was the ideal of femininity constructed by the Communist parties? What was the female counterpart to the productive, powerful, and combative male proletarian? Certainly the idealized woman was a proletarian committed to the cause of socialism and a full participant in all realms of social life. She worked in a factory, for participation in the productive realm constituted the necessary path to emancipation. At the same time, she was a housewife attuned to rationalized methods of work in the home and dedicated to constructing a supportive environment for the proletarian family—for the man when he came home from a hard day of labor and political struggle, for the children as they matured with consciousness of and confidence in their class and political identities. She was young and energetic and an object of beauty, most often in a proletarian manner—not luxurious and ostentatious beauty, but a beauty that derived from athleticism and health. In the 1920s she was sexually emancipated in that she had a right to sexual pleasures, and could choose,

57. See esp. Liliana Lanzardo, "Il Consigli di gestione nella strategia della collaborazione," in Problemi del movimento sindacale in Italia, 1943–1973, ed. Aris Accornero, Fondazione Giangiacomo Feltrinelli, Annali 16 (1974–75): 325–65; and for the example of Fiat, Renzo Gianotti, Lotte e organizzazioni di classe alla FIAT (1948–1970) (Bari, 1970), pp. 29–41.

58. See also L'unità, April 18, 1948, which depicts a mother bathed in light serving the family meal to her husband and son.

59. Contrast L'unità, March 8, 1948, and March 8, 1946.

13.20. Within a few years of the end of World War II, the PCI adopted far more conventional gender images, as in this campaign poster for peace, with the Madonna-like mother in the forefront and male workers in the background. (*L'unità*, April 10, 1948)

by her own volition, to limit the size of her family. By the latter part of the 1930s and after World War II, when the parties sought at almost all costs to maintain political alliances, Communist movements propagated maternalist images that differed hardly at all from prevailing social norms. Throughout the period the Communist construction of femininity most often rendered women in a passive rather than active fashion— as objects of pathos in a melodramatic genre in the 1920s, as recipients of protective, maternalist social welfare policies in the 1930s and 1940s.

Still, the Communist parties did articulate an emancipatory message. They defended women's right to work in paid jobs even when they promoted elegance and maternity.[60] Their call for equal pay for equal work, social reforms, and the full participation of women in all realms of life challenged most directly the prevailing gender codes of European societies—a challenge that became increasingly important in the 1930s, when the demand that women return to the domestic sphere found a newly shrill and powerful voice in the fascist parties. Communism vastly broadened the "political imaginary" in a different direction, one that enabled people to envisage a world of egalitarian relations between the sexes. The Comintern parties also provided some women with an avenue of activism and a vigorous forum that enabled them to articulate their oppressions and desires. At least in the 1920s, the parties also defended women's right to abortion in ways that offered them, potentially, far greater control over their own bodies.

Indeed, nothing better depicts communism's dilemmas in relation to women than reproductive issues. In Germany the KPD helped initiate a great public movement against the prohibition of abortion, paragraph 218 of the criminal code.[61] The campaign flowered in earnest in the midst of the Depression, and the KPD, for one of the few times in its history, found itself at the head of a broad and popular multiclass and multipolitical alliance. But these were uncomfortable allies—women, for example, who articulated an autonomous feminism that challenged the primacy the KPD placed on class.[62] Within the ranks of the party women

60. See also Laura L. Frader, "Engendering Work and Wages: The French Labor Movement and the Family Wage," in this volume, for the Communists' commitment to women's right to work.

61. See Atina Grossmann, "Abortion and Economic Crisis: The 1931 Campaign against Paragraph 218," in *When Biology Became Destiny: Women in Weimar and Nazi Germany*, ed. Renate Bridenthal, Atina Grossmann, and Marion Kaplan (New York, 1984), pp. 66–86; Usborne, *Politics of the Body*, pp. 156–213; Kontos, *"Die Partei kämpft wie ein Mann!"* pp. 84–120.

62. Grossmann, "Abortion and Economic Crisis," pp. 74–80. Note also Petro's comments on the ambiguity of the messages in *AIZ*, which potentially enabled a reader to develop an identification with women and women's issues despite the overt emphasis on class: *Joyless Streets*, p. 139.

increasingly gave voice to an independent position that placed greater weight on gender than the party leadership was prepared to countenance. Nor was the KPD free from the eugenics-based population politics that many other groups, right and left, advocated. At the same time, by raising the slogan "Your body belongs to you," the KPD "implicitly and rather nervously defended the individual woman's right to choose.... The Communist left at least partially broke through the motherhood and eugenic consensus that extended into the ranks of left, feminist, and Sex Reform movements."[63]

Yet, as Atina Grossmann has shown so well, the KPD found itself in a dilemma. It had set in motion a broad-based coalition around women's issues, yet resisted the development of an autonomous women's politics; indeed, it feared any actions that lay outside the realm of party-controlled cadre politics and that challenged the primacy of class.[64] The French Communists, as we have seen, learned from the mistakes of their German comrades: they took the safer and politically more successful road of adapting to the pronatalist consensus. Similarly, the PCI rapidly withdrew from a trenchant reconsideration of gender and avoided the entire realm of reproduction. It, too, retreated to the safety of maternalist politics.

But one is left to wonder whether the Communist parties' weak support among women had as much to do with particular policies as with the construction of images so far removed from attainability. Many men could attain the party's construction of masculinity—they could be and often were combative, politically committed workers—but the feminine ideal was elusive. The double burden of paid work and housework left little time and even less energy for daily exercise, political involvement, establishment of a nurturing home environment, attention to beauty, and a full sex life.

At the same time, the specific construction of masculinity may also have served to limit the parties' appeal among males. Communism in its formative decades found support primarily among younger men. Its ethos of tough male proletarianism reverberated with those ready and willing to engage in street fights and revolutionary warfare. Those less inclined to establish their masculinity through battle scars may have found far more amenable political homes in social democracy and the Catholic labor movement.

In the end, communism's emancipatory position, the construction of an alternate femininity, was largely vitiated by the parties' prevailing construction of masculinity. Certainly the general Marxist-Leninist

---

63. Grossmann, "Abortion and Economic Crisis," p. 77.
64. Ibid., pp. 78–80.

enthrallment with the productive sphere, the "heavy metal" sector in particular, contributed to communism's strongly masculine tenor. Even the recipe for women's emancipation reflected the ideological denigration of the reproductive sphere—in order to become free, women had to become more like men: they had to work in the sphere of production. But the varying constructions of gender were shaped also by the particular spatial locations of labor and Communist politics. Driven by the coalition of order from the workplace, the KPD made the streets its primary space of political engagement. In combination with the party's incessant invocation of revolution as the path to the future society and its denigration of the legislative arena, the turn to the streets made male physical prowess the essence of political action and commitment. The PCF, working through the existing political institutions of the Third Republic, adopted a pronatalist position that it could implement at the local level, which enabled it partly to break out of the proletarian milieu. The politicization of all arenas of social life in the Resistance, including the household, made the PCI for a time the advocate of transformed gender roles. Its subsequent commitment to political coalitions as vehicles of power led it to abandon its radical position and to return to a far more conventional understanding of gender and families.

The shifting constructions of femininity by European Communist parties stand, then, at the interstices of political strategies and social histories. Gender served as a critical marker of the more general political strategies through which parties sought to accomplish their breakthroughs to popular status. In the case of those parties that became mass or ruling parties, their constructions of gender illuminate also the efforts by Communist parties to navigate their ways through formal Communist ideology and practice, on the one hand, and more generalized societal understandings and practices, on the other.

Contributors

LAURA L. FRADER is Associate Professor of History at Northeastern University and Senior Associate at the Center for European Studies, Harvard University. Author of *Peasants and Protest: Agricultural Workers, Politics, and Unions in the Aude*, she is currently preparing a book on gender and the labor movement in interwar France.

SONYA O. ROSE is Professor of History and Sociology at the University of Michigan. She is the author of *Limited Livelihoods: Gender and Class in Nineteenth-Century England* and numerous articles on gender and class and on household economic strategies. Her current project is on sex and moral citizenship in World War II Britain, in which she explores how race, class, gender, and national identity were linked to the cultural meanings of "the good citizen."

KATHLEEN CANNING is Associate Professor at the University of Michigan, where she teaches modern German history and European women's history/gender history. She is the author of *Languages of Labor and Gender: Female Factory Work in Germany, 1850–1914*. She is currently working on a book on gender and working-class citizenship in Germany between 1890 and 1930.

HELEN HARDEN CHENUT is a historian working in the field of urban, gender, and labor history. She is one of the founding members of a women's interdisciplinary research group on gender and work in Paris at the Centre National·de la Recherche Scientifique. She received her doctorate from the University of Paris VII and has taught modern European and women's history at Harvard University and Mount Holyoke College. She is currently working on a book on gender, socialist politics, and working-class culture in the textile town of Troyes.

ANNA CLARK is the author of *The Struggle for the Breeches: Gender and the Making of the British Working Class* and *Women's Silence, Men's Violence: Sexual Assault in England, 1770–1845*, as well as several articles and book chapters on gender and franchise reform, Chartism, wife-beating, religion, Queen Caroline, and melodrama. She is now working on an anthology of the history of sexuality in Europe, and on a book on the sexuality of politics in Britain from the eighteenth to the twentieth centuries. She is Associate Professor of History at the University of North Carolina at Charlotte and lives in Durham, North Carolina.

JUDITH G. COFFIN got her Ph.D. at Yale University and teaches European and French history at the University of Texas, Austin. She has published articles on women's labor, social science, and political economy in the *Journal of Modern History, Journal of Economic History*, and *French Historical Studies*. Her book *The Politics of Women's Work: The Paris Garment Trades, 1750–1915* is a social and cultural history of issues surrounding female wage labor in the nineteenth century.

JANE GRAY is Lecturer in Sociology at St. Patrick's College, Maynooth, where she teaches courses on gender, family, and social change and development. She has published several articles on gender, plebeian culture, and uneven class formation in the Irish linen industry, including "Rural Industry and Uneven Development: The Significance of Gender in the Irish Linen Industry" in the *Journal of Peasant Studies*. She is currently working on two projects: on individual life stories and social change in eighteenth-century Ireland and on the significance of flax and linen in the eighteenth-century world economy.

TESSIE P. LIU is Associate Professor of History at Northwestern University, where she teaches modern European social history and comparative women's history. Author of *The Weaver's Knot: The Contradictions of Class Struggle and Family Solidarity in Western France, 1750–1914*, she is currently focusing on the role of suffering and personal loss in the construction of a gendered memory of the Vendée counterrevolution. She is also doing research for a book on family metaphors and racial thinking in France in the early nineteenth century.

KEITH MCCLELLAND is Senior Lecturer in Social History at Middlesex University, London. He is also co-editor of the journal *Gender and History*. His research and teaching have been mainly in nineteenth-century British labor and gender history and in historical theory. He has published articles on these subjects and also co-edited E. P. Thompson's *Critical Perspectives* (1990). His current research is within a collaborative project on aspects of class, gender, and race in relation to the reform politics of 1967 in Britain.

JUDITH F. STONE is Associate Professor of History at Western Michigan University. She approaches political history from the perspectives of political nature and gender. Her book *The Search for Social Peace: Reform Legislation in France, 1890–1914* examines the ideological and political debates surrounding the "social question" as well as the implementation of major labor reforms. Her *Sons of the Revolution: Radical Democrats in France, 1862–1914* analyzes the political culture of democracy in a particular time and place.

LAURA TABILI received her Ph. D. from Rutgers University in 1988 and currently is Associate Professor of Modern European History at the University of Arizona. Her research has explored the specific forms of gender, race, and class formation and of labor migration in the process of European global expansion. She is the author of *"We Ask for British Justice": Workers and Racial Difference in Late Imperial Britain*. Her current project reconstructs migrant networks and institutions to illuminate questions of labor migration, racial formation, and British identity in the period 1870–1940.

ERIC D. WEITZ is Associate Professor of History at St. Olaf College, Northfield, Minnesota. He is the author of *Communism in Germany: Worker Movement and Socialist State, 1890–1990*, and is the co-editor of a forthcoming book on German socialism and communism from 1840 to 1990. He has published articles on European communism and on German social and labor history in the *Journal of Modern History*, *Journal of Contemporary History*, *Central European History*, and *Social Science History*.

ELIZABETH A. WOOD is Assistant Professor of History at the Massachusetts Institute of Technology. Her book on gender and state formation in Soviet Russia from 1917 to 1930 is soon to be published.

Index